THE UNI[
WINCHESTF[D]

D1760710

81 8
DRE

Theodore Dreiser

Political Writings

THE DREISER EDITION

Sponsored at

the University of Connecticut

by

the Department of English,

the Thomas J. Dodd Research Center,

the College of Liberal Arts and Sciences, and

the University Research Foundations

and by

the University of Pennsylvania Libraries

Thomas P. Riggio

General Editor

Theodore Dreiser

Political Writings

Edited by
JUDE DAVIES

University of Illinois Press
Urbana, Chicago, and Springfield

Photos on pages 98, 102, 165, and 230 from the Theodore Dreiser Papers
and the W. A. Swanberg Collection, Annenberg Rare Book and Manuscript Library, University of Pennsylvania, courtesy of the Trustees of the
University of Pennsylvania.

Excerpts from *Tragic America* and *America Is Worth Saving* are printed by
permission of the Dreiser Trust.

Research for this publication was funded by the University of Winchester
and the Arts and Humanities Research Council, ahrc.ac.uk.

Arts & Humanities
Research Council

Library of Congress Cataloging-in-Publication Data
Dreiser, Theodore, 1871–1945.
Political writings / Theodore Dreiser ; edited by Jude Davies.
p.   cm. — (The Dreiser edition)
This volume gathers Dreiser's most important political writings from
his journalism, memoirs, and long out-of-print books.
Includes bibliographical references and index.
ISBN-13: 978-0-252-03585-2 (hardcover : alk. paper)
ISBN-10: 0-252-03585-2 (hardcover : alk. paper)
1. Dreiser, Theodore, 1871–1945—Political and social views.
I. Davies, Jude. II. Title. III. Title: Theodore Dreiser : political writings.
PS3507.R55A6   2011
818.'52—dc22   2010040852

CONTENTS

ILLUSTRATIONS

PREFACE

Theodore Dreiser's considerable fame as a novelist has overshadowed much of his other writing. Of the twenty-seven books he published during his lifetime, only eight were novels—and two of these, one unfinished at his death, were issued posthumously. Although much of Dreiser's fiction and autobiographical writing can be mined for its political significance, his lifelong insistence on a strict division between creative writing and "propaganda" makes the task difficult. He self-mockingly told a friend that when the last volume of his fictional portrait of a financier was published, "most of my critics will pounce on it as decidedly unsocial and even ridiculous as coming from a man who wants social equity" (Dreiser to Dorothy Dudley, 7 April 1932).

Dreiser anticipated his critics and biographers in recognizing the paradoxes that riddled his career. By temperament a bundle of contradictions, Dreiser was especially hard to pin down when it came to his political opinions and loyalties. He could secretly edit the freewheeling *Bohemian* magazine while serving as editor-in-chief of the cautious, patently bourgeois *Delineator*; he would write for the *Masses* one week and the *Saturday Evening Post* the next; he was a working associate of the leftwing Trotskyite Max Eastman, but was as content hobnobbing with writers as different as the Tory H. L. Mencken and the apolitical bohemian George Sterling.

Into his fifties, Dreiser consistently paraphrased Chekhov and declared that "it was not so much the business of the writer to indict as to interpret." The social implications of this artistic credo are seen in this edition, which isolates a cross-section of his overtly political thought. During the first half of his career Dreiser assumed the role of an interpreter of the spectacle of life, a stance that in both his political writing and fiction allowed him to admire amoral capitalists like his financier Cowperwood and, simultaneously, to express pity and the need of reform for the impoverished masses. They were all, in this view, part of the "color" of life, each depending on the other's presence for existence and providing a kind of "balance" inherent in the natural order of things. The personal attacks he endured during World War I, as both a German American and a pacifist, intensified his liberal proclivities; but his protest remained within the limits of generally accepted progressive politics.

Dreiser's position changed dramatically during the second half of his career, in the years after the stock market crash of 1929. He moved from irresolute political involvement to an openly activist stance, identifying with the aims of various leftist political movements. Like others in the 1930s he idealistically looked to the Soviet experiment as a model for a new democratic order, particularly after the rise of fascism abroad. He abandoned the precarious social balance he had once maintained, rejected what he now called the "myth of individuality," and vociferously advocated support for the "people" as a means of bettering society here and abroad.

Dreiser certainly was not alone in his revision of long-held beliefs. He was one among other mainstream writers—such as Sherwood Anderson, Edmund Wilson, and John Dos Passos—who helped to make radical politics respectable among intellectuals in the 1930s. Like Dreiser they embraced socialist and communist enterprises, often with a great deal of ambivalence, and at times with an underlying nostalgia for an older social order. Their hesitancies were perhaps most intense when they confronted the tensions between their aesthetic and political allegiances.

Dreiser's ambivalences are on full display in this edition, the first to present the complete range of his political thought. The neglect of this aspect of his writing had little to do with lack of significant material. Although not formally a political theorist, Dreiser wrote as a citizen who spent his creative energies observing the American scene. He was prolific in this field and influential in his day. He published three books on political subjects—*Dreiser Looks at Russia* (1928), *Tragic America* (1931), and *America Is Worth Saving* (1941). Add to these a mound of journalism, broadsides, contributions to books, speeches, and introductions, and one could assemble a multivolume set of his political commentary. Two factors led to a lack of interest in this work. First, his leftist politics was, to greatly understate the matter, out of favor during the long Cold War decades. Second, there is the matter of his methodology. It is still fashionable to routinely dismiss a book like *Tragic America* for its hasty composition and its amassing of data that are not always accurate. Even in his own day, of course, the novelist was attacked on stylistic grounds. But as Edmund Wilson pointed out, although Dreiser's polemical style "is always collapsing the man behind it remains sound. His prose has a long and steady rhythm which continues to convey his feelings and ideas." Wilson felt that Dreiser's importance lay in his ability to translate doctrinaire Marxist theory into an American idiom: "It will thus have back of it the immediate conviction of such unrusssianizable Americans as Dreiser" (*New Republic* LXX, 30 March 1932, pp. 185–86).

For all Dreiser's idiosyncrasies, there are a number of important constants in his thought. From his first efforts as editor of *Ev'ry Month* and *The Delineator* to his activist period during the Great Depression, his major target was American exceptionalism. He fought, in one way or another, against the widespread assumption that all American citizens were being treated equally and justly. Even when he expressed admiration for the ruthless careers of the rich and famous, he unfailingly indicted the extremes of poverty and wealth in a society whose core documents and social myths were too often at odds with empirical evidence. In the end, his real heroes belonged to what he called "our revolutionary tradition" (see 201). They were individuals who defended the rights of the common people against vested interests—from Thomas Paine and Abraham Lincoln to Eugene Debs and Emma Goldman.

This volume offers readers the essential primary documents that trace Dreiser's evolution as a political thinker. The editors trust that the texts will spark reevaluations, particularly of such complex issues as his relationship to communism, Soviet Russia, and American Jews. The edition was undertaken in the belief that much of what Dreiser's generation experienced is pertinent to the present political landscape, and that his responses remain valuable to this day.

* * *

Political Writings is part of an ongoing series in the Dreiser Edition. Each book is a product of cooperative efforts. The general editor appoints an editor for each project. The general editor and the volume editor select copy-text for each edition and establish the project within the framework of current editorial practice. They determine the relevant documents and devise the historical and textual principles for the edition. The general editor verifies all transcriptions and oversees the volume editor in gathering the pertinent textual, historical, and bibliographical documents. At each stage of preparation, the editorial staff proofreads the text and authenticates its contents.

The volume editor has presented a representative sample of Dreiser's political commentary, arranged chronologically. Some texts occasionally discussed by critics or biographers—such as the complete exchange of letters with Hutchins Hapgood on the topic of anti-Semitism and excerpts from books long out of print—have not been available to the general public. Other essays—"American Idealism and German Frightfulness" is a good example—have never been published, and many others have hitherto remained buried in the files of specialized archives. In keeping with the general guidelines of the Dreiser Edition, selections are edited as public documents and appear as clear texts emended for typographical slips, misspellings, and demonstrable errors. Essays found only in manuscript are treated similarly, under the assumption that Dreiser had prepared the typescripts for publication. Substantial differences between the published and manuscript versions of a text are discussed in the notes. There are a relatively small number of

Dreiser's letters included in the collection; they were either intended for publication or became public documents with Dreiser's consent, and have been standardized accordingly. These editorial practices are more fully discussed in "Editorial Note."

The editor's introduction offers a general account of Dreiser's political thought. Each major division of the book is prefaced by an extended exposition of the historical, compositional, and biographical factors that influenced Dreiser's opinions at specific times in his career. Suggestions for further reading are listed at the end of the historical commentaries, offering guides for readers to explore more fully the themes and concerns of the texts at hand. Annotations identify significant figures and references, providing readers with the necessary information for understanding the text.

* * *

Political Writings continues the Dreiser Edition's tradition of publishing texts that are not easily accessible, even to the specialist. Such an undertaking would be unimaginable without the sponsorship of two institutions: the University of Connecticut and the library of the University of Pennsylvania. Several individuals at the University of Connecticut deserve special mention for their initiatives and continuing generous support of this project: Janet Greger, vice provost and dean of the Graduate School; Ross D. MacKinnon, dean of the College of Liberal Arts and Sciences; Wayne Franklin, head of the English Department; and Betsy Pittman, director of the Thomas J. Dodd Research Center. Anthony R. Vecchiarelli has contributed his valuable services as a proofreader. The goodwill and special training of the staff at the University of Pennsylvania's Annenberg Rare Book and Manuscript Library have been essential to the progress of the Dreiser Edition. Director David McKnight generously devoted his own time and the resources of his staff to facilitating the work of the Dreiser Edition. Curator of Manuscripts Nancy M. Shawcross continues to contribute her expertise and special service to the project. John Pollack has consistently and untiringly assisted Dreiser Edition editors in their work. Finally, Dr. Willis Regier, the director of the University of Illinois Press, continues against high odds to provide imaginative guidance and commitment to the project.

Thomas P. Riggio
General Editor
The Dreiser Edition

ACKNOWLEDGEMENTS

Previously unpublished works by Theodore Dreiser and illustrations from the Theodore Dreiser Papers and the W. A. Swanberg Collection at the Rare Book and Manuscript Library, University of Pennsylvania Libraries, are published courtesy of the Trustees of the University of Pennsylvania. I am indebted to the Dreiser Trust and Harold Dies for permission to print excerpts from *Tragic America* and *America Is Worth Saving*.

This volume has been supported by research leave from the University of Winchester and the Arts and Humanities Research Council of Great Britain (Matching Leave Scheme), and the McCorison Fellowship awarded by the Bibliographical Society of America. My grateful thanks to all of these bodies, and to Professor Liz Stuart, pro vice-chancellor at the University of Winchester.

It could not have been completed without the generous, cordial, and expert aid of the staff of the Rare Book and Manuscript Library at the University of Pennsylvania. I would especially like to thank Curator of Manuscripts Nancy M. Shawcross for her continuing contribution of expertise to the Dreiser Edition, and John Pollack for his particular interest in this project and for his help, which went far beyond reasonable expectations.

A great debt of gratitude is owed to Tom Riggio—who has done more than anyone to demonstrate Dreiser's continuing relevance in the twenty-first century—for his enthusiasm, knowledge, and attention to detail. I am particularly grateful to Clare Eby for her perceptive comments and very helpful suggestions on a complete draft of the book. For their illumination of Dreiser more generally, I would also like to thank Stephen C. Brennan, Richard Lingeman, Jerome Loving, Keith Newlin, and Donald Pizer; and for advice on matters ranging from Taoism to the Communist Party of America, I thank Chris Aldous, Ian Bell, John Bentley, Janet Beer, Anna King, Lisa Merrill, Alasdair Spark, and Graham Thompson. At the University of Illinois Press, I would like to thank Dr. Willis Regier, Angela Burton, Tad Ringo, and Douglas Clayton.

Finally and most deeply, I would like to thank Carol Smith for her inexhaustible support, patience, criticism, and insight, and Rosa Davies, "seed corn of the future," for her inspiration.

INTRODUCTION

Struggles over Theodore Dreiser's political significance and the importance
of politics for Dreiser's reputation were evident at his memorial service on
3 January 1946. The funeral party was addressed by both the communist
John Howard Lawson, later to become one of the "Hollywood Ten" indicted
by the House Un-American Activities Committee, and Dr. Allan Hunter,
a minister in the Congregational Church. Though representative of contrasting views on the importance of politics to Dreiser—and of Dreiser to
politics—both men concurred that his life and his work could be seen as
a whole. Hunter acknowledged Dreiser's "limitations," but he also insisted
that Dreiser "had going in him, like a fire in his bones, not just a wistful
desire but a demand that power be cut up and passed around among men,
and that the dignity of these men be recognized, and that they be given a
chance to fulfill themselves in this world, beginning now." Dreiser's political
writing makes explicit these demands.

Like his novels, Dreiser's political writing concerns itself with human
dignity and self-fulfillment, and the obstacles to both. It extends the scope
of his fiction, seeking what he called "the Golden Rule" or "equity" between
people, classes, and nations, in what he believed to be an amoral universe. A
substantial, multifaceted, and often passionate engagement with the major
controversies, themes, issues, and movements of the half-century from the
mid-1890s to 1945, it remains relevant to contemporary political debates.

If the essential subject of Dreiser's literary work is the American scene,
the overarching concern of his political writing is America-in-the-world.
From the outset, his keynote as a social critic was his attack on American
exceptionalism—that is, entrenched beliefs that American institutions, and
capitalism in general, held a monopoly on what was moral, democratic, or
liberating. Throughout his career, Dreiser devoted himself to unmasking
the invidious effects of institutionalized moral frameworks, especially in the
forms of religion and what he called "moralistic mush," and later expanded
to include critiques of nationalistic and individualistic ideologies. Yet Dreiser's view of society as fundamentally amoral in no way precluded a sense of
responsibility for others—a combination that differentiated him from fellow
skeptics such as his friend H. L. Mencken, and that both complicates his
political engagements and adds to their interest. He therefore concerned
himself with campaigns on behalf of victimized individuals and groups from

destitute children to women denied the vote, from the Scottsboro boys to civilians bombed during the Spanish Civil War, and supported a series of specific campaigns to reform "abuses" and extirpate "evils." Over the course of his career, these commitments brought Dreiser into contact with successive political movements that in very different ways sought to invigorate American democracy. Many of the issues he engaged, ranging from racial problems to responsibility for childcare, from the United States's military interventions abroad to the relationship between its political and financial institutions, are of continuing importance. In addition to recording these engagements and making these criticisms, Dreiser's political writings seek positive values, a search that would ultimately lead him to a philosophy of socially beneficial work, creativity, and a democratic internationalism that drew heavily on radical American traditions. Dreiser's political trajectory is outlined in the preface to this volume; here follows a more detailed overview of the development of his political thought in its historical contexts.

Dreiser's earliest social criticism, in his 1890s editorials for the magazine *Ev'ry Month*, employed an empirical measuring stick based on the workings of "Nature" to unmask what he viewed as the corrupt or compromised character of American politics, finance, economics, and urban life in the age of the robber barons. At *Ev'ry Month* Dreiser gave critical support to reform movements such as suffragism and William Jennings Bryan's populism. A decade later, while editor of the prestigious fashion magazine *The Delineator*, Dreiser adopted a "humanitarian editorial policy," promoting Progressive campaigns to reform the care of destitute children and to promote child health. Commending the examples of activist reformers like Jane Addams and "municipal housekeeper" Caroline Bartlett Crane, Dreiser regarded such women as playing a crucial role in ensuring that the aims of Progressive reform were realized in the face of resistance from male elites. This overt appeal to women's political agency, and its underlying assumptions about the importance of women as social actors, is particularly significant since, aside from the suffrage issue and a chapter in *Dreiser Looks at Russia*, Dreiser seldom explicitly treats gender as a politicized category.

In 1910 Dreiser left his editor's desk. As a full-time writer, he quickly became a significant player in the literary and social ferment of the day. His personal rebellion from middle-class respectability, marriage, and outworn literary conventions mirrored the larger social revolution of the period. He settled in Greenwich Village and befriended, among others, *Masses* publisher Max Eastman, anarchist Emma Goldman, feminist Crystal Eastman, avant-garde artists such as John Sloan and Eugene O'Neill, bohemian author Floyd Dell, Bolshevik activists John Reed and Louise Bryant, and radical labor leader "Big Bill" Haywood. Over raucous meals at Polly's Restaurant and the Liberal Club, he engaged in vigorous discussions on issues such as a woman's right to vote and to have access to birth control, the right of labor to unionize, and the recognition of the Soviet experiment in Russia, for which they were dubbed "Reds." Most important for Dreiser, his cohorts championed the freedom to depict censored subjects, especially sexuality, in the arts.

Dreiser's critique of "puritanism" reached its apogee in "Life, Art and America" (1917). The essay attacks the overt idealism of the American mind and what Dreiser sees as the national obsession with sexual morality, and holds these traits responsible for keeping "the American in his highly romantic state of self deception," blind to the realities of sexuality, material-ism, class conflict, and corporate power.

On another front, Dreiser expressed his opposition to American entry into World War I in "American Idealism and German Frightfulness." Writ-ten in 1917, but suppressed under the Espionage Act and unpublished until this edition, the essay contests Woodrow Wilson's claims for America's unique global role in defending democracy, asserting that "America is largely the land of *the free corporation,* not of the individual." Dreiser's thesis de-rived in large part from his longstanding interest in the power of dominant individuals, which also informs the Cowperwood trilogy of novels. This led him to argue that there was no significant difference in social organization between Germany with its titled bureaucrats and army lords, Britain with its hereditary aristocracy, and America with its monopoly-owning millionaires and billionaires. With the privilege of hindsight, Dreiser's antipathy toward the English has come to appear more eccentric than it was at the time, yet it might be argued that this perspective allowed Dreiser to see similarities between America and the imperial nations of Europe, which were obscured by the rhetoric of exceptionalism.

In any case, for Dreiser at this point, it was futile to oppose the economic hierarchy that assured corporate power, since "the world is ruled by force, guided by superior intelligence or ability . . . big brains rule little ones everywhere." Acknowledging the dynamism and strength of capitalism, Dreiser's fundamental challenge in the 1910s and 1920s was to the capital-ist system's reliance on discourses of moral right and individual freedom. Eschewing such appeals himself, he wondered in a 1919 essay whether America needed "More Democracy Or Less?" Thus it was that, as late as his 1927–28 visit to Russia, as an official guest of the state to evaluate progress in the decade after the October revolution, Dreiser angered his hosts by praising American individualism.

Dreiser's attitude toward Russia shifted as soon as he returned to New York and learned that breadlines had appeared amidst the ostentatious consumption of the "roaring twenties."[1] Still, it took the upheavals of the Great Depression for Dreiser to consider "individuality" as an antisocial "myth" and Soviet Russia as a model of social organization. As unemployment spiraled, reaching over fifteen million in 1933, Dreiser rethought the Soviet experiment and what appeared increasingly to be the failure of America's free market system. Among intellectuals, he was far from alone in this, but for Dreiser it was a very personal matter. "I will never forget," he had announced in the concluding chapter of *Dreiser Looks at Russia* (1928) "that via Communism . . . it is possible to remove the dreadful sense of social misery in one direction or another which has so afflicted me in my own life in America and ever since I have been old enough to know what social misery was."[2]

As the young "Prophet" of *Ev'ry Month* he had proclaimed, "Surely the lever that moves the Universe is pain." In the early 1930s the American scene appeared to be changing into a large Dreiserian novel. The country was witnessing soup kitchens, the social displacement of families, the revival of racism, bloody battles between unions and big business, violent conflicts between miners and corporations, the plight of farmers in the dust bowl, the imprisonment of political radicals, and the threat of a world war. For the first time Dreiser viewed such ills as systemic to the American way of life.

As it did for many Americans, the Great Depression propelled Dreiser toward the political left. Dreiser's trajectory was, however, unusual in several ways. First, his critique of individualism was originally launched out of a sense of the contradiction between the historical reality of the competitive and exploitative nature of American capitalism—whose "force" and positive dynamics Dreiser recognized in novels such as *The Financier* (1912), *The Titan* (1914) and *The "Genius"* (1915)—and the official morality of self-discipline, epitomized by the American emphasis on sexual respectability.

Moreover, the question of "What to Do" (the Tolstoyan title of a late poem) about the country's social ills perplexed Dreiser. He praised the ideas of the Communist Party, but he could not abide the party's lectures on the "correct" political lines to follow. Although he supported many of their initiatives, Dreiser felt most party members were ideologues who blindly followed Russian norms and did not adapt their platform to American realities. Nevertheless, he received much practical support from the party—and in turn argued for its legitimacy and right to run candidates for office. Dreiser's identification with the left led to publications such as *Tragic America* (1931), which offers wide-ranging criticism of American institutions from the Supreme Court to the federal system, from the railroads to the Church, largely on the basis that their overt commitment to democracy, individual freedom, and morality only camouflaged corporate power.

In the early 1930s, with organizational help from Communist Party members, Dreiser founded and chaired the National Committee for the Defense of Political Prisoners, which publicized cases of class and racial injustice and raised money to provide humanitarian and legal aid for victims. Lending his name to several protests against the violent suppression of distressed labor under Herbert Hoover, Dreiser was prominent in the campaign on behalf of the Scottsboro boys, nine African American children and youths sentenced to death on questionable evidence, and led a committee to Harlan County, Kentucky, to investigate claims that members of Communist-organized miners' unions had been violently attacked, their meetings broken up and soup kitchens dynamited, with the complicity of the local police, judiciary, and press. The results were published in *Labor Defender* and other leftwing publications, and in the volume *Harlan Miners Speak* (1932), which also contained Dreiser's critique of "grim and rapacious individualism." Throughout the early 1930s Dreiser wrote in defense of such victims of legalized and often violent persecution as Tom Mooney and Warren K. Billings, incarcerated on perjured testimony during the postwar Red Scare and not released until 1939, and Yetta Stromberg, a communist children's camp organizer imprisoned for flying the red flag. In the 1930s and 1940s Dreiser also campaigned vigorously against militarism and war, attending a July 1938 conference in Paris at which a broad spectrum of political figures, from conservative British and French politicians to communists, protested the bombardment of Spanish and Chinese civilians, and subsequently tried to organize war relief for Spain.

By this point Dreiser's belief that corporate capitalism was "an inevitable law of nature," as he had called it in "American Idealism and German Frightfulness," had become obsolete. The turning point for him was the conjunction of the Great Depression with the latter half of Herbert Hoover's presidential term, from 1930 to 1932. For Dreiser, Hoover's America did not simply demonstrate the economic failure of capitalism but showed that in this moment of crisis those in power would try to protect their privileged status even if it added to the distress of those already at the bottom of society: industrial workers, displaced farmers, poor white miners, and African Americans.

Although Dreiser was ambivalent about many of the tactics of the communists, he realized that they constituted one of the few organized parties that actively supported these victims of the social order. He supported the Communist presidential campaign in 1931, and subsequently engaged with a variety of leftist groups, including nonaligned communists and socialists, technocrats, and Upton Sinclair's End Poverty in California (E.P.I.C.) campaign. Dreiser worked with the political activist Max Eastman to try to unify various nonaligned groups in February 1934, and he contributed four essays to Alfred M. Bingham and Selden Rodman's monthly *Common Sense*, which was aimed at providing a radical alternative to the New Deal by synthesizing an independent socialist movement from the farmer-labor and technocracy movements. At the same time Dreiser tried to interest mainstream readers in leftwing ideas and issues in the pages of the politically eclectic *American Spectator*, the literary newspaper of which he was joint editor from 1932 to 1934.

As political freedoms and economic conditions improved under Roosevelt's New Deal, Dreiser devoted more time to considering wider questions of political and social values. Essays such as "Flies and Locusts" (1933) combine fierce criticism of the narrow pursuit of economic profit, with an appeal for genuinely innovative, social, and creative activity, a perspective extended to international scope in the 1938 speech "Equity between Nations." Despite his connections to extreme left activists, Dreiser supported Roosevelt's reelection campaign in 1936 and subsequently corresponded directly with F.D.R. and Eleanor Roosevelt on a variety of issues, from the provision of relief to the civilian victims of the Spanish Civil War to the welfare of American children. Visiting Barcelona in July 1938 he witnessed at first hand the destruction wrought by the bombing of civilians. The experience confirmed Dreiser's negative view of Britain and France, who he felt had abandoned Spain's democratically elected socialist government to the forces of fascism. This was a decisive factor in his rejection of their appeal for support once Hitler turned on them in 1939.

Between 1930 and his death in 1945 Dreiser became well known for speaking out on behalf of communist campaigns, and for staunchly defending the internal and foreign policy of the Soviet Union. Yet he was largely indifferent toward, and even critical of, two of the main intellectual and emotional appeals that Marxism-Leninism made in the 1930s: its promise to deliver a scientific theory of history, and its rhetoric of class solidarity. In *Tragic America* and other writings, Dreiser repeatedly emphasized the importance of adapting Marxian ideology to American traditions, "even if it has to lose its own identity," as he put it in his contribution to the 1936 *Partisan Review* symposium on Marxism and the American Tradition, "What is Americanism?"

As a result, Dreiser was often out of step not only with the political mainstream but with others on the left (his overtures toward Communist Party membership in 1931 were rebuffed). In contrast to American writers who were attracted by the coalition-building of the Popular Front, Dreiser supported communism most vocally at the moments of its greatest isolation from the American mainstream—in the period between the revelation of the nonaggression pact between Germany and Russia in September 1939 and Hitler's invasion of Russia in June 1941, and during the birth of Cold War tensions in mid- and late 1945. Dreiser's belated membership in the Communist Party just before his death in 1945 demonstrated how different his trajectory was than that of former cohorts such as Max Eastman and John Dos Passos, who were by then already embarked on the rightward movement that would typify much American intellectual life in the 1950s. As ever, Dreiser's motives, described in "Theodore Dreiser Joins Communist Party," were highly personal.

* * *

Dreiser's political writing contains important parallels to his fiction. In both he pursues the plotting of human agency against social, economic, and ideological forces and circumstances. Especially in the earlier phases of his career, when he addressed a mainstream audience, key ideas in his fiction and social criticism overlapped and intersected. Figures such as the "Captain," described marshalling Manhattan's homeless in journalism and in *Sister Carrie* (1900), cross the boundaries between fiction and political writing. Such boundaries are further blurred in the hybrid short story/ philosophical meditation "The Toil of the Laborer" and in short fiction such as the 1904 city sketch "Cradle of Tears." The latter confronts readers with the pain suffered by destitute or unmarried mothers who give up their children to the New York Foundling Hospital, asking repeatedly, "Here is a condition. What will you do about it?" It is a question that is implicit in the novel *Jennie Gerhardt* (1911). Dreiser's preoccupation in *Ev'ry Month* and *The Delineator* with the sociopolitical agency through which abuses could be abolished and social conditions improved is the counterpart of the ways that novels such as *Sister Carrie*, *Jennie Gerhardt*, and the Cowperwood trilogy set individuals against social pressure and convention. His address to Progressive women in *The Delineator* envisions a synthesis, in the realm of social activism, of the examples of the independent woman in novels such as *The "Genius"* and *The Financier*.

At intervals throughout his career, Dreiser took up in the political sphere specific issues depicted in his fiction. The legal banning of contraception—whose asymmetrical effects on different classes and ethnic groups are central to *An American Tragedy* and *A Gallery of Women* (1929)—is forcefully contested in "A Word Concerning Birth Control" (1921). Dreiser's campaigning on behalf of the Scottsboro boys in the 1930s, whom he feared would fall victim to a "a lynching concealed in the forms of law," was informed by his own experience of witnessing a lynching in Missouri while a newspaper reporter in 1894, fictionalized in the short story "Nigger Jeff" (1901). The interest in Asian culture and philosophy, manifested in the closing chapters of *The Stoic* (1947), has its political expression in 1939's "The Dawn Is in the East."

Like his fiction, Dreiser's political writings constitute a "twentieth century quest."[3] Central to that quest is the attempt—sometimes implicit, sometimes explicit—to marry his critique of worldviews derived from moralistic frameworks with his commitment to what he called "equity." Dreiser therefore constantly returns to engage with the social outsider, or what he called "the underdog." As early as the November 1896 *Ev'ry Month*, Dreiser asserts that "there is no charity outside of that existing in the heart, the eye and the hand of one toward the suffering and woe of a visible *other*."[4] This kind of charity is similar to that exercised and demanded by the "Captain," described in *Sister Carrie* as "an ex-soldier turned religionist, who, having suffered the whips and privations of our peculiar social system, had concluded that his duty to the God which he conceived lay in aiding his fellow-man."[5] These examples initiate a trope—the visible presence of the other, which makes an implicit demand for recognition and aid, without recourse to conventional moral and ethical frameworks—that appears repeatedly in Dreiser's fiction and in his political writing. Almost forty years later, in his speech "Loyalist Spain—July 1938," Dreiser depicts another set of "others" encountered, like the Captain and the homeless men he assembles, on city streets. There it is the inhabitants of war-torn Barcelona, whose biographies and inner lives can only be matter for speculation, yet whose plight still cries out for ameliorative action. Typically, Dreiser frames his appeal for aid by reference to a direct engagement with these people, explicitly contrasting this with Christian models of organized charity.[6] He closes the speech by distinguishing between war relief and the activities of Church missionary societies, arguing that help be given to Spanish civilians without "any of that smug glow that suggests that such conditions can never come here, or are not made here."

This was one way, on a personal level, to harmonize the pursuit of equity with a critique of conventional moral frameworks. But Dreiser goes further, connecting the responsibilities of individuals with national and international politics—in this case America's role in the struggle between Spanish Loyalists and fascist-supported Nationalists. In doing so, Dreiser registers the historical emergence of the United States as "a world weather-maker" in "wars and international affairs," which had taken place over the decades since he first wrote about the nation's responsibilities with regard to Cuban independence in 1896 (see "America, Europe, and Cuba").

Dreiser's hopes for postwar cooperation between America and the Soviet Union already looked doomed by the time of his death in December 1945.

But his political writing does more than evoke a road not taken by history, and amounts to more than the record of a remarkably wide-ranging series of campaigns and criticisms. His last political works especially respond to their moment in ways that resonate well into the twenty-first century. In wartime broadcasts to Europe, and in pieces such as "Interdependence" and "What to Do," Dreiser explores the global role of the United States and links individual action to global politics, in the context of the "One Worldism" of the time.

In the suppressed essay of 1917, "American Idealism and German Frightfulness," Dreiser asks of America, "But what are you going to do with a nation of persistent idealists who are so ignorant of history and of natural law as to imagine that they are called upon to play the part of a moralistic and Puritanic Messiah, not only to the world, but to the universe, no less?" The heightened rhetoric implies his alienation from the nativism and nationalism dominating wartime America, but it is a question Dreiser meant for his readers to take seriously. His political writing continues to pose such unsettling questions of individual morality, national responsibility, and global relations.

Notes

1. See TD to Ruth Kennell, 24 February 1928, in Theodore Dreiser, *Letters to Women. New Letters, Volume II*, ed. Thomas P. Riggio (Urbana: University of Illinois Press, 2009), 200–201; and see Theodore Dreiser, *Interviews*, ed. Frederic E. Rusch and Donald Pizer (Urbana: University of Illinois Press, 2004), 165–66.

2. Theodore Dreiser, *Dreiser Looks at Russia* (New York: Horace Liveright, 1928), 252.

3. Lawrence E. Hussman, *Dreiser and his Fiction: A Twentieth-Century Quest* (Philadelphia: University of Pennsylvania Press, 1983).

4. Nancy Warner Barrineau, ed., *Theodore Dreiser's Ev'ry Month* (Athens: University of Georgia Press, 1996), 203.

5. Theodore Dreiser, *Sister Carrie*, ed. John C. Berkey, Alice M. Winters, James L. W. West III, and Neda M. Westlake (Philadelphia: University of Pennsylvania Press, 1981), 465. See also the historical 1900 text in Theodore Dreiser, *Sister Carrie*, ed. Donald Pizer (New York: Norton Critical Edition, 3rd ed., 2006), 329.

6. In these examples, Dreiser anticipates the prominence given to the "face of the other" in the ethical philosophy of Emmanuel Levinas. Like Levinas, Dreiser experiences the encounter with the other as making a direct ethical demand, which requires that the other's absolute difference from the self is recognized. Levinas's insistence on the phenomenological nature of the self-other encounter, as distinct from the sanction of an abstract system of ethics or morality, may also be considered as elaborating philosophically on the central crux of Dreiser's political thinking. See Emmanuel Levinas, *Totality and Infinity: An Essay on Exteriority*, trans. Alphonso Lingis (Pittsburgh: Duquesne University Press, 1969); Emmanuel Levinas, *Otherwise Than Being: Or Beyond Essence*, trans. Alphonso Lingis (Pittsburgh: Duquesne University Press, 1999).

EDITORIAL NOTE

The corpus of Dreiser's political writing and social criticism comprises more than two hundred editorials, articles for magazines and newspapers, essays, broadsides, and speeches, and much or all of four books, *Hey Rub-a-Dub-Dub* (1920), *Dreiser Looks at Russia* (1928), *Tragic America* (1931), and *America Is Worth Saving* (1941). With very few exceptions, these works have been long out of print. This edition presents selections that have been newly edited from published work and from Dreiser's private papers, preserved at the Van Pelt Library at the University of Pennsylvania (abbreviated to DPUP throughout). Selections are assembled in chronological order of composition, divided into four periods. Detailed historical commentaries put the selections into the context of Dreiser's times and his other output, principally his fiction. Each part also contains a list of additional writings by Dreiser that could not be included for reasons of space. The aim throughout has been to make available the core of Dreiser's political writing, to demonstrate its range and depth, and to provide the resources for readers to make their own judgments on debated issues.

For the most prominent of these debates—over the significance of Dreiser's close relationship with the Communist Party after 1930, and the accusation of anti-Semitism first leveled by Hutchins Hapgood in the 1930s—see the historical commentaries to parts 3 and 4. Alternative views on Dreiser's communism can be found in Lionel Trilling, *The Liberal Imagination: Essays on Literature and Society* (New York and London: Harcourt Brace Jovanovich, 1950), 11, and W. A. Swanberg, *Dreiser* (New York: Charles Scribner's Sons, 1965). For a different view of Dreiser's alleged anti-Semitism, see Donald Pizer, *American Naturalism and the Jews: Garland, Norris, Dreiser, Wharton, and Cather* (Urbana: University of Illinois Press, 2008), 31–49.

All of the texts in this edition were intended to be public documents and have therefore been edited as such. (Dreiser's 1933 letters to Hapgood constitute a partial exception, since they originated as private letters, but Dreiser later acceded to Hapgood's request to publish them, providing him with fair typewritten copies.) Texts have been newly edited from Dreiser's final typescripts, where these are extant, with reference to the published versions. Each selection is introduced by a headnote that gives the place of first publication, and each is followed by a textual note giving further information.

Typographical errors have been corrected. Spellings and punctuation have been silently standardized to contemporary American usage (for example, sweater-shop to sweatshop; to-day to today; moralic to moralistic; co-operation to cooperation; Roumania to Romania; Marti to Martí; Tchicherin to Chicherin; Czar to Tsar). Where capitalization signifies a particular political conceptualization, notably when referring to Communists/communists, Communism/communism, and Fascism/fascism, Dreiser's usage, or that of the editors of his chosen publication, is retained. Where Dreiser uses alternative forms in different places, these have been silently standardized (Lao-tzu for Lao Tze and Lao-Tse). Expressions of number have not been normalized; rather, the variety of original forms of publication has been respected.

Where substantive differences occur between published versions, or between a published version and the latest typescript, efforts have been made to ascertain Dreiser's intentions with reference to his general objectives at the time of composition. Significant differences are indicated in the notes and the textual notes to each selection, and in the headnote if particularly important. A full list of emendations is lodged with the Dreiser Papers at the Rare Book and Manuscript Library of the University of Pennsylvania.

Incidental factual errors, such as the misattribution in "American Idealism and German Frightfulness" of the Panama Canal Zone to Bolivia rather than Colombia, have been corrected.

Dreiser occasionally, as in "American Idealism and German Frightfulness" and *Tragic America*, made disputatious use of statistical information. In such cases Dreiser's formulations have been retained while further information is cited in notes.

Some material has been cut to avoid repetition and for reasons of space. Cuts of less than one paragraph are indicated by a row of three points. Longer cuts are indicated by a row of four asterisks (* * * *).

The notes identify specific people, events, works, allusions, and quotations when these are not part of common knowledge. For example, President Woodrow Wilson is not identified, but members of his administration and specific policies or speeches are identified and explained. In order to avoid repetition, such notes are provided only for the first citation in the volume. Specific references are given for sources of information on controversial topics; otherwise the sources of historical data are so numerous and diverse as to preclude separate listing. Two reference works, however, have been invaluable: *A Theodore Dreiser Encyclopedia*, edited by Keith Newlin (Westport, Conn.: Greenwood Press, 2003), and *Theodore Dreiser: A Primary and Secondary Bibliography*, 2nd edition, edited by Donald Pizer, Richard W. Dowell, and Frederic E. Rush (Boston: G. K. Hall, 1991).

The following abbreviations are used for political organizations or policies:

A.F.L.	American Federation of Labor
Comintern	Communist International
C.I.O.	Committee for Industrial Organizing; after 1938, Congress of Industrial Organizations
E.P.I.C.	End Poverty in California
I.L.D.	International Labor Defense
I.W.W.	Industrial Workers of the World
N.A.A.C.P.	National Association for the Advancement of Colored People
N.M.U.	National Miners' Union
N.C.D.P.P.	National Committee for the Defense of Political Prisoners
N.R.A.	National Recovery Administration
R.U.P.	Rassemblement Universel Pour La Paix
U.M.W.	United Mine Workers of America

The following are abbreviations used for works cited in the editor's notes:

Barrineau, *Dreiser's Ev'ry Month: Theodore Dreiser's Ev'ry Month,* ed. Nancy Warner Barrineau (Athens: University of Georgia Press, 1996).

Dreiser Looks at Russia: Theodore Dreiser, *Dreiser Looks at Russia* (New York: Horace Liveright, 1928).

Dreiser's Russian Diary: Dreiser's Russian Diary, ed. Thomas P. Riggio and James L. W. West III (Philadelphia: University of Pennsylvania Press, 1996).

Elias, *Letters: Letters of Theodore Dreiser: A Selection,* ed. Robert H. Elias, 3 vols. (Philadelphia: University of Pennsylvania Press, 1959).

Hakutani, *Art, Music, and Literature: Theodore Dreiser: Art, Music, and Literature, 1897–1902,* ed. Yoshinobu Hakutani (Urbana: University of Illinois Press, 2001).

Hey Rub-a-Dub-Dub: Theodore Dreiser, *Hey Rub-a-Dub-Dub: A Book of the Mystery and Terror and Wonder of Life* (New York: Boni and Liveright, 1920).

Riggio, *Dreiser-Mencken Letters: The Correspondence of Theodore Dreiser and H. L. Mencken 1907–1945,* ed. Thomas P. Riggio, 2 vols. (Philadelphia: University of Pennsylvania Press, 1986).

Riggio, *Letters to Women:* Theodore Dreiser, *Letters to Women. New Letters, Volume II,* ed. Thomas P. Riggio (Urbana: University of Illinois Press, 2009).

Rusch and Pizer, *Interviews: Theodore Dreiser: Interviews,* ed. Frederic E. Rusch and Donald Pizer (Urbana: University of Illinois Press, 2004).

Part One

1895–1910

Historical Commentary

In the decade and a half around the turn of the century, Dreiser addressed political issues in three main ways. As editor of *Ev'ry Month* from 1895 to 1897 he expressed trenchant criticism of contemporary American society, largely in moralistic and philosophical terms. *Ev'ry Month* also evaluated various attempts at social improvement on the part of individuals and groups, a focus that Dreiser went on to extend as a freelance writer, and on his return to editorship in 1905. From 1907 to 1910, as editor of the mass-circulation *The Delineator*, he adopted a "humanitarian editorial policy" that favored a feminist and Progressive agenda.

Ev'ry Month belonged to a wave of cheap illustrated magazines starting publication in the 1890s, spurred by population growth and advances in printing technology, especially the numerous illustrations made viable by cheap halftone engraving. Its original raison d'être was to publicize the songs of Howland, Haviland and Company, in which Dreiser's brother Paul Dresser was a partner, and was thus notionally aimed at middle-class housewives with access to a piano, though it doubtless also appealed to women aspiring to this status.[1] Dreiser's tenure as editor coincided with a severe economic depression that exacerbated political dissensus, setting wealth against labor, farmers against financiers, Southerners and Westerners against the East, Populists against the political establishment, and those who wanted "free silver" to ease the money supply against those who wished to retain the gold standard to protect banks and lenders. He took sides, ranging himself with suffragists, Westerners, farmers, striking garment workers, and immigrants, against centralized wealth, corruption, privilege, and social prejudice.

For his editorials Dreiser adopted a title, "Reflections," and a persona, signing them "the Prophet"; both signaled a critical distance from which to comment upon contemporary America. The editorial columns habitually opened with a topical or seasonal reference, for example, to the marriages of wealthy Americans to European nobles (December 1895), the bond issue intended to resolve the 1896 financial panic (February and March 1896), upcoming presidential elections (September and November 1896), the true meaning of patriotism (October 1896), Christmas sentiment (December 1896), or the Bradley-Martin Ball (March 1897), and went on to put it into a wider philosophical and historical context. This was then followed by between five and nine commentaries on various topics, in which

Dreiser frequently expressed sympathy for many of the marginalized groups of the period and made stinging moral criticism of the wealthy, privileged classes, who, he suggested, had usurped control of the nation's economy and its political and juridical institutions. "It has been the curse of every age," he argued, "this centralization of wealth—gathering where it least belongs" (November 1896).[2] Dreiser offered "a good word" on the "great and sure-to-be-victorious cause" of "woman suffrage" (see 15–17), sympathized with striking garment workers (October 1896), defended immigrants (April 1897), and polemicized about the state of public schools (May and June 1897). He inveighed against what he saw as the intrigues of the Republican Party (October 1895); systematic political corruption (January, April, and July 1896); "the evil of money influence in the courts" (July, November, and December 1896); and, in what would be a long-term concern, corrupt charitable organizations (November 1896). He also picked up on and recast the popular press rhetoric that called for military intervention in support of Cuba's struggle against Spanish colonial rule (November 1895, April 1896, July 1896, and January 1897).

The "Reflections" column's moral condemnation of wealth and power often embraced Populist criticism of the power of trusts (April 1896, March 1897), and occasionally employed overtly Populist rhetoric mistrustful of the "silent company" of financiers and capitalists who controlled the money supply (February 1896). *Ev'ry Month* focused closely on William Jennings Bryan's 1896 campaign for the presidency on a populist "free silver" plat-form. In the five months leading up to the election, "the Prophet" evaluated Bryan's potential to bring about significant change without ever referring to him explicitly, in ways that a politically aware readership (and Dreiser obviously assumed the readership of *Ev'ry Month* was politically aware) would have easily decoded. Thus, on the eve of Bryan's triumph in winning the Democratic Party nomination, the July 1896 "Reflections" opened with a meditation on the contradiction between the "ceaseless demand of the good citizen for pure politics" and "politics themselves." The distinction between reforming the political apparatus and using it in its current state was pertinent to Bryan's attempt to use the machinery of the Democratic Party in a two-horse presidential race, rather than mounting a third-party challenge. Bryan's famous oratorical skills—his victory at the Democratic Party convention was widely attributed to his "Cross of Gold" speech—prompted two discussions of oratory as a force in national politics. The September 1896 "Reflections" listed "loud-mouthed oratory" as one of the "huge national nothings" by which the population was diverted from paying attention to graft and fraud closer to home. The following month, however, oratory was considered as a means of inspiring people to action, and the orator "one of those hero-beings in whom the meaning of life finds its highest expression." This implicit support for Bryan was qualified by the discussion of true patriotism with which Dreiser had begun the column, and in which he concluded that no one in the current crop of politicians could qualify as a true patriot, since the contemporary political scene was dominated by wealth and "the patriot has invariably appeared with no wealth other than that of an abundantly generous nature." Dreiser opened the November 1896 "Reflections," the last before the election, with an openly Populist attack on "incompetence, bribery and blackmail" at the state level, "one of the questions not discussed in this campaign."[3] Typically, he was concerned that concentration on a single issue, the money supply, should not detract from the necessity of more sweeping change.

Ev'ry Month's coverage of social problems explored various means by which positive change could be brought about. "It is to the masses, not to the classes, that the appeal for the reform of the school system must be addressed," Dreiser argued in November 1896.[4] Six months later he reflected that the privileged also had a role to play: "One's duty consists, these days, in arousing a working sympathy among those whom the tide of fortune has elevated, for those whom the undertow of adversity has swept to the lowest depths of the sea of misery."[5] Dreiser frequently returned to the topic of charitable work to benefit the urban poor, with an ambivalence characterized by the February 1897 description of Rose Hawthorne Lathrop's mission to the Lower East Side. "Although her single efforts are meager in result," Dreiser writes, "it is still inspiring to see some one trying to do good, be it ever so weakly, for so many do not try at all."[6]

Several of the "Reflections" intermingled personal experience, feelings, desires, and morals with politics, in ways that anticipate *Sister Carrie* and subsequent novels. For example, discussion of the garment workers' strike in October 1896 was embedded in a cautionary tale that began, "To those who are infatuated with the thought of living in a city and of enjoying the so called delights of metropolitan life, the recent strikes in the sweat-shops of New York might furnish a little food for reflection."[7] In December 1896 another exemplary story cast a certain Weber, the profligate son of a millionaire, as a latter-day prodigal son, whose "progress . . . through gilded and glittering resorts, into the asylum and Potter's Field, must ever arrest the attention of the eye and the mind."[8] Cautionary tales such as these treat political issues (strikes, the abuse of wealth and privilege) as materials for narrative in a manner similar to Dreiser's fiction, evoking urban pleasure and danger, depicting individual lives as spectacles for others, and offering short life-stories as the basis for wider social, philosophical, and moral speculations.

In the four years following his departure from *Ev'ry Month* in the fall of 1897, Dreiser published over one hundred freelance articles in magazines such as *Ainslee's*, *Demorest's*, and *Cosmopolitan* on a tremendous variety of contemporary topics.[9] In several of these, Dreiser documented the conditions of the urban poor and various attempts to ameliorate such conditions by factory owners, charity workers, political representatives, and lone individuals, whether charitable, as in "A Touch of Human Brotherhood" (*Success*, March 1902) and "A Doer of the Word" (*Ainslee's*, June 1902); on the part of the dispossessed themselves, as in "Christmas in the Tenements" (*Harper's Weekly*, 6 December 1902); by political representatives, as in "A Mayor and His People" (*Era*, June 1903); by officialdom, as in "Our Government and Our Food" (*Demorest's*, December 1899) and "Atkinson on National Food Reform" (*Success*, January 1900); or from the perspective of industrial organization, as in "It Pays to Treat Workers Generously" (*Success*, September 1899), "The Railroad and the People: A New Educational Policy Now Operating in the West" (*Harper's Monthly*, February 1900), and "The Transmigration of the Sweat Shop" (*Puritan*, July 1900).

Questions of the agency through which positive change might be effected are highlighted in "A Mayor and His People," which presents what Dreiser calls "the story of an individual which possesses a political and social significance for every citizen of the United States."[10] Based on the career of Thomas P. Taylor, a reforming mayor of Bridgeport, Connecticut, from 1897 to 1899, the article describes the mayor's initial success in fighting municipal corruption and his subsequent defeat by forces of the railroad in combination with the political establishment. Taylor's story was important enough to Dreiser for him to rework it for the 1919 collection *Twelve Men*, where he reports the ex-mayor's response to electoral defeat in the following terms: "What has happened in my case is that, for the present, anyhow, I have come up against a strong corporation, stronger than I am. What I need to do is to go out somewhere and get some more strength in some way, it doesn't matter much how. People are not so much interested in me or you, or your or my ideals in their behalf, as they are in strength, an interesting spectacle."[11] An investigation into the possibilities for human agency and solidarity in the face of such spectacular, materialistic, and individualistic social relations informs the spectrum of Dreiser's output at this time. Questions of the individual's capacity to change society were paramount in his documentary reportage, such as "Curious Shifts of the Poor" (1899) and "The Tenement Toilers" (1902), and the philosophical, autobiographical, and political hybrid "The Toil of the Laborer" (1913, see 17–25). One form of ameliorative action was undertaken by the charitable individual known as the "Captain," a man who each evening collected donations on New

York's Broadway to fund beds for the homeless. In some ways the epitome of Dreiser's ideal of charitable work, the Captain was first described in a magazine article, "Curious Shifts of the Poor" (*Demorest's*, November 1899), then in the famous depiction of urban poverty in the latter stages of *Sister Carrie*, and again in "A Touch of Human Brotherhood," which appeared in Orison Swett Marden's *Success* magazine in 1902. Here and in several more of the thirty pieces he contributed to *Success*, Dreiser enlarged the scope of the individualistic ideology promoted by Marden—essentially the celebration of powerful individuals and advice on how readers might emulate them—to include examples of charity and industrial cooperation that emphasized social solidarity. Another *Success* piece from 1902, "The Tenement Toilers," described visits, alongside an official, to an immigrant home where garment work is being done under illegal conditions, and to the small factory run by the contractor who had given out the work. "The Tenement Toilers" and "Curious Shifts of the Poor" came to the same conclusion: that the existence of poverty was a symptom of a wider social malaise, a false belief in the power of money. While their form, tone, and content echoed Jacob Riis's 1890 exposé *How the Other Half Lives* (Dreiser would later enlist Riis as a contributor to *The Delineator*), this sweeping diagnosis of social ills sounded a different note than Riis's campaigns for specific reforms.

Between 1902 and 1913 Dreiser wrote numerous city sketches and short stories depicting life in New York's poorest districts. His observations of urban poverty regularly provided evidence for some moral or philosophical point, lesson, or comment, which in many cases is critical of some aspect of contemporary society. Dreiser called explicitly for change in "The Cradle of Tears" (1904), a short sketch describing the crib at the New York Foundling Hospital, into which women would place the human fruits of unwanted pregnancies. The story closes:

> Still, the tragedy repeats itself, and year after year and day after day the unlocked door is opened and dethroned virtue enters—the victim of ignorance and passion and affection—and a child is robbed of a home.
>
> I think there is a significant though concealed thought here, for nature in thus repeating a fact day after day and year after year raises a significant question. We are so dull. Sometimes it requires ten thousand or ten million repetitions to make us understand. "Here is a condition. What will you do about it? Here is a condition. What will you do about it? Here is a condition. What will you do about it?" That is the question each tragedy propounds, and finally we wake and listen. Then slowly some better way is discovered, some theory developed. We find often that there is an answer to some questions, at least if we have to remake ourselves, society, the face of the world, to get it.[12]

This concern for the welfare of destitute children, and the same kind of sentimental appeal for reform, would be features of Dreiser's editorship of *The Delineator* later in the decade.

Other sketches touched upon issues of economic inequality, social solidarity, and alienation. "The Man Who Bakes Your Bread" and "The Silent Worker" (both written in the mid-1900s and, like several others, published a few years later in the Sunday magazine of the socialist *New York Call* newspaper) depict workers whose labor was often invisible to middle-class Americans yet was crucial to everyday life. The short story "The Mighty Burke" (*McClure's*, May 1911) describes an Irish section foreman who initially seems to bully the Italian workers set under him, but who is revealed as heroic when, after a building collapses, he sacrifices himself for their sake. A 1903 manuscript bemoaned the results of "our modern congestion in cities," where not only "is the whole energy of our lives turned into a miserable struggle for the unattainable, namely, the uninterrupted and complete gratification of our desires, but our hearts are soured and our natures warped by the grimness of the struggle."[13] Warming to the theme of social alienation, Dreiser continues as follows:

> The effect of such an unnatural order of existence is the almost complete disappearance of the social amenities. We do not interest ourselves in the hardships, discomforts and toil of our fellow-citizens, or rather, neighbors. We fail even in the superficial cordiality that might pass for friendship and which, for want of something better, will sometimes fill the void of despair. Men do not really interest us. The humor and tragedy of their social impulses do not attract, save as a spectacle. We have no time and no patience for anything but what are considered the larger interests—music, the drama, society in its most blatant and impossible phase, and life as a whole.[14]

The manuscript's title, "A Call for a New Relationship," suggests the strand of social criticism in Dreiser's literary work at this time, though it was not adopted in the published version.

Dreiser returned to editing at *Smith's Magazine* from 1905 into 1906, where he served up a mix of fashion, fiction, and, riding the contemporary vogue for muckraking journalism, articles on socialism, the railroads, and the reorganization of the post office. Moving on to *Broadway* magazine in the middle of 1906, in its September issue Dreiser covered Anthony Comstock's persecution of publishers and interviewed sixteen-year old socialist firebrand Elizabeth Gurley Flynn, prefiguring what would become major concerns in the 1910s and 1930s, respectively. In June 1907 he accepted a lucrative position as editor of *The Delineator*, a prestigious women's fashion magazine published by the Butterick pattern company. With Dreiser's appointment as editor, company president George Warren Wilder saw the commercial potential of allying the magazine with the Progressive reform agenda that was energizing many women at the time. Like *Ev'ry Month, The Delineator* mingled the personal with the political, and even more than its predecessor, it did so by reference to the agency of women in effecting positive change. "*The Delineator*'s message is human betterment," Dreiser announced in a September 1907 editorial, "Its appeal is to the one great humanizing force of humanity—womanhood."[15]

Under this "humanitarian" editorial policy, Dreiser commissioned articles from feminists such as Ida Husted Harper and Mabel Potter Daggett, which covered the work of reformers Jane Addams (October 1907) and Caroline Bartlett Crane (June 1909), investigated municipal politics, and exposed the inhumane treatment of orphans in children's homes. His editorials, which were unsigned, called for a series of reforms, primarily concerned with the health and welfare of children, but also ranging across employers' liability legislation (October 1908 and April 1909), gun control (October 1908), temperance (July 1909), and an ecological concern with the over-production of timber (January 1909). Alongside the coverage of fashion, etiquette, features for girls (the "Jenny Wren Club" or the "Junior Delineator"), a little fiction, and other ephemeral material, *The Delineator* depicted an America beset by ignorance, vested economic interests, municipal corruption, and outdated organizations of various sorts, of which the preeminent examples were the charity-run orphan asylums. Against these, Dreiser's *Delineator* mustered typically Progressive values of organization, education, and the application of science, including technology and the emerging sociology, as well as the expansive sense of women's abilities as "housekeepers" and mothers that was common to much contemporary feminist and Progressive thinking.

During his editorship, Dreiser oversaw two campaigns of national prominence: Child Rescue, launched in November 1907, and in 1909 the Schools for Mothers. In addition, he published symposia on "What Is the Matter with the Churches?" and the state of public schools, and repeatedly called attention to issues of children's health: clean schools, the provision of safe milk and drinking water, the prevention of tuberculosis, and the dangers of infection from house flies. At a time of considerable debate over the "New Woman" as a political, social, or cultural figure, *The Delineator* addressed women directly, enlisting their support for its various projects of social improvement individually and collectively, through Women's Clubs, the National Child Rescue League, and educational organizations. As Dreiser wrote in a November 1907 editorial on "Twentieth Century Charity": "If you would help your fellow-man permanently, pause not to sympathize with his wrongs, but sally forth determined to get him pure water, sanitary houses, fresh air, educational advantages, humane working conditions."[16] Adding that "this radical change in the charitable temper has been admirably met by women," Dreiser connected the professionalization of charitable work with the wider emergence of women as active agents in American society.

Tapping into the suffrage and Progressive reform movements, Dreiser's *Delineator* pushed at the boundaries of contemporary notions of domesticity. The injunction to "sally forth" was put into historical context by "What She Did for Us," a short series on a previous generation of women's rights campaigners, featuring Elizabeth Cady Stanton and Susan B. Anthony. Embracing the feminist and Progressive view that "municipal government is domestic housekeeping on a broader scale," the magazine announced a "notable series of articles on women's suffrage" in February 1908.[17] The latent abilities of women were suggested by the emblem chosen to decorate the editorial columns—what looks to be a sewing needle, partially wrapped in cloth. In the editorials, entitled "Concerning Us All," Dreiser set about releasing this potential and coordinating women's abilities for the good of society as a whole.

The Child Rescue Campaign—"for the child that needs a home and the home that needs a child"—was at the center of contemporary debates over women, class, immigration, "race," national development, and the role of religion in American institutions, since many orphanages were run by Catholic or Protestant organizations. It was launched with two articles: "The Child Without a Home" by Mabel Potter Daggett, in the October 1907 issue, and Lydia Kingsmill Commander's "The Home Without a Child," in November.[18] Daggett's piece contains verbal echoes of both Dreiser's 1896 polemic in *Ev'ry Month,* and his 1904 sketch of the New York Foundling Hospital, "The Cradle of Tears." Commander, by contrast, was a prominent writer on "race suicide," a notion taken up by President Theodore Roosevelt, which constructed motherhood as a civic and national duty of middle-class "native" women. This was an anxious response to the reported statistics that two million married women were childless, while "ethnic" immigrants from places like China and Eastern Europe were reproducing twice as frequently as "Anglo-Teutons."[19]

During 1908 and early 1909, the activist elements of the Child Rescue campaign came increasingly to the fore as it ran up against the vested interests of the municipal and charity-run children's homes. In a coup that *The Delineator* would dwell upon at length over the ensuing months, Roosevelt's support was secured for a conference at the White House in January 1909 on "The Care of Dependent Children." The following month, as reported in the magazine, the president sent a special message to Congress, recommending various steps to bring orphanages in the District of Columbia and the Federal Territories under tighter supervision: regular inspections by the Boards of Charities, children's education to be overseen by Boards of Education (not the orphanages themselves), and compelling the orphanages to keep records.[20]

By 1909–10 Dreiser was moving toward a more radical position than that permitted by *The Delineator*. He found a congenial home away from home in Greenwich Village, where he socialized with radicals such as Emma Goldman and Max Eastman, who would have found the nativist elements of Child Rescue anathema. Though the editorship of what was essentially a fashion magazine jarred with his later self-image as a literary and political radical, Dreiser would remember the magazine's constraints rather than disowning it altogether, complaining retrospectively of the conditions imposed upon "the things we were trying to do" by the "raw commercial force and theory that underlay the whole thing."[21] In 1921 he referred specifically to "Roosevelt with his race suicide mush" (see "A Word Concerning Birth Control," 93).

In 1909 Dreiser secretly (he was under exclusive contract to the Butterick Company) took control of a small magazine, *The Bohemian*, overseeing the issues for September, October, November, and December. "At the Sign of the Lead Pencil" was its unsigned editorial department, presented as "our viewpoint of the worthwhile events of the times" and intended to contain, Dreiser told a potential contributor, "broad interesting shots at current conditions from any point of view so long as it is clever."[22] The principal contributors were Dreiser himself, nominal editor Fritz Krog, and H. L. Mencken.

This sense of freewheeling critical wit was Dreiser's way of addressing *The Bohemian*'s readership of would-be urbane sophisticates. The magazine advertised itself on the basis that "we're *different*" and the "At the Sign of the Lead Pencil" editorials do indeed take a variety of "interesting shots at current conditions." There was a detailed discussion of corporate land-grabbing in the far West, and several topics from *Ev'ry Month* and *The Delineator* are revisited: the defects of organized charity, the repeated attempts to eradicate the corrupt influence of Tammany Hall, the state of the public schools, and the class divisions attendant upon industrialization.[23] "The State of the Negro" (see 32–35), "The Day of Special Privileges" (see 35–37), and "The Death of Francisco Ferrer" (see 37–40) either raise new topics or add a significant dimension to issues Dreiser had already broached. Another editorial, "The Superior Sex," makes fun of contemporaries who insisted that men were innately more intelligent than women. "It is a human characteristic," it argues, "wide as the race, long as history, to consider those who hold an inferior position to be necessarily inferior by nature."[24] Although it is not possible to precisely ascribe authorship of this particular piece, the combination of dispelling prejudice and trying to understand its historical roots recurs frequently in Dreiser's later output.

Notes

1. See Joseph Katz, "Theodore Dreiser's *Ev'ry Month*," *Library Chronicle of the University of Pennsylvania* 38 (1972): 46–66; Barrineau, *Dreiser's Ev'ry Month*, xviii–xix.

2. Barrineau, *Dreiser's Ev'ry Month*, 199.

3. Barrineau, *Dreiser's Ev'ry Month*, 49, 116, 164, 190, 184, 196.

4. Barrineau, *Dreiser's Ev'ry Month*, 46, 200.

5. The Prophet [Theodore Dreiser], "Reflections," *Ev'ry Month*, May 1897, p. 21.

6. The Prophet [Theodore Dreiser], "Reflections," *Ev'ry Month*, February 1897, p. 3. Dreiser covered Lathrop's work in more detail the following month, under the pseudonym S. J. White, in "A Social Samaritan: Rose Hawthorne Lathrop's Mission to the Afflicted," *Ev'ry Month*, March 1897, p. 25.

7. Barrineau, *Dreiser's Ev'ry Month*, 190–91.

8. Barrineau, *Dreiser's Ev'ry Month*, 213–16.

9. For a complete list of Dreiser's freelance articles in this period see Hakutani, *Art, Music, and Literature*, 285–89.

10. Theodore Dreiser, "A Mayor and His People," *Era* 11 (June 1903): 578.

11. Theodore Dreiser, "A Mayor and His People," *Twelve Men* (New York: Horace Liveright, 1919), 341.

12. Theodore Dreiser, "The Cradle of Tears," *The Color of a Great City* (New York: Boni & Liveright, 1923), 241.

13. Theodore Dreiser, "A Call for a New Relationship," holograph manuscript, DPUP, 1, 2. A revised version was published as "The Loneliness of the City," *Tom Watson's Magazine* 2 (October 1905): 474–75.

14. Dreiser, "A Call for a New Relationship," 2–3.

15. Unsigned editorial, "Between You and Your Editor: Personal Talks with the Delineator Family," *Delineator* 70:3 (September 1907): 284.

16. Unsigned editorial, "Concerning Us All," *Delineator* 70:5 (November 1907): 733.

17. Unsigned article, "Announcement of a Notable Series of Articles on Women's Suffrage, Prepared under the Direction of Bertha Damaris Knobe," *Delineator* 71:2 (February 1908): 244.

18. Mabel Potter Daggett, "The Child without a Home," *Delineator* 70:3 (October 1907): 505–10; Lydia Kingsmill Commander, "The Home without a Child," *Delineator* 70:4 (November 1907): 720–23, 830.

19. On Child Rescue as a program of Americanization, see Julie Berebitsky, *Like Our Very Own: Adoption and the Changing Nature of Motherhood, 1851–1950* (Lawrence: University Press of Kansas, 2000), chapter 2.

20. Unsigned article, "The President Acts: Full Text of His Message to Congress in Relation to the Care of Dependent Children," *Delineator* 73:5 (May 1909): 696.

21. Quoted in F. O. Matthiessen, *Theodore Dreiser. The American Men of Letters Series* (New York: William Sloane Associates, 1951), 107.

22. Unsigned editorial, "At the Sign of the Lead Pencil," unpaginated section, *Bohemian* 17 (September 1909); TD to H. L. Mencken, 8 August 1909, DPUP.

23. Unsigned editorials, "Ballinger vs. Pinchot," *Bohemian* 17 (November 1909): 556–58; "The Defects of Organized Charity," *Bohemian* 17 (October 1909): 429–31;

"Tammany Hall," *Bohemian* 17 (November 1909): 558–60; "How Our Public Schools Are Run," *Bohemian* 17 (November 1909): 560–61; "Pittsburgh," *Bohemian* 17 (December 1909): 712–14.

24. Unsigned editorial, "The Superior Sex," *Bohemian* 17 (October 1909): 420.

Further Reading

Nancy Warner Barrineau, ed. *Theodore Dreiser's Ev'ry Month*. Athens and London: University of Georgia Press, 1996.
"Curious Shifts of the Poor." *Demorest's* 36 (November 1899): 22–26.
"A Mayor and His People." *Era*, June 1903, pp. 578–84. Revised version in *Twelve Men*. New York: Boni and Liveright, 1919, 320–43.
"The Tenement Toilers." *Success* 5 (April 1902): 213–14, 232. Reprinted as "The Toilers of the Tenements," in *New York Call*, 24 August 1919, *Call Magazine*, pp. 1, 6–7.
"The Cradle of Tears." *New York Daily News*, 27 March 1904, Colored Section, p. 4. Reprinted in *The Color of a Great City*. New York: Boni and Liveright, 1923, 239–41.
"The Philanthropy of the Poor." *The Delineator* 71:5 (May 1908): 776.
"Your Christmas Gift to Your Country." *The Delineator* 74:6 (December 1909): 494.
"Go Thou and Do Likewise." *The Delineator* 74:6 (December 1909): 494.
"Pittsburgh." *The Bohemian* 17 (December 1909): 712–14.

America, Europe, and Cuba

Ev'ry Month: An Illustrated Magazine of Popular Music, The Drama, and Literature, November 1895.

The Cuban insurgency against Spanish colonial rule and Spain's repressive military response were widely reported in the American press between 1895 and 1898. The Hearst and Pulitzer newspapers conducted a sensationalistic campaign for military intervention on behalf of the Cubans, which was decried by anti-imperialists such as Mark Twain and William James. Dreiser sets a foot in each camp, using heavy irony to solicit support for the heroic and persecuted Cubans and to highlight the combination of arrogance and deference in American attitudes toward the Old World. In 1898 the United States entered the war, swiftly defeating Spain and, after a very heated congressional debate, taking colonial control of Guam and the Philippines.

We are getting to be a very great people, I think. Everything points that way. We are marrying our millionaire daughters off to foreign dukes and earls, and bonding our cities in the interest of our loving protectors, the bankers of Europe.[1] We are chasing off to foreign capitals every spring-time 100,000 strong, and spending $100,000,000 all told, so that when the bankers begin to call for the settlement of our checks left with them, in gold, our treasury supply sinks below the confidence mark and we suffer a panic. We have a great society navy with twenty-five battleships as ornaments for our summer resorts, and a great National Guard to watch and downtread our 5,000 troublesome Indians. In all our greatness we are no longer worried by the affairs of smaller American nations. Our citizens may be seized and murdered by the cheap Chinese and the groveling powers of the Old World generally, while we wave our national hand over it all in silent disdain. We are too large to fool with any nation outside of England. There comes the ignorant and intolerant Spanish to our door, despoiling the fairest Isle of our shores, and we hear not the cries of the downtrodden. There come the sons of the Inquisition and the sponsors of murder and rapine, dragging with them the cruel implements of greed and hatred, and we hear not the moans of the patriots nor their earnest pleadings for aid. The children of liberty are being despoiled at our door, the smoke of feudal cannon and the drip of American blood are in our ears and nostrils, but we are too great to pulsate anew with the fiery blood of liberty. While busily engaged in allying ourselves with the nobility of Europe, how can we be expected to look after the nobility of Cuba. Pshaw! We have had enough of patriots. What needs the western hemisphere with Maceos and perished Martís when it has already had Washington and Bolivar, Lincoln and Sucre.[2] Why more revolutions when all are free except Cuba? There is no need. Let Cuba struggle alone.

Textual Note: "Review of the Month," editorial signed "The Prophet," *Ev'ry Month: An Illustrated Magazine of Popular Music, The Drama, and Literature*, November 1895, p. 2. Dreiser's editorials for *Ev'ry Month* were either unsigned, or more frequently, signed "The Prophet," in part to camouflage the extent of his contributions to the magazine. Title supplied by the present editors.

1. Dreiser expanded his criticism of "the vigorous and disagreeable struggles of some wealthy Americans to become as un-American as possible" in the August 1896 *Ev'ry Month*. As here, his central example of Europhilia was the contracting of marriages that involved the exchange of American money for old-world prestige. Wealth, he went on to argue, "will cause the possessor of it to see the lowness and cheapness of Americans and the grandeur and superior beauties of Europeans."

2. Brothers Antonio Maceo Grajales (1845–96) and José Maceo Grajales (1849–96) returned to Cuba from exile in 1895 to help lead the insurgency. The former, nicknamed the "Bronze Titan" due to his heroism and mixed racial heritage, was pictured in the January 1897 issue of *Ev'ry Month* after his death in battle on 7 December 1896. José Julian Martí (1853–95), a poet, teacher, and anti-imperialist activist of continuing significance, had been killed by Spanish forces in May 1895. *El Liberator* Simón Bolívar (1783–1839) was the celebrated hero of South American independence movements and is named alongside presidents George Washington and Abraham Lincoln and his lieutenant, Antonio José de Sucre (1795–1830), the first president of Bolivia.

Women's Suffrage

Ev'ry Month: An Illustrated Magazine of Popular Music,
The Drama, and Literature, August 1896.

Woman Suffrage is a very old, and, in reason, undisputed subject, but a good word on behalf of a great and sure-to-be-victorious cause is never out of place, so be it set down here that the activity of women in every quarter is but a sign that she is coming out of her dark ages, and beginning to take to herself the half of life that belongs to her. Of course, it is said that so long as woman looks to man as her sole support and enters into matrimony convinced that her lot in life is to be devotion itself, in return for which she is to be supported, so long will she be the inferior in power and position, and, that is true. So long as she is brought up rigidly and carefully preserved from all but theoretical knowledge of the world, so long will she give cause for the sentiment concerning widows and orphans, which is no other than the charitable regard of a superior for an inferior. So long as the German idea brings its stand-still influence into the question, and women are advised to attend to "religion, children and kitchen,"[1] so long will the helplessness of women be one of the first arguments offered by men against her equal enfranchisement. Women are not helpless, but it will take a long time to convince some of them that they are not. The present sphere of the home is not exactly all that befits them, though it will take years of explanation before all of them appreciate the fact. They are not exactly dolls put on earth to be gloriously dressed and admired, but three fourths of them would prefer that impression to hold good, and the average man has for centuries been growing in the belief that such is their highest and most befitting state. They are capable when equally trained with their brothers, of doing any but manual labor, and neither man nor woman was ever intended to toil physically, and to delve and hew and draw, though they have not learned that fact because they have not learned very much about the possibilities of machinery. Introduce the proper machinery and men and women stand on equal ground.

There is no use talking about the superiority of women in some phases of necessity. Gray matter is gray matter, and it will work about as well through masculine as it will through feminine hands. Eyes are about the same in either sex; ears usually gauge accurately a moderate range of sound, and the other senses average up pretty fairly in the two sexes, though there are thousands who will not believe it. This general equality of the senses and sentiment speaks fairly well for the possible progress of women in the fields that do not involve hard manual labor, and as before stated, manual labor has nothing to do with the case. As soon as the wits of man have been properly sharpened by proper effort, machinery will come and do away with manual labor, when the sexes will be on a very fair starting basis. Such are the basic principles which underlay the question.

But there is no reason to suppose that the spheres of the two sexes are going to clash for long. There is, of course, some confusion at present owing to the desire of woman to take to herself as many rights as possible regardless of male opposition, and in this anxiety to gain her rights she will overshoot the mark, and take more than her rights, when, of course, the reaction will set in. Again, not having a full and clear apprehension of what her rights are *in toto,* she will be very apt to mistake a number of privileges as hers which do not rationally accrue to her, and these after some discussion and bitter experience, she will at length be willing to relinquish. Just at present she is reaching out and doing some very strange things, which time alone can justify or discredit. At present, there are so many to argue for or against her every move that a fair judgment is almost impossible, excellent authorities being at war, so to speak.

From a liberal point of view, she has a right to turn her hand to almost anything which her strength and mental capacity will permit of, but it is to be believed that in time she will drift into those fields of effort and usefulness which best agree with the gentleness and charity of her nature. The control of schools is one such field, and the conducting of great charitable institutions is another. Vast asylums for the poor, the physically afflicted and the insane, it will generally be agreed should be placed in her care. Considering her motherly capacity, it will be naturally supposed that in time women will gravitate into such earthly labor as involves this motherly sentiment most, and one such labor is that of purifying the politics of the land, under the laws of which her sons and daughters are to grow up, and which it is her duty to teach them to honor and obey. She will stand for goodness and purity in all things, and with her will stand the husband and father. On the subject of the good of the children, they will in their mutual intelligence, be united, and from such unity must naturally result the purer and brighter home, the better school and college, the kinder and more charitable asylums, the better hospitals and public institutions generally. She will not be less motherly, nor less attentive to home and the little ones, nor less interested in her husband's success, and back of it all will be her vast intelligence assisting to direct and control. Surely the old saw about two heads being better than one is a good and agreeable one, and the wonder of it is that it has never before been offered to the solution of the suffrage question.

Textual Note: "Reflections," editorial signed "The Prophet," *Ev'ry Month: An Il-lustrated Magazine of Popular Music, The Drama, and Literature,* August 1896, pp. 3–4. Title supplied by the present editors.

1. Adapted from the German phrase, "kinder [children], küche [kitchen], kirche [church]."

The Toil of the Laborer

New York Call, 13 July 1913.

Composed in late 1903 and early 1904, and based on Dreiser's experiences work-ing as a laborer for the New York Central railroad from June to December 1903, as he recovered from a physical and mental breakdown.

When revising the text for inclusion in Hey Rub-a-Dub-Dub *(1920), Drei-ser registered the lapse of time since his direct experience of laboring and adopted the reflective, philosophical tone of the volume. The direct plea toward the end of the second section—"That none should suffer, that none should want! This after all seemed the worthiest thought that sprang at the sight of a toil-weary man"— became "I wondered, and still do, for in spite of endless personal inconvenience I have never been able to believe that an unbreakable dead level of equality should maintain, that none should suffer overmuch, that none should want to the extreme. And yet at this time, at this place, the less varied seemed the all-to-be-desired."* (Hey Rub-a-Dub-Dub, *98.) In the 1920 version, a series of small revisions and additions in the third section reiterate the theme of how "the two elements of capital and labor would not adjust themselves within my consciousness," tending to shift the emphasis from class tension itself to the conscious contemplation of it.*

I.

The toil of the laboring man is artless. There is in it neither form nor color nor tone. For months I have been working as only working men work, and in the dreary round of the hours, it has come to me that the thing which was wearisome and disheartening about it was that it was utterly devoid of art. In the construction of a building whereat we labored for three long months, I discovered that with each day's labor I was in contact with only that which was formless and colorless and toneless. Huge, misshapen, dis-heartening piles of bricks; commonplace, indifferent and colorless masses of stone; wood, iron, sand, cement—bone and sinew of what was to be, but in themselves devoid of all that could appeal to the eye or touch the heart, and scattered about in such an aimless way as to bring to the mind nothing but a wearying sense of disorder. This disorder, it struck me, was not apparent in a distinguished way to all those who worked amid it. These mixers of mortar and carriers of brick toiled in the grime and dust without seeming to realize that it was a wretched condition—hard, grim, and so far as the sum of their individual lives were concerned, but meagerly profitable. Carpenters, masons and iron workers went sturdily about their work, but the artless and unlovely quality of it was over it all, and, despite the seeming unconsciousness, one felt the drag of its absence, the eagerness to get away—the innate yearning to be where things were not in the making—the urge to be out in the larger and more perfect world, where form and color and tone abound.

And seeing this to be so, and not being able in my own consciousness to explain why, my heart was sad for a time and I wondered why life should be thus grimly organized: why formlessness in the parts of the things to be formed: why tonelessness in that which when laboriously organized would be all tone: why colorlessness in that which in the end would enliven the heart with color and dance before the eye, a perfect thing.

In the progress of the work, however, it was given to me to see that in the production of all things there is at the bottom this very formlessness innate. For to organize and perfect one thing we must take from and destroy another. And in taking from or destroying anything, we fly in the face of that which we most desire—order and harmony. Therefore, if we would have that which the inexplicable urge for something new and more beautiful commands, we must steel our hearts against the old and destroy it, but having committed the offense of destruction repay by the labor of construction.

It is not given all of us to follow the ramifications of nature's planning, nor to see wherein the justice or the seeming injustice lies. Most of the men, average short-reasoning creatures, took their labor drearily enough and were not permitted to see in a definite inspiriting way the approaching beauty of that which their hands were building. Many of them came and labored a little while, seeing only the mass and chaos of it without ever obtaining one glimpse of the loveliness which was to be.

But when the labor had been completed; when the mortar had been mixed and the bricks and stones removed from their uneven masses and set in order; when the wounds of the ground had been smoothed over, the scattered debris removed; and the grass allowed to grow; when in the light of the restful evening there rose high in the air a perfect tower, buttressed, arched and pinnacled, with here a window reflecting the golden western glow, and there a pillar standing out in delicate relief against the perfect background of the sky, the meaning of the indescribable chaos came home. Here it was: color, form, tone. The labor of the shoveler, the toil of the iron worker, the irritating beats of the carpenter's hammer, all blended together and made into a perfect thing. And as I looked, my heart rose up and I was thankful to have been in part a worker, to have worked a little, to have wearied a little, to have sighed a little, that this lovely thing might be.

II.

The toil of the laborer is thoughtless. There is in it neither conception nor initiative nor the development of that which is new. Though the hands labor and the body bend, the heart is not in it. It is all a weariness and a travail of the flesh and the profit is not visible.

In a certain factory not far from the heart of the City of New York I worked as a laborer. My duty in this capacity was to carry shavings and lumber and to sweep the floor. All day from the blowing of the whistle at seven in the morning to the welcome blast from the same at six at night, my body was busy lifting and bending, the need of keeping the floor clean of shavings and of supplying a half dozen machines with lumber, being an unending task.

In this period, the idea with which I prefaced these facts had time to sink into my very soul. The slow unchanging imperative nature of the work, the fact that it went forward whether one man came or another one stayed away, the dreary persistence with which it was necessary to repeat the same motion day after day, week after week, month after month and year after year was to the thinking and restless mind maddening.

In this factory there ruled a foreman who fitted in well to the scheme of things. He was a peculiar creature—a strange, egotistic, vainglorious soul— with a mind so set up by the fact that he had been made foreman of this little shop, that there was no living with him. He was arbitrary. His word was law. With an air that might well have become a tragedian he walked about his confined domain and glared upon each and all. Every word was either a command or a reproof, and in times of excitement or depression, such as naturally flow from the hurry or the lack of work, he was always about venting his wrath or humor as the moods dictated.

This situation, coupled with the meagerness of the wages attached, was a difficult thing to endure. It was so apparent to anyone who thought for a moment, that it was without point save as a means of subsistence. To lift and carry, to start and stop, to move along certain given lines and within certain limits—this was the sum and substance of wisdom desired, and it mattered little who did it. Some small personal characteristics figured in, such as whether a man was naturally quick or slow, good-humored or ill-humored, and the like, but the main point was to do the work as required—as

conceived, planned, initiated and developed by someone else. What you thought or how you felt was not involved. It was the rule, the method, the manner, that was all. All this could be acquired until it was not a matter of thought, but of rote. You did not have to think.

One of the most pathetic things about it was that it was involved with the maintenance of a condition which was not necessarily beneficial or worthy of approval. This great corporation (of which this little shop was but a minute figure), while a vast lever, making for a condition which was interesting, was one which could hardly be called useful. Some of the owners for whom the thousands upon thousands of individuals labored, were mere idlers in society, daily bulletined as the chief factors in a dozen trivial amusements, and as unconscious of the condition which made for their situation and pleasure, as if it did not exist at all. For every motion and every bend here some one else was deriving the privilege not to move and not bend there. It was as if some untoward power was momentarily taking something from each of these, and giving it, uncalled for, to someone who did not even know whence it came. The measured increase of their profit was so plainly visible.

And the saddest part of it was that these men, born for the most part to a condition, were visibly affected by their situation. Most of them were mechanics—mere machine regulators in fact—who had acquired the little they knew by observing others, and who really did not think, in the sense of originating anything. Some of them, it is true, had the capacity in a limited degree, but the nature of their labor almost precluded the possibility of utilizing it. It was one of those situations in which labor—a mere routine of motions—took the place of thought and left them weary and disinterested at the close of the day—not fit to originate a thought had it been necessary.

And yet it occurred to me after a time that it was not perhaps the thoughtlessness of it that was so wretched, as that any human being, laboring to his full capacity, should not receive the profits of his toil. These men, ignorant and, in a way, without direction, were nevertheless useful creatures, and in this sense, if no other, were deserving of a far more reasonable share of the profit which their efforts created. That it should not be so; that despite their willing or not willing, they should be driven early and late to create a surplus which was not directly applied to the pressing needs of a man, seemed hard.

And yet, sometimes, when I looked out upon the world as it glimmered before my windows, when I saw, as it so chanced that it should be, the waters of the river flowing nearby, the splendid boats riding at anchor or steaming peacefully by, and the wonder of the hills and hollows all set suggestively before the eyes, it occurred to me that perhaps, variety was as essential to happiness as justice, and that the very inequalities which I was bemoaning in labor were the things which I was admiring in nature.

To blot out the light and the shadows, to remove the hills and dales, to take away the far reaches which spread between luxury and want, idleness and toil, might not these be the things which, after all, would rob life of its value and charm?

And then as I turned to the weariness of my labor again, I could not help wishing for each, some better solution than this necessity for variety— that the heights and hollows might not be so vast. To see a mountain, to view a desert: was not this the privilege of but a few; and is not the true beauty of life to be found in the way places, where are neither heights nor depths, but only a tender and appealing undulation? That none should suffer, that none should want! This after all seemed the worthiest thought that sprang at the sight of a toil-weary man. That it might not be sought in so widely diversified a world as here offers did not lessen the value of the ideal. Rather, to work, to wait, to hope, to pray—these things loomed large in the hour of weariness. And the charm that they cast over effort was as though the difference had already in part been overcome, and that the realization of the ideal was almost at hand.[1]

III.

The toil of the laborer is without mercy. Its grim, insistent durance unrequited by anything save the meager wages with which it is paid. There is no beauty in it—no tenderness. The last vestige of effort is the sum required. There is no thought of anything save what muscle and the strength of the individual can be made to yield. More than this, the sum of what is accomplished passes almost entirely into other hands. There is no provision made for the future of those who will be as tattered remnants when the things· they labored for have been accomplished.

For several months I have been working with the laborers who do the work of a great railroad. It has been the kind of labor that falls to the lot of every man who is unskilled and whose sense of honesty, as well as duty and need, commands that he labor. We were compelled to carry lumber, load bricks, shovel earth and mix mortar. Our work was requited at the rate of fifteen cents an hour, with nothing more than this allowed for overtime. We worked from nine to ten hours a day, as the light permitted.

During this service I found that there was no rest for those employed save in the form of subtle subterfuge which was as wearisome to one not accustomed to it by long years of practice as the toil itself. It was possible to be deliberate, to hang first on one foot and then on the other. There was a way of idling in the manner in which one could hold his pick at rest before lifting it, but the gain was hardly worth the pain. At the close of the day, the sum of idleness secured in this way would not be sufficient to produce a restful feeling, and the thought that a watchful foreman was well aware of the spirit of your labor was not conducive of peace.

In the progress of this labor as an underling, it was also made perfectly plain to me the heartless persistence with which the work of the world is accomplished. We were under a foreman whose conception of life was that it meant toil, and who was perfectly equipped physically to meet it. He did not stop to parley or to temper the necessities with tenderness, but shouted his commands, the fulfillment of which was as much of a burden on his mind as upon our bodies. Work there was to be done, vast quantities of labor extending into the weeks and years, and the only thought which the conclusion of one hard day's toil could bring was that there was another tomorrow.

I pondered over this, wondering at the fierceness of the temper of the foreman, the persistence of his frown, the manner in which when anything was delayed, or the work went wrong, he visited the blame upon the heads of those who were the carriers and serfs of his commands. Life did not demand it, I said. The wealth of this big corporation was proof that it was an unjust exaction. A man should be a man despite the orders of his superiors. Mercy and tenderness should qualify our every deed.

I held to this persistently through a thousand wearinesses, saying that if I were made a foreman I would do differently. There would be no harshness in my tone. I should not swear. A moderate effort would be demanded of my men, but nothing more.

Then I was made foreman.

My duties in this latter capacity were of a different nature. Here, instead of running at the bark of another, I had men running at one from me. I had from a dozen to fifteen men under me, and my principal labor was to see that they did not shirk. I was to see that the work set aside for us was done quickly and well.[2]

I accepted this with a light heart. It was so easy to do. I took my position beside my gang, humming a tune, and I thought to watch their progress with a gentle as well as a merry heart.

How speedy and how sad was my disillusionment!

Before a single day was gone, I was made to feel the pressure which was on me from above. There were orders to be complied with, periods to be observed, standards of quality, in so far as certain kinds of work were concerned, which had to be reached. I did not dare to fall below this, if my superior's regard or my position were worth anything to me, and at every turn there were rules, rules, rules.

How hard I tried to adjust my new relationship to the ideal which I had held before myself, and at the same time comply with the rules of the company, I shall not say. For a time I did manage to keep a cheerful attitude and to speak gently. In my observation of the men, I tried to overlook the indifference and subterfuge, which I knew they were practicing, and it seemed to me as if I would succeed. The memory of my own recent feelings was too fresh not to influence me deeply.

There came a day, however, when the pressure of work was so much greater than it had been before, that the usual subterfuge of the men became an irritation to me. A heavy rain had washed in a trench that we had been excavating. It was essential to hurry the reopening of this. Concrete had to be prepared, a large foundation laid by a given date. We were under urgent surveillance from our superiors, and could not but do as they said, or resign.

In this situation, I confess, I did not do much parleying with my sense of justice. Although I knew these men to be in the main underpaid and overworked, and in so far as the corporation was concerned, mere machines, to be pushed to the limit of their capacity and discharged when no longer useful, still I stood beside and ordered and commanded, urging first one and then the other with shouts and gruff words until at last they were as wrought up and as troubled by me as they had been by the man of whom I had complained. At last one of them turned on me.

"Yes, 'Hurry, hurry.' You did not work so yourself, though."

I paused in my ordering and walked aside a little space to consider. How true was the thing he said! I had not worked so. It had been my one complaint that so much insistence and heartless driving was not necessary. And here I was outdoing the driver who had seemed most brutal to me.

For that day and many others I canvassed the situation carefully, and tried hard to discover in just what way it was that I had drifted into so brutal an attitude. Why was it, I asked myself, that I had become so? Did I not know now, as well as before that the corporation was enormously rich? Had I not more evidence, if anything, that the men were overworked and underpaid? Could I not see in the orders given men, that there was no consideration for them but only the thing to be accomplished, and that at the least possible expense? I acknowledged freely that I saw this, and that it was absolutely true, and yet now I pleaded with myself that I saw no way to remedy it, and that if I did not fulfill the company's orders, someone else would. The work which was given to us to do had to be done. There was no way of allowing these men to shirk and take their time without noticeably delaying the work. If the railroad was to be run and the public served, it would have to be done at a profit or no man would undertake the matter, and then there would be no labor at all for these men to do. Besides, if at any time I let one shirk, I must, in justice, let all the others do so, and this, I reasoned, would be the destruction of all effort. I did not feel that I could reasonably do so.

The retort of the laborer proved a great shock to me, however. I could not recover my exterior equanimity, and never my mental peace. Try as I would, the two elements of capital and labor would not adjust themselves within my consciousness. I was forced, in spite of myself, to choose sides. Either I must relinquish my former attitude of sympathy for the men and opposition to the indifference of the railroad, or I must side with them and against the railroad. There was no middle ground, and until I should choose, my conscience would give me no peace.

It was after a particularly hard day's work that my decision was eventually made. We had been mixing concrete, as on the former occasion, and with a touch of my old cynical uncertainty dominating me I had been driving them all day long. Urging one to shovel faster; calling another to bring the wheelbarrows of stone even before they were needed; sending this one for water and that one for cement, until it seemed as if the men were mere tools to me, and I, the god of their destiny. About four o'clock it began to rain. It had been gray and lowering all day, but now the moisture began to descend in a fine drizzle and we were compelled to work or to leave the batch of concrete we were just beginning unfinished. In a sullen mood, because of my own dreary part in the matter, I stood beside them and held them to their task, not caring much what became of them or myself, either, until at last the work was completed. Damp and dreary, I took my lunch box and tramped doggedly along the tracks toward the depot, comforted by the one thought only, that the day was over and that I, myself, was free.

It was at that hour when the traffic from the great city outward assumes its most imposing aspect. Along this magnificent highway of steel were speeding the trains of one of the wealthiest corporations in the world. Limiteds were passing, their splendid interiors aglow with a half hundred lights. On each of the five or six tracks that glistened side by side were hurrying locals, expresses and specials, the warmth and comfort of their interiors possessing an almost pitiable fascination for the eye. Passengers were reclining in comfort. The more thoughtful were gazing idly out. The expensive dining cars were set with silver and white linen.

As I paused near the station to turn my eye on this truly inspiring scene and to gather the rich significance it always possessed for me, there passed by a little procession of Italians, bearing the tools with which they had been laboring. There was Phillip, whom I had often noted as I stood by the trench in which he worked, his body all twisted and bent from long years of unremitting toil; there was Angelo, old and leathern in feature, whose one boast was that he had never missed a day's work in seven years; there was Matteo, thin, worn-looking, whose eye was always alight with a kindly humor and whose willingness to work I had never been able to question. There were John and Collarbrace (as we called one Calabrian), Mussolin and Jimmie, all trudging patiently on like cattle, the day of labor having brought forth nothing but a night of weariness.

And as I stood there looking at them, I could not help contrasting the weariness of their labor with the flower which it had produced. There was this immense corporation with its magnificent equipment, its palatial depots, its comfortable trains and the host of those who found service and pleasure in them, and here were these humble trudgers making their way homeward in the night and rain. And as I thought of the meagerness of their wages, the manner in which I had driven them, and the, so far as they were concerned, slightly profitable luxury to which their labor trended, I resolved that I, for one, would have nothing to do with it. Not to drive where I could not release, not to exact where I could not repay, not to be a tool in the hands of those who were tools themselves, only that they were closer to the owners who did not think, was something, even though by quitting I could not relieve the situation of its pain.

Textual Note: New York Call, 13 July 1913, p. 11. Sent out by 16 January 1904, "The Toil of the Laborer" was rejected by several publications before it finally appeared in *Call*. A revised version was published in *Reconstruction* 1 (October 1919), 310–13, and in Dreiser's book of philosophical speculations, social criticism, and reading plays, *Hey Rub-a-Dub-Dub* (New York: Boni and Liveright, 1920), 98–111. A further typescript, dating from between July 1914 and October 1919 (DPUP folder 8230), contains revisions in Dreiser's hand that were not adopted in *Hey Rub-a-Dub-Dub*. Copy-text is the first published edition, emended for typesetting errors by reference to the extant holograph manuscripts of sections one (DPUP folder 8229) and two (DPUP folder 12431).

1. Dreiser gave the title "The Realization of an Ideal" to a city sketch composed within a few years of "The Toil of the Laborer" and included it in *The Color of a Great City* (1923). Focusing on a church on the Lower East Side, the sketch presents the urban poor who use it as demanding a response of "tenderness" according to human ideals of living decently, if not of Christian belief.

2. Dreiser exercises some freedom with his autobiographical material—his duties as a foreman were largely clerical—which he used differently again in "The Mighty Burke" (1911).

Helps the Municipality Owes the Housewife

The Delineator, February 1909.

In several editorials for The Delineator, *Dreiser celebrates the achievements of Progressive women reformers and calls upon readers to engage in works of social improvement as individuals and at the municipal level. Here he draws upon Ida*

*Husted Harper's article "Woman's Broom in Municipal Housekeeping," which
immediately follows Dreiser's essay in the pages of the magazine. Under this
facetious title—the image of the woman with the broom, and women's abilities
as municipal housekeepers, were clichés of Progressive feminist rhetoric—Harper
highlighted "the entrance of women into public life" and presented patriarchy as
a proven obstacle to municipal reform:*

> *This [the frustration of reform by male politicians and business leaders] is what
> the women come up against continually in their efforts for practical improve-
> ment in municipal affairs. They did not realize the situation when they were
> only theorizing about the needs of the community and using their much-lauded
> "indirect influence." This was all-sufficient for the sewing-circle and the Ibsen
> society, but when these evolved into civic clubs and legislative committees,
> and great bodies of women organized for a vital purpose constantly found
> themselves confronted by the unyielding stone wall of a city council or a State
> legislature, they began to look for a ladder. Long before another decade has
> passed, these large associations of women will unite in one strong, determined,
> uncompromising demand for suffrage, and then the biggest monopoly in this
> country today—the masculine voting trust—will see its finish.[1]*

This is the day when the municipality is finding itself. A sense of active
responsibility for the environment of its citizens is a rapidly developing
conviction with city governments. Even to the home life this jurisdiction
extends. The milk and the water and the meat that supply the household
must now be right or there are regularly commissioned officials to know the
reason why and make them so. And such Government control of conditions
that vitally affect the home, women, particularly, may appreciate. But there
are some other helps that the Government owes the housewife. Men are
blunderingly carrying on their municipal housekeeping so that it is materially interfering with the home housekeeping. What, pray, will it profit the
most diligent housewife to scrub and polish all day long, when dirt comes
in at the windows faster than she can send it out of the back door?

There is the street-sweeping, which a great many cities are still doing in the
wrong way. Men seem to know how to use a broom only to stir up a great dust.
And they send out the sweeping-machines that lift the dirt from the pave-
ments only to send it flying into the houses. Out in Kalamazoo, Michigan, this
was the only way they knew until a woman, the Rev. Caroline Barlett Crane,
said, "I'll show you!" and, taking charge of the city's street-cleaning brigade,
she instilled into their consciousness the simple fact which every housewife
knows.[2] That with every broom belongs a dust-pan. A number of city councils
have been instructed in this elementary principle of cleanliness and are now
having the dirt from the streets carefully swept up and removed.

But there's another even worse violation of the simplest sort of economy of human energy. It's the smoke nuisance, that in so many cities undoes nearly all of the most careful housekeeper's efforts. There have been congresses and conventions, and public agitation has even progressed so far as engrossed resolutions and neatly framed ordinances. There are mayors and aldermen and health officers who show you these with considerable pride to prove that their towns are in the vanguard of progress. But to the feminine mind these exhibits are not satisfying. From these very gentlemen's office windows a woman looks at the smoking chimneys and persists in declaring that still the smoke doesn't seem to be suppressed.

Why isn't it? is what the housekeepers everywhere have a right to demand of the city fathers. Indianapolis affords about the sorriest illustration. Once it had natural gas for fuel and was clean. Now, the supply having given out, all the factories are burning soft coal. And the city, once white, is enveloped in clouds of soot constantly falling in black flakes over everything and everybody and obscuring the sunlight so that it is difficult to determine whether the day is pleasant or threatening rain. Rich furnishings in beautiful homes are covered with a soil that comes off on the hands. And not all the house-servants that money can hire can keep these things clean.

Indianapolis is not the only city. There are others. A city cannot prevent its manufacturers from burning soft coal so long as it is cheaper than anthracite. They simply won't be prevented. But every city can compel a factory to use a smoke-consumer. Many cities have ordinances to say that factories must do this. Why don't they make them obey? That's what the women want to know. It's a help the municipality owes the housewife.

Textual Note: Unsigned editorial, "Concerning Us All," *Delineator* 73:2 (February 1909): 211. Attributed to Dreiser as editor of *The Delineator*.

1. Ida Husted Harper, "Woman's Broom in Municipal Housekeeping," *Delineator* 73:2 (February 1909): 214.

2. Caroline Bartlett Crane (1858–1935), who had successfully campaigned for the reform of slaughterhouse hygiene in Kalamazoo and who was engaged in reforming meatpacking regulation in Michigan, would become a nationally renowned activist for public health and women's suffrage. Bartlett Crane's reputation as "America's housekeeper," and her appeal to the middle-class women's clubs, to the social gospel, and to the emergent sociology, epitomized the Progressive reform movement with which Dreiser identified *The Delineator*. She was the subject of Mabel Potter Daggett's "One Woman's Civic Service," (*Delineator* 73:6 [June 1909]: 767–68), and was taken up as an exemplary figure in Dreiser's editorial for that month, under the subtitle "You Might Do It, Too."

THE CHILD-RESCUE LEAGUE

The Delineator Starts a New and Aggressive Campaign for Doing Away with the Old-Fashioned Orphan Asylum.

THE time has come in the Delineator Child-Rescue Campaign when a stand of considerable importance has to be taken. For a year and more THE DELINEATOR has presented the facts in connection with the child,— its homelessness, its loneliness, the deficiency of its childhood life. The hour has now come when the evil which the old-fashioned institution in almost all cases unconsciously does must be forcefully and vigorously emphasized. We have always said that the child, when possible, should be in a home where it can have the advantage of individuality and variety. We now say that, except in cases where medical or corrective supervision is absolutely necessary, the child should not be kept in an institution. The latter, for all except the purposes of a receiving and temporary examining agency, is an anomaly and should be done away with just as rapidly as the various home-placing organizations demonstrate their ability to care for the children now in these institutions, in the family home under thorough supervision. Already there are such organizations in most of the States. Some of these need to be strengthened. In a few States home-placing agencies have yet to be organized. Our experience with these agencies reveals that their problem is to get a sufficient number of children for the desirable homes available. Many people are willing to take children by adoption and many are willing to board them. As a rule the orphan asylums refuse to give their children up. THE DELINEATOR does not consider this fair to the child.

THE DELINEATOR wants the institution done away with as soon as possible. The great mother-heart of America wants it done away with, and we say now that as rapidly as the women and the men of this country come to understand what the institution means to the child and its future, they will join hands to see that it is done away with. THE DELINEATOR, and behind it the BUTTERICK PUBLISHING COMPANY, is in this educational campaign to stay.

We hope and believe that the kind-hearted and unselfish people who have given of their time and means in the support and management of the institution, in their desire to do the best possible for the children in their care, will be among the first to ap-

GRACE AND BILLY

preciate the advantages, not only to the child but the State, in developing this modern method of caring for dependent children. The problem is to get their attention and thought.

THE DELINEATOR is willing and anxious to help any of these institutions. It is prepared to furnish data and substantiate every claim that has been made, and to show to Boards of Directors the practicability of carrying into effect the reforms advocated.

The National Child-Rescue League is now an accomplished fact. The actual members now number several hundred and every mail brings a material increase. Every new member asks the same question: What can I do to help? We were prepared for that question. There is ready a complete and carefully-thought-out program of active service for every League member. One step of that plan will be outlined in that portion of these pages given to the National Child-Rescue League every month.

The first step is to get new members. A membership of several hundred is gratifying, but far from sufficient to accomplish the purpose of the League—to place every normal child now in an institution in a family home. This is a matter requiring a national sentiment; the fused desire of millions of people is necessary to accomplish such an object.

You who have expressed your willingness to help, have therefore, this your first task set before you. Get into the National Child-Rescue League your next door neighbor, your friend, your pastor, your grocer, every intelligent human being with whom you come in contact. We need them; the League needs them; the one hundred thousand children who are waiting for us to release them from soul starvation need them. Use the sympathy aroused in you to this end. On another page of this issue you will find a copy of the constitution of the National Child-Rescue League; also a reproduction of the certificate of membership. Use these as your propaganda. Let the next issue that goes to press number the National Child-Rescue League by thousands, and we shall be ready for the next step in behalf of the homeless child.

The Child Rescue League is launched in *The Delineator*, January 1909.

The Problem of the Dying Baby

The Delineator, August 1909.

In this Delineator *editorial, Dreiser discusses the Progressive rationale for the* Schools for Mothers, *or* Mothers' Conference, *a campaign announced in March 1909. This was the second major campaign initiated by the magazine under Dreiser's editorship, the first,* Child Rescue, *having attained national prominence. Like* Child Rescue, *which sought both to place destitute children with families and to abolish the municipal and charity-run orphanages,* Schools for Mothers *combined a kind of charitable outreach coordinated by the magazine, with political pressure on city and town authorities to better provide for children's health. In December 1909 Dreiser would announce that* The Delineator *had requested that the Children's Aid Society take over the work on a permanent basis and that it had asked the Department of Education and the Department of Health in New York City to run schools for mothers.*

This is the hot season. It is now that the problem of maintaining our physical equilibrium is at the highest. Those who have money go to the seashore or the mountains. The cities are left, sweltering and uncomfortable, to those who must remain. In the long streets and the narrow area-ways you see that mass of humanity who by process of nature are of poor constructive ability, not so good as they might be—not so strong, not so shrewd. These people are left fighting in the ranks; husbands toiling for from seven to fifteen dollars a week and supporting in many instances a wife and two or three children; wives, their anemic, dispirited bodies pottering around among a rag-tag array of household utensils, fighting a pitiful fight for subsistence. They are keeping house (save the mark!). They are raising families! Some of them, it is true, make a right respectable showing on these sums under these conditions. Others, handicapped by their own vices, stagger through the mire and dirt of wretched surroundings and fade away eventually before the helpful forces which they do not understand. All through these conditions you find, mewling and toddling, the little child, new-born, unconscious, weighted with God knows what inherent vices and weaknesses, but a little child nevertheless.

The world has come at this problem in various ways recently. It has established children's aid societies for the particular care of neglected children. It has established children's courts, child-rescue bureaus, anti-cruelty-to-children organizations, but, somehow, with all these, it has not yet reached the little child in the cradle, the new-born babe, who, by reason of being voiceless, is, therefore, considered by some miracle of nature to be under divine protection. Mother-love is supposed to be the saving element in this situation. The inherent sympathy that extends in all right-minded people to the child is supposed to answer. No harm can come to the child, once we prevent the parents or the neighbors from being cruel and unnatural. All we have to do, according to the old theory, is to keep the child in the care and sympathy of the mother, and the problem is solved.

The error here is incalculable. The enemies of child-life are not necessarily acts of intentional cruelty on the part of strangers or of parents. The real enemy is ignorance, and it masquerades in the most subtle form—ignorance of the simplest laws of hygiene; ignorance of the protective value of pure milk, of clean food, of cold storage; ignorance of the fact that dirt breeds disease, that flies carry filth and vermin, that contagion lurks in dark rooms and crowded chambers; ignorance of the things that relate to the child's eyesight, its need of fresh air. All of these things are the dark, subtle enemies that are prowling about the rooms of a thousand tenements of every city and in the more or less thousand towns and villages, killing seventeen out of every hundred children, and weakening and making defective a noticeable percentage of the remainder.

This is a stern indictment of the condition in which we find ourselves, but when you have said all this you have not got at the bottom of the problem. The bottom of the problem is that, knowing all these things, we are not yet reaching these people. Human service based on human sympathy would do it. But the average human being shrinks from dirt and ignorance. He will not wade through mire, even to save a child.

And yet these children should be saved. Back of all this wretchedness and poor furniture and cheap ideas are human spirits capable of a sense of suffering and facing hopelessly a condition which they do not know how to remedy. They are ignorant, and so they put the rubber nipple, that has been rolling about on the floor, and is reeking with germs, into the baby's mouth, thus conveying disease by the straight avenue; they are ignorant, and so they put the baby in an open baby-carriage or box and let it be trundled by the children in the hot sun until its eyes are ruined and its feeble constitution impaired; they are ignorant, and so they feed the baby meat or tea or coffee or cake, or quiet it with soothing syrup and dope teas, when only fresh air and pure milk and clean water for bathing and clean clothing are all it needs.

Who is to blame for this? The individual who, housed in squalor, is fighting an anemic battle for subsistence in a hurrying, vigorous, intelligent world? Not always. "The sins of the father shall be visited upon the children even unto the third and the fourth generation"[1]—and these are the children. What are you going to do in such cases? Leave them in their wretchedness to breed disease and suffering and to let the children die? Or are you going to enter in through sympathy and tenderness, clean up the wretched hovels, compel intelligent action on the part of the mother and save the State from its criminals and cripples of the future?

The Delineator has started a campaign for the education of mothers. We have printed in this magazine and in pamphlet form the rules and the regulations which go with the intelligent care of infants.[2] We have striven to have conventions called in various cities, to have mothers' classes inaugurated in the schools, to have the various agencies which make for child protection and aid united and made effective in each of the various cities of this country, but we can not do anything without human sympathy. We must have you, the readers of this magazine and the public at large, see the significance of this situation. The case of the individual mother must come home to you. And unless in imagination or in fact you can stand by the cradle or the potato-box of the tenement-born child, unless you can feel the heat, sense the foul air, see the wasting paleness, and know that hour after hour and day after day this is going on, we can do nothing. The mothers all over the country can not be made wise and efficient just by our writing in *The Delineator*. You must know that it is individual contact which is the answer: the going yourself or hiring someone to go who can intelligently and forcefully indicate to the ignorant mothers the way and the truth. Are you going to do this? If not, are you going to make your city or your town do it? After all it is a municipal function, but it will not be put into force until you personally see that it is done.

Remember that the great thing is to put yourself in the other person's place. Supposing you were the ignorant mother. Supposing your rooms were dark and dirty, and your facilities for improving them depended on a drunken husband or an income of eight dollars a week. Suppose it was your child who was sickly and, although there was a remedy, you did not know it. And supposing, in spite of its scrawny neck and its big wobbly head and weak little body, you loved it—loved it so dearly that you carried more illness to it with your constant fondling and your anemic, microbic kisses—what would you do? And when the heat came, and the Summer-disease came, and Death stalked at your heels as it stalks at hers, what would you do?

This is a rich world. There are loads of ideas and lots of strength in it. If some of the Thomas F. Ryans and J. P. Morgans and E. H. Harrimans of financial ability would only turn their attention to organizing our social forces so as to look after these things, we would soon be out of the darkness.[3] But meanwhile, here is this problem, here and now in these hot days. Here are the ignorant mothers, the sick children, the pathetic little funerals, the darkness and sorrow. What do you think you ought to do about it? Sit by the seashore or the mountain-side and sympathize? Society is a great organized, working association. Its basic, underlying idea is that each shall help the other. This is religion—this is social economy. What do you think that, as an honest member of that society, you should do? What *will* you do?

Textual Note: Unsigned editorial, "Concerning Us All," *Delineator* 74:2 (August 1909): 113. Attributed to Dreiser as editor of *The Delineator.*

    1. There are various Biblical sources for this quotation; Exodus 20:5; Numbers 14:18; Deuteronomy 5:9. Biblical language is often used in the "Concerning Us All" editorials to borrow authority and, as later in this piece, to appeal to ideas of the social gospel, but its use here is more redolent of "scientific" notions of inherited characteristics or conditions.

    2. See Edith Howe, "The Baby and the Public School," which appeared under the headings "The Delineator Mother's Conference: 'To teach the mother is to save the child': A National Department, Representing Over a Thousand Health Departments, Schools, Philanthropic Institutions and Mother's Clubs, To Lower the Needless Death-Rate Among Babies," *Delineator* 73:6 (June 1909): 783.

    3. Prominent and extremely wealthy financiers. John Pierpont Morgan (1837–1913) and Thomas F. Ryan (1857–1928) were controversial figures, to whom Dreiser would return in "The Day of Special Privileges" (see 36). E. H. (Edward Henry) Harriman (1848–1909) had built up a considerable fortune on the stock market and controlled the Union Pacific and Southern Pacific Railroads, among others. Close to death he had initiated negotiations to give substantial landholdings in New York State to extend the Palisades Interstate Park, a charitable work completed by his widow, Mary Williamson Averell. In the 1930s Dreiser would return to the idea that successful people should be induced to use their energies and expertise for the public good with more urgency.

The State of the Negro

The Bohemian, October 1909.

In the satirical style of The Bohemian *magazine, Dreiser contrasts mainstream white hostility and indifference to African Americans with the achievements and potential of Black culture. Having depicted a lynching and its devastating effect on a Black family in the 1901 short story "Nigger Jeff," Dreiser would reiterate the complaint that "the American has no plan for the negro" in "Some Aspects of Our National Character" (1920), going on to attack racial injustice directly in 1930s works such as* Tragic America *(see 151) and "Speech on the Scottsboro Case," (see 139–44).*

There is nothing so interesting today in our civilization as the condition of the negro. Here is this vast body of people, citizens in name only, who live and have their being among us and who yet by the intelligent and respectable elements are entirely ignored. We hardly know of their existence socially. We rarely consider them financially. They slip about among us doing our washing, our cooking, our waiting and cleaning and we all but forget that they are with us.[1] A race without a country, a people without a national ideal. We laugh at their humor. We build up fiction out of their quaint wisdom. We hang and burn them when they interfere with our women.[2]

It is a curious situation. Not long ago a dinner was given in New York to which were invited a number of intelligent blacks, men and women, and a number of intelligent white people to meet them.[3] The idea was conceived in a high philosophic spirit. Those who came of the negroes were refined, broad-minded, cleanly in body and spirit. These who came of whites were equally able socially—editors, artists, magazine writers, college professors. The public got wind of it through the newspapers and at once there were low mutterings. The deeps of society were really stirred. There was something so threatening in the social air that those who had innocently and foolishly participated ran to cover. Most of them denied vigorously, scared white by the fear of social ostracism.

And yet we have these people with us. They are a social menace—a danger to the established order, breaking out in mulatto hues upon our body politic and yet we linger. No one knows what to do. Our alleged significant statesmen haven't a single idea to their names. We drift, drift, seeing them grow in numbers, increase in wealth, gather in intelligence and yet neither we nor they have a program of any kind whatsoever.

It is wonderful, this problem of the black race. We find it injecting strange doubts into the significance of Christianity, the workableness of the Christian virtues, the possibilities of a humanitarian program of any kind when it meets the color line. Who is my neighbor? Not the negro. Who is my fellow-servant in the field of righteousness? Not the negro. Who is my co-heir in the heavenly sense—the negro? Not in any noticeable way. We admit the negro to labor and labor only—and that is as it should be from the standpoint of self-preservation, but, alas, we cannot make it exactly so. The negro at the bottom is exercising a destructive influence upon the whites and that is where the trouble lies.

If only some prophet of the race would lead them out of bondage. This is a great world. There is room for a black republic or a black empire. We can imagine such a thing, magnificent beyond the dreams of fancy. We all know how this race loves color. We know how rich they are in emotion, in imagination. The poems of a Paul Laurence Dunbar, the decoration of a Henry Ossawa Tanner, the vigor of a Booker T. Washington or a Menelik give us a suggestion.[4] But in a real empire with ambition to rule and power luring men on, what might not come to pass? These people are not devoid of intellectual power. There are rising among them authors, editors, financiers, artists, musicians, only we do not hear of them. Their day has not come. But in a real empire, with their love of color, their sense of music, their taste and show, might they not flower out a great, gorgeous orchard of nationality—yellow and red, black and gold, which would outstrip all our puny conceptions of regal significance? It might be.

And yet among us they run the elevators, they answer the door bells, they sit in dark halls and serve. Paul Laurence Dunbar running an elevator! And he did this till he died.

Textual Note: Unsigned editorial, "At the Sign of the Lead Pencil," *Bohemian* 17 (October 1909): 432. This and the two following selections appeared in the unsigned editorial department of *The Bohemian* titled "At the Sign of the Lead Pencil," to which the principal contributors were H. L. Mencken, all of whose pieces have been identified, the nominal editor Fritz Krog, and Dreiser. In the absence of definitive evidence, "The State of the Negro," "The Day of Special Privileges," and "The Death of Francisco Ferrer" have been attributed to Dreiser, partly on the basis that they are not claimed by Mencken or Krog, and for further specific reasons, in this case the similarities in phrasing and argument with the discussion of the "race problem" in "Some Aspects of Our National Character," *Hey Rub-a-Dub-Dub*, 42–43.

1. Dreiser had been given some idea of the frustrations experienced by African Americans attempting to develop their professional and personal capabilities through his friendship and correspondence with J. E. Bowler, a black presser of Bedford City, Virginia.

2. Dreiser had reported as eyewitness to the lynching of one John Buckner in rural Missouri ("This Calls for Hemp," St. Louis *Republic*, 17 January 1894, p. 1; "Ten-Foot Drop," St. Louis *Republic*, 18 January 1894, pp. 1–2; rpt. T. D. Nostwich, ed. *Theodore Dreiser, Journalism Vol. 1: Newspaper Writings 1892–1895* [Philadelphia: University of Pennsylvania Press, 1988], 249–58); and transmuted the narrative into one of his earliest published fictions, the short story "Nigger Jeff" (1901), which is sympathetic to the black victim and his mother.

3. The dinner is undoubtedly that of the Cosmopolitan Society of America, commonly known as the Cosmopolitan Club, at Peck's restaurant in New York, 27 April 1908. Among the one hundred or so guests was Mary White Ovington (1865–1951), whose brainchild the club was; also present were antilynching campaigner, editor, and cofounder of the club Hamilton Holt (1872–1951), Oswald Garrison Villard (1872–1949) of the New York *Evening Post*, and socialists such as André Tridon (1877–1922), and John Spargo (1876–1966). Much of the reporting of the event in the white press did profess to be scandalized, describing it as "loathsome," a "miscegenation dinner," and calling Ovington the "high priestess" of a "Bacchanal feast." Unfazed, by the time "The State of the Negro" was published, Villard and Ovington had gone on to help found the National Association for the Advancement of Colored People. In focusing on white embarrassment, Dreiser may have been thinking particularly of the Presbyterian Rev. Madison C. Peters (1859–1918), who was booked to speak at the dinner, but left precipitately, allegedly when he saw that young white women had been seated next to black men.

4. Paul Laurence Dunbar (1872–1906), author of *Majors and Minors* (1895), was one of the first internationally recognized African American poets. Although he struggled to make a living from his writing, Dunbar did make a reading tour of England for six months in 1897 and later gave up a job at the Library of Congress

in part for health reasons and in part to concentrate on writing. Henry Ossawa Tanner (1859–1937) was the foremost African American painter of the nineteenth century and the subject of a one-man exhibition at the American Art Galleries in New York City in 1908. Tanner produced a variety of work, including landscapes, portraits, and religious paintings, to which the term "decorations" does little justice. He also rejected being labeled primarily in terms of race. Booker T. Washington (1856–1915), author of *Up From Slavery* (1901), was a prominent campaigner for racial equality through peaceful means. An ex-slave, he had gained a measure of behind-the-scenes political influence by the early 1900s. Washington rejected the Cosmopolitan Club's strategy of mixing middle-class blacks and whites, and he clashed with the N.A.A.C.P. Dreiser had enlisted Washington's public support for *The Delineator*'s "Schools for Mothers" campaign. Menelik II (1844–1913) was the major military and political leader of Abyssinia [Ethiopia] in the late nineteenth and early twentieth centuries, expanding its land area and instituting ministerial government. In 1896 his troops inflicted military defeat on Italy, forcing the Italians to recognize Abyssinia as an independent state.

The Day of Special Privileges

The Bohemian, November 1909.

Dreiser discusses themes of individualism and inequality that would inform novels such as The Financier *and* The Titan.

It is amusing or disturbing, just as you feel about our national life, to see how people take the growing privileges of the wealthy and the consequent diminution of the opportunities and privileges of those who are not so wealthy. Some of us are quite sure that we are slipping our moorings in regard to what is deemed our natural rights. Others that we are doing what has always been done before. Certain it is that we are seeing some interesting examples of class consideration and some other equally interesting examples of class oppression. As a matter of fact, there has never been a time in the history of the world when there has been really less class distinction and class oppression. Heretofore the world has gone naturally about this business of showing the little fellow that he did not amount to much and making the big fellow feel that he was almost divinely called to his privilege. There does not appear to be any way now by which we can prove that the big fellow is not almost divinely called. He has more strength than the small man, as a rule, both physically and mentally, and these were given him not by man but by nature. It is easy to say these come by accident—it is the best we can say in the face of a political philosophy which demands the subordination of the individual to the will of the masses—but we have not as yet proved that they are accidental. It may be that men are born to rule, that they come stamped with the imprint of hierarchies and powers of which our philosophers know nothing. At any rate, they come.

Does anyone really, honestly suppose that a man like J. P. Morgan or Thomas F. Ryan can be ruled by the same principles and ideas which govern the carpenter or the cobbler in the back street?[1] One has a physical and nervous organization so much superior to the other that they are not to be mentioned in the same breath, and as for ideas, the one sees the whole working organization of society where the other merely grasps, after much effort, the idea of patching shoes. These men cannot be made equal. They cannot be governed alike. The best you can say—the best honest government can say—is that their interest, their value to society will be considered and judged according to their respective merits. Thomas F. Ryan must have the consideration which his ideas and his force deserve. Antonio Galuzio, the shoemaker, must have the consideration which his ideas and his service deserve.[2] Because Thomas is rich Antonio must not be allowed to take a bomb and blow him up. Because Antonio is poor Thomas must not be allowed to swindle him out of property or take it by main force. There must be balance maintained.[3] How this balance is to be maintained is a question of great moment, a very subtle question, and one which has never yet been even partially solved. We have the idea firmly fixed in our minds now that our government is superior to any of our individual selves, but we have not yet clearly fixed in our minds what it is that we owe to the individual. Is it protection in all his efforts, all his ambitions, or merely the right to work or to apply for work with no protection other than he can provide for himself by strength and brain? A subtle question surely. We are not within many decades of solving it as yet.

Henry George had the idea that all natural facilities, such as land, water, air, coal, gold and the like should be held in common and worked for the good of the individual.[4] The socialists go a little further and want all our industrial system put on a national basis. There are those who insist that there should be a re-division of property and facilities at stated periods. Meantime the big individual remains big in brain and brawn, and the little individual remains little in these things. You are all the time figuring that you are going to head the big individual off; keep him from taking undue advantage of the little individual. This may be done partially, never entirely. The big individual will always get in and regulate the natural and national facilities for the little individual. There can be no other way. The little individual never tries to seize what he cannot hold.

And so we have come back to this problem of class distinction. It is not a matter of might against right, or brain against muscle, or evil against good, but mere brain or force as opposed to the lack of it. When you have plenty of brain and the force to back it up, the doors open. Society does not want to keep you out, men do not want to keep you down—they merely want to find out where you are. Here and there you will find powerful individuals who will fear and oppose you, who will come out like the successful knights of old to give you battle, but our fight is with these individuals, not with the world in general.

And, as a matter of fact, if you did not seize upon special privileges the world would rush forward and bestow them. See how it crowns the author, the poet, the inventor, the creator of anything. It is immensely gratified when one representative of its type rises and demonstrates that it, as epitomized in him or her, can do something. We have, so far as this country is concerned, no orders to bestow, but we have the freedom of our cities and we make up by actually forgiving sins. Our heroes can do no wrong. We would rather ignore their private shortcomings than not. It has always been so.

What folly then to talk of drifting from our moorings. We have never been really fastened up. It remains that we will do and have done about as much justice and fair play as we see, locally and nationally. And where our pride or our affection or our vanity enter in we will always swerve in the direction not of fair play but unfair play. We will give our heroes the best of it whether they want it or not.

Textual Note: Unsigned editorial, "At the Sign of the Lead Pencil," *Bohemian* 17 (November 1909): 565–57. Attributed to Dreiser for reasons stated in the textual note for "The Problem of the Negro" and on the basis of its thematic continuity with editorials in *Ev'ry Month* and the novels *The Financier* and *The Titan*.

1. Controversial financiers previously mentioned in "The Problem of the Dying Baby," (see 31–32). Morgan was publicly criticized for his manipulation of the financial panic of 1907, while in 1908 Ryan had been investigated for corruption, but not charged.

2. Antonio Galuzio has not been identified. The name connotes Italian immigrants who often worked in the shoe-making trade, and also possibly political radicals.

3. Dreiser's sense of "balance" here and elsewhere is primarily derived from his reading of the English social theorist Herbert Spencer. A central concept in Dreiser's philosophical writings, it is discussed at length in "Equation Inevitable" in *Hey Rub-a-Dub-Dub*.

4. Henry George (1839–97), author of *Progress and Poverty* (1879), which proposed the "Single Tax" on land. George, a crusading journalist against social Darwinist policies, was an early political hero of Dreiser.

The Death of Francisco Ferrer

The Bohemian, December 1909.

The biased trial and subsequent execution of the Spanish anarchist educator Francisco Ferrer (1859–1909) in October 1909 caused an international outcry. In America, protest was led by the anarchist and feminist Emma Goldman (1869–1940), whose photograph and that of her fellow activist Alexander Berk-

man (1870–1936) Dreiser printed in successive issues of The Bohemian. *In part due to Goldman's efforts, Ferrer became the figurehead of the Modern School movement in America.*

If there is one recent significant happening which the American people ought to impress indelibly upon their brains it is the shooting with official sanction at Barcelona, Spain, of Francisco Ferrer, the exponent of modern education in Spain. Ferrer was a philosophic anarchist. That is, he believed that the state is an unnecessary excrescence of comparatively modern growth—that the total abolition of kings, policemen and courts would leave the world free to engage in voluntary cooperation, and that human brotherhood and prosperity would follow. A terrible doctrine, isn't it? He didn't believe in assassination. He never assassinated anybody. And what is more he stood sponsor for the only known form of modern education now existing in Spain—the Escuela Moderna—his modern schools, which he established, for the founding and forwarding of which he used all of his private fortune, and for which he begged and canvassed trying to drag Spain out of its benighted condition.

The one thing that he didn't do was to teach that Jesus Christ was the son of God. He had no personal opposition to the beautiful tenets of the Hebrew teacher. He simply said that religious education as it is inculcated in Spain is false and teaches foolishness, and he cited the noble theories handed out from the average pulpit, particularly the average pulpit of Spain. He also stated that the soldier's uniform conceals crimes against humanity, and the misery of its own existence. This is very fatal in Spain. The soldiery is all that is left to keep an outworn and degraded aristocracy in power. If it weren't for the soldiers Spain might have a decent system of education, a relieved and rehabilitated farming class, a healthy commercial and social situation. Nothing like that. Spain must have a king and a large number of grandees. It must have a priesthood, living in monasteries. It must see to it that the Holy Roman Catholic Church loses no ground. That is the situation in Spain, and that is why it was a dangerous place for a man like Ferrer to live and think. But he did live and he did think. He took the $500,000 left him by his first wife and invested it in one hundred modern schools where the children were educated in the actual facts of history, science and government.[1] He wanted the modern scientific and economic works translated into Spanish, and so he organized a Spanish publishing house and had the works translated at his own expense. He worked hard to bring a sense of what was going on in the world to this benighted country, and as a result he earned the displeasure of royalty—such as it is in Spain—and the priesthood and, of course, the soldiery, because soldiery has to be displeased when royalty is.

What happened? In the simple words of our American language, they "laid for him." On May 31, 1901, one Morral tried to assassinate the king and queen of Spain.[2] Ferrer had nothing to do with that, but it seems that a man by the name of Nakens, who had formerly boarded with Ferrer, assisted the man Morral, not to escape entirely, but to get along the road toward his destination. Morral applied to Nakens for shelter. Nakens gave it to him. Ferrer knew Nakens. Hence Ferrer was guilty of trying to kill the king and queen of Spain. How is that for legal evidence?

And he had a hard time getting loose. They kept him in prison, abused and browbeat him and tried to frighten him into false admissions. They had a difficult man to handle in Ferrer, however, and finally, when scientific Europe was fairly excited over his fate, they let him go.

But he couldn't escape long. The priests were after him. His schools were teaching that evolution brought about our present intellectual state, and that the noble theories on which our modern religions are built are mostly moonshine or worse. This meant that the Catholic Church and, for that matter, any other kind of a church, if there is any other in Spain, wouldn't flourish eternally. The priests wouldn't be so powerful, the rank and file so lean and ignorant. So they made another attempt.

When the great uprising of last July[3] took place the first thought of the authorities was "here is a chance to get Ferrer." At the time he was busy extending his schools, but he was arrested upon a trumped-up charge of inciting riot, treason and so on, and brought before a court martial. No civil jury for him, no, no. Twelve good men and true might have seen through the ruthless scheme to "do" him. He was brought before a court martial, a lot of trumped-up affidavits filed, no witnesses produced, and then he was condemned to be shot. No Catalonian soldiers were allowed even to shoot him. They had to get trusted men from the king's own household to do it. The ordinary soldier might not have wanted to. And this is A.D. 1909. And we have a free and untrammeled press in America—or we think we have.

Well, they shot him. He asked that he be allowed to die with his eyes unbandaged, but they wouldn't stand for that. "A traitor has no right to look upon the faces of soldiers," said the general commanding. How's that! And from a little two-by-four, moth-eaten, rack-rented military power. A traitor. As though any man with two eyes in his head could help but be a traitor to such a cheap, ignorant, oppressive, behind-handed, little squeak of a country as Spain. Well, they shot him, and now the world has a good lesson in what can happen when priests and aristocrats are allowed to rule. A great man has been murdered. A hundred worth-while schools—the only ones in Spain—suppressed. Alfonso is safe and Rome needn't fear the theory of evolution—not in Spain, anyhow, for a while yet. And, as I said before, this is A.D. 1909, and we have Lloyd George of England[4] and the flying machine.

But what this country needs to learn is to look out for the clergy. The world has seen enough of their fat-headed, clerical politicking. We can have it here. We are having it now. The Catholic Church's eager solicitude for its parochial schools is a fair example. The Catholic, Lutheran and other denominational desire to hold all the orphan children is another. They would like to teach history their way and to stamp the mind of the child with their theories. This will never do. A nation cannot prosper and have such religiously educated children. It needs general education and the facts of life only. We should take a warning from Ferrer.

Textual Note: Unsigned editorial, "At the Sign of the Lead Pencil," *Bohemian* 17 (December 1909): 710–12. Attributed to Dreiser for reasons stated in the textual note for "The Problem of the Negro" and on the basis of contextual evidence for his interest in anarchists and anarchist ideas, anticlericalism, Spain, and the care of orphan children. In 1934 Dreiser would write to Henri Barbusse that "From the days of Ferrer and his schools . . . I have followed the machinations of the idle, brutal, grafting, leisure-loving nobles and their allies the grandees and loafers of the Catholic Church." Elias, *Letters*, II: 704.

1. Some of this essay's minor assertions reflect limited contemporary access to the factual record. The money for Ferrer's schools derived from a legacy from one of his students, not from a deceased wife.

2. Dreiser refers to a 1906 attempt on the life of Alfonso XIII by one Mateo Morral. This name has been corrected from "Morales" given in *The Bohemian* text.

3. A general strike was called in Catalūnya when, in July 1909, the Spanish government announced conscription in that province and no other part of Spain in order to fight a colonial war in Morocco. Violent clashes followed, with street battles in Barcelona. Many churches were burned down, and two hundred workers killed. Ferrer was not involved, and indeed his philosophical opposition to violence was criticized by some members of the Solidaridad Obrera (Workers' Unity), which had called the strike.

4. David Lloyd George (1863–1945), Chancellor of the Exchequer in the British parliament from April 1908 to May 1915, was engaged in a series of reforms that polarized British political life. His plan to increase taxes on the wealthy to pay for old-age pensions in the 1909 "People's Budget" sparked a constitutional crisis that is described in "The Threatening British Revolution," "At the Sign of the Lead Pencil," *Bohemian* 17 (December 1909): 716–17. Lloyd George went on to serve as British Prime Minister from December 1916 to October 1922.

Part Two

1911–1928

Historical Commentary

Dreiser's fiction, travel writing, and plays of the 1910s examine, among other things, industrial organization at various levels of society. His interest in the workings of finance capitalism is evident in the first two volumes of the Cowperwood trilogy, *The Financier* (1912) and *The Titan* (1914), which fictionalize the career of financier Charles Tyson Yerkes (1837–1905). In response to the industrial conflicts of 1912–13, Dreiser wrote "The Girl in the Coffin," a play set among labor activists involved in a strike. Centering upon two men torn between their personal feelings and their wider duties to fellow workers and to social justice, "The Girl in the Coffin" shows the influence of Greenwich Village radicals with whom Dreiser had been associating since his final year at *The Delineator*. These included the socialists Floyd Dell and Max Eastman, the labor organizer "Big Bill" Haywood, and the anarchist feminist Emma Goldman, at the height of her notoriety and shortly to be deported from the United States when Dreiser called her, in a 1918 interview, "one of the noblest women who ever lived."[1] Dreiser's political writing of 1911–28 echoed in its own way the Village's eclectic cultural and political radicalism, targeting a range of social, political, and economic problems, and exploring the links between different forms of power. Thus, when his fifth novel, *The "Genius,"* was effectively suppressed late in 1916, Dreiser regarded the threat of prosecution for obscenity as part of a wider struggle with political implications for American democracy. "We Americans," he argued "borrowed or retained from lower English middle-class puritans all their fol-de-rol notions about making human nature perfect by fiat or edict. . . . So although by reason of our coarsest and most brutal methods we have built up one of the most interesting and domineering oligarchies in the world, we are still by no means aware of the fact."[2]

The "most brutal methods" referred to in 1916 intensified with the increasing conservatism of mainstream American politics, which became a marked rightward swing after the United States entered the First World War in April 1917. In line with the hardening of nationalist ideologies, censorship was further tightened by the Espionage Act (1917) and the Sedition Act (1918). New social movements such as socialism and communism, discussed quite openly in the decade up to 1914, were stigmatized as "alien" and repressed, culminating in the draconian official response to postwar labor unrest known as the "Red Scare." While some Progressives like Jane

Addams resolutely opposed the rising tide of chauvinism and paranoia, over the 1913–19 period the xenophobia and hostility to political and cultural radicalism that had long been explicit in the preaching of Billy Sunday and other fundamentalists became part of mainstream thought, setting the scene for many Progressives' involvement in the postwar repression of labor. In response, Dreiser's sympathies shifted to the left of the generally Progressive orientation of his previous intellectual allegiances, though he identified no specific political affiliations and retained his belief in the importance to society of powerful individuals.

During the later 1910s and the 1920s, Dreiser fought a wide-ranging battle against repressive, xenophobic, authoritarian, and censorious tendencies in American life. In short articles for newspapers, and for magazines such as *The Nation* and Margaret Sanger's *Birth Control Review,* he argues for the liberalization of divorce (see "Deeper than Man-Made Laws" in Further Reading) and birth control (see "A Word Concerning Birth Control," 89–95), and he returns several times to the issue of censorship. A series of longer pieces written in 1917–20 expand upon Dreiser's sense of the disjuncture between Americans' beliefs in freedom and democracy and the realities of censorship and social and economic power, the most influential of which, "Life, Art and America," develops Dreiser's response to censorship, which he views as suppressing a true understanding of American life. On this basis Dreiser takes aim at censors, white slave chasers, and antivice crusaders, including Anthony Comstock's New York Society for the Prevention of Vice, which had coordinated the campaign to suppress *The "Genius."* In the 1920 essay "Neurotic America and the Sex Impulse," Dreiser goes on to attack attempts to regulate sexuality according to Christian precepts, arguing that they are doomed to failure and can lead only to repression and hypocrisy. Worse, he suggests, the Puritanical strand in America stultifies its cultural development and fosters the national preoccupation with narrowly materialistic values.

The target of many of these criticisms, the "Puritans," referred in part to the censors and campaigners against vice, headed by Comstock, his successor John Sumner, and figures such as the bible-thumping evangelist Billy Sunday. Dreiser, along with his friend and ally H. L. Mencken, also indicted under the tag of Puritanism a more general American tendency to frame political discourse according to the dictates of Christian morality. Dreiser was especially hostile to the intellectual Protestantism of Woodrow Wilson and his secretary of the interior, Franklin Lane, and especially to their use of it to bolster exceptionalist discourse and to justify entry into World War I.

During the "preparedness" period, nativist fears were stoked by the loss of American lives to German submarine warfare, and Dreiser and Mencken were caught up in the widespread resentment against Germany and those perceived to have German roots or affiliations. After the United States entered the war, thousands of Germans were interned, "Teutonic" culture was anathematized, and a narrow, propagandistic nationalism—"one hundred per cent Americanism," in the slogan promoted at first by the American Legion and the Ku Klux Klan and subsequently adopted by former president Theodore Roosevelt—was enforced by legislation and social pressure. In consequence, Dreiser's ethnic roots became a focus of personal and professional attack,[3] notwithstanding that he had previously demonstrated little affiliation with German ethnicity or culture. Mencken—who had celebrated Dreiser as a writer in the "Teutonic" tradition, popularized Nietzsche, and semi-satirically wrote of "Prussianizing" America—was pilloried and accused of spying for Germany.

In their private letters, Dreiser and Mencken expressed fear of persecution and made uneasy jokes about German victories.[4] Ambivalent about Germany as a visitor in *A Traveler at Forty* (1913), Dreiser made mention in *A Hoosier Holiday* (1915) of "my German ancestry on one side and my German name and my German sympathies" in a passage that was excised shortly after publication for fear of giving offense.[5] He responded to the United States's entry into the war on the side of Britain and France with a fourteen-thousand word essay, "American Idealism and German Frightfulness." Written in the late summer of 1917, the essay ironizes both of the tendencies described in its title, disputing stories of German atrocities and describing America as "a nation of persistent idealists . . . [who] imagine that they are called upon to play the part of a moralistic and Puritanic Messiah." Its main target is Woodrow Wilson's rhetoric of America's special role in a "war to save the world for democracy," which Dreiser contests by reference to repressive wartime legislation, instances of economic inequality, the venality of state legislatures, police and militia collaboration with the corporations in their struggles against organized labor, the United States's engagement in colonialism in the Philippines, and its complicity with Imperial powers such as Britain, France, and Japan. Combining detailed attention to the country's economic inequalities and the domination of its politics, police, and judiciary by corporate power, with internationalist concerns about imperialism, militarism, and war, this is Dreiser's most sustained piece of political writing outside of the volumes *Tragic America* and *America Is Worth Saving*. Rendered unpublishable by the 1917 Espionage Act, the bulk of "American Idealism and German Frightfulness" is printed for the first time in this edition.

A sense of the extremes of wealth and poverty in America runs through almost all of Dreiser's writing in this period. Drawing on his own experience of the consolidation of corporate power in the face of Populist, Progressive, and other reform movements, and on his reading of Gustavus Myers's *History of the Great American Fortunes* (1909–10), Dreiser criticizes the concentration of wealth and the unbridled power accorded to capitalism and to capitalists by the American political system. What remains an open question, at least until the beginning of the 1930s, is how corporate power can be tempered by the "mass" of common people. Discussing this problem in correspondence with Myers and with others on the political left, Dreiser dismisses appeals to moral right, class solidarity, and the courts as potential agencies of social change, and he expresses little confidence in labor unions and politics.[6] Regarding implicit faith in American democratic traditions as, at best, misguided, Dreiser wonders whether the country needs "more democracy or less"—that is, an autocracy powerful enough to curb corporate power, given the inability of its weak and fragmented labor movement to do so. Such radical questioning could leave contemporary readers unsure of Dreiser's position, and some reviewers of the essay collection *Hey Rub-a-Dub-Dub* attributed confusion to Dreiser himself;[7] yet it also stems from his refusal to choose what appeared to be the lesser of two historical evils. This latter stance is elaborated in several essays published in *Hey Rub-a-Dub-Dub*. "Balance" and "Equation Inevitable" take philosophical perspectives, "The Reformer" considers politics directly, while "The American Financier" insists on the importance of both the powerful individual and the "mass."

The refusal to accede to the either/or frameworks in which political questions tend to be put became a habitual pose in Dreiser's political writing of the 1920s. After the critical and popular success of *An American Tragedy* enhanced his reputation as a novelist and social critic, Dreiser's opinions were sought by the liberal, radical, and mainstream press on topical issues such as freedom of speech (see 94–95) and presidential elections. In 1927–28 he published a series of six syndicated articles surveying such aspects of the contemporary scene as American restlessness, America's global role, and "the rebellion of women."[8] Dreiser visited the Soviet Union in late 1927 and early 1928 as a guest of the Russian government, returning with much praise for the Russian project but characteristically ambivalent, emphasizing that he was "an incorrigible individualist—therefore opposed to Communism."[9]

In September 1928, Bruce Bliven of the *New Republic* inquired as to Dreiser's voting intentions in the presidential election. Dreiser's reply, published in the *New Masses*, dismisses the Republican Herbert Hoover as "little more than a hall boy for American corporate powers whose national and international wisdom halts sharply at the corporate profit line." He also rejects the Democratic candidate, Governor of New York Alfred E. Smith, out of a combination of anticlericalism and disgust at Smith's connections with the corrupt Tammany Hall machine. There were candidates who challenged the Republican/Democrat duopoly, such as Norman Thomas of the Socialist Party, and the Workers [Communist] Party nominee William Z. Foster. But Dreiser does not mention them, instead reserving his enthusiasm "for some individual who in a better day, I trust, will put the advancement of the human mind first—[and] that of any dogmatic religious organization or party last."[10]

Notes

1. David Karsner, "Theodore Dreiser," *New York Call, Call Magazine*, 3 March 1918, p. 20.

2. Theodore Dreiser, "America's Foremost Author Protests against Suppression of Great Books and Art by Self-Constituted Moral Censors!" Syndicated Article, *Los Angeles Record*, 7 November 1916, p. 4. The passage reappears in "Life, Art and America."

3. See Stuart P. Sherman, "The Naturalism of Mr. Dreiser," *Nation* 101 (2 December 1915): 648–50; repr. as "The Barbaric Naturalism of Theodore Dreiser," in Sherman, *On Contemporary Literature* (New York: Holt, 1917), 85–101. See also Thomas P. Riggio, "Theodore Dreiser: Hidden Ethnic," *MELUS* 11 (Spring 1984): 53–63.

4. See Riggio, *Dreiser-Mencken Letters*, 1: 187–320.

5. Theodore Dreiser, *A Hoosier Holiday* (New York: John Lane, 1915), 173.

6. TD to Gustavus Myers, 31 March 1916, in Elias, *Letters* 1: 208–09; TD to James Bann [after 23 September 1920], in Elias, *Letters* 1: 283–87; TD to Hammond Defense Fund Committee, M. W. Martin, Chairman, 4 October 1921, in Elias, *Letters* 1: 375–83.

7. See Jack Salzman, *Theodore Dreiser: The Critical Reception* (New York: David Lewis, 1972), 378, 390.

8. Theodore Dreiser, "America's Restlessness is Symbol of Our Hidden Power," New York *American*, 10 April 1927, section E, p. 3; "Are We in America Leading Way Toward a Golden Age in the World?" *New York American*, 22 May 1927, section E, p. 3; and see "Dreiser Analyzes the Rebellion of Women," in Further Reading.

9. *Dreiser Looks at Russia*, 9. This, from the opening sentence of the book, echoes Dreiser's first public statement on Russia, in an interview as he was about to leave the country. See Riggio and West, *Dreiser's Russian Diary*, in Further Reading.

10. Dreiser to Bruce Bliven, 14 September 1928, printed as "Theodore Dreiser on the Elections," *New Masses* 4 (November 1928): 17.

Further Reading

"Deeper than Man-Made Laws." *Hearst's Magazine* 21 (June 1912): 2395.

"Freedom for the Honest Writer." *Cleveland Leader*, 12 March 1916, p. 7.

"Our Greatest Writer Tells What's Wrong with Our Newspapers." *Pep* 2 (July 1917): 8–9.

"Some Aspects of Our National Character." *Hey Rub-a-Dub-Dub: A Book of the Mystery and Terror and Wonder of Life*. New York: Boni and Liveright, 1920, 24–59.

"Neurotic America and the Sex Impulse." *Hey Rub-a-Dub-Dub*, 126–41.

"The Reformer." *Hey Rub-a-Dub-Dub*, 206–11.

"Dreiser Analyzes the Rebellion of Women." *New York American*, 5 February 1928, Section E, p. 3.

Dreiser Looks at Russia. New York: Horace Liveright, 1928.

Thomas P. Riggio and James L. West, eds. *Dreiser's Russian Diary*. Philadelphia: University of Pennsylvania Press, 1996.

"Theodore Dreiser on the Elections." *New Masses* 4 (November 1928): 17.

From "The Girl in the Coffin"

Smart Set, October 1913.

This one-act play was written for the Little Theater movement and was first performed in St. Louis, San Francisco, and New York in 1917. Set in a "large mill town" at a pivotal moment during a labor dispute, it centers on two figures, loom foreman William Magnet and strike leader John Ferguson. Magnet's inspirational speaking, his respected status as a skilled and hard worker, and his ability to address Italian workers in their own language, are portrayed as being indispensable to the labor cause. However, he is distraught over the death of his daughter Mary, in connection, it is strongly hinted, with the termination of an unwanted pregnancy. Consumed with grief and anger toward the girl's lover, whose identity is unknown, Magnet claims the "privilege" to be "left alone with my own trouble." Ferguson, however, demands that Magnet attend a crucial mass meeting, arguing that "it's a privilege no man ought to want to claim at the expense of fourteen thousand of his fellow-workers." Recounting his own personal and political story, the visiting activist reveals that he has himself just experienced a personal tragedy, the death of his lover. After this passage, at the very end of the play, it is revealed that Ferguson's lover was Mary Magnet herself, "the girl in the coffin."

FERGUSON

You said to me I don't know how it feels to be a father. You're right about that, Magnet, dead right. I don't know. Being the kind of man I am, nobody seems to think I'm entitled to any connection with a family. A court-room or a jail cell is supposed to be the place where my disposition thrives to the best advantage. The only kind of a father I've ever had a chance to be you wouldn't call a father at all. You'd call him a beast, a low-down scoundrel, a man that ruins other men's daughters. Since my mother died, when I was a ten-year-old kid working on the bunkers in a coal mine out in Colorado,[1] I've never known but one home, and that's in a dead woman's heart. I'm alone now and likely to stay so. I haven't any more hope of happiness in this world than I have of going to heaven when I die, and that's none at all.

[*With sudden, passionate emphasis.*]

But there's one thing I don't ever forget, Magnet—unhappiness is a lot easier to bear when you've got clothes to cover your back and food enough to hold your body and soul together. When I come to a town in the dead of winter and find twenty-five thousand people on the edge of freezing and starvation, I remember the time when my own mother went cold and hungry, and it don't seem to make very much difference to me whether I'm happy or not.

[*He takes up his hat as if to leave, and moves a little toward the door.*]

As long as I can keep alive to fight for those poor devils, I'll fight for 'em. There was a while I expected others to feel the same way, but I've got over that. Nobody knows any better than I do how few men you're likely to run across in a lifetime that'll join the ranks to stay. I used to take it pretty hard when an old comrade fell out, but it don't make so much difference any more. I've swallowed that kind of a disappointment with my daily bread for so many years now that it's got to be a pretty old story. There's one thing that always helps me to stand it. If there's nobody else in this world I can count on, I know I can always count on myself. As long as there's breath in my body I'll never lose heart and I'll never give up the game. A good part of the world seems to look on me as a kind of a devil. Well, if that's the way they feel about it, let 'em think so. I don't mind being the kind of an individual that can walk through hell without being scorched any so's you'd notice it. Life can kill and bury my happiness, but it can't kill and bury my courage. This strike that's on in this town is the biggest I've ever handled. Without you to help me, Magnet, maybe I'll lose it. Or maybe I won't lose it. Maybe I'll win it anyhow. This night may mean the beginning of the end for me or it may mean the beginning of the biggest success I've ever known. But whichever way it is, you can be sure of one thing—if ever I go down it'll be with every man's hand against me and my back shoved up against a hard high wall.

[*There is a knock.* FERGUSON *opens the door and* McGRATH *steps just inside.*]

MCGRATH

Are you ready, Mr. Ferguson? Time's getting short.

FERGUSON

All ready, McGrath.

MAGNET

[*Rising suddenly.*]

Hold on there a minute, Tim. (*He walks to the dining room door and calls to* MRS. LITTIG.) You needn't set the table till I get back, Mrs. Littig. I'm going down to the hall.

Textual Note: Smart Set 41 (October 1913): 127–40. Rpt. in *Plays of the Natural and the Supernatural* (New York: John Lane Company, 1916), 7–53; and in Keith Newlin and Frederic Rusch, eds., *The Collected Plays of Theodore Dreiser* (Albany, N.Y.: Whitston Publishing, 2000), 1–24. This selection is taken from *Plays of the Natural and the Supernatural*, pp. 50–52.

1. These biographical details broadly resemble those of the labor activist William D. "Big Bill" Haywood (1869–1928), cofounder of the leftwing union, the Industrial Workers of the World (I.W.W.). Haywood organized among English- and Italian-speaking textile workers during strikes in Lawrence, Massachusetts, in 1912, and Paterson, New Jersey, in 1913. Dreiser visited Paterson during the 1913 strike to carry out research for the play.

From "Life, Art and America"

The Seven Arts, February 1917.

During its short run between November 1916 and October 1917, the magazine The Seven Arts, *with its motto "An Expression of Artists For the Community," epitomized the blend of political, cultural, and sexual radicalism associated with its base in Greenwich Village, New York. This essay, which has become one of Dreiser's best-known critiques of the "Puritan" influence on American culture, appeared alongside pieces by, among others, Louis Untermeyer, Kahlil Gibran, and Robert Frost. It was reprinted with minor revisions and cuts in* Hey Rub-a-Dub-Dub.

* * * *

No country in the world, at least none that I know anything about, has such a peculiar, such a seemingly fierce determination, to make the Ten Commandments work. It would be amusing if it were not pitiful, their faith in these binding religious ideals. I, for one, have never been able to make up my mind whether this springs from the zealotry of the Puritans who landed at Plymouth Rock, or whether it is indigenous to the soil (which I doubt when I think of the Indians who preceded the whites), or whether it is a product of the federal constitution, compounded by such idealists as Paine and Jefferson and Franklin, and the more or less religious and political dreamers of the pre-constitutional days. Certain it is that no profound moral idealism animated the French in Canada, the Dutch in New York, the Swedes in New Jersey, or the mixed French and English in the extreme south and New Orleans.

The first shipload of white women that was ever brought to America was sold, almost at so much a pound.[1] They were landed at Jamestown. The basis of all the first large fortunes was laid, to speak plainly, in graft—the most outrageous concessions obtained abroad. The history of our relations with the American Indians is sufficient to lay any claim to financial or moral virtue or worth in the white men who settled this country. We debauched, then robbed and murdered them. There is no other conclusion to be drawn from the facts covering that relationship as set down in any history worthy of the name. In regard to the development of our land, our canals, our railroads, and the vast organizations supplying our present day necessities, their history is a complex of perjury, robbery, false witness, extortion, and indeed every crime to which avarice, greed and ambition are heir. If you do not believe this, examine at your leisure the various congressional and state legislative investigations which have been held on an average of every six months since the government was founded, and see for yourself. The cunning and unscrupulousness of American brains can be matched against any the world has ever known, not even excepting the English.

But an odd thing in connection with this financial and social criminality is that it has been consistently and regularly accompanied, outwardly at least, by a religious and a sex puritanism which would be scarcely believable if it were not true. I do not say that the robbers and thieves who did so much to build up our great commercial and social structures were in themselves inwardly or outwardly always religious or puritanically moral from the sex point of view, although in regard to the latter, they most frequently made a show of so being. But I do say this, that the communities and the states and the nation in which they were committing their depredations have been individually and collectively, in so far as the written, printed and acted word are concerned, and in pictures and music, militantly pure and religious during all the time that this has been going forward under their eyes, and, to a certain extent, with their political consent.[2] Why? I have a vague feeling that it is the American of Anglo-Saxon origin only who has been most vivid in his excitement over religion and morals where the written, printed, acted, or painted word was concerned, yet who, at the same time, and perhaps for this very reason, was failing or deliberately refusing to see, the contrast which his ordinary and very human actions presented to all this. Was he a hypocrite? Oh, well! Is he one? I hate to think it, but he certainly acts the part exceedingly well. Either he is that or a fool—take your choice.[3]

Your American of Anglo-Saxon or any other origin is actually no better, spiritually or morally, than any other creature of this earth, be he Turk or Hindu or Chinese, except from a materially constructive or wealth-breeding point of view, but for some odd reason or another, he thinks he is. The only real difference is that, cast out or spewed out by conditions over which he had no control elsewhere, he chanced to fall into a land overflowing with milk and honey. Nature in America was, and still is, kind to the lorn foreigner seeking a means of subsistence, and he seems to have immediately attributed this to three things: first, his inherent capacity to dominate and control wealth; second, the especial favor of God to him; third, to his superior and moral state (due, of course, to his possession of wealth). These three things, uncorrected as yet by any great financial pressure, or any great natural or world catastrophe, have served to keep the American in his highly romantic state of self deception. He still thinks that he is a superior spiritual and moral being, infinitely better than the creatures of any other land, and nothing short of a financial cataclysm, which will come with the pressure of population on resources, will convince him that he is not. But that he will yet be convinced is a certainty. You need not fear. Leave it to nature.

One of the interesting phases of this puritanism or phariseeism is his attitude toward women and their morality and their purity. If ever a people has refined eroticism to a greater degree than the American, I am not aware of it. Owing to a theory of the doctrinaire acceptance of the Mary legend (Maryolotry, no less), the good American, capable of the same gross financial crimes previously indicated, has been able to look upon most women, but more particularly those above him in the social scale, as considerably more than human—angelic, no less, and possessed of qualities the like of which are not to be found in any breathing being, man, woman, child, or animal. It matters not that his cities and towns, like those of any other nation, are rife with sex; that in each one are specific and often large areas devoted to Eros or Venus, or both.[4] While maintaining them, he is still blind to their existence or import. He or his boys or his friends go—but—.

Only a sex blunted nature or race such as the Anglo-Saxon could have built up any such asinine theory as this.[5] The purity, the sanctity, the self-abnegation, the delicacy of women—how these qualities have been exaggerated and dinned into our ears, until at last the average scrubby non-reasoning male, quite capable of visiting the gardens of Venus, or taking a girl off the street, is no more able to clearly visualize the creature before him than he is the central wilds of Africa which he has never seen. A princess, a goddess, a divine mother or creative principle, all the virtues, all the perfections, no vices, no weaknesses, no errors—some such hodgepodge as this has come to be the average Anglo-Saxon, or at least American, conception of the average American woman. I do not say that a portion of this illusion is not valuable—I think it is.[6] But as it stands now, she is too good to be true: a paragon, a myth! Actually, she doesn't exist at all as he has been taught to imagine her. She is nothing more than a two-legged biped like the rest of us, but in consequence of this delusion sex itself, being a violation of this paragon, has become a crime. We enter upon the earth, it is true, in a none too artistic manner (conceived in iniquity and born in sin, is the biblical phrasing of it),[7] but all this has long since been glozed over—ignored—and to obviate its brutality as much as possible, the male has been called upon to purify himself in thought and deed, to avoid all private speculation as to women and his relationship to them, and, much more than that, to avoid all public discussion, either by word of mouth or the printed page.[8]

To think of women or to describe them as anything less than the paragon previously commented upon, has become, by this process, not only a sin—it is a shameful infraction of the moral code, no less. Women are too good, the sex relationship too vile a thing, to be mentioned or even thought of. We must move in a mirage of illusion. We must not know what we really do. We must trample fact under foot and give fancy, in the guise of our so-called better natures, free rein.[9] How this must affect or stultify the artistic and creative faculties of the race itself must be plain. Yet that is exactly where we stand today, ethically and spiritually, in regard to sex and women, and that is what is the matter with American social life, letters and art.

I do not pretend to say that this is not a workable and a satisfactory code in case any race or nation chooses to follow it, but I do say it is deadening to the artistic impulse, and I mean it. Imagine a puritan or a moralist attempting anything in art, which is nothing if not a true reflection of insight into life! Imagine! And contrast this moral or art narrowness with his commercial, or financial, or agricultural freedom and sense, and note the difference. In regard to all the latter, he is cool, skeptical, level-headed, understanding, natural—consequently well developed in those fields. In regard to this other, he is illusioned, theoretic, religious. In consequence, he has no power, except for an occasional individual who may rise in spite of these untoward conditions (to be frowned upon), to understand, much less picture, life as it really is. Artistically, intellectually, philosophically, we are weaklings; financially, and in all ways commercial we are very powerful. So one-sided has been our development that in this latter respect we are almost giants. Strange, almost fabulous creatures, have been developed here by this process, men so singularly devoid of a rounded human nature that they have become freaks in this one direction—that of money getting. I refer to Rockefeller, Gould, Sage, Vanderbilt the first, H. H. Rogers, Carnegie, Frick.[10] Strong in but this one capacity, the majority of our great men stand forth as true human rarities, the like of which has scarcely ever been seen before.[11]

* * * *

The American, by some hocus pocus of atavism, has seemingly borrowed or retained from lower English middle-class puritans all their fol-de-rol notions about making human nature perfect by fiat or edict—the written word, as it were, which goes with all religions. So, although by reason of the coarsest and most brutal methods, we, as a nation, have built up one of the most interesting and domineering oligarchies in the world, we are still by no means aware of the fact.

All men, in the mind of the unthinking American, are still free and equal. They have in themselves certain inalienable rights; what they are, when you come to test them, no human being can discover. Your so-called rights disappear like water before a moving boat. They do not exist. Life here, as elsewhere, comes down to the brutal methods of nature itself. The rich strike the poor at every turn; the poor defend themselves and further their lives by all the tricks which stark necessity can conceive. No inalienable right keeps the average cost of living from rising steadily, while most of the salaries of our idealistic Americans are stationary. No inalienable right has ever yet prevented the strong from tricking or browbeating the weak. And although by degrees the average American is feeling more and more keenly the sharpening struggle for existence, yet his faith in his impossible ideals is as fresh as ever. God will save the good American and seat him at His right hand on the Golden Throne.

On earth the good American is convinced that the narrower and more colorless his life here the greater his opportunity for a more glorious life hereafter. His pet theory is that man is made useful and successful and constructive—a perfect man, in short—by the kinds and numbers of things he is not permitted to do or think or say. A pale, narrow, utterly restrained life, according to his theory, is the perfect one. If one accepted the King James version and kept utterly unspotted by the world, entirely out of contact with it, he would be the perfect American. Indeed, ever since the Mayflower landed, and the country began to grow westward, we have been convinced that we were destined to make the Ten Commandments, in all their arbitrary perfection, work. One might show readily enough that America attained its amazing position in life by reason of the fact that, along with boundless opportunities, the Ten Commandments did not and do not work, but what would be the use? With one hand the naïve American takes and executes with all the brutal insistence of Nature itself; with the other he writes glowing platitudes concerning brotherly love, virtue, purity, truth, etc. etc.[12]

A part of this right or left hand tendency, as the case may be, is seen in the constant desire of the American to reform something. No country in the world, not even England, the mother of fol-de-rol reforms, is so prolific in these frail ventures as this great country of ours. In turn we have had campaigns for the reform of the atheist, the drunkard, the lecher, the fallen woman, the buccaneer financier, the drug fiend, the dancer, the theatergoer, the reader of novels, the wearer of low-neck dresses and surplus jewelry—in fact, every human taste and frivolity, wherever sporadically it has chanced to manifest itself with any interesting human force.

* * * *

Textual Note: Copy-text is *The Seven Arts* 1 (February 1917): 363–89. These selections are taken from pp. 373–78; 384–85. Rpt. as a pamphlet in 1917, and in *Hey Rub-a-Dub-Dub*, 252–76. Several cuts and revisions were made to the *Hey Rub-a-Dub-Dub* text, the most significant instances of which are indicated in the notes. Some revisions avoid duplication with other essays in the volume; others are often only partially successful in resolving slight ambiguities or irregular syntax, and one, "disillusioned" for "illusioned" on p. 266 (*Seven Arts*, 377), introduces confusion.

1. Ninety British women arrived in Jamestown, Virginia, in 1620 on the "Bride Ship." They were "sold" to colonists who had to pay for their passage.
2. Dreiser revised this passage for the republication of the essay in *Hey Rub-a-Dub-Dub* to read "in so far as the written, printed and acted word are concerned, most loud in their pretensions" (263–64).
3. The two sentences at the conclusion of this paragraph are cut from the 1920 text.
4. Public meeting places for people desiring sexual activity. Eros, the ancient Greek god of lust, love, and sex, is associated primarily with male desire, while Venus, the Roman goddess of love and beauty, is associated with female desire. Dreiser is also distinguishing between prostitution (Eros) and other forms of extramarital sexual activity (Venus).
5. The following is inserted into the 1920 text at this point: "One would suppose that as they did, so they would have the courage to say, or at least cease this endless pother as to superior virtue. But no" (*Hey Rub-a-Dub-Dub*, 265).
6. The phrase "I think it is" is cut from the 1920 text.
7. Psalm 51, verse 5.
8. Dreiser was frequently pressured by publishers to edit his fiction, and his work faced increasing attack from antivice and "watch and ward" societies, culminating in the withdrawal from sale of *The "Genius"* under threat of prosecution for obscenity in late 1916. The case against the novel involved the citation of almost ninety instances of "lewd, profane, or blasphemous" matter. Dreiser subsequently both polemicized against and organized resistance to various initiatives to tighten censorship still further.
9. This passage was revised in 1920 to "Women are now so good, the sex relationship so vile a thing that to think of the two at once is not to be thought of. They are supposed to have no connection. We must move in a mirage of illusion; we must trample fact underfoot and give fancy, in the guise of our better natures, free rein" (*Hey Rub-a-Dub-Dub*, 266). Several further revisions were made to this and the following paragraph, including the elimination of the break between them, and minor changes of phrasing.
10. John D. Rockefeller (1839–1937), Jay Gould (1836–92), Russell Sage (1816–1906), Cornelius Vanderbilt (1794–1877), Henry Huddleston Rogers (1840–1909),

Andrew Carnegie (1835–1918), and Henry Clay Frick (1849–1919) were prominent American businessmen, bankers, and industrialists of the nineteenth and early twentieth centuries.

11. This sentence, which reads confusingly "Strong in all but this one capacity" in the original, was cut from the 1920 text.

12. All but the final sentence of this paragraph was cut from the 1920 text.

American Idealism and German Frightfulness

August 1917.

Written in response to a commission for an antiwar essay from the Seven Arts, *this essay was rendered unpublishable under the terms of the 1917 Espionage Act, which forbade the "transmission of information . . . to the advantage of any foreign nation." By drawing attention to Germany's combination of national unity, technological development, and social legislation, and calling for Germany to be treated on a par with Britain and France, it was inevitable in the wartime context that the essay would be interpreted as "pro-German," despite Dreiser's protestations to the contrary within and outside the text. The extent to which his sympathies extended to an actual affiliation with the German state remains debatable. Viewed in the immediate context of the comparative considerations of political structures in "Life, Art and America" and "More Democracy Or Less? An Inquiry," it is clear that Dreiser was more concerned with exposing what he saw as the hypocritical manipulation of democratic and moralistic rhetoric by Woodrow Wilson's administration than with endorsing German autocracy. Nevertheless, the ugly face of "Anglo-Saxon" dominance revealed by the wartime persecution of German-Americans, and Dreiser's view of World War I as a struggle to maintain established empires, especially that of Great Britain, would shape his perspective on the international tensions of the 1930s and 1940s.*

In the opening two thousand or so words, Dreiser deals skeptically with stories of German atrocities and contrasts Woodrow Wilson's rationale for the war "to make the world safe for democracy" with the imperialism of Britain, France, and Japan.

* * * *

For myself, I sincerely fear that our entrance into this war, (selfish and self-aggrandizing as it was and is on the part of England, Germany, Austria, Russia, Italy, and even Romania and Serbia) is a mistake—one of the greatest if not unfair blunders ever made by a great nation. Led by pro-moralistic Puritans and unreasoning Anglophiles, we are at this moment making a spectacle of ourselves, the folly and ridiculousness of which may cost us much, and possibly make us a laughing-stock, if not a slaughter pen, for generations to come. Actually instead of entering this war, we should have considered, I think, that we have Germany, Japan and England to deal with—nations that do not love us at all, and that envy our wealth, and which may some day lead them into hostile relations with us, in which case all our strength, economic and otherwise, will be needed here. Oh, the folly of America! And, in addition, I think we may eventually be compelled to retreat with ignominy, or the price of our victory will be so staggering as to weary us for many a year.

Actually, we are busy making statements and doing things which have no real relationship to life, liberty, or the pursuit of happiness, as these concern the true interests of ourselves or the world at large. We have our Cuba, our Philippines, our Santa Domingo, our Canal Zone (the last seized ruthlessly from a friendly power)—and we have not freed them by any means (read the true story of the recent uprising in Cuba)[1]—and yet, with all these interesting examples of the predatory, mercenary and selfish tactics of ourselves as well as our Allies and our foes, we are going to establish universal peace and make the world safe for democracy.[2]

And by what authority, I should like to know? Is America such a success as a form of government that it can boast of carrying the blessings of liberty, equality, and the like, to all foreign lands, or nearly all? I wonder? Already in this land of freedom, two per cent of the people own sixty-five per cent of all the wealth.[3] Thirty-five merchant financiers rule New York, we are told, and they do. Less than one half of one per cent of our citizens have enough income to be subject to the drastic tax of 1917![4] In addition, the purchasing power of the dollar is being cut in half, and only the cheapest, the worst, foods are being bought by the poor—the very worst. Naturally, this war is being favored by the very rich, for their business has doubled and trebled in the last few years, and by some this is looked upon as the reason for our entrance into this war—this and the propagandizing power of England—its able press-agent work in its own behalf. In addition, many believe that our financiers compelled our aid in order to get back from Europe—the Allies—the money they had invested there. Whether this is true or not, I do not know, but certain it is that a portion of our Americans believe this. The West and South were not eager for the loan. But New York and Wall Street were wildly enthusiastic. Do you actually believe that the average financier cares very much how many Americans die so long as he gets his foreign investments back?[5]

But let us grant that the financiers and the moneyed element are truly patriotic. Are they going to pay for the war? Have you studied the new tax bills? Are our American incomes going to be taxed as much as those of England? Tea, coffee, sugar, the movies, postage, etc. are on the list, but how about war profits over fifty per cent? Did you note our Congressional action as to that? And there were in 1916 twice as many people with incomes of over one million as there were in 1915. Does not that fact tell you something?

In so far as I can see, this land has not done so much better than any other by its population, considering that it was and still is in a measure virgin soil, an unoccupied territory, full of opportunities for even the dullest and most disinterested. We are always confusing America's natural opportunities with the benefits its form of government is supposed to have brought us, but personally and seriously, I believe its government has done little so far save allow the big dog free rein to pounce upon the little one, in spite of all that we think to the contrary. We are a great nation, a rich one, but in so far as our boasted freedom is concerned, it has consisted mainly in this: that whenever the little dog has felt too much "bit up" he could move into some section where there are or were other dogs even smaller than himself. There he has been free to bite them up. But this condition will not always endure. You have only to consult your current expenses to prove it. Instead of one Tsar, we have fifty or a hundred who squabble among themselves as to which one shall be allowed to tax us most. Who made $250,000,000 out of wheat alone in 1916—the rank and file?[6] If so, why bread at fifteen cents a loaf? Look at the food prices, the food riots, the labor wars.

Actually, I think half the rage of a certain element in America as in England—the strongly Anglo-Saxon element against the German—is due to the fact that they have been compelled to see a purely autocratic form of government do as well, if not better (really much better, considering the handicap of the lack of a new land and boundless opportunity) by itself, and its people, than they have, all things considered. Germany has really done much better, and a few years ago our ears were full of the praises of all things German—their schools, officials, homes, shops, factories, their efficiency, patience, thoroughgoing-ness, their music, philosophy, science, logic, their home life, and what not—and this by no less a country than England itself. It could not praise Germany enough, until Germany became ambitious for a little world territory too. And then look at them! Dogs, pigs, savages, snakes, barbarians, murderers, what not! And all because—and all because—if you want the plain simple truth, Germany wanted to expand a little: into China, which England felt that she owned, into Turkey and Mesopotamia, which England felt she ought to own, into Africa, about which England felt much the same.

And on what grounds, pray? Or, in other words, why should we become so excited fearing that England will not be permitted to do this? Is there so much more true democracy in England than there is in Germany or Japan or here? Have you ever been in England? Do you know what the British autocracy, the English aristocracy, think of the rank and file there and everywhere else, and how they manipulate it? Have you ever read a book entitled *The History of Canadian Wealth*,[7] wherein is set forth the looting of Canada by British aristocrats and those who became aristocrats? Do you know that actually in England a tradesman may never aspire to be anything more than a tradesman, because, forsooth, he began as a tradesman? That once a governess or clerk, always a governess or clerk? England allied herself with autocratic Japan to rule the seas and the world, and before that with autocratic Russia to partition Asia, but when she is endangered, we rush to her aid, crying that we are "saving the world for democracy!" Imagine the guffawing in English high circles over that phrase.

But how much did she love American democracy before we decided to come to her aid? Will your memory reach back so far as a year? We were to be shut out of any participation in anything, were we not, and that by no less a power than democratic England, aided by autocratic Russia and Japan. The threats! The comments on America and Wilson! The plot to put in Hughes to help England![8] Is it not a fact that all the democratic reforms which Lloyd George introduced into England before the war, and which were so bitterly denounced by the English aristocrats as "demagogic socialism," were borrowed from policies actually in operation in Germany? Where did our new farm loan bank come from—England? France? Russia? Or Germany? Which? The British old-age pension system? Where was that first tried out? Our proposed labor regulation laws? Our revised insurance laws? Our workingmen's compensation acts—one of the best features of our new Federal banking law? All these came from where? Germany, of course.[9] Is it not entirely possible that it is the democratic character of such laws and measures, (the general public benefit that has been derived from them), that has caused the people of Germany to be so devoted to their government? Which has enabled them, for the time being anyhow, to withstand the onslaught of the whole world? But, on the other hand, if the German people have had nothing to do with these democratic and socialistic laws, as some seem to think, what is wrong with an autocracy that seeks to look after the mass so well?

The trouble with America, as I see it, is that it is "cracked" on the subject of England,—its greatness, its import to the world—while failing entirely to understand true democracy, "republicanism," "individual freedom." We do not seem to grasp in the least—most Americans anyhow—that along with our boasted independence, etc., must go a full measure of individual and national self-discipline which must tend to benefit the mass, not the few, and that religious illusion and moral hysteria or Puritanism (all the trash, in short, which has passed for self-righteousness and individual and national perfection during the last nineteen hundred and seventeen years, no less) have nothing to do with true democracy. We seem to know little or nothing about that true Greek or pagan[10] discipline which understands

that individual and national independence or perfection, or what you will, are related to intelligent and forceful organization and control in favor, and for the benefit, of the mass—autocratic control, I mean, willed and delegated by the people themselves. This last is not, or should not be at least, concerned with who is moral or immoral in the religious or Puritanic sense, but rather with who is fittest to survive, not by slaying or burning entirely, (except in self defense), but by winning to his side by reason of intelligence, the power to conceive and execute a reasonable and intelligent and constructive system of social procedure. If any nation can scheme out a system of living that is best for itself, its largest number, and does not betray itself to impossible ideals and fol-de-rol notions, it is entitled, I suppose, to be let alone, or should be without being pestered by other nations desirous of extending willy-nilly, the blessings or advantages of democracy to the uttermost limits of the world, "to make the world safe for democracy." Well, Germany, let us say, believes that it has such an ideal scheme for itself. What is wrong then with its being allowed to live in its own way? England is living its own way. Japan is living its special way. Why not Germany? Is her system so much worse than ours or England's? We seem to think so—some of us—but is it? Or are we merely led by ancient prejudices into imagining that it is? Remember, for instance, all the benefits we have derived from Germany—not England. In this case, I believe the American people do not really understand what they are fighting for—whom. Also, I believe that if they did, they would refuse to fight, for it is not their chestnuts that are going to be raked out of the fire, by any means, I fear.

The whole trouble with our English-speaking world, as I see it—that is, when it is tinged with the ideas of Anglo-Saxon domination, the greatness of England and so forth—is that on the one hand it is "hyped" on the subject of the moral or Christian code—trying to make the Sermon on the Mount work, or imagining that it is—while on the other hand, it is busy commercially and in every other way doing just the opposite, making of the whole thing, the whole system, a laughing stock and a joke. The English, any more than the Americans, are not Christian, any more than is Germany, or Japan, or Turkey, or Siam. They are pagan, the ruling element, the same as the despised German ruling element. We all know, or should, that England has no more love for democracies than she has for autocracies save only as they will benefit her. And as for the Christian and Western pro-moralistic codes being dominant in either England or America any more than they are in Germany or Turkey or Japan, well they have nothing to do with either our private or trade lives, as I see it. They do not work. We do not practice them. Our Western world has built upon certain human instincts—mercy, tenderness, a sense of fair play, and social relationships which every animal has and has had since the dawn of life, perhaps—a vast system of tinkering religiosity which has had nothing to do with real life, and never has had. People pray principally because they are frightened or helpless. They spout social maxims because it is advantageous to them—when they are weak. They cry for fair play and justice and mercy—all those instincts which operate anyhow in nature according to a law of balance and adjustment—not nearly so much when they are in a position to give or compel them, as when they themselves are in need of them. Our religious principles and maxims, so-called, are literally the mouthings of the underdog, and as such should be heeded, but never to the destruction or undoing of the manhood or brain force (true and executive) of the race or the world. The crowd can sense and feel. It is entitled to consideration on that score. But if it can not think and plan—as it plainly can not—it must not be allowed to hold back or dictate too much to those individuals who can. Individuals are required, leaders, great ones, but not everyone can be a leader, and for that very reason life can not escape a certain measure of autocracy, any more than it can escape a certain measure of democracy. Both are necessary, inherent in the scheme of things. Life will never again tolerate, unless it has even less brains than I give it credit for, that system of brutal tyranny seen, let us say, in a country like Russia of yesterday, or the minor satraps[11] of Asia and Africa, but on the other hand it will bow, and gladly, to the need of hard, forceful, educative leadership, whether it be Teutonic, Anglo-Saxon, Oriental, or any other.

And in regard to this same matter of justice, Christian or otherwise, which we say we are so eager to establish in the world; Germany insists that that is just what we do not deal in and what it has not had since the beginning of this war—and makes out a pretty fair case for herself—as witness her contention that from the very beginning we have been anything but fair or neutral. All along she has insisted, until of late her voice has been more or less shut out of the telegraphic world, that British command of the seas had become absolute and had long since abolished any neutral rights which interfered with it, and this is true. We ourselves protested feebly (because of our feeling against Germany) against the illegal blockade of Germany by the British at the opening of the war, the detention of our ships and the opening of our mails coming from countries other than Great Britain, but with what result? Our ships are still being detained, our mails opened, by the British censor.[12] Think of it! And we are going to war to save England— help her maintain her control of the seas, along with Japan, with whom she appears to be willing to divide the control of the world—Imperial Japan, not Democratic America, mind you! We have done nothing but protest feebly, not willing to disturb British sovereignty. On the other hand, when Germany, recognizing our unfairness in the matter, retaliated, saying that if England could starve her illegally, she could starve England in the same way, we proceeded to use the threat of war, and actually to declare war. We refused to withhold our supplies from England—munitions, for instance. We refused to ask our citizens to keep off un-neutral English ships. That would have been giving aid and comfort to barbarians, I suppose. On the other hand, we would not guarantee the freedom of the seas. That would have disturbed England. If England said we must not use certain areas of the North Sea, we did not use them; if England said we could do only a certain amount of trade with Holland, that is all the trade we did. Great Britain illegally beleaguered Holland, Norway, Sweden, Denmark, Greece, ourselves, even Argentina and Brazil, and is still doing so, and we have never said a word. She actually commandeered all Greek shipping, dethroned the King of Greece,[13] ordered Holland and Sweden to cease trading with Germany, threatened Argentina with retaliation in case she ceased giving up most of her wheat to England, and of late has been attempting, and with some success, to dictate the internal policy of Russia, a fact which should teach us that she is well able to take care of herself—but—no. To us Great Britain is literally sacred. To quote Mr. Secretary Lane in one of his wildest flights, our "laws, traditions, standards of life and inherent love of liberty, which we call Anglo-Saxon civilization, come from England," and we cannot afford to do anything but fight for England.[14] He says so.

In other words, it seems to have come down to this, that the vile Germans having attempted to disturb that Anglo-Saxon supremacy of which we are so gloriously the tail, it is our duty to fight them, to tear up root and branch this rival Teutonic civilization—or hard, successful common sense—and throw it into the sea. No worry about autocratic Japan which is steadily swallowing up China, and telling us to mind our own business while she does so, none about Russia (before her change),[15] none about Italy or Spain, only Germany and her Kaiser. Why? Because Germany, at the worst, wants to set up a middle Europe agreement, as opposed to English and (we add) American domination of the world, and to take her place in life as a truly great and interesting power. And why not, pray? And why not? Must we or England always control—preferably England? Or Japan instead of Germany? Personally, I can see no glorious love of justice here. No desire to guarantee "the undictated development of all peoples" in this instance.[16] In short, as I have shown, and as has recently been affirmed and reaffirmed under the mildest of the conceived plans for a world peace, Germany is to lose not only her present share of Poland and Alsace and Lorraine, but "Bavaria, Saxony, and other states of the German Empire," which are to be permitted "to resolve themselves again into their separate entities as they were before the Franco-Prussian war," while England, with

India, Egypt, Burma, the Boer Republic, and her new German colonies, as well as a finger in China and Persia, is to remain intact. Why? Because of her superior moral worth? Well, she may have it, although I cannot see it. And as for France, Russia, Japan, Italy, and ourselves, being better than Germany and therefore entitled to dismember her, well—

What rot! What pharisaism! What unbelievable tosh and pecksniffery! Could American rag-bag Puritanic balderdash and British pecksniffery be carried further?

The trouble with us Americans is, as I have often pointed out in other places, that we do not know the history of European politics any more than we know the true genesis of this war. Actually, it dates back to the sixteenth century, when the policy of carving the world into what are now called "spheres of influence" began. There was practically not even a rest to this until the end of the Napoleonic period, when the Spanish, Dutch, and French navies being swept from the seas, British imperialistic control was fully established.[17] I shall not go into the details of this accomplishment, which may be found in any school history. The philosophy of it is a different matter. Those who know anything about such things know that as usual in human life, the ever active greed of individuals, corporations and nations in those days, as in these, began this sort of thing and is continuing it to this day. Human nature has not changed much. It is, as far as one can tell by history, no worse and but little better. Dreamers and idealists read all sorts of fantastic improvements into the nature of man, but back of man and his so-called improvements is nature itself—and is man going to make over nature, the universe itself, or is the universe going to make over man? We read of improvements, but consider, if you please, man himself as to his character and moods and actions as you find him in your daily contact with him. Is he constitutionally fitted to exercise fair play and love and the Golden Rule only? Can he? Will life permit him? Then consider that the world has seen a war regularly every thirty years throughout recorded history. We had a war with England in 1776, another in 1812, one with Mexico in 1848, an unjust war on our part. We had another in 1865, justifiable perhaps, with the South. We had another in 1898—Spain—very laudable on our part, though we kept the Philippines and Cuba for our share. We could have had one ten years ago with Colombia if she had been strong enough when we took the Panama Canal Zone from her by trickery.[18]

Allons![19]

The seventeenth and eighteenth centuries were spent in wars to re-arrange world ownership. France had occupied a large part of North America and many of the West Indian Islands; Holland was also an owner in North America, possessing a great colony in what is now New York; England occupied later in the seventeenth century all of what is now our Atlantic seaboard, except Florida. In the middle of that century she had destroyed Holland's sea power, both mercantile and naval; had seized New York, and a little after the middle of the eighteenth century had driven France from Canada and practically held nearly all the territory east of the Mississippi.

The peace of 1763 left but two owners in North America: Great Britain and Spain.[20] Florida was given to Britain as an offset to the relinquishment of Havana, taken in 1762. The peace of 1783 established the United States. Florida was returned to Spain, and there were again three nations in North America: the United States, Great Britain, and Spain.[21] There was to be no permanent settlement by Russia in Alaska until 1784.[22]

In 1803 France had again, though but for a year or so, become an owner in North America. Napoleon had forced Spain to retrocede Louisiana, with a promise that it should not be alienated to another power. But, as always, international promises are of small moment in the face of national necessities, and the great region then known as Louisiana was practically given to us by Napoleon, we paying the nominal sum of $15,000,000.[23]

The reason for this action was the new outbreak of war between France and England, and the almost certainty of Louisiana's going to England in case France should attempt to hold it. Our going beyond the Mississippi was thus due to Napoleon; Jefferson had not wished such an extension; he only as President accepted what was thrown into our lap.

We all know how we developed in the next fifty years into a great and almost regular rectangle which stretched from ocean to ocean, and bought Alaska, which added 700,000 square miles to our territory.[24] In 1898, we became an overseas power and started a moderate effort in imperialism on our own hook, a thing which we are now denouncing Germany for. We may be right or wrong, accordingly as we believe that intelligent force or larger brains must rule weaker ones, etc., but if our policy is peace, and if the aim of the world is peace, we shall yet learn that imperialism has very little to do with that idea.

The fact is, the world is ruled by force, guided by superior intelligence or ability, and until we come down to a *brass tacks* acceptance of that fact and see ourselves as we really are, we shall be sculling about in the miasmatic back waters of life, without a true chart or compass. Big brains rule little ones everywhere, and largely in their own way; big strengths master small ones. The individual or nation which can lead and wants to lead is the one entitled so to do, and does do so, all moralistic and religious theories to the contrary notwithstanding. Why rage so wildly at a nation which wants to rule and which shows a great capacity for so doing, when we ourselves are at this moment trying to dictate to a very large portion of the world what it must and must not do, and without, as I see it, the intellectual force or skill to do it. For instance, how really silly it is to talk of guaranteeing the integrity of all nations great and small. The Monroe Doctrine is much more a guarantee of our own integrity than that of any of our other American nations—Santa Domingo, for instance, and Cuba, and as for our guaranteeing the life of China, our "open door," how quickly that has been abrogated by Japan.[25] Also how about Japan's power and determination to rule in Asia, anyhow? We talk much of virtue, justice, truth, democracy, freedom for all nations great and small, what Christ or someone else has taught, but we do not seem to see our true position in this situation, how illogical it is and how aimless and groundless our whole program really is. If autocracy is to be put down in Germany, then it should be put down in Japan, England, and everywhere else.

But aside from all this, does America really want to fight Germany, now? Have we a just cause? Could we not have waited and armed, kept ourselves out of this row, and then when a quarrel was justly ours, step up and say "Here—thus far and no further?"

Must we of necessity save England, and to what end? Or Russia, or France? Affection might lead us to fight for France, the mother of our republican ideals, or Russia, the new stumbling infant of democracy, but why England with her imperialistic ideas and her autocratic contempt for America and every other nation? Is it not really a fact that England, commercially and autocratically, desires the destruction of Germany for purely selfish reasons? Would she not desire ours in precisely the same way if ever we crowded her too closely? Isn't it true that up to the present she has considered us a nation easily swayed, one cleverly to be dominated in England's interest by our amazing reverence for our so-called British extraction? But let us show our independence clearly, let us try to push England aside, as England is constantly pushing us aside, discounting us. Then what?

Has England offered any reasonable peace terms? Will she? Has she not been going about the world rather binding up the nations to a death-to-death fight with the so-called German autocracy and all its plans for purely selfish and individual reasons? Did not England stir up Russia to help her to curb Germany in the Balkans and Turkey? Did she not stir up Japan to help her in the Far East and elsewhere, and have they not at this moment an offensive and defensive alliance, of which, by the way, it is rumored that Japan is growing weary? That England stirred up France, Italy, Spain, Portugal, Norway, and did her best to throw Greece into the balance, and finally succeeded in dethroning the Greek King, and at last, by divers hooks and crooks, financial, commercial, literary, managed to embroil America, on the ground that our liberties are at stake, can scarcely be denied. Privately the

English boast of this. But are our rights or liberties involved any more than are those of Chile, Argentina, Mexico, Peru, none of which have entered the war, although their neutral ships have been sunk? Our liberties may be at stake before this war is over, that is true enough now. But up to the time we moved into it they certainly were not. The wrongs, as I see it, were as much on our side as any: our neglecting to protect our neutral commerce, and that of every neutral nation; to keep the seas open for our ships, if not those of other neutrals; to protest against the starvation of Germany as well as the invasion of Belgium, if we did either. Have we any real proof that once Germany defeats England our liberties will be at stake? Are we so weak, then, that we cannot maintain ourselves without England or Europe? And if we are, should we deserve a separate existence? Why should England rule the seas, looking at it from our point of view? To protect her Empire, of course (mark the word Empire). But why should we want her to rule the seas any more than Germany? Are we the British Empire? Why help England any more than Germany?

But what are you going to do with a nation of persistent idealists who are so ignorant of history and of natural law as to imagine that they are called upon to play the part of a moralistic and Puritanic Messiah, not only to the world, but to the universe, no less? We actually hear it said that God is speaking through America. Has not the President and one million Fourth of July orators and ambitious Puritans so stated? "This is a war for Christ," no less. The Secretary of the Interior has said so. We are His anointed, called upon to bring the world to justice, truth, mercy, light, sweetness, etc., although, as Mr. Lane neatly phrases it, He has, up to date, been "a neglected though not a rejected Christ." I should say yes. We have persistently been told—I have, at least—that from out the darkness of the ages the torch of liberty which now blazes here so perfectly has slowly been growing to a flame, never fully blazing, however, until America appeared.[26] Liberty everywhere, in monarchies and older republics, Greece and Rome, for instance, was nothing compared to that which has flourished here. Greece, we are told, championed the cause of freedom against the encroachment of Asiatic despotism (as she did), only the helot, the slave caste, remained a feature of Greek civilization after the victory of Salamis, making it not a true Democracy, and I might add in passing, the Spartan theory of State control and the astounding victories of Alexander are imperial, not democratic, in character.[27] The Roman republic built up the doctrine of the freedom and inviolability of Roman citizens, it is true, "only those who were not born free and were not given their freedom or were captured as slaves, remained slaves," and the greatest period of Rome was imperial, not republican. "The structure of the Roman republic was reared upon the subjection of the plebs, or common people, and upon a still lower caste in the community, whose condition of slavery was affirmed and maintained." France revolted in 1789, but obtained no real freedom at once. England earlier, but with no better result. It remained for America to perfect and broaden the scheme of liberty toward which the world had been struggling "through silent suffering or the turmoil of battles." It remained for America to formulate the all-comprehensive doctrine that "all men are born free and equal," to enunciate as a principle that all men are alike entitled to "life, liberty, and the pursuit of happiness." And here in America these things have flourished ever since, if you will believe it. We are free. No one interferes with our conscience. We have liberty of speech, liberty of action, liberty of thought. We are not unjustly put upon in any way.

I would not have a word to say if this were true, but is it? Are we free? Are we not put upon in many ways? Have we liberty of speech, liberty of action, true liberty of conscience? Isn't this actually one of the most narrow, the most moralistic, the most Puritanic and pecksnifferic nations in the whole world, barring only Puritan England? Has the Japanese, the German, the Swede, the Norwegian, any less liberty of thought or action than we have? Does he love his country any less? Are his ideas of life any less clear than ours? Does he not think and write as he chooses, far more daringly than we? Are we not literally brow-beaten from day to day by our neighbors, our fellow churchmen, our newspapers, our large commercial organizations, all in leash to the most narrow and selfish ideals, our English and American Puritanism? Has there been any real liberty of conscience since this war began? Any liberty of speech or action? Will there be? Consider the proposed press laws, the espionage laws, the food control laws, the alien residence laws![28] Is comment on the Kaiser any more dangerous in Germany than criticism of the President here? If I am arrested and punished for what I write here or say elsewhere, will you kindly remember this? Could autocracy do better if it tried? Will we prove any more efficient in enforcing all these things than Germany or Japan, for instance?

In regard to this same country of Japan, let me have your attention for a moment. Speaking of autocracies that are wrong, and democracies that are right, how comes it that the Japanese display so much enthusiasm for their autocracy, as much, if not more than we do for our democracy? Ignorance? Oh, if you choose. But is it not entirely possible that their government is an agreeable and helpful one to them all? If so, is it the duty of enlightened democracy to shatter that?

Do you remember the captain of the shattered Japanese warship who, finding his ship sinking and being called upon to surrender, calmly lit a cigarette and went to the bottom with it between his lips? Do you remember the lieutenant who all alone towed a torpedo in a boat at night in order to make an end of the mole at Port Arthur?[29] The searchlights were turned on, and all that remained of the lieutenant and his boat was a bloody stain on the concrete wall. Yet the next day all the midshipmen and lieutenants of the fleet overwhelmed Admiral Togo[30] with applications offering to repeat the exploit. To what end? To destroy autocracy? Have our American heroes ever done any better? I am not advocating autocracy. I am arguing that nations may have a right to live their own lives in their own way. And that signature of the Samurai, the first finger cut from their left hand and attached to their respective letters requesting the honor of leading in a charge which would certainly end in their death.[31] Has our democracy produced anything more heroic, if you will? We have had Hobson, yes, and Paul Jones, and many others, but have the Germans had none?[32] Have we actually proved that democracy is the only answer to life? What folly to talk about crushing autocracies that do not want to be crushed! Are we really better, or just different?

Truly, when I think of these United States, their history during the past fifty years, I wonder what it is that we have to offer the world that is so different or so very much better than the dreaded autocracy of Germany, or Japan, or any other country. The beef trust? The Standard Oil Company? The railroad trust? The electric light trust? The telephone trust? The telegraph trust? The political rings of our cities and states? Our thieving, brutal food monopolies and combinations of all kinds, licensed by venal legislatures of different states to prey upon the public? The exactions of all, great and small, licensed under a benign republic to prey? We hear that things have been so perfectly equalized for all of us that we are free, equal, happy, well cared for, and yet in a little over a hundred years we have produced the richest men and as poor people as are to be found anywhere, and all right within our own borders. Nowhere in the world at this moment, as I have pointed out before, is freedom of speech less a general privilege than in America, and even now we are not wholly done with the espionage bill, which does away with the freedom of speech and the freedom of the press during the war.[33] If you have ever stood up on a street corner and attempted a few radical remarks, even with a license in your pocket, or if you wish to say that you do not believe in conscription or a war without a reasonable aim, you will understand what freedom of speech in America means.

It means, to be exact, to talk as a monopoly-governed, religiously-controlled, Puritanically dictated-to press, or a strangely Puritanic and idealistic administration thinks you should speak, not otherwise. The Methodist Church, the Baptist Church, the Lutheran Church, and the Catholic Church, in so far as the newspapers are concerned, represent circulation, just as the beef trust, the steel trust, the street railway trusts, etc., etc., etc., *ad infinitum*, represent advertising in those same newspapers, to say noth- ing of political control at Washington and elsewhere, outside of them, and these dictate to the newspapers the policies they are to pursue, as well as the thoughts they are to think. Actually, our newspapers browbeat us. They threaten our citizenry with all sorts of dire punishment, jail, espionage, ostracism, political, social, financial defeat. They sniff, snort, pursue, harry. Our boasted newspapers and magazines do this. You may well have freedom of speech to agree with them, but no farther. If you think otherwise, write otherwise, or talk otherwise, than they wish, or than those who control them wish, the trashy newspapers, (aided by the moral censors and the petty judges and politicians and "interests" generally), denounce you and invoke the aid of the police and the courts. Of such is the freedom of speech in America.

Shall we turn to freedom of action? Did you ever hear of the labor troubles at Paterson, in Lowell and Lawrence, in Pittsburgh, (the Carn- egie Steel Works), in Colorado (The Fuel and Iron Company and Cripple Creek), in San Francisco, in Chicago, Philadelphia, New York, and what befell those who sought freedom of speech and action in those and other places?[34] Take so recent a case as that of the I.W.W. leader, Frank Little, at Butte, Montana, where he was lynched, for his freedom of speech.[35] Is that a typical American case or is it not? But it is useless to attempt any detailed statements here. They are by now open books. You can get the details by consulting various labor papers and the court proceedings that have fol- lowed. Ettor and Giovannitti detained unjustly and without bail on false charges for seven months in a Massachusetts jail, Tom Mooney sentenced to be hanged for a crime he never committed, for being an agitator really, whole communities of laborers "deported" in Colorado and elsewhere without authority of law, protestors seized and searched without due process of law in New York, Colorado and elsewhere, the Chicago "anarchists" hanged for a crime that was only theoretically a child of their views, Emma Goldman and Alexander Berkman sent to the penitentiary for opposing conscrip- tion.[36] Need I go on? Hundreds of writers and protestors have insisted that no country in the world has seen more brutal outrages against the freedom of action in so far as the individual is concerned, and it is true. Ought we not first make democracy work in America before we shout so wildly about imposing it upon the whole world or destroying autocracy elsewhere?

As a matter of fact, as I see it, America is largely the land of *the free corpora- tion*, not of the individual, and this is why, perhaps, nearly all our corporations are so enthusiastic for war. The corporation has been and is the be-all and the end-all of legislative concern in America. If you do not believe this, look up the legislative record of any legislature in any state since the foundation of the republic, and see for yourself. Nearly all our laws are prepared and enacted to guard the rights of corporations. More and more the individual has been shoved off in a corner in America, until at last he is exactly what he has been in all countries, monarchic or autocratic, an underpaid working machine for one powerful corporation or another. He has no liberty that cannot be invaded or set aside at will or that a German or a Japanese has not. He is *not* really free, any more than the ordinary individual anywhere is free. That myth ought to be laid by about now. In America, as elsewhere, the corporations, our privileged autocrats, own the railroads, fix prices, dictate the laws and avoid taxation whenever and however they please. This is literally true. Here, as elsewhere, the owners of corporations have done what they would naturally do anywhere, taken the money and established themselves as a ruling class at the top. Germany has its titled bureaucrats and Army lords; England its hereditary aristocracy entrenched in privileges and "rights;" America its monopoly-owning millionaires and billionaires; and there you are. The one is as much concerned over the welfare of the average citizen, or the working-man, as the other. No more and no less.

Now I, for one, am not opposed to this if it is an inevitable law of nature, as it appears to be, but why all this pother about a so-called entrenched and domineering aristocracy in Germany, (not Japan or England, mark you), when we have exactly the same thing here, or are fast getting it? And what, pray, in any of the respects in which either we or England or France have been so successful, has Germany failed? Is she, as I have asked before, any less democratic than ourselves in looking after the welfare of her population? Are her people contented? Do they love her? Are they willing to fight and die for her? If they were not, would she have survived and triumphed so in this great war? Is her intellect any less powerful than that of England or France or Italy or Russia, or these same United States? I will not take up these different lands *seriatim* and contrast them. No suitable space would permit. But take America, which is most loud in its denunciation of "the sodden German mind" and contrast it with Germany at the present moment, its power to lead intellectually and survive physically. If America had had England, France, Russia, Italy, Serbia, Romania, Japan, Canada, Australia, New Zealand, South Africa, Spain and Portugal against her, how would she have fared by now? I am an American first, foremost, and all the time, and I want America to survive, but on what basis? As a tail to England's kite? Never! As an appendage to the exploded Christian ideal, with all that that entails—Puritanism, pecksniffery, or moral belly-ache, over the commonest facts of nature? Never! If America is to survive, why should she not survive on exactly the same grounds that Germany is surviving, Japan is surviving, England is surviving, namely, efficiency—mental, moral, commercial, physical—on the basis that she is useful and comforting to all her people. All—not a few.

Germany is surviving because she is able so to do, against England, France, Italy, Russia, Spain, Portugal, America, Japan, and I am even inclined to believe that she will continue to do so. Why? Because autocracy, as we have seen it worked out there, is efficient—as efficient, for instance, as are our private autocracies, our trusts and corporations—the railroads, for instance. And because Germany knows more about living, economy, self-sacrifice, energy, constructive organization, than we or England or France or Russia or Italy do, is that any reason for our being so incensed? For one thing, in 1912 Germany raised on 5,558,000 farms averaging less than fifteen acres each 40 per cent more of wheat, rye, barley, oats and potatoes than we on 6,340,000 farms averaging 138 acres each. Think of it. She has a population of only 67,000,000 to our 110,000,000, yet out of this she has maintained and drilled a citizen army of nearly four millions of men, which is capable of being amplified in emergency to one of eight millions, all drilled and armed, while we so far have drifted along with a paltry army of 100,000 or less, and a lot of fine-spun theories of universal and permanent peace. Imagine! I do not say that a great standing army is either necessary or desirable if the world can get along without quarrelling, but if it cannot, (and where is there any real evidence that it can?), what is the use of blinking the fact? Even if war were abolished, isn't it conceivable that there would still be a need of some form of necessity or compulsion to cause people to discipline themselves, set themselves tasks, mental and physical, lest the world run to seed or become the wishy-washy thing which we appear to have become already. In the recent examinations for fitness for army service here in America, it was shown that by our happy-go-lucky policy of allowing the American to dream of universal peace and no military or physical service of any kind, seventy-five per cent (note that) of the applicants so far examined have been rejected as unfit, unable to pass a satisfactory military examination, and the reason given was over-self-indulgence, twentieth century American habits! Imagine that in Japan or Germany! If a peace-dreaming, money-loaning, luxury-loving life, undisturbed by any necessity, will do this, where, I ask you, is it to end?

What is the advantage? Would Germany have gotten an army of 4,000,000 or 8,000,000, constantly refreshed every spring by 650,000 more available for military duty, if she had any such dreams as this? And would we not now be better off physically and morally and in every other way if we had always had a large army and navy; universal military service and a spirit for our national welfare such as animates Germany and Japan? Has any suitable substitute yet been found for war, or fear, or necessity, as a character-builder and a life-maker? Has it? Have envy, greed, ambition, lust, been substituted by any higher moving forces as yet? If so, where? For war, ambition, necessity, greed even, we are constantly being told to substitute love, self-sacrifice, personal solicitude for others; the Golden Rule. These last are beautiful in their way, useful, needful and always have had and always will have a place in life. But do you think really that they are any less common under tyrannies or autocracies than they are here in America, or more so? Do not imagine a vain thing. They are common as their antitheses, and everywhere have always existed and always will in equal or balancing proportion to the others. I would be for the beatitudes wholly if everybody followed them wholly, or if, outside of a limited percentage, they helped humanity to survive and be truly vigorous, but I don't think they do. They are good as antidotes to the rougher forces, not otherwise.[37] They will never govern life—never. That is how the black morass of the dark ages came to be: false moralistic tosh. Impossible ideals of conduct weaken people. They produce lies or self-deception. By degrees they actually destroy efficiency and make milksops of us all. We must be driven, harried at times, otherwise we sink back and end in slumber and death.

But even if this were not true, where is the sense in our entering this war? In what way have we been abused really? France had a chance to stay out in the beginning. Why didn't she? Ditto Russia. Ditto England. Why was it necessary to push Germany back so swiftly?

The answer to it all, as far as I can discover, lies in just one place. England! Through the refusal of England to allow Germany to have any share in the development of Mesopotamia or the spoils of Asia and Africa was this war brought on. Apparently various students of European diplomacy are now about ready to admit this. Japan, Russia, France, Italy, and even various minor countries were apparently entitled to expand only they did not appear as dangerous to England as Germany, but once the Germans began to move, the world must be set aflame. Why? Was it because England was more afraid of Germany than any other nation? It would seem so. England would not compromise with Germany because apparently she feared her, hence hated her. Hence, because we love England above all other nations, we must rush to her defense. Is that it? But why should we save England which really does not care for us and in all likelihood would not assist us in the same way? Two of our wars have been with England. Why not let England go, and we ourselves prepare to deal with Germany separately, as well we may, since we have treated her so indifferently, and as we can if we are worth our salt? Or better yet, negotiate a sensible peace. It can be done. A counsel of the nations that would suggest to England and Germany that they effect a sensible compromise would bring about a compromise, and if not we might well let them go on and fight without expending a dollar or a man except on our own defenses and to protect our own interests.

I hold no brief for Germany, and I do not want the Germans to rule America. I do not think they will, because America has or should have a destiny of her own, but how are we going to prepare ourselves to maintain our place in the world if not by some such national enthusiasm for our own private welfare as now animates Germany and Japan and England, by saving ourselves for our own troubles, all our forces, all our strength? Are the rank and file in America anxious for this war? Do they want to fight? Do you feel right about your boy going to the firing line? Does the boy? Is he wildly enthusiastic? And if not, why not? England, my dear sirs. The greed of foreign powers for spoils, that is all. He knows, or if he doesn't, he feels. This isn't his war and you will never get him to feel it. Let Japan strike at America some time or other, or England, or Germany direct. Then see. I tell you, under such circumstances there would be no need to worry over the fighting spirit of America or conscription. There are boys who would cut off their forefinger and affix it to their letters of appeal as signatures. The spirit of America is not dead, it is only wrongly guided at present, that's all. If this were really a popular war, what reason was there for refusing to submit the decision as to whether we should fight or not to the people at large? That suggestion was made earnestly and with force but it was persistently ignored. Why?

In so far as Europe is concerned, we are a distant power. The Western Hemisphere is our domain. Why not stick to it? Why not make America and the Western Hemisphere great, as Germany wants to make middle Europe and neglected and brutalized Asia Minor and the Euphrates great? Has England ever done anything for Asia Minor or Mesopotamia? Is it not a wilderness, a robbers' den? Why should not Germany be allowed to make it over, as she would, to make it bloom like a rose? What is wrong with that, and why should we be so opposed to it, if we really are?

Why are our people divided in sentiment in this hour, whereas Germany and all her Allies are a solid unit? I can tell you why: because Germany believes in herself even more than we have ever believed in ourselves, and she has grown tired of seeing England and Russia eat up all the available spaces of the earth while we sit by and spout maxims about universal peace, and England and the other countries plot to reduce Germany to nothing, while Germany believes herself entitled to grow and hold a place in the world's sunlight. Can you blame her? I can't. Instead of preaching eternal peace and the soporific end of things (which will never occur and which we do not want to occur), it would be better, much better, if we imitated England and Russia and Italy and Japan and France, and planned to stand by our own destiny and to carve out a place for ourselves, put ourselves into vigorous fighting and economic trim for that international struggle which is certain to go on even if Germany is swept down to defeat and England and Japan and ourselves become the dominant economic factors in life. England is not America. She does not love us—wants no more to do with us than she wants with Germany at this very moment. England wants England to rule the world, not us. She doesn't even want to share it with us. Never. England actually wouldn't wipe her feet on us, intellectually or socially, and once this war is over, and if she has any luck, and if we do not steer a much more practical and pagan course than we have, she will deal with us later.

England is for England, as Germany is for Germany, and Japan is for Japan—only England feeling a little doubtful of her supremacy at times seeks to effect combinations which will guarantee her supremacy and divide the counsels of the other powers. Hence her alliance with Japan, with Russia, with any power that will help to keep her position secure. She would combine with us if it were feasible or useful, or she would combine against us. Why should we worry over England?

And as for Japan, she is selling us silk and buying our steel. Why? England is borrowing our money at three and three and one half per cent and re-loaning it at five and six, and getting us to let her dictate to us on the seas and elsewhere, while she tries to starve and cripple Germany.[38] We are struggling to furnish her men and supplies in order to win a victory which can do us personally no good. Really, are we not all fools? Will we be any stronger after this contest, or weaker—which? England having induced the whole world to fight her battle for her, will be much stronger than she is now, or should be if she wins. And Japan—consider Japan, gentlemen. Both these latter nations are even now laying the keels of a sufficient shipping tonnage to control the shipping trade of the world. England is organizing and forwarding the Royal Dutch Shell (Oil) Company, the great and even victorious rival of the Standard Oil Company, in order to control the oil trade of the world and so have the oil to run the ships, which in the future are to be fired by oil. Japan is laboring constantly for the control of the Pacific and China and possibly the Philippines and Hawaii—and why not? It is her natural domain. England wanted the gold and diamond mines of South Africa, and got them.[39] She desires the rubber trade of South America, and is getting that. Japan desires a large sphere of influence in South America, Brazil, for instance, and is moving heaven and earth to get it. Both powers are inimical to American trade. England has shut out our American Tobacco Company wherever she can, our wheat milling interests, our beef-packing and cattle-raising interests. Japan is doing nearly as much against a score of our Asiatic trade interests. Both England and Japan are countries that we have to fear quite as much as Germany, and while it may be wise to curb Germany's power some, and to hold Japan in check, why should we waste our substance in saving a power, I mean England, which is as indifferent to us as Germany and as guilty of autocratic and imperialistic crimes?

But, to return to this matter of autocracy for one more final argument. It is one of the humors and anachronisms of the situation that all of the countries that are protesting most lustily against Germany and her autocratic central-izing methods, (and in the forefront of these must be placed America), are most energetic and enthusiastic in copying those very methods. Germany has a definite autocratic censorship; England has a worse one; the powers at Washington desire one equally rigorous. Germany has a standing army of tremendous efficiency which reaches from the boy of seventeen to the old man of sixty, all trained in the most effective methods of making war. England, France, Russia, Italy, and now the United States,[40] have set out to imitate her, to reach the efficiency which autocracy has perfected, and by the same methods.

Germany at the beginning of the war seized all her railroads and oper-ated them in the interest of the Empire. What did England do? What did France do? What did Italy do? What did Russia? What does America want to do? Germany sensibly and vigorously and autocratically seized all food and the sources of food production, administering it in behalf of all units of the Empire, and with an eye to the future. What did England, France, Italy, Russia do, and what does the United States now want to do? (Only in our case we have so far succeeded in controlling the food in favor of the monopolies, not in favor of the mass.) Avoid autocracy? Not a bit of it. They want autocracy apparently in these matters because a successful autocracy has shown them the tremendous efficiency, if not value, of cen-tralized power. To quote Senator Newlands: "If we have got to Prussianize America in order to beat Prussia, I am willing to do it."[41] Well, so am I, but not to save England. Never!

Personally, in so far as America is concerned, I would like to see more autocracy of a sensible Teutonic kind. For instance, I would be in favor of a standing army, or at least universal military service, in order to train all our men and even our women physically. I would be and am in favor of the state owning the railroads and running them intelligently and cheaply, but not without power to make the workers courteous and respectful as well as comfortable financially. I am in favor of telephone and telegraph opera-tion in the same way. As far as I am concerned, I would have permanent national food control, not only as to most prices, but as to the rearing of certain crops and their amounts in accordance with our greatest needs, and, in addition, I would have conscription to compel the proper working of the farms—every boy and girl to spend at least a year in that service, no less. I would have national control of the mines, the highways (their arrangement and maintenance)—all natural monopolies, in fact; and, in addition to that, I would have national inspection of the schools and the houses of all our people, their kitchens, bathrooms, parlors, bedrooms, not in order to look after their spiritual or moral welfare in the religious sense, but to compel cleanliness and proper sanitation, the health of the country. When will we learn to let people's brains and emotions alone? It will come, of course. Yes, I would let the tastes and the so-called morals of the people severely alone. Quit worrying and harrying them about their eternal souls. Let them go to the devil if they want to, in their own way, but don't let them drag down others via disease and ignorance, when those others distinctly do not want to go. There is such a vast difference between so-called moral and spiritual efficiency and worth, and material and social ability to live and be a worth-while member of the community. We have had Christianity . . . Japan has had ancestor worship. Which of the two nations is better at this moment? The one relates to a mythical heaven, the other to a very real state which has to be lived here and now.

Our government was built in a period which was antipathetic to leadership, in a time when leaders were tyrants, and when the only defense against them seemed to be to take power from their hands and put it upon those who can never be expected to exercise it without leadership—the crowd. Nearly all the so-called fathers of the republic were terrorized by the thought of a dictator. They feared nothing so much as the man on horseback or the crafty Richelieu who would wreck things.[42] Unfortunately, they left no formula for discovering exactly the right man at the right time, though in Washington, Jefferson, Jackson, Lincoln, and even Roosevelt, we have had men who could and did do things and did not become really too ambitious— amazing men, all of them. So far, so good. Yet times appear to be changing a little. The mass is becoming slightly unwieldy. Delegated autocratic authority may not be such a bad thing after all, if you can control your autocrat, and sometimes even if you can't. It depends on the man—the spirit of a nation. Yet the man who at present is protesting loudest against dictatorship and autocracy in Germany—I refer to President Wilson—is apparently the one who is most anxious to exercise as much of it as anyone, to concentrate in his own two hands all the reins of power. But to what an end! To save another nation which actually despises us. To prevent one greedy power from being compelled to play fair by another greedy power. And, what is worse, which is very different, to the autocrats whom he has so far imitated, he has not as yet permitted entrance into his counsel of any save second-rate individuals, not a real outstanding American among them—secretaries and hall-boys, all. Your autocratic Kaiser, at least, tolerates a Hindenburg, a Ludendorff, a von Mackensen, a von Bethmann-Hollweg, a von Beseler, and seems to take no harm from it.[43] England has its Balfour, its Lloyd George, its Northcliff.[44] But our democratic President! A man like Gerrard, an ex-Tammany Judge, Ambassador to Germany; a man like Page (Walter H.), a mediocre publisher, Ambassador to England; a man like Baker, an unheard of nonentity, Secretary of War; a man like Daniels, a wild-eyed theorist and idealist, full of eternal peace notions and how to make the navy drink grape juice, Secretary of the Navy; Mr. Lansing, whose name you can scarcely keep in mind from day to day, Secretary of State; Mr. Lane, shouting that this is a war for Christ, no less, Secretary of the Interior; a Mr. Somebody—I forget his name—quarrelling with the newspapers over what they must or must not print, and then Wilson himself, full of idealistic college notions of the history and supremacy of England and the destiny of the Anglo-Saxon race, and permanent peace, and the dominance of Democracy without Autocracy, or even intelligent leadership, while men like Roosevelt, Johnson, Rockefeller, Luther Burbank, sit on the side lines and wonder whither we are drifting and what the ultimate outcome is to be.[45] Wonderful! Wonderful! Wonderful! And now we are going to force two or three or four or five million American boys to face an almost impregnable autocratic firing line. God speed! I only hope they don't die.

But actually, I think we are sending them to die in an unjust cause. We are standing by, foaming over autocracy, when we have never really worked out democracy here or curbed our own autocrats, never even enjoyed the benefits of a centralized autocracy such as is the German Empire—and that while we are permitting England, Japan, Italy, France and ourselves to go their and our imperialistic and even autocratic ways, and all without a murmur. England may and does rule the seas, dominates our ships, and orders an American trading vessel trading between Argentina and Florida or New York, for instance, to call at an English port and be examined as to its cargo—opening our mails and ordering a starvation blockade against Germany, in defiance of so-called international law, and we have never a word to say. Japan rifles China under our eyes, although China has been seeking to make itself into a republic, and never a word do we say. Russia and England could and did seize Persia and destroy it in order to keep Germany out of Mesopotamia and the Persian Gulf, and never a word did we have to say. But let Germany seek additional territory, a place in the sun, try to open the seas to all and make the misgoverned Euphrates Valley or Mesopotamian plain into a habitable happy world once more, and we rise, screaming that "the world must be made safe for democracy," and that the integrity of small nations must be protected.

The situation is all wrong. We haven't the right answer to this in any way. If England wants to keep Germany out of Turkey and Mesopotamia, let England do so, at her own expense. If Japan wants to help her, well and good. Let Japan do so. If Russia also, let her. But let us for our part pick out the things we object to, if any, call a conference with Germany and the other powers and ask them plainly their ultimate aims and how they want the world run, and seek to find out why they can not be adjusted. If England is asking too much, and we cannot make her stop asking it, let us not sacrifice another dollar in her cause. If France is demanding anything unfair, or Italy, or Japan, let them cease, or quit asking our aid. Determine Japan's policy as to China, for China desires to become a republic, unless we have no legitimate interest there. Ask England to allow Germany a part of Mesopotamia, or if not that, let her cease to demand the disintegration of the German Empire. Let the Kaiser stay if the German people want him. If we cannot get a reasonable deal for all, let us sit by while they fight until they are willing to listen to reason, in the meanwhile arming ourselves to the teeth and saving our strength for the great contest which may come later, in case either Germany or England wins. Japan, I am sure, would be pleased to see us exhaust ourselves in this futile contest. England also. Germany also. Why be fools—suckers, to use a homely American word? Why not demand a conference of the Allies now, formulate sensible terms, and then, if we cannot obtain a reasonable acceptance of them, something to test Germany out with, quit? This dismemberment business is too silly for words. It seems that all the countries now fighting together: Germany, Austria, Bulgaria, Turkey, will fight to the last dollar and the last able man, while we and the others exhaust ourselves, with the possible exception of England. In the meanwhile, Japan will be sitting on the sidelines waiting. We need not try to establish universal peace now (think of that as a fighting cause!) or seek to end autocracy in one place only to permit it to flourish in another. Let us, for heaven's sake, be sensible. Stop England from being a hog. Demand of Japan what her aims are in China, if we want to. Tell the Kaiser he can rule if he will stop trying to rule the whole world and disarm with the rest of us. Why not? If we can't get anything fair out of anybody, let us arm, *arm, arm*, and when ready, and unfairly treated, strike, and strike so hard that those who have dealt unfairly with us will all know what it means to disturb a great nation anxious for peace but willing to fight to the last man and the last dollar for what it thinks is fair—equable—

No more—and no less.

Textual Note: Unpublished essay, composed summer 1917. 44-page typescript, DPUP. Solicited by Waldo Frank, associate editor of the *Seven Arts* but rejected as unpublishable under the provisions of the 1917 Espionage Act by both *Seven Arts* and the

Century magazine, to whom Dreiser subsequently offered it. The first seven pages or so of typescript, which deal principally with historical accusations of German atrocities and war aims, have been cut for reasons of space.

1. Examples of the United States's colonialism in the Caribbean and Central America. American forces had been battling a Filipino independence movement since taking over political control of the islands from Spain in 1898, and frequently intervened in the independent Cuba, most recently when marines were put ashore in February 1917 to help suppress an insurrection against President Menocal (1866–1941). Santa Domingo on the island of Hispaniola (now the Dominican Republic) was occupied by marines from 1916 to 1924. The Panama Canal Zone was under occupation from 1903 until 1999.

2. President Woodrow Wilson had argued that "the world must be made safe for democracy" in his 2 April 1917 speech to Congress urging war with Germany. The phrase crystallizes Wilson's vision of the nation leading a global struggle for democracy, the "American idealism" Dreiser opposes in this essay.

3. The United States Commission on Industrial Relations had reported in 1915 that the richest 2 percent of the population owned 35 percent of total wealth.

4. The War Revenue Act of 1917 raised income tax on incomes of over $1.5 million to 67 percent.

5. Wall Street had closed for four months in 1914 for fear of a collapse, but the war effort proved highly lucrative for business, and the Dow Jones hit a new high in 1916. Suspicion of the prowar influence of financiers and business leaders was widespread, as Dreiser suggests.

6. Commodity prices were massively inflated by the outbreak of war in Europe. According to Bureau of Labor statistics, the wholesale price of wheat increased by a factor of two and a half between July 1914 and June 1916.

7. Gustavus Myers, *History of Canadian Wealth* (Chicago: Charles H. Kerr and Co., 1914).

8. Charles Evans Hughes (1862–1948) had run unsuccessfully as the Republican Party's presidential candidate in 1916. Hughes was associated with Theodore Roosevelt's prowar rhetoric and lost to the incumbent Wilson, who campaigned on the basis of having kept the country out of the war.

9. Dreiser refers to the raft of social legislation, including sickness, accident, and old age insurance, and limitations to child labor and working hours, introduced by the German Chancellor Otto von Bismarck (1815–98) in the 1880s, twenty years in advance of Lloyd George's reforming British government. Bismarck's motivations were largely to secure the support of the working class for the newly created German state, and the social legislation was accompanied by severe repression of socialists and social democrats—elements of the autocracy to which Dreiser subsequently refers. In rejecting "American Idealism and German Frightfulness" on behalf of *Century* magazine, Douglas Z. Doty made the point that "it is not the nature of Germany's liberal laws that counts but the motive back of those laws; and those motives have now been clearly revealed" (Doty to William Lengel, 12 July 1917, DPUP).

10. Here Dreiser looks to Ancient Greece for a model of democracy that acknowledges conflict and self-interest, as an alternative to the moralism he associates with the Christianized democracies of America and Britain. The term "pagan" carried a

complex set of associations for Dreiser, including the mystical, unconditional giving he associated with his mother. See Shawn St. Jean, *Pagan Dreiser: Songs from American Mythology* (Madison, N.J.: Fairleigh Dickinson University Press, 2001).

11. Originally a term for provincial governors in ancient Persia, by Dreiser's time "satrap" was used more generally to indicate a ruler under the sway of a more powerful state.

12. In February 1916 Dreiser had complained to H. L. Mencken that "all letters addressed to me from Holland, where I have friends, are regularly taken off lines sailing directly from here and Holland and read and resealed by the *English* Censor. In other words we are a political appendage of John Bull" (Riggio, *Dreiser-Mencken Letters* 1: 222).

13. In June 1917 Britain and France engineered the replacement of King Constantine I of Greece (1868–1923), who had maintained neutrality in the war.

14. Secretary of the Interior Franklin K. Lane (1864–1921). The speech quoted from here was widely circulated under the title "Why We Are At War With Germany."

15. The February Revolution of 1917, as a result of which the Russian Tsar Nicholas II (1868–1918) abdicated and a provisional government was installed.

16. The commitment to guarantee "the undictated development of all peoples" and the peace terms quoted subsequently are Woodrow Wilson's, from the period of "armed neutrality," 1914–17.

17. The Napoleonic period, 1799–1815, was a particularly intense phase of conflict between European imperial powers. France under Napoleon Bonaparte (1769–1821) was involved in military, political, and economic struggles with Britain, Spain, and Russia.

18. Dreiser refers to the American Revolutionary War (1775–81), the 1812–15 conflict with Great Britain and the 1846–48 war with Mexico, the American Civil War (1861–65), the Spanish-Cuban-American War of 1898, and the 1903 seizure of the Panama Canal Zone from Colombia (mistakenly given as Bolivia in the typescript).

19. French for "Let us go on!"

20. The Treaty of Paris (1763), signed by Great Britain, Spain, and France, ended the Seven Years' War and established British colonial control in North America and India.

21. The (Second) Treaty of Paris (1783) formally ended the American Revolutionary War, recognizing the independence of the United States, while Florida reverted to Spain and Britain maintained control of Canadian territory.

22. A Russian expedition founded a settlement at Three Saints' Bay on Kodiak Island, Alaska, in 1784.

23. The Louisiana Purchase, during Thomas Jefferson's presidency in 1803, involved 530 million acres (828,000 square miles) at a cost of around three cents per acre.

24. Alaska was purchased from Russia in 1867 for $7.2 million.

25. The Monroe Doctrine was issued by President James Monroe in 1823, at a time when new republics—Argentina, Chile, Colombia, Mexico, and Peru—had emerged in Central and South America with the weakening of the Spanish Empire. It essentially proclaimed the independence of the Americas from European colonization, without committing to specific actions. The United States would resist any European attempts to recolonize the Americas, regarding any military action

by European powers on American soil as a threat to its national security, but it was otherwise unconcerned with relations between the European powers and between the Empires and their current and former colonies. In his "Peace without Victory" speech to Congress on 22 January 1917, Woodrow Wilson had cited the Monroe Doctrine as a blueprint for his own vision of a world of independent nation-states allowed to develop freely. Dreiser cites examples—Santa Domingo, Cuba, and China—that highlight both the inconsistency of its application and the subjugation of democratic principle to American commercial and political interests. The "open door" policy was formally adopted by President McKinley in 1898 to further American business interests in China, reiterated after the Boxer Rebellion in 1900, and had been abrogated by Japan in 1915.

26. For the rest of this paragraph, Dreiser outlines the teleological history of democratic progress, culminating in the United States, that he is criticizing.

27. "Asiatic despotism" refers to the Persian Empire, which was resisted successfully by Greek city-states such as Athens, culminating in the battle of Salamis in 480 BCE. Alexander the Great, or Alexander III of Macedon (356–323 BCE), one of the most successful military leaders ever, conquered most of Asia. The ancient Spartans defeated the neighboring state of Messenia and held the Messenians and their descendants as a slave caste known as "helots," or captives.

28. A raft of measures called for or enacted in the wake of the Declaration of War on Germany, in order to further the war effort and to suppress dissent.

29. Dreiser alludes to what he regards as various acts of naval heroism during the Russo-Japanese War of 1904–5 as evidence of loyalty and dynamism within an autocratic regime.

30. Togo Heihachiro (1848–1934), commander-in-chief of the combined fleet of the Imperial Japanese navy from 1904.

31. Dreiser refers to the "bushido," or code of conduct, of the Japanese warrior class, which he associates with extreme loyalty and self-sacrifice. In the Samurai practice of "yubizume," the final joint of the little finger is severed as a form of atonement or apology; in battle this would be virtually suicidal since this finger was critical in manipulating the samurai sword.

32. Richmond Pearson Hobson (1870–1937) became famous during the Spanish-Cuban-American War for his unsuccessful mission to block the Spanish fleet in the harbor of Santiago de Cuba. Scottish-born John Paul Jones (1747–92), a captain in the Revolutionary War, was the first great naval hero of the United States.

33. The Espionage Act, passed in June 1917, was drafted so widely as to ban the dissemination of any information that might interfere with the operation of the armed forces or give comfort or aid to the enemy. It was used to incarcerate an estimated 450 conscientious objectors and opponents of the war. Substantiating Dreiser's warning, the labor leader Eugene V. Debs was sentenced to ten years in jail for criticizing the Act itself; Rose Pastor Stokes received the same sentence for asserting in a letter to the *Kansas City Star* that "no government which is for the profiteers can be for the people, and I am for the people while the government is for the profiteers"; and Floyd Dell and Max Eastman were prosecuted for the *Masses*'s antiwar stance. The Espionage Act also effectively made "American Idealism and German Frightfulness" unpublishable.

34. Major labor struggles, many of which involved the employers' manipulation of the judicial system, state police, and state militia. Textile strikes in Paterson, New

Jersey, and in Lowell and Lawrence, Massachusetts, took place in 1912 and 1913. The 1892 Carnegie Steel Strike in Homestead, outside Pittsburgh, was broken by the Pennsylvania state militia. In 1902–3, Colorado state militia, paid with money from the Iron and Fuel Company, were used to suppress a miners' strike in the area surrounding Cripple Creek. Dreiser would return to the role of state police in labor disputes in chapter 12 of *Tragic America* (1931), "The Growth of the Police Power."

35. Frank Little (1879–1917), a member of the General Executive Board of the I.W.W., was lynched on 1 August 1917 in Butte, Montana. Little had vociferously opposed the war while also helping organize a strike at the local Anaconda Copper mines.

36. Joseph Ettor (1885–1948) and Arturo Giovannitti (1882–1959) were leaders of the strike of textile workers at Lawrence, Massachusetts, in 1912. They were arrested as accessories to murder by the local authorities, held until after the strike had ended, and eventually acquitted in November 1912. Another I.W.W. activist, Tom Mooney (1882–1942), and his fellow trade unionist Warren K. Billings (1893–1972) would spend more than twenty years in prison after being convicted on perjured testimony of bombing the July 1916 Preparedness Day parade in San Francisco. Dreiser later took up Mooney's case (see "Mooney and America," 127–31). Emma Goldman (1869–1940) and Alexander Berkman (1870–1936) had been arrested in June under the Selective Service Act of 1917 and charged with organizing a "conspiracy" of young men to avoid the draft. They would remain in prison until being deported in 1919. Dreiser also refers to the Haymarket tragedy, the bombing by persons unknown of a meeting in Chicago in May 1886 and the deaths of seven policemen, after which eight anarchists were convicted of murder—and four hung—on the basis of their expressed views on political violence.

37. This argument is expanded in "The Reformer," *Hey Rub-a-Dub-Dub*, 206–11.

38. Dreiser repeats rumors that war loans to Britain made at preferential rates of interest were loaned again by the British at higher rates.

39. Britain's military conquest of indigenous South Africans and the Boers, colonists originally from the Netherlands, whose two independent republics were forcibly incorporated into the British Empire in 1902.

40. Wilson had pressured Congress to expand the Regular Army to 140,000 men late in 1915. Conscription of men aged twenty-one to thirty was introduced in May 1917.

41. Francis Griffith Newlands (1848–1917), a Democratic Senator for Nevada. The charge of Prussianization (that entry into the war would mean emulating the autocracy and militarism of Prussia-led Germany) had originally been brought by protestors against the war.

42. Armand-Jean du Plessis, Duke de Richelieu (1585–1642), known as Cardinal Richelieu, was a statesman under King Louis XIII of France, famous for his political maneuvering in support of the French crown and the Roman Catholic Church at a time of religious and international tensions.

43. Kaiser Wilhelm II (1859–1941) and the military and political leaders of Germany, Paul von Hindenburg (1847–1934), Erich Ludendorff (1865–1937), August von Mackensen (1849–1945), Theobold von Bethmann-Hollweg (1856–1921), and Hans von Beseler (1850–1921).

44. Arthur James Balfour (1848–1930), author, philosopher, and British foreign secretary; David Lloyd George, prime minister; and Alfred Harmsworth, Lord

Northcliffe (1865–1922), newspaper baron and, briefly, in charge of propaganda in Lloyd George's cabinet.

45. Dreiser contrasts the members of Wilson's cabinet—James Watson Gerrard (1867–1951), Walter Hines Page (1855–1918), Newton Diehl Baker (1871–1937), Josephus Daniels (1862–1948), Robert Lansing (1864–1928), and Franklin Lane, all of whom he considers weak, inexperienced, and Anglophile—with more dynamic leaders in the fields of politics, business, and science: President Theodore Roosevelt, Standard Oil boss John Davison Rockefeller (1839–1937), and agricultural scientist Luther Burbank (1849–1926). Gerrard had been appointed as ambassador to Germany after helping to finance Wilson's 1912 presidential campaign; he would become notorious in November 1917 for suggesting that to prevent any possible insurgency, half a million German-Americans could be hung from lamp-posts. As a partner in Doubleday, Page, it was Page who had communicated directly with Dreiser about the company's vacillations over the publication of his first novel, *Sister Carrie*, in 1900. Baker and Daniels were both appointed by Wilson on the basis of their pacifist tendencies. Lansing had protested the British blockade of shipping more vigorously than Dreiser implies. "Mr. Somebody" may be George Creel (1876–1953), head of the Committee on Public Information, which disseminated propaganda and implemented "voluntary guidelines" for the press; the identity of "Johnson" is unclear.

From "More Democracy or Less? An Inquiry"

Reconstruction, December 1919.

One of several essays in social criticism collected in Hey Rub-a-Dub-Dub. *Dreiser begins by arguing that the United States has neglected its political, social, artistic, and cultural development by dedicating itself to commerce.*

* * * *

In my personal judgment, America as yet certainly is neither a social nor a democratic success. Its original democratic theory does not work, or has not, and a trust- and a law-frightened people, to say nothing of a cowardly or suborned and in any case helpless press, prove it. Where in any country not dominated by an autocracy has ever a people more pathetically and ridiculously slipped about afraid to voice its views on war, on freedom of speech, freedom of the press, the trusts, religion—indeed any honest private conviction that it has? In what country even less free can a man be more thoroughly browbeaten, arrested without trial, denied the privilege of a hearing and held against the written words of the nation's own Constitution guaranteeing its citizens freedom of speech, of public gathering, of writing and publishing what they honestly feel? In what other lands less free are whole elements held in a caste condition—the Negro,[1] the foreign-born, the Indian?

When one considers the history of American commercial development, the growth of private wealth, of its private leaders—the Rockefellers, Morgans, Vanderbilts, Goulds, Ryans, *et al.*, indeed all the railroad, street-car, land and other lords—a, until the war, practically stationary wage-rate, an ever increasing cost of living, cold legislative conniving and robbery before which the people are absolutely helpless, Tammany Hall, the New York Street Car Monopoly,[2] seven hundred and fifty-three different kinds of trusts that tax people as efficiently and ardently as ever any monarchy or tyranny dreamed of doing—I should really like to know on what authority we base our plea for the transcendent merits of democracy, and I am as good a democrat as most Americans, if not more so.

Government everywhere, in monarchies and republics, as well as tyrannies and despotisms, has, other things being equal, always kept step with the natural development of the intelligence of the mass, a thing which has been as much developed by the goads of tyrannies as by the petting of republics. But could you ever convince a full-fledged American, raised on Fourth of July orations and the wonders and generosities of the American Constitution, of this? For him, of course, liberty began in 1775 at Bunker Hill or somewhere near it.[3] Before that was not light anywhere. Since then we have gone on—doing better and better, making all men richer, happier, kinder, wiser.

But have we? Is our land and its progress so absolutely flawless? Aside from love of country and individual vanity which might make us want to think so, have we not developed as many flaws, anachronisms, social and governmental irritations and oppressions as any other country? I call attention to the deliberation and ease with which the trusts organize our legislatures, dictate to the jurists of the land, deny even the permanence or sacredness of contract when it concerns them; rob, pillage and tax to their hearts' content while a pitiful mass at the bottom march to and fro wondering where or to whom to turn for relief. And, on the other hand, life here, as much as elsewhere—the struggling mass—is as savagely pushed by necessity as any mass anywhere. Our labor unrest is as great, our poverty as keen; five per cent, or so it is alleged, of the population controlling ninety-five per cent of the wealth; thirteen per cent of the population illiterate; at the top gorgons of financiers as fat and comfortable and dictatorial as any the world has ever seen and as unpatriotic and un-American, in so far as its original theory goes, as may be. Worse yet, it is absolutely true that ours is, or was, materially at least, a rich land, boundless in its opportunities at first, which latter fact has contributed greatly to our optimism but not to our comfort. More rapidly here than anywhere in the world the rich have divided themselves from the poor, and now here as elsewhere necessity and pain are and will remain no doubt the goads to comparative ease. Yet the tramping American when he utters the marvelous word democracy believes

that he has it, and when he is not complaining and the newspapers tell him
so, believes that he is perfectly happy.

At the same time, considering our aggressive and progressive financial leaders—and heaven forbid (on humanitarian grounds, at least) that I
should defend them, for a more selfish, cruel and undemocratic pack never
lived (consider the packers, the street-car corporations, the railroads alone,
not to mention a thousand others)—there is this to be said, that although
nearly every crime in the decalogue[4] may be charged to them, bribery,
perjury, murder, even a total indifference to individual welfare (twelve and
a half cents an hour, for instance, up to six years ago for hard, grinding day
labor on a railroad or in a canning factory), as well as greed, love of power,
and lust after it, much if not all of America's boasted financial supremacy
is due to them and to none other. We jeer at John D. Rockefeller at home
perhaps, or Morgan, but when abroad among envious strangers who is first
to thrust out his chest and boast of what America has done—its financial
leaders, no less? Who? The average American? You know so. Such being the
case one often wonders what is to be done with a country or a people that
can so readily blow hot and cold out of the same mouth. Can it be made
to follow an austere democratic program—the sharp, taut socialization of
everything—or will it succumb to autocratic or to financial domination, and
if so, which? At the present moment the air hums with the rival theories.
To me the chief problem in connection with America, if it has one, and as
I see it, is that of finding itself mentally as well as finding a formula that will
allow and encourage leadership without submitting to the abuses which in
the past and even the present the latter tends to give rise. For here as much
as anywhere else the average small American is as much a petty tyrant as
may be found. Consider only the food profiteer, the small dealers, jobbers
and wholesalers. And here, as elsewhere, are all the petty tyrannies of small
and large enterprises in regard to wage-earners, the scorns, the brutalities,
the exactions. Can these be outrivaled if readily duplicated in any autocracy or democracy ruled by a dictator anywhere? At the same time, is it not
true that, if the country is to succeed or at least progress materially, a place
must be made for the selfish, self-aggrandizing individual either as leader
politically or as creator? Will life go forward without some such process or
opportunities for immense rewards or honors to the individual—the right
to satisfy his feverish if ridiculous ambition for supremacy? Will patriotism,
love of country, alone do it? Can it be discovered?

* * * *

Our Federal Constitution, theoretically at least, gives us a crowd government; only, owing to the wholly undemocratic character of the American

people, this has long since been replaced by money or trust government, the rule of the wealthy by right of subornation. And our state and municipal governments, modeled on that of the nation, have gone the same way. Even such little individuality and leadership for the mass as might possibly exist under these conditions is lost or discarded nearly every two or four years in the regular and money-controlled changes of administration. The old and experienced are replaced with the new and untried. Perhaps under conditions as they are this is best. I am not sure. But for efficiency, after the manner of the great successful private corporations, is it? Personally, I think not—not yet, at any rate. As yet democracy does not take sufficient interest in itself, is too indifferent to its real interests and needs. It is too easy going, not sufficiently self-compelling. Everyone wants to be his own boss and to be a great, undemocratic, individual success, hence there is very little true effective organization outside private institutions and what they compel in a public way. We make no provision for the continuation of leadership even under emergency.

Personally, I think the defect cannot for ever go on un-remedied. Democracy must do at least as well as autocracy, or it ought to shut up shop. And if it cannot obtain the efficiency exemplified by the private corporation it will, and it will deserve to. Perhaps our recent sad experiences in meeting the expanded demands on governmental efficiency should show us how to lay a new basis for that efficiency in modifications of our governmental structure.[5] But will they? What I think is that more autocracy, behind which should be a livelier sense of power and control on the part of the people, should come into our democracy, or our democracy will really cease to be. The present drift toward money control cannot go unchecked. Our leaders will either become much more forceful, and the mass more watchful and jealous, as it should be, or we will have no democracy of any kind. There is scarcely any now. Congress should be used more against the President and the Supreme Court, and the latter against both, only the judges should be plainly responsible to the people, closely and fearsomely beholden to them—as much so, at any rate, as they now are to the corporations and wealth. Both the leaders and their weapons—the laws—should become more vigorous. Democracy will have to step up, and step lively. Then will it be any more of a democracy than some of the older and more historic autocracies and monarchies? Will it?

Textual Note: First published in *Reconstruction* 1 (December 1919): 338–42, and *New York Call*, 30 November 1919, *Call Magazine*, 5–7. Copy-text from *Hey Rub-a-Dub-Dub*, 228–32, 236–37.

1. Dreiser discussed the continuing marginalization of African Americans in "Some Aspects of our National Character," *Hey Rub-a-Dub-Dub*, 42–43.

2. The Democratic Party's machine in New York, Tammany Hall, had become a byword for municipal corruption. The construction and ownership of the initial New York subway in 1900–1904 was monopolized by the financier August Belmont Jr. (1853–1924), who had become President of the Interborough Transit Commission and worked closely with Tammany Hall. The scandal was exposed by the muckraking journalist Ray Stannard Baker, in "The Subway Deal," *McClure's Magazine* 24 (March 1905): 451–69.

3. The Battle of Bunker Hill, 17 June 1775, during the American Revolution.

4. The biblical Ten Commandments.

5. The government's assumption of control over industrial infrastructure, such as the railroads during the First World War.

Dreiser Sees No Progress

New York Globe and Commercial Advertiser,
22 February 1921.

Solicited as part of a projected symposium on the question "Are the interests, social freedom, and post-war activities of the younger generation a sign of decadence or the breaking of hampering and unnecessary shackles of convention demanded by a vastly extended world outlook?" Printed as a letter to the editor, dated 14 February 1921.

I can truthfully say that I cannot detect in the post-war activities or interests, social, intellectual or otherwise, of the younger or other generations of Americans, poor, rich, or middle class, any least indication of the breaking of hampering shackles of any kind—intellectual, social, monetary, or what you will. The American as I encounter him, young or old, is the same old American, thin lipped, narrow-minded, money centered, interested in the Ten Commandments as they apply to the other fellow, and absolutely blind to everything that would tend to enlarge, let alone vastly extend his world outlook. Here and there, there may be an individual, one or two maybe to a town or city, who by some accident of nature is interested in something outside his business, his store, or his church. But, as I say, he is an accident. The vast majority are interested in but one thing—to get into business where they will be able to "sting" the other fellow good and plenty. And after that their dream is to build a stuffy house wherein they can lie down and take the count. He hopes to be a Rotarian, a Shriner, an Elk, or an Oddfellow, and wander off with trainloads of others like himself to conventions, picnics, reunions, where his outstanding hope is to parade in an astounding uniform. World outlook? Now, really? Are you kidding me?

He still forms, daily, outside some fourth-rate moving picture house immense queues in which he waits for hours in order to be permitted to see Blossom Springtime or Cerise Fudge[1] illustrate the honor, virtue, heroism, self-sacrifice, charity, etc. of American manhood and American womanhood. And he is only happy when for the billionth time at the end he has seen that no one has done anything wrong and that all the really good people have come off pure and uninjured, if a little naked, as it were.

And in his cities his politicians still continue to give away his franchises, where there are any left to give, the while they lecture him in his nearest church on the duty of patriotism, thrift, morality, virtue, guarding the home, fulfilling his civic duties, etc. His gas company sells him carbon monoxide for pure gas and charges him for eight hundred and fifteen thermal units as against seven hundred and fifty delivered. His street railways raise his fare from 5 to 7 or 10 cents—on account of rising prices—and then, when prices fall, his wages included, keep it there. His railroads raise his freight and passenger rates on him, ruin his business or his district, making it impossible for him to travel or to ship, and then when their own business slumps rush to his government with a plan to reduce wages and to have their own annual income guaranteed. His telephone company lets his business and his home wait months without a telephone, the while it retains his large deposit without interest and should he complain meets him with the sobriquet: Socialist or Bolshevist.

The lumber trust taxes him 80 per cent profit whenever he seeks to build one of his dear American homes. His landlord adds 75 to 100 per cent to his rent. The milk trust jumps the price of his milk from 5 to 20 cents the quart. The clothing trust stings him three prices for his clothes. (And to defeat them he threatens to wear overalls—just like that.) His shoe trust charges him four prices for his shoes and makes them of imitation leather. And if he gets too outspoken in his complaints his local district attorney arrests him for being a Socialist or a Bolshevist—particularly if he suggests that his government do something for him as opposed to his 971 might-is-right trusts.

His lawyer refuses to take his case unless he can put up a retainer of $1,000. His banker, if he has one, advises him to let well enough alone. His preacher assures him that Christ reigns, the while his doctor and his undertaker raise prices and so make his exit heavenward difficult. His newspaper and his magazines assure him that he is all right; that he is living in the best of all countries, the land of the free and the home of the brave, and that all he needs to get on is grit, nerve, honor, decency, thrift, spunk, wit, tact, brains, patience, etc. His librarian locks up every decent book relating to politics, economics, and life, and then urges him to inform himself. Lastly, in face of it all, he himself insists upon subscribing to a conservative paper wherefrom he comes to favor a blue Sunday[2] and the censoring of the already brainless movies and the stage, to say nothing of his one refuge, a decent book.

No, frankly, I see no least sign of those post-war activities on the part of the younger or the old generations which threaten the hampering and unnecessary shackles, social, economic, and religious which now hold the good American safe and sound. I see no change in the point of view that looks upon all phases of art as essentially immoral and upon political change as dangerous and even evil. In the eyes of the American, young and old, the salvation of the world lies more in religion—more spiritual activity—not in any widening of his social and economic faculties. He seems to feel that all he needs to do is to trust in God and the innate goodness of his fellow men—especially his allies. God is on his throne. The less one knows of life and the more of Heaven, the better. In God we trust. Oh, well—

Textual Note: New York Globe and Commercial Advertiser, 22 February 1921, p. 6. Letter to the editor, opening "Dear Globe" and closing with the dateline Los Angeles, Feb. 14.

1. Blossom Springtime and Cerise Fudge (Cherry Fudge) are names invented to suggest the banality and excessive sweetness of contemporary Hollywood, which Dreiser is viewing as a distraction from postwar profiteering, censorship, and the maintenance of corporate wealth.

2. A Sunday free of all activity except for religious observance, as prescribed by fundamentalist Christian influences on state legislatures.

A Word Concerning Birth Control

The Birth Control Review, April 1921.

The Birth Control Review *was edited for the American Birth Control League by Margaret Sanger (1879–1966) as part of her campaign to make contraception freely and legally available. The dissemination of advice on contraception and the distribution of devices such as condoms were banned under the 1873 Act for the Suppression of Trade in, and Circulation of, Obscene Literature and Articles for Immoral Use, known popularly as the Comstock Law after its proponent, the antivice and censorship campaigner Anthony Comstock (1844–1915). The possession of wealth often enabled the ban to be circumvented, an unfairness touched upon in two Dreiser novels,* Jennie Gerhardt *and* An American Tragedy. *Although motivated primarily by a concern for overburdened working-class women, Sanger regarded birth control as a single-issue campaign, and adapted her arguments to different constituencies. Dreiser had already discussed the eugenic control of "defectives" in "The Right to Kill" (1918). He gave Sanger permission to reprint his one-act play "The Blue Sphere" and subsequently wrote offering support during her frequent arrests and trials. Largely due to Sanger's efforts, legal bans on distributing the means of contraception were eventually lifted, though in some states not until the 1960s.*

I have never been able to understand why anything so obviously beneficial and essential as Birth Control—the knowledge of the means of preventing conception—should need a champion or a movement to foster it. Nature apparently understands the importance of it—or, at least, the pointlessness of waste in connection with life at any level as I will later indicate. And certainly the shrewd and intelligent in all ranks of society are not stopped by religious or moral theory from exercising that care in regard to the number of offspring which they feel themselves decently and intelligently able to provide for. And again it would seem to me, that anything so plainly advantageous to the very poor would be most enthusiastically welcomed by them. And I am inclined to believe that ignorance and religious and moral theory aside—(the dogmatic and commercial beneficiaries of the same estopped from exercising an undue influence on the ignorant and the religious)—the same would gladly welcome and profit by such intelligence. But, as it stands, this natural and advantageous knowledge appears to collide most sharply with present day religious, corporate and social theory in general and is even taboo as a subject in most of the so-called conservative circles of all walks.

Why, I wonder?

To what or whose advantage?

I can readily understand why a certain type of state, depending for its existence upon a large standing army and (as opposed to another state or army of greater numerical strength) anxious to maintain its place, might be opposed to Birth Control in any of its social grades—might even proceed to enforce its mood in regard to the matter. Again I can understand why some very powerful and huge manufacturer or group of manufacturers or growers controlling some product the profit from which might depend upon cheap if not exactly ignorant labor—the rubber interests operating in Africa and Brazil, let us say—might be very much opposed to anything which would tend to lower the birth rate in his or their respective preserves, however much a larger rate might torture the lives over whom, for the time being at least, he or they chanced to exercise economic control. And again, I can understand why shrewd and well conducted organizations such as the Roman Catholic, Mohammedan, Methodist, Baptist, and other churches interested as each must be in its own numerical growth, might be violently opposed to Birth Control in the ranks of its followers at least—and by reasons of fear of contagion of knowledge from other sources be opposed to Birth Control in the ranks of society anywhere. But knowing all this, or once having had it pointed out, I cannot see why the poor or those economically uncertain, should ever again allow themselves to be influenced by such alien considerations.

For after all their own lives and their own economic welfare and that of their children should plainly come before that of any religious or commercial organization, however much one might be willing to bow to the social necessity of the state. I am a believer in strong and intelligent states and I would not wish to hinder their intelligent development in any way. But it seems to me that Birth Control should be as good for the truly intelligent state, as it is for the individual and his progeny, contributing as it must to a better nurtured citizenry. I may be wrong, but I think so.

My personal feeling about life and education in every form is this, that the more we know, *exactly*, about the chemic and biologic and social complexities by which we find ourselves generated, regulated and ended, the better. It cannot be drummed into too many ears and brains too soon. Few of us have sufficient capacity to know much or to do anything with what we do know as it is. Quite all of us know much, much too little of all that we should know. Man has never progressed either self-defensively or economically via either blind faith or illusion. It is exact knowledge that he needs. And as I see it contraceptal means are not only exact but most beneficial economically and so socially of course. The individual should be better cared for at every turn if he is to do better, and where better to begin with him and his proper care than at the source—by regulating the number of him to as many as can be intelligently cared for. This seems to me so plain that the thickest of dunces should be able to see the point.

* * * *

[Dreiser "pause[s] a moment" to "take a look at nature and see how she works." Adducing evidence of the relative fertility of different species, he argues that "as intelligent parental care increases the number of offspring needed for the perpetuation of the species decreases."]

Indeed, to me it glows as a plain bit of common sense that no human being should indifferently or lustfully, or because of some religious or moral emotion bring a line of offspring into the world for whom he or she can make no adequate economic provision. That smacks of ignorance and real vice—criminal brutality in my judgment and worthy of the cat-o-nine-tails. Yet in the face of ragged and unintelligent children, a constant increase in the number of defective, the criminal and the insane, we hear the squawk of the moralist and the religionist and the boom of the dull timeserving politician to the point that contraception is wrong. Millions dying in India, China, Egypt and elsewhere of starvation. Other millions everywhere, who find themselves because of poverty and ignorance to begin with undernourished, poorly clothed, bondservants to men their lives long, underpaid, despised socially and morally and yet they, and even those who brought them into the world, continuing to usher in others as wretched or more so than themselves—weaklings who will ever find the hands of the strong at their backs and necks ushering them unwillingly to their unwelcome tasks.

But why, I should like to know?

Where the intelligence?

Where the much vaunted Christian or moral generosity, charity, decency even when in plain view lies a remedy?

Would it not really be more intelligent and humane and moral for that matter, to allow or compel even the ignorant and the criminal and the hopelessly incompetent of all walks to waste themselves in idle unproductive pleasuring, if such be their bent, rather than that they should be permitted to spawn a helpless or criminal brood afterward to be looked after by the police, the hospitals, the asylums and the homes for the defective? Or to be worked in huge and hopeless droves by those who have no other ambition in life than to "cut financial melons" the substance of which is to be used to take even more from those who have all too little and waste it among those who have already too much. I think so. I have all the respect in the world for the individual who collects from among thousands and millions even who don't know how to manage their own affairs some hundreds of millions of dollars and then distributes the same in the shape of education or science—improved means of living—to all those and more from whom he has collected his wealth. That is one thing. He suggests a practical Providence. But how about those who do not? And why shouldn't the worthless be prevented from being so worthless or at any rate so numerous. How about reaching the evil at the source?

Whenever I hear a Catholic priest or a Protestant minister or some flabby, half-educated judge or journalist spouting from the altar, the pulpit, the bench or the editorial page solemn tosh about the manifest scandal of so many parents refusing to have more than one or two children, or none—all they can decently support in any case perhaps—I would like to rise in my place and say to the very good father or the grave and reverend bunkus or dub of whatsoever persuasion that he is about an ignorant if not a tricky or self-aggrandizing business in this urging of his docile followers, if any there be, to undertake what, in too, too many instances can only prove not only financially but intellectually and ethically beyond them. "Increase and multiply." As though the numerical or physical size of anything—a state, a religion, or a family were the measure of its import. If that were true, what would one have to say for India with three hundred millions as against England with forty?

What an inane or deceptive or criminal suggestion. To what end? Who is to pay? The state or the individual? And with what? In the case of the state with other people's money of course. In the case of the individual thrown out without care or education by irresponsible parents with his very life perhaps. A fine business for a priest or a judge or an editor to be in. Such men besmirch not only their professions and organizations but the intelligence of life itself. They ought to be drummed out of the work which they profess.

For if religion or the bench or the newspaper and periodical have nothing better than this to offer—a deluded consciousness of moral well-being in rags and squalor, they had better shut up shop. For their business is or should be to make life more tolerable for all, since they all so boldly profess to have the best interests of life at heart, if not in charge. They should be helping man to understand and meet his very human difficulties and necessities here—not urging him to complicate them by the bearing of a number of children whom he may be in no wise fitted to aid or instruct. Roosevelt with his race suicide mush.[1] And the preachers and judges with their solemn bletherings against the sin of childlessness. If a home is anything it ought to be a place in which children can be physically and mentally assisted to the end that they will prove a comfort to themselves and to others. And if any so-called home is overcrowded with ignorant and helpless children thoughtlessly spawned by ignorant and economically inadequate parents, how is the same to fulfill this function? I sometimes suspect the wealthy and powerful of various persuasions and interests, especially those who might hope to profit from the presence here of vast and docile hordes of having more of an interest in blind unregulated reproduction on the part of the masses than they would care to admit. It is a sinister thought to be sure and I hope, untrue. But when one finds so many of them so enthusiastic in their suggestions and urgings to this end, what is one to think? For surely they cannot be blind to the economic and social difficulties not to say horrors which too often trail ignorant self reproduction. If they are, believe me, they are blind indeed—judges, priests, editors and public leaders all.

Personally I would rather think that the latter rather than the former is true, for the latter is so much easier of remedy. And perhaps such is the case. But in either case an earnest campaign looking to the enlightenment of all is in order. And it has my unqualified endorsement.

Textual Note: Copy-text from *Birth Control Review* 5 (April 1921): 5–6, 12–13. In the footers of the published text appear quotations from such commentators as Ralph Waldo Emerson, Herbert Spencer, and Robert Ingersoll. Since they do not appear in the typescript carbon (8 pages, signed and dated 23 February 1921, DPUP folder 12479) and are related to the article only in a very general way, they are not reproduced here.

1. While president from 1901 to 1909, Theodore Roosevelt articulated fears that "Anglo-Teutons" were committing "race suicide" by failing to reproduce at the rate of immigrants, and he encouraged middle-class women to regard reproduction as a racial and national duty.

Contribution to "The Rights of a Columnist: A Symposium on the Case of Heywood Broun *versus* the *New York World*"

The Nation, 30 May 1928.

The journalist Heywood Broun (1888–1939) had been dismissed from the staff of Joseph Pulitzer's New York World *for criticizing the paper in his column in* The Nation. *Dreiser's view of the case as symptomatic of wider social problems contrasts with most of the other contributors to* The Nation's *symposium, who confine themselves to the specifics of Broun's case.*

I have long observed that it is a rare American newspaper or magazine that offers any space to anyone who has a vital criticism of our American life to offer. A soothing prosperity now appears to reduce the American mass to an almost hoggish indifference to everything mental—to look upon as negligible any and all such ills as may affect an unsuccessful minority. The devil take the hindmost. By all means smother the plaintive yowl of the underdog. Whatever else you do, touch on no vital issue. Instead furnish the mob with a constant clatter in regard to sports, radio, the races, patriotism— indeed, anything and everything about purely material developments while a financial oligarchy runs things for the good or ill of all.

Indeed, to me, at this writing, it would seem as though it is the high percentage of prosperity, in no way related to culture or intensive thought, that has snuffed out the interest of the majority in anything save comfort and pleasure. Unquestionably there are men, even today, who, slightly encouraged by a national alertness or thoughtfulness in regard to any hovering national ill, would speak in no uncertain terms. But where is there such a minority—any really important group concerned with any outstanding American problem? I cannot feel its presence.

Yet there are approaching ills—the gradual subornation of the American mind by the Catholic program for one thing; the gradual but certain reduction of the American freeman to an infinitesimal unit in the lock-stepping majority, easily and dictatorially guided by a purely financial and by no means mental money crew. More and more wealth and power for a few corporations and their officers and directors. More and more thoughtless subservience on the part of the limitless majority.

Yet truly, and apart from thought, of course, a not unpleasing panorama for the average man. Plenty—or nearly so—of food and clothing for the many; even houses, automobiles, radios, phonographs, newspapers, and magazines conducted in the interest of those who feel material comfort is the be-all and the end-all of life. As for those who think, who foresee impend-ing ills—sudden and enormous and possibly catastrophic changes[1]—they can wait. Out on them for the radicals, firebrands, Reds that they are. Give them no voice. Discharge them from all responsible positions. If possible subvert their means of living.

And yet approaching ills; assured and possibly disastrous changes now pending. And solutions possible. But the newspapers! Is not circulation—numbers of subscribers of whatever character—their very blood; and money for their exchequer, from those who control the many, the food of their blood? Who doubts it? Yet conditions being what they are I cannot savagely censor any individual paper or its misdeeds. But a land flaccid because of material ease, indifferent to a reasonable equation between the states of men and their individual sorrows; a land that winks at injustice, more and more modifies the liberty of the individual to think for himself, is not worthy of those who, planning this nation, dreamed a great dream. They led men to believe that by thought and the effort that flows from generous and equable thought in regard to all things is a proper accord among men to be maintained. But never, by what one sees in America at this hour, is man to be moved nearer toward an understanding of his strange and at present anomalous relation to nature; or his perhaps futile hope that he may not pass as meaningless dust may yet lift his spirit as a distinguished force which need not die.

Textual Note: The Nation 126: 3282 (30 May 1928): 608.

1. Wall Street crashed, precipitating the Great Depression, a year later, in October 1929.

From *Dreiser Looks at Russia*

New York: Horace Liveright, November 1928.

Dreiser visited the Soviet Union from early November 1927 to the middle of January 1928 as a guest of the state, to observe its progress in the ten years since the 1917 revolution. The trip was extensive in comparison with those taken by other Americans at the time, taking in Moscow, Leningrad, Nizhi-Novgorod, and parts of Ukraine, the Caucuses, and Georgia, returning via Yalta, Sebastopol, and Odessa on the Black Sea.

Dreiser's observations on Russia were syndicated in eleven newspaper articles and then, with the help of Ruth Kennell (1893–1977), who had acted as a guide, translator, and secretary on the trip, assembled, revised, and expanded to form the volume Dreiser Looks at Russia. *In Russia Dreiser frequently insisted upon the importance of the individualism associated with the United States, while on his return he praised the achievements of the Russian communal approach. The book is similarly ambivalent.*

Chapter 6: Communism—Theory and Practice

* * * *

But, have I been converted to Communism? No, not to the brand that is operating in Russia at this time. (Of course, all official Communists explain to you that true Communism has not yet arrived; that the dictum of Marx, father of the present experiment, or whoever invented this slogan, much quoted by all Communists— "From each according to his ability; to each according to his need"—is something to be approximated, not necessarily achieved.)[1]

But why not? Is Communism all wrong? Far from being all wrong, I consider, as I have said, many of its aspects and developments to be very much right and progressive,[2] and if it were in my power so to do I would this day dispatch to Russia as large a number as possible of present-day American and English enthusiasts for things as they are—the rankest individualists, say, of America, England, France, Germany, in politics and out—in order that they might observe for themselves and come to understand that something besides unlimited private rights for the strong and capable—their privileges, pleasures, etc.,—is possible, and not only possible but in Russia actually in existence and, with modifications, likely to endure. One of the things they would have to look upon, if not mentally accept for themselves (and which would cause many to return in a state of high dudgeon, vowing that Russia is upside down), would be the enjoyment by labor of a maximum of consideration or privilege consistent with the economic success of the country as a whole.

I myself, ordinarily most sympathetically inclined toward the underdog and the minor individual everywhere, was inclined, and still am, to decide that a little too much was being done for labor and too little for the brains necessary to direct it; that labor was being given an undue share of the fruits of the land; and that the elimination of the old-time creative or constructive business man, with all that his self-interest and consequent industry, ingenuity, etc., implied, was likely to result in a kind of slowness or seeming indifference or quiescence which would not be likely to work out for the best interests of all concerned. And as one goes about any city or town apart from Moscow, where naturally center most of the political and official if not exactly mental opportunities of the country at this time, there is to be noted just this ease or slowness, not to say indifference. In factories, in order to speed up production and prevent slack, piece-work is the rule. But in offices, on trains, in stores, you will find that ease which one might expect in a society from which the urge and tang of competition has been extracted.

But is this best? Wise? Can society endure unless everybody works, and works hard? Coming from America, where nearly everybody works and likes to—in order to pass the time—and in consequence piles up an amazing amount of material possessions, I, for one, was inclined to quarrel with this slowness and predict this, that and the other fatal result for Russia. Yet why, exactly? Must we have or do we need really all the speed and energy and material plethora which is now being heaped up before us in America? Might we not do with less and are we not already a little weary of too much of everything and sighing for a simpler, less plethoric state of affairs? I, for one, am beginning to think so.

And so, after observing these slow, easy-going Russians for a time, I was not so ready to criticize as at first. True, there is a great deal to be done before the actual necessities of Russia are met—before it is brought up to the modern level of living and usage—(I calculate that it is now about three hundred years behind in many ways)—but need it all be done overnight? Cannot a leisurely and wise nation take its time and get quite as much fun out of so doing as we who feel we must hurry so? To be sure, want and warmth and sanitation which means the elimination of disease should not be made to wait. But beyond these, just what? Must they have a rapid increase in population, immense apartment houses and hotels, crowded trains and overstuffed highways, resorts, and places of amusement? I hope not. And so I am in no hurry to see Russia changed in this respect, although they are— the leaders, at least. They all want Russia to be like America—its cities like Chicago and Detroit, its leaders and geniuses like Ford, Rockefeller, Edison and Gary.[3] God! I pray not.

Tenth anniversary celebrations of the 1917 Revolution,
from Dreiser's trip to Russia, November 1927.

Chapter 9: The Tyranny of Communism

Unquestionably, one of the most disagreeable phases of Communist Russia—
from an American or English point of view—is the inescapable atmosphere
of espionage and mental as well as social regulation which now pervades
every part of that great land.

* * * *

You must believe, or pretend to believe, that collectivism is right, individualism wrong; that holding or wishing for private property is an evil and the
curse of the rest of the world; that it is not right to want anything that all
cannot have; that upon the worker more than the intellectual rests the burden of maintaining the world. Also that to work together, "one for all and
all for one," is the only way to collective or State happiness; that to want
special things for yourself—even rare or different articles of adornment—is
wrong. And that mass wants (for likeness rather than difference) should
control. That the machine is the worker's as well as Russia's friend. That
the shorter working day, with the consequent longer period for recreation
or study, is for the great good of all. That there must not and shall not be
any classes; and that the establishment of this fact, either by war or peace,
falls to the lot of Russia because of its present intellectual or humanitarian
leadership in the world.

   Oh, very well! Let it be so, if you will! Only I wish to remark here that the
phrase: "Dictatorship of the Proletariat," in so far as Russia is concerned, is a
misnomer. There is a dictatorship of the Communist Party in the interests of
the Proletariat. This Party (fifty per cent of whom are workers and peasants
and fifty per cent public officials, about half of whom were formerly proletar-
ian) consists of no more than (in 1927) 1,200,000 members who rule the
rest of Russia. They insist that it is the workers who rule them, but that is a
pleasant theory only. The Government, directed by the Communist Party,
employs labor just as might a capitalist trust. It seeks not only efficiency but
mental loyalty and conformity, and unless it gets it there is trouble. Let any
one show disloyalty in any way, and he loses his job. What befell Trotsky,
Radek, Rakovsky,[4] and others once they failed to agree with the present
powers of the Communist Central Committee? They were exiled, and that
quite swiftly. And at the very time that this process of excommunication
and silencing was under way I was in Russia—in Moscow—and seeking
appointments with not only Radek and Rakovsky, but Trotsky also. Only,
in the case of Trotsky, I was told that it was quite impossible, that the mere
seeking of such an interview by me would do harm not only to myself but
to Trotsky. Already he was being watched and anything he had to say

intercepted and censored or destroyed. So anything that I might possibly obtain from him would also be examined and censored.

In the case of Radek whom I did see and talked with, the situation was somewhat different. At that time both he and Rakovsky still occupied quarters in the Kremlin (the official or state residence of leading executive Communists) and were assumed to be in Party favor. At the same time, they really were not, although the public did not know that, and it was impossible for me to see them. They would telephone or leave word for me to call on them, but when I did so I was informed at the outer gate of the Kremlin that they were not in. Yet when I would return to my hotel and call up, there they were, and at my invitation would come to see me. And at last it was Radek who indicated (truly diplomatically, of course) that all was not well, but that soon he would have rooms outside where his friends could call.[5] But before that could happen, they were already tried by some secret process and ordered to the Mongolian frontier, where, for all the world knows, or at the time this book goes to press, they still are.

Chapter 12: Women in Present-Day Russia

* * * *

The economic independence of women in Soviet Russia is not merely an official theory but a fact. Women are encouraged and educated in the idea of supporting themselves, be they single, married or even mothers, and every facility of an impoverished state is contributed to make this possible. First of all, there is no difference in the valuation put on the industrial labor of women and men. Trade union laws make equal pay for equal work of the two sexes absolutely compulsory, and every form of employment, from ditch digger to engineer, is open to women. There are even women soldiers in the Red Army, and, notably, a young woman, married to an officer and the mother of two children, who has just been graduated from the Military Academy in Moscow with the rank of general.

Prostitution, which to a great extent is an indication of the economic condition of women, shows itself to be steadily decreasing in new Russia. . . .

What constitutes the important difference between the women of Soviet Russia and those of other countries is that public opinion, plus official sanction which makes a fact of the equality of the sexes, places no social stigma on the unmarried mother or on unregistered marriages or divorces, makes motherhood not only voluntary but the responsibility of the State, and gives equal educational opportunities for women and men and equal remuneration for labor.

It does not follow that the material condition of women is better in Russia than in the outside world. On the contrary, the majority of women in the United States undoubtedly live far better than the Russian women. But, primarily, this is due to the vast difference in the standard of living which in turn is due to the backward industrial state of Russia. It must be admitted that the public attitude in America toward women, while on the whole liberal, nevertheless contains a definite disapproval of a married woman, and especially a mother, working outside the home. This attitude has its own psychological effect on the woman, who from her childhood is brought up with the idea of marriage being her ultimate profession. The resulting waste of trained workers as Communists at least see this is appalling. There is not only the great evil of the "stop-gap" professions for women, for which girls take a half-hearted, superficial training in order to support themselves until they can find a husband to support them, but there is the intelligent woman who earnestly trains herself for a useful profession and then finds herself compelled to abandon it when she marries. Many such women remain childless because of their dread of being tied irrevocably to the home, since a nurse for the baby is out of the question for any but the rich. They expend their mental energy somewhat futilely in social work or women's clubs. If they have children, by the time the children are old enough to free them, it is too late to return to their profession.

So in spite of the infinitely higher standards of living for women in America, they are, to a much greater extent, household drudges. Of course, the vastly more modern equipment of the American home as compared with the Russian home is a great labor-saver, but this is offset by the enormous complication of housework in America compared with the simplicity of the one- or two-room apartment in Russia, where cooking and eating are quite often done in community kitchens and dining rooms.

But there still remains the question of the sanctity of the home, which, it would appear, is going out of existence in Russia. Whether or not this is a step backward, only time will tell. If the American woman chooses the profession of housewife and mother and voluntarily keeps to it, well and good. It is an honorable profession and possibly best for society in the long run. But there are widespread indications that intelligent American women do not voluntarily choose this profession and are, in part at least, in rebellion against it.

All this may explain, to some extent, why some American women can live more contentedly in Russia, under conditions of life amounting to almost physical hardship, than in their own rich and comfortable land. Madame Litvinov,[6] an English woman and the wife of the Foreign Minister, told me that when she was out of Russia she was always restless—running here and there, competing with whosoever was competing for anything—clothes, contacts, what not. But once in Russia again all these things seemed to fall away; nothing mattered much. Clothes were poor, to be sure; social advance all but impossible; wealth impossible. "And yet I am happier," she said. "Like everybody else, I work, part time for my husband as typist and translator, part time for one of the Government bureaus as translator. I get 200 rubles a month. You see how I dress. And I have no social life here. There is none to speak of. Yet I am happier here than anywhere, I think, much happier, and I often wonder why."

I could not answer her at the time, but now I think I can. It is due to the absence of national worry over one's future or the means of subsistence. In Russia one's future and one's subsistence are really bound up with that of the entire nation. Unless Russia fails you will not fail. If it prospers, you are certain to prosper. Therefore a sense of security, which for some at least replaces that restless, painful seeking for so many things which here you are not allowed to have.

Another view of the tenth anniversary celebrations of the 1917 Revolution from Dreiser's Russian visit, November 1927.

Chapter 18: Random Reflections on Russia

* * * *

Yet ambling about here and there—looking at the true Russians in Moscow, the White Russians of the Ukraine, the Tartar and half Chinese in Siberia, the Uzbecks in Uzbeckistan, the Arabs, Persians, Turks, and Armenians in the region of the Caspian—I could not help thinking, suppose they are all really wrong? Suppose, as Darwin and his theory insist, a measure of chance and gamble is really right? That man, in order to get even a measure of joy out of this mysterious and inexplicable world, must really dice and gamble and trick and waste and show off or strut before his fellows who now have less but tomorrow may have more? Suppose? For is it not possible that once these very Russians have all a fair measure of property and comfort, they may begin to think back on and crave the good old days when one could knock a man down (in some sly, concealed way, of course) and rob him? Or will they always, because of the new training now being provided prefer to deal fairly and generously or justly with their neighbors? I wonder.

Mr. Stalin, Mr. Bukharin, Mr. Kalinin, and Mr. Chicherin[7] will tell you yes. Mr. Darwin, Mr. Haeckel, Mr. Spencer, and Mr. Voltaire[8] will tell you no, and that these Russians are fools, dreamers, and that some day they will wake up.

I wonder.

* * * *

On the other hand, it is entirely possible that once the Russian temperament has succeeded in equipping itself with life's material necessities and some of its luxuries (those that we in America already enjoy), it will turn from them with a phase of loathing to the things which I really think matter to it most—phases of mental research and development. For unless I mistake entirely the feel of the land, it is a thinking and perhaps—and that is not so good—a brooding nation. The Russian likes to speculate and dream. You can see it in his eyes. And he will drop any matter in hand, even now in all the hurry and pother of this grand industrialization business that is going forward, as he thinks, with so much speed—to discuss anything he can discuss—art, literature, science, politics, or the ways and doings of his neighbors, and, above all, the mystery and meaning, or meaninglessness, of life. (If anything, I think it is this last that engages him most.) And from his lips, in ordinary conversation, will fall the most colorful proverbs, which could only grow out of speculation and meditation. "The dog barks and the wind carries it farther." "The old is fat; the new is lean." "When you wait, you listen." "No one laughs but another cries." These are but a few that dropped, like bright coins that clink and shine, from the lips of Russians who were speaking in English to me.

And more, even as they talk of the glorious material prosperity that they dream is to come to them, I never met one who spoke of it in purely personal or selfishly possessive terms. On the contrary, it was always a general prosperity that was to be, and in which all were to share, plenty for everybody, everybody happy or free to do this and that. And almost as instantly it took the form of leisure to think. If society—not self—say these Russians, can be supplied by everybody working eight, or seven, or six hours, well and good—then everybody will have more time to do that which he most wishes to do—study, play, think, travel. And if society can supply itself with all that it needs by working only three or four hours a day, then so much the better—more time to do the real and delightful things which have nothing to do with either laborious toil or the hoarding of mere possessions. "Oh," said one old Volga peasant to one of my interpreters, "I shall not live to see it, but my son tells me that no one will have to work more than four or five hours a day after a while, and then every one can study and get a good education." And that, rather than material possessions in the new day, seemed the great point to him.

And truly, talking to the principal statesmen and leaders of Russia as well as many of the industrial workers everywhere, I was persistently impressed by the fact that they also seemed to see this new development in just this way—in terms of general improvement, and always with the goal in view not of luxury but of an intellectual leisure which is to follow upon the acquisition of sufficient material equipment. One could always get ten, twenty, thirty to join in such a discussion anywhere, but never with a dissenting voice from this program of general prosperity and general culture.

And this finally led me to fancy that possibly Russia—and that in the near future, should its present program succeed—is destined to enter upon an intellectual labor which will go farther than has any other thing as yet toward solving the strange mystery of our being here at all.

I wonder.

Textual Note: New York: Horace Liveright, November 1928. These selections are on pp. 74–76, 115, 122–24, 166, 168–70, and 259–61.

1. The quotation, from Karl Marx, *Critique of the Gotha Program* (1875), refers to Marx's conception of life "in a higher phase of communist society," that is, after productive relations have been transformed and technology developed much further than was the case in 1920s Russia.

2. These progressive aspects, listed in the first chapter of *Dreiser Looks at Russia,* included full employment; the elimination of idleness at both ends of the social scale; the limitation of individual workloads; the practical system of education in Russian schools; the prevention of the accumulation of wealth by individuals; the legal and economic emancipation of women; liberal, secular marriage and divorce; and the general improvement in the working conditions of industrial labor.

3. Industrialists Henry Ford (1863–1947) and John D. Rockefeller ; inventor and industrialist Thomas Alva Edison (1847–1931); Elbert Henry Gary (1846–1927), erstwhile chairman of U.S. Steel. Dreiser's Cowperwood trilogy of novels fictionalizes the career of another "old-time creative or constructive business man," Charles Tyson Yerkes.

4. Leon Trotsky (1879–1940), Karl Radek (1885–1939), and Christian Rakovsky (1873–1941) had all held prominent posts in Russia, but during Dreiser's stay they were expelled from the Communist Party and sent into exile for opposing Stalin. Trotsky eventually settled in Mexico, where he was assassinated on Stalin's orders in 1940. Radek was readmitted to the party in 1929 after admitting his "errors," but both he and Rakovsky were arrested and convicted of treason during the "Great Purge" in 1937.

5. Radek's visit to Dreiser and their conversation are described in *Dreiser's Russian Diary,* 102–4.

6. Ivy Low Litvinova (1889–1977) had met and married Maxim Litvinov (1876–1951) in London during the latter's exile from Tsarist Russia. According to his diary, Dreiser's discussion with her took place in Moscow in November 1927 (*Dreiser's Russian Diary,* 108–9).

7. Nikolai Ivanovich Bukharin (1888–1939), coeditor of *Pravda,* was interviewed by Dreiser at some length on 5 December 1927; Mikhail Ivanovich Kalinin (1875–1946), head of state of the Soviet Union; Georgy Chicherin, (1872–1936), Commissar for Foreign Affairs until succeeded by his assistant Litvinov in 1930.

8. Naturalists Charles Darwin (1809–82) and Ernst Haeckel (1834–1919), and philosopher Herbert Spencer are listed here as proponents of the importance of accident and competition in the development of species, and by extension societies; the French philosopher Voltaire (1694–1778) is cited for his disbelief that state authorities could influence the beliefs of their people.

PART THREE
1929–1937

Historical Commentary

In response to the economic crisis, labor conflicts, and international tensions of the 1930s, Dreiser increasingly devoted his time and energy to politics. Moving markedly to the left in 1930–31, he campaigned on behalf of some of the most oppressed members of American society and interested himself in radical solutions to economic problems, working closely with groups affiliated with the Communist Party. Until the fall of 1932, Dreiser regarded orthodox communists as effectively the sole advocates of positive change. When the country emerged from the worst depths of the Great Depression, Dreiser allied himself with a range of leftwing groups, including orthodox communists, supporters of the exiled Leon Trotsky, nonaligned labor and farmers' groups, and representatives of the technocracy movement. He polemicized for peace and against imperialism on the international scene and maintained his support for the victims of racial oppression and corporate power. As the 1930s wore on, Dreiser also began to reflect more widely upon social values and programs of transformation. Dreiser positioned himself as a staunch critic of "grim and rapacious individualism," and with "equity" as an ideal, he validated scientific and technological innovation and creativity applied for the good of society as a whole.

After the Wall Street crash in October 1929, unemployment spiraled, eventually peaking in March 1933 at 15,071,000—between one quarter and one third of the working population. The existing provisions for relief, administered on a local basis by private charities, proved completely inadequate, and the result was widespread poverty and even starvation. Already critical of the economic inequities in 1920s American society (see "Dreiser Discusses Dewey Plan," 122), Dreiser regarded the Great Depression as evidence not only that American capitalism had failed as an economic system, but also that it had engendered the abuse of political power and inflicted grievous damage on society. In earlier work such as "Life, Art and America" and "American Idealism and German Frightfulness," Dreiser had acknowledged the dynamic force of capitalism and individualism; the object of his criticism was the contradiction between this competitive reality and the moralizing frameworks through which it was mystified, especially the ideologies of social mobility and self-restraint. The anticompetitive practices of corporate capitalism had already partially undermined claims for its efficiency, and for Dreiser the depression discredited them utterly. He was radicalized by the sheer scale of suffering and by the inefficacy of mainstream responses to it. The Hoover administration was slow to acknowledge the severity of the depression, and when it finally acknowledged the need for federal intervention, proposing the Reconstruction Finance Corporation in 1931, it aimed to shore up private companies. The American Federation of Labor (A.F.L.), declining in membership and power throughout the 1920s, was unable to protect even the members of its affiliated unions. Out of its commitment to voluntarism, the A.F.L. had rejected centralized unemployment insurance, and in the early 1930s it opposed militant strikers and organizers. In Dreiser's view at the time, just as the most vulnerable members of American society (blue-collar and unskilled workers, and marginalized racial and ethnic groups) were bearing the brunt of the economic crisis, they were more than ever isolated, exploited, harassed, and suppressed. Only the far left consistently defended those who were suffering most.

Dreiser's immediate response was to try to defend the freedoms of expression and organization. After decrying political repression in several public statements in 1930 (see "John Reed Club Answer," 124), Dreiser served as founding chair of the National Committee for the Defense of Political Prisoners (N.C.D.P.P.) from April 1931 to January 1932. The N.C.D.P.P. publicized the cases of victims of economic, political, and racial repression, such as the Scottsboro boys in Alabama; the Kentucky miners shot by strike-breaking vigilantes, who also dynamited soup kitchens; and the incarcerated I.W.W. activists Tom Mooney and Warren K. Billings. In addition to campaigning on their behalf, the N.C.D.P.P. raised money for their legal expenses, which was channeled through a Communist Party auxiliary, the International Labor Defense. Under the auspices of the N.C.D.P.P., Dreiser made fact-finding visits to mining communities in Pennsylvania and Kentucky, where he was shocked by the poverty and the violent repression suffered by miners organized into the Communist-supported National Miners Union, and shaken by the complicity of local police, judiciary, and press with the mine operators. He concluded that most American institutions, from mainstream politics to the A.F.L. to law enforcement and local judiciaries, were dominated by business interests, to the extreme distress of labor, as well as to the detriment of middle-class Americans who lost civil liberties and were forced to pay inflated prices.

The experiences of 1930–31 had far-reaching effects on Dreiser's philosophical and political beliefs and on his sense of his own role and responsibilities. Throughout 1931, Dreiser wrote articles for the communist and leftwing press—*Labor Defender,* the *Daily Worker,* the *Progressive*—and had statements printed in mainstream newspapers and journals, protesting passionately against political and racial repression. The N.C.D.P.P.'s view of the Scottsboro case as "a lynching concealed in the forms of law" enjoined both practical campaigning in the present and the necessity to understand racism in historical perspective. Thus Dreiser argues in the June 1931 *Labor Defender* that

> the Negro as well as the white, before the law, should be treated with understanding, and liberality. Through no fault of their own, a century or two ago, some of them were drafted as slaves by the white powers and yet that, instead of invoking sympathy, has produced belittlement and hatred. Because Negroes are not, at present, a dominating race, some unthinking members of the white race manifest prejudices toward them and their conduct. And, finally, the prejudice-makers have grown to include even the more intelligent leaders who do not stop to analyze the standards and ideas under which they, themselves, were brought up. Hence, not only laws unduly severe concerning the human relations of Negroes have been made, but these laws in the eyes of the unified Southern population have become so near perfection itself, that the people almost justify mob-rule to enforce them. . . . These eight boys must at least have a just trial even though they are oppressed by a law unduly severe and emotionally enforced at this time in Alabama. Study the Negroes' past in America first, and then judge.[1]

In the same month, in the *Daily Worker*, Dreiser urges sweeping economic change, insisting that successive reform movements had been outmaneuvered by corporate power and therefore "a change in the treatment of property is necessary . . . to restore the balance of power which has so rapidly favored the wealthy few at the great loss and expense to the masses."[2] Notwithstanding his solidarity with the victims of capitalism and of corporate and racial persecution, this is as close as Dreiser comes to calling for the overthrow of capitalism along orthodox communist lines. More often he describes the Great Depression as symptomatic of a multifaceted need for change: "something more than a mere crisis of politics and economics," necessitating "new social forms, new mental directions and interests, and, in consequence, a new social code" (see "America," 171).

At the center of this crisis, Dreiser argues repeatedly in the 1930s and 1940s, lay the individualism associated with capitalism in America. Here was a major shift in his own thinking, since as recently as his 1928 reportage on Russia Dreiser had identified himself with individualism against communism. Less than four years later, he writes in the January 1932 *New Masses* that "it is well enough to study such instances of economic and social injustice as Harlan and the mining districts of Illinois, Eastern Ohio, Western Pennsylvania, and cotton mills of the South, and the textile and other phases of New England and elsewhere, but far more important to me as a subject is the complete collapse of individualism which, as it seems to me, lies at the bottom of it all."[3] In the substantial volume *Tragic America* (1931), in the Introduction to *Harlan Miners Speak* (1932) (a record of the Kentucky visit), in 1934's "Will Fascism Come to America?" (see Further Reading), and in other works of the 1930s and early 1940s, Dreiser attacks individualism on economic and ideological grounds. At one level, "grim and rapacious individualism" signifies the competitive social and economic relations engendered by American capitalism, which have allowed corporations to amass unbridled power and have precipitated the Great Depression. At another level, Dreiser contests the ideology of individualism, which he sees as a ruse of corporate power that prevents people from acknowledging the truly social nature of existence. In *Tragic America* and elsewhere, Dreiser argues that the pursuit of "equity" is the true goal of "organized society" and ranges it against corporate power, class privilege, and economic individualism. Equity was a prerequisite for the resolution of political, ethnic, and national conflict, and was thus a higher value than peace ("Interview with Nazife Osman Pasha," see 144–46; "Statement on Russia and the Struggle Against Fascism in Spain," 208–9). While Dreiser continued to invoke the "Golden Rule" as he had in essays such as "American Idealism and German Frightfulness," in the 1930s he refined this rather general notion into the idea of "equity," which became a touchstone of his political philosophy. It was still at base a simple concept of economic justice, defined in *Tragic America* as "participation in produce and such for effort expended." Equity functioned both as a social ideal and as the basis of appeals to people of talent in all classes of society to dispense with purely individual aggrandizement, and instead to find fulfillment by using their abilities for the common good. Equity thereby went hand in hand with Dreiser's invocation of "human" and "mentally creative" values, set against individualism and materialist acquisitiveness. As to the means of achieving equity, Dreiser brought together several political programs: the socialization of key services (see "America," 171–72); the synthesis of American individualistic traditions with communism (see Contribution to "What is Americanism?" 200–202); the socialist End Poverty in California movement (E.P.I.C.); and technocracy (see "Epic Technologists Must Plan," 202).

From 1930 until 1942, political writing and campaigning took up much more of Dreiser's time than did the production of fiction, and he came to be seen as one of the left's most prominent voices. *Tragic America* sets out his most detailed criticism of the nation's economic, political, judicial, and social institutions, drawing upon a variety of sources, including Gustavus Myers and Walter Wilson, reports by independently minded senators and state governors, the Labor Research Association, and research by his own assistants, such as Kathryn (Kay) Sayre. After 1930 Dreiser often drew heavily on research sponsored by the Communist Party; he corresponded with and met with its top leaders, Earl Browder and William Z. Foster; and more often than not he gave explicit support to party campaigns. Yet he did not accept party discipline and at times rejected party policy on matters of principle, strategy, and detail. Even when working closely with the Communist Party in the summer of 1931, Dreiser continued to insist that the Harlan miners should try to obtain justice through the courts, in the face of express advice from Foster and Browder that such appeals to the "capitalistic" judiciary undermined "mass struggle among the workers."[4] A few months later, Dreiser maintained his support for victimized labor unionists in China after the Communist Party had branded them counter-revolutionaries.[5] As a result, his overtures toward Party membership, made early in 1932, were rebuffed by Browder. Continuing to assert his independence, in April 1932 Dreiser refused to sign a draft letter to Tom Mooney prepared by Melvin Levy of the N.C.D.P.P., on the grounds that "it would still align me directly and awarely with the motivating Communistic directorate in this country and that, as you know, is entirely false."[6]

The visit to Harlan and Bell counties in November 1931 thus marked the high-water mark of Dreiser's relationship with the Communist Party, until he successfully applied for membership under the very different circumstances of 1945. Resigning as chair of the N.C.D.P.P. early in 1932, Dreiser continued to allow his name to be used in connection with many of its campaigns, including those on behalf of workers in the fur trade and of unemployed workers fired upon during a demonstration at Ford's Dearborn automobile plant.

While he continued to support Communist-led campaigns, after 1931 Dreiser embraced wider perspectives upon social change and how it could be brought about. An unpublished essay from the early 1930s titled "What To Do" sets out a multifaceted agenda rooted in communism and feminism with some left-liberal elements. It calls for freedom of speech, a seven-hour work day and a five-day work week, unemployment insurance, the abolition of child labor, the right to strike and to join a union, equal pay for equal work irrespective of gender or race, employment rights and "bursaries" for pregnant women, a good public education for all, curbs on speculation, government ownership of railroads and utilities, and an end to imperialist economic and financial exploitation abroad.[7] In April 1931, Dreiser proposed to the Communist Party the formation of "The Society of Karl Marx," which would promote Marxist philosophy as distinct from political action, and shortly afterwards he discussed a Party initiative to institute "Dreiser Clubs" along the lines of the John Reed Clubs.[8] Dreiser fully embraced communist opposition to corporatism and capitalism and its critique of the A.F.L. as being compromised and exclusionary, but he seems to have had little faith in the working class as agents of change, and fought shy of embracing the vanguardist project of the Communist Party.[9] By October 1932 he was moving away from Soviet-sponsored communism and toward modernizers in American radical and progressive traditions. He wrote to the Russian editor and critic Sergei Dinamov that "I see some things now which I did not see anywhere near as clearly when I was in the midst of it last year, and one is the enormous significance of the machine in any equitable form of society, and the need of the technician as a part of a newer kind of state. The technician, the chemist, the physicist, the mathematician, the inventor and the economic student and expert are not quite the same as the factory hand or the farmer, but the introduction of the working formula which is to remedy their troubles is not quite clear."[10]

The search for that "working formula" for social transformation led him in the mid-1930s to nonaligned communist and socialist groups and the technocracy movement, whose faith in scientific management developed directly from the Progressivism which had attracted Dreiser during his editorship of the *Delineator*. In February 1934, working with Max Eastman, Dreiser tried unsuccessfully to broker the unification of various leftwing dissidents and groups, including Alfred M. Bingham of the Farmer-Laborer Political Federation, A. J. Muste of the American Workers Party, other radicals such as *Modern Monthly* editor V. F. Calverton, and technocrats Lewis Mumford and Harold Loeb. Dreiser was especially interested in the attempt of Bingham and Selden Rodman to forge connections between technocracy and the farmer-labor movement in their journal *Common Sense*, to which he contributed four articles, including "Flies and Locusts" (see 188–93) and "Challenge to the Creative Man" (see Further Reading). The deliberately innovative and even visionary outlook of *Common Sense* suited Dreiser, now in his sixties, and these essays supplement his still plangent criticism of the distortions produced by the "profit motive" with an appeal to creative people from the arts, business, science and technology, and politics to channel their abilities for the betterment of society as a whole. In the middle of the decade Dreiser corresponded with technocracy's main proponent, Howard Scott. He wrote enthusiastically to one technocratic organization, the "Committee for Unified Action for a Plan of Plenty Throughout the Nation" that "personally I believe that the key organization in the whole business should be Technocracy, although it might be surrounded and aided by many other organizations, since whichever group, if any, succeeded in obtaining power, would need Technocracy as the key implement for proper social reconstruction."[11] Dreiser also supported the campaign of Upton Sinclair to become Governor of California in 1934 on the E.P.I.C. platform (see "The Epic Sinclair" in Further Reading). In 1936 he called for the advocates of technocracy to ally themselves with E.P.I.C. as it sought to expand across the country, and thereby to involve themselves with practical political action (see "Epic Technologists Must Plan," 202–3).

This ferment was symptomatic of how, after the overt class conflicts of 1929–32, the political map of America was reshaping itself. Key developments were the increasing radicalization of Franklin D. Roosevelt's New Deal; the rise of fascism in Europe; the continuation of the Comintern's disruptive and divisive "Third Period" policy until the advent of the Popular Front in 1935; and the 1933 split in the Communist Party and the expulsion of supporters of Trotsky, some of whom, such as James P. Cannon and Rose Karsner, a long-time correspondent of Dreiser's, had been prime movers in the International Labor Defense. While he supported the Communist presidential candidates in 1932 against F.D.R., Dreiser subsequently tried to engage strategically with the New Deal. He wrote one activist in June 1933, asking her to "drop the idea of the Dreiser Clubs for the present, because I am interested to see how this Roosevelt experiment works out." Characteristically, Dreiser added "that does not mean that if I get a chance to cooperate on some issue that is worthwhile I would refuse, but I am interested to see how this thing works out, without comment of any kind."[12]

In interviews and letters Dreiser cautiously supported the New Deal, explaining to the skeptical Sergei Dinamov that "what I support in the N.R.A.[13] is its result in making Americans conscious, as they have never really been conscious before, of the economic workings of their own country. That it is not enough, I agree, but compared with the abyss of Hoover's administration, for instance, it is certainly something."[14] For orthodox communists, at a time when Third Period policy was branding social democracy as "social fascism," this was at best wishful thinking. Isidor Schneider pointed out to Dreiser in a 1934 review that the New Deal was aimed at saving capitalism, not abolishing it.[15] Selden Rodman's response to Schneider on Dreiser's behalf suggests some of the tensions within the left, and criticizes, backhandedly, the Third Period tactics of disrupting the nonaligned left: "Your implication that Dreiser has swallowed the N.R.A. hook, line and sinker is absolutely untrue. Dreiser is just as basically and completely a Communist as he ever was. But just as he never could have been taken in by the butterfly art of the Left Bank, so he is not impressed when people who consider themselves followers of Lenin break up antifascist meetings.[16] Dreiser has said that Roosevelt is an improvement on Hoover, that his huge budgets are mortgaging away the future of capitalism, that the N.R.A. has given the worker a new incentive to organize and strike. Anyone who denies these things must be as blind as a bat."[17]

An index of the changing political landscape was the new militancy of virulently anticommunist union leaders, such as John L. Lewis, whose Union of Mine Workers of America (U.M.W.) had excluded the Harlan miners and were bitter rivals of the Communist-organized N.M.U. in the early 1930s. Lewis launched new recruitment drives in mining areas and cofounded the militant C.I.O. (Committee for Industrial Organizing). Communists subsequently worked alongside and within the C.I.O., especially after its reconstitution in 1938 as the Congress of Industrial Organizations, a national body in direct rivalry with the A.F.L. As popular pressure thus pushed New Deal Democrats to the left, Dreiser reacted by openly supporting Roosevelt in 1936, albeit with a caveat. "It is with the more liberal and radical parties that my real sympathies lie," he wrote in response to Bruce Bliven's customary enquiry on behalf of the *New Republic*, "but just now, I feel that they are so mismanaged that I cannot support them. Besides this, I do feel that at this election there is such a great difference between the candidates, a difference which is so overwhelmingly in favor of Roosevelt, that it seems of major importance to me that he be elected."[18]

Part of that difference lay in "the foreign relations of this country," which, Dreiser warned, "will need increasingly able handling during the next years." The militarism of the interwar years, along with fears over the security of the Soviet Union and the expansion of the United States's economic and political interests in South and Central America, stoked Dreiser's concern with international relations. He wrote, sometimes using material supplied by the N.C.D.P.P. secretary Joseph Pass and other Communist Party members, on various international problems. Articles for the leftwing and pro-Soviet press deplored American imperialism in Panama and in Chile, condemned the misuse of Red Cross funds to help White Russians, argued against the restoration to Hungary of territory excised after World War I, expressed fears that the Hoover administration saw militarism as a means of escaping the economic crisis, and alleged that American banks and companies were benefiting from selling armaments to Imperial Japan.[19] In general, Dreiser urged the importance of working for international peace and attacked the distortion of foreign policy by the power of the "money lords," who feared the autonomy and example of communist Russia and required markets and resources abroad.[20]

Dreiser always strove to address the widest possible audience, and his political work appeared in a remarkable variety of publications in the 1930s. Across the spectrum of the political left, these included the Communist Party's *Daily Worker* and *Labor Defender*, the Moscow-sponsored *Soviet Russia Today* and *International Literature*, the nonaligned leftwing *Common Sense* and *Modern Monthly*, and the liberal *Nation*. He wrote to the *New York*

Times on general and specific issues,[21] and his appreciation of Sinclair and E.P.I.C. appeared in the pages of *Esquire* magazine. An early version of the *Common Sense* essay "Flies and Locusts" appeared in August 1933 as a column in the *New York Daily Mirror*, substituting for the vacationing Walter Winchell. In 1935 Dreiser published a lengthy five-part essay, "I Find the Real American Tragedy," in *Mystery Magazine*, describing a certain type of murder that was, he argued, caused by the national obsession with wealth and social mobility (see Further Reading). He gives a detailed account of the 1934 murder conviction of Robert Edwards, a case which bore some resemblances to Dreiser's 1925 novel, and pleads for the reform of judicial procedures. Other projects, such as a film based upon the 1907 rebellion of tobacco growers against the Duke tobacco trust, remained unrealized or unpublished.[22]

Dreiser also addressed the mainstream in the *American Spectator*, a "literary newspaper" that he edited jointly with George Jean Nathan, Ernest Boyd, James Branch Cabell, and Eugene O'Neill. During his time on its editorial board from November 1932 to February 1934, Dreiser continually tried to give the *American Spectator* a "left" political agenda. He solicited contributions from, among others, the Labor Research Association, his Russian contact Sergei Dinamov (from whom Dreiser wanted an account of the life of the ordinary Russian worker and "anything" that Stalin might see fit to contribute), the Marxist painter Diego Rivera, and veterans of the Harlan committee such as John Dos Passos and Bruce Crawford, as well as Max Eastman and the technocracy leader Howard Scott.[23] Dreiser explained his strategy of preaching to the unconverted in a June 1933 letter to Dos Passos: "My desire has always been to inject into the paper a spirit of social criticism and also valid arguments in favor of mass dictatorship, and, to quite an extent, I have succeeded with it. The value of this is that social criticism and argument for change in this paper reaches mentally valuable people who are not as readily swayed by the more direct arguments of the Left."[24] This desire remained largely unfulfilled.

Dreiser did publish in the *American Spectator* short articles on reforming the railroads, on education (see "The Child and the School," 175–76), and on birth control, and the monthly ran an account of Tom Mooney's prison experiences signed by the prisoner of sixteen years himself.[25] The *American Spectator*'s ironic detachment—its "clear orientation toward the aesthetic, the ironic, the purely clever," as Dreiser described it to Dos Passos—was deliberately provocative and continues to pose uncomfortable questions. For example, the August 1933 front-page editorial was one of several that deplored the electoral victory of Nazism in Germany: "That recently naturalized German, Herr Adolf Hitler, has undertaken to define Germanism and Aryanism with such a complete disregard for the ascertainable facts of biology, anthropology and German history that one wearily realizes that nothing but a reversal to medieval methods can help him and his followers in an intellectually indefensible position. . . . In brief, we turn back the clock of history, but the smell of tortured, burning flesh, the shadows of the Dark Ages, hang about it still." Dreiser and his coeditors were thus among the first Americans to express unease at fascism's domination of Germany, yet Nazism is the principal target among a range of contemporary religious, political, and economic "dogmas" at which the editorial swipes, including Anglo Catholicism, "devotees of the Strong Man," "the cult of the proletariat," and the "glorification of the American Tractor."

The following month's editorial led to high controversy that has continued to cast a shadow upon Dreiser's reputation. The spark was an "Editorial Conference (With Wine)" published in the September 1933 *American Spectator,* which discussed "the Jewish question" with a mixture of flippancy and seriousness. The writer Hutchins Hapgood wrote to the *American Spectator* editors, accusing them of being reactionary and irresponsible. Dreiser responded forcefully, arguing that Hapgood's avowedly "liberal" position was an inadequate response to the tensions generated by the strength of Jewish ethnic solidarity. While much of Dreiser's argument echoes American Zionism of the period, he expressed concern over the large numbers of unassimilated Jewish immigrants, and he employed the ethnic stereotype of "money-minded" Jews that many regarded as offensive. A second exchange of letters followed in October and December 1933, in which Hapgood accused Dreiser of anti-Semitic prejudice and interpreted his support for a Zionist homeland as a desire for Jews to be expelled from the United States, charges that Dreiser furiously denied. The bulk of this correspondence was eventually published by Hapgood in the 7 April 1935 issue of *The Nation,* under the title "Is Dreiser Anti-Semitic?" The two exchanges of letters are printed in full here, along with Dreiser's statement published in the *New Masses,* addressing the controversy that ensued. Also printed here is Dreiser's June 1936 letter to *The Nation* titled "Mea Culpa." Previously neglected in discussions of Dreiser's alleged anti-Semitism, "Mea Culpa" is a significant part of the historical record. Still rebarbative, Dreiser nevertheless acknowledges what he had previously resisted: the possibility that his argument that Jews should either assimilate to American society or be granted an independent homeland might give succor to those intent on persecuting Jews. In addition, he begins to understand anti-Jewish feeling as being caused by individuals' needs for a "scapegoat," rather than as a direct reaction to Jewish religious and ethnic solidarity. Dreiser's contribution to *"We hold these truths . . . ,"* the American Writers' League 1939 volume protesting against Nazi anti-Semitism, appears in part 4.

From the early 1930s on, Dreiser committed himself to defend the internal and foreign policy of the Soviet Union, evoking Russia variously as achievement, principle, or aspiration. His private letters suggest that he adopted this role out of loyalty to Russia as the best historically existing project of establishing "equity," but both his letters and published work make it clear that he regarded the Russian example as neither sufficient nor infallible. Dreiser's role as a "propagandist" has tended to obscure his deep engagement with the political tensions and contradictions of the 1930s. At one level, Dreiser simply tried to ignore tensions within the left, continuing to work with Eastman and other Trotskyists such as Rose Karsner, and with the technocracy movement, as well as with orthodox communists. In 1933 he seriously considered, but ultimately decided against, joining the condemnation of Stalin's persecutions when invited to do so by Max Eastman. But by 1937, he was publicly expressing doubts and severe criticisms of Soviet Russia, as in his contribution to the *Modern Monthly* symposium "Is Leon Trotsky Guilty" (see 209–11), one of two articles Dreiser published in a magazine that was denounced bitterly and at length in the same issue of *International Literature* that had carried Dreiser's contribution to "Where We Stand" (see 196–99).[26] By December 1937, Dreiser was sufficiently perturbed by the purges within Russia—and by the Communists' persecution of the anarchists, syndicalists, and socialists fighting against fascism in Spain—as to acknowledge in print that "I was strong for Russia and for Stalin and the whole program, but in the last year, I have begun to think that maybe it won't be any better than anything else" (see 212).

Notes

1. Theodore Dreiser, "Dreiser on Scottsboro," *Labor Defender*, June 1931, p. 108.

2. Theodore Dreiser, "Why the *Daily Worker* Should Live," *Daily Worker* (New York), 24 June 1931, p. 4.

3. Theodore Dreiser, "Individualism and the Jungle," *New Masses* 7 (January 1932): 1.

4. William Z. Foster to TD, 17 July 1931, DPUP; Earl Browder to TD, 4 August 1931, DPUP.

5. TD to *Daily Worker*, 2 November 1931, DPUP.

6. TD to Melvin P. Levy, Secretary, National Committee for the Defense of Political Prisoners, 11 April 1932, DPUP.

7. Theodore Dreiser, "What To Do," typescript, DPUP.

8. Theodore Dreiser, "A Suggestion for the Communist Party," typescript, DPUP.

9. See the call for the "socialization" of key economic institutions in "America," (171). Dreiser's most explicit description of his preferred mode of government and social institutions in chapter 22 of *Tragic America* is to an extent modeled on Soviet Russia, but it sidelines the issue of how this transformation may be brought about.

10. TD to Sergei Dinamov, 11 October 1932, DPUP.

11. TD to Rolland H. Hollbrook, 16 July 1934, DPUP.

12. TD to Esther McCoy, 21 June 1933, DPUP.

13. The N.R.A., or National Recovery Administration, instituted by Roosevelt's National Industrial Recovery Act and passed by Congress in May 1933, empowered the government to legislate codes of employment across industry. It was declared unconstitutional by the Supreme Court in 1935 and replaced by the more radical Wagner Act.

14. TD to Sergei Dinamov, 29 November 1933, DPUP. Dreiser's changing hopes are reported in "Dreiser Says N.R.A. is Training Public . . . " *New York Times*, 28 August 1933, in Rusch and Pizer, *Interviews*, 266–67, and "Interview by Allen Chase for Central Press, December 1933," repr. in Rusch and Pizer, *Interviews*, 268–70.

15. Isidor Schneider, "Theodore Dreiser," *Saturday Review of Literature*, 10 (10 March 1934): 533–35.

16. One such incident took place on 16 February 1934, when an antifascist protest meeting in Madison Square Garden, New York, called by the Socialist Party, was broken up by Communist Party sympathizers after they had failed to take it over.

17. Selden Rodman to Isidor Schneider, after 10 March 1934, DPUP.

18. TD to Bruce Bliven, 9 September 1936, DPUP.

19. Theodore Dreiser, "Should Capitalistic United States Treat Latin America Imperialistically," typescript, DPUP; "The Red Cross Brings Poverty and Misery," typescript, DPUP; "Should Hungary Have Been Crunched under Heel," typescript, DPUP; and "War and America," *International Literature* 2–3 (April-June 1932): 110–11.

20. Dreiser, "War and America," 110–11.

21. Theodore Dreiser, "Where Is Labor's Share?" *New York Times*, 13 May 1931, p. 24; "Dreiser Defends Norris on Power," *New York Times*, 2 July 1931, p. 16.

22. The film project, undertaken with Hy Kraft, was called *Revolt* or *Tobacco*. Further examples include "Unemployment in New York," a long 1930 essay criticizing the authorities' failure to provide relief; it was rejected by *The Nation*, which had wanted something shorter and more of a "graphic and pictorial story" like that of Hurstwood in *Sister Carrie* (Dorothy Van Doren to TD, 30 October 1930, DPUP). Dreiser also tried and failed to rally the Hearst newspapers behind the Mooney campaign, already supported by the Scripps-Howard papers (TD to William Randolph Hearst, 24 January 1933, in Elias, *Letters* 2: 621–23).

23. See James T. Farrell, "Introduction" to *American Spectator Numbers 1–21, 1932–34* (New York: Greenwood Reprint Corporation, 1968), n.p.; TD to Robert Dunn, 8 February 1933, DPUP; TD to Sergei Dinamov, 22 September 1932, in Elias, *Letters* 2: 607–8; TD to Diego Rivera, 30 December 1932, in Elias, *Letters* 2: 618–19; TD to Bruce Crawford, 22 September 1932, in Elias, *Letters* 2: 605–6; TD to Max Eastman, 14 June 1933, DPUP; TD to Howard Scott, 17 September 1932, in Elias, *Letters* 2: 601–3.

24. TD to John Dos Passos, 14 June 1933, in Elias, *Letters* 2: 631.

25. Theodore Dreiser, "A Writer Looks at the Railroads," *American Spectator* 1:5 (March 1933): 4; "The Child and the School," 1:6 (April 1933): 2; and "Birth Control," 2:14 (December 1933): 1. Tom Mooney, "Sixteen Years," *American Spectator* 1:4 (February 1933): 1.

26. A. Stork, "Mr. Calverton and His Friends: Some Notes on Literary Trotskyism in America," *International Literature* 3 (July 1934): 97–124.

Further Reading

"Dreiser on Scottsboro." *Labor Defender* 6 (June 1931): 108.

"An Open Letter to the Governor of Alabama." *Labor Defender* 6 (June 1931): 109.

"Why I Believe the Daily Worker Should Live." *Daily Worker* (New York), 4 June 1931, p. 4.

"America and Her Communists." *Time and Tide* 12 (31 October 1931): 1247–48.

"War and America." *International Literature* 2–3 (April—June 1932): 110–11. Reprinted as "America—And War," in *Labor Defender* 8 (August 1932): 143, 157, and *Labor Defender* 8 (September 1932): 169, 175.

"Challenge to the Creative Man." *Common Sense* 2 (November 1933): 6–8.

"What Has the Great War Taught Me?" *New Masses* 11 (7 August 1934): 15.

"Will Fascism Come to America?" Contribution to Symposium, *Modern Monthly* 8 (September 1934): 459–61.

"The Epic Sinclair." *Esquire* 2 (December 1934): 32–33, 178–79.

"I Find the Real American Tragedy." *Mystery Magazine* 11 (February 1935): 9–11, 88–90; (March 1935): 22–23, 77–79; (April 1935): 24–26, 91–92; (May 1935): 22–24, 83–86; (June 1935): 20–21, 68–73. Reprinted in *Resources for American Literary Study* 2 (Spring 1972), 5–74.

"I am Grateful to Soviet Russia." *Soviet Russia Today* 6 (November 1937): 11. Reprinted as "I am Grateful to the Red Marx and Red Russia," in *International Literature* 12 (December 1937), 107–8.

Dreiser Discusses Dewey Plan

New York Telegram, 28 September 1929.

One month before the Wall Street crash, Dreiser echoes calls for a third political party, expressing concern for economic equity and suspicion of media manipulation under the two-party system. The educator and pragmatist philosopher John Dewey (1859–1952) had been sponsoring the establishment of a third party under the auspices of the League for Independent Political Action since 1928. In the 1930s Dewey wrote extensively for political magazines such as the New Republic *and* Common Sense, *supplying the Introduction to the* Common Sense *anthology* Challenge to the New Deal *(1934).*

Considering the old parties and how they function, one would be justified in having small hope for a new one. As it stands today, it looks to me as though the rank and file the world over needs only to be fed with sufficient data of a given color and texture to make them think and act as the devisers of the data desire. In this connection one thing that interests me is the way that Mr. Coolidge, via a well-oiled press service, is being groomed for a third term.[1] So simple a thing as the washing of the family dishpan becomes a national event, important to all voters, while the right of free speech by the same process becomes an ineradicable crime.

Still, being alive and not wishing to sit down and fold my hands, I find myself interested in the idea of a third party, however hopeless. It is possible, even probable, that there are a large number of people who look past the fol-de-rol propaganda that issues so glibly from one source and another to the economic and social conditions by which they find themselves surrounded. If there chances to be a considerable number of these people it would be most interesting and valuable if they could be combined under the leadership of such a man as Dewey, or if not directly under his leadership at least according to his plan.

I am not absolutely sure that economic disaster is to follow the present wave of prosperity,[2] but I am sure of one thing, and that is that very few drops of the large and fascinating wave of prosperity which is so much talked of eventually dribble down to the man at the bottom.[3] As I see him on the streets, in the stores and factories—except for those economic mercenaries and freebooters, the union men—he seems to me as poorly taken care of as ever. He or she tries to get by on 15 or 20 cents for a meal and from $8 to $10 or less per week for a room. Their clothes are nothing to speak of and their labor apparently as arduous as ever. If by some such process as Dr. Dewey outlines the economic fullness of the world could only dribble down a little more nourishingly to the man at the bottom, I for one would be satisfied.

As I have stated and restated and re-restated, the big mind the world over is destined to rule the little one, but, after all, it need not be a swinish big mind. It might wish to see that apart from its own distinction and position, the little fellow at the bottom was at least comfortable and sociologically and in other ways well looked after—about as well looked after, for instance, as a good horse or a tractor, or any animal or thing from which the owner expects profit.

Textual Note: Letter to the Editor, *New York Telegram*, 28 September 1929, p. 4. Printed as "By Theodore Dreiser," with his address, 200 W. 57th St., appended.

1. President Calvin Coolidge (1872–1933) held office from 1923 to 1929. He did not run for a third term in 1928, but speculation continued that he might seek the Republican nomination for the 1932 election.

2. The stock market crashed in late October 1929, one month after this letter was published.

3. According to contemporary figures, in the decade of the 1920s, corporate profits rose by more than 60 percent, industrial production increased 40 percent, but average wages grew by only 10 percent.

John Reed Club Answer

Broadside, June 1930.

The John Reed Club of New York had been started in 1929 to encourage the development of literature, art, and culture sympathetic to communism. Its members included writers and artists such as John Dos Passos (1896–1970), Michael Gold (1893–1967), and Hugo Gellert (1892–1985). In March 1930 Dreiser gave it a statement defending the Soviet Union against a campaign of "moral pressure" orchestrated by Western religious leaders. On 28 May the club cabled Dreiser, asking for a public statement protesting the "current American suppression [of] free speech and assembly." This "Answer" was published as a broadside. Dreiser calls for significant change to address the world economic crisis, admonishing economic and political leaders to end political persecution and instead to devote themselves, alongside "all men of brains," to the benefit of all.

I have been asked by the John Reed Club of New York to express my opinion concerning the present hysterical and all too savage and unreasonable persecution for economic and political opinion everywhere in America. It is as follows:

As everyone knows, there has been by now two centuries of economic and social, or as the phrase runs, material development, not only under the leadership of men of science, but of inventors, statesmen and men of genius in the fields of organization and trade. More recently—and here in America particularly—there has been a tendency for discovery—as well as time and money saving organizations and individuals to (in their productive capacity) outrun the purchasing and even the consuming power of the consumer. Witness this in connection with the development of electricity, gasoline, labor saving devices of all kinds, as well as pleasure giving things such as the automobile, the radio, the phonograph, even the telephone. These privileges and pleasures have come so rapidly to so many that at last not nearly as many as were originally yearly required and in fact struggled for are now needed. In short, over-production. We have become almost too efficient. But—at the very time when industry is almost perfectly fitted to deliver in enormous quantities, reduction in the number of men and women needed to manufacture on the old basis. And so a reduced purchasing power on the part of many—almost all. And so hard times for all who depend not on investments but a steady wage to keep them going. Hence soup kitchens, bread lines, marching crowds descending on mayors and "representatives" generally and a general and irate inquiry as to why this should be.

But in the capitalistic and directive world now functioning almost wholly through various corporations and banks, no desire to do anything but earn more money, or at least to keep things as they were—the corporations and their particular directors and owners contented and even happy. And among the voting poor no economic or political intelligence. And among the politicians, neither brains nor decency in connection with those who elect them to office—only a lively desire to serve those—the corporations of course—who pay them. And so, from those who are unhappy economically, protests—talk of socialism, communism, a desire to do away with the chain stores—and to make the rich corporations carry them or at least help them during the hard times. But on the part of the corporations and their powerful backers and profiteers no such intention. Down with the ignorant, inefficient, idle. Up with the strong, the creative, the capable. And in many directions the notion—most lunatic indeed—that the man who by now has inherited, not earned, a fortune or a part of one, is "capable"—better than the fool who has inherited nothing.

Having used government, the politicians and the peoples' "representatives" generally—to say nothing of their own brains—for the purpose of developing and controlling the enormous and effective corporate and other mechanisms with which we have been busily creating the machine age, the corporations and money owners, their banks and servants do not now propose to see that control slip away—not even modified or weakened in any way—and that in the face of the by now rival economic systems such as communism, socialism, even the small fry individualism of our earlier days, functioning in other lands. Rather, having control of legislatures, the police, the newspapers, the movies, the radio, the railroads, the high priced lawyers and in all too many instances, the courts, they propose to fight in order to stay where they are. And do.

In fact, you may see for yourself how dangerous it has recently become—and that under a government that in its constitution guarantees the right of assembly and free speech and opinion—for anyone to even so much as mention communism, socialism, or, indeed, any local ill whose airing might tend to stir in anyone the notion that the present corporate capitalist system with its individual favorites, is not perfect—that it is not all right for every rich man to will his spineless heir millions of age old economic properties while denying to the underling who comes with nothing (and frequently for the lack of birth control) the right to complain when he is starving. I call your attention to the campaign of Robert Gordon Duncan of Portland, Oregon, against the present evils of the chain store, bank and what-not systems and what befell him in his desire to aid his fellow men;[1] of William Z. Foster, Robert Minor, Harry Raymond and Israel Amter, suffering indeterminate sentences which may run three years in New York for heading a protest march down Broadway without a permit; to Joseph Carr and H. M. Powers, arrested in Atlanta, Georgia, charged with "inciting to insurrection," and that carrying with it the possible penalty of death, for distributing leaflets demanding "work or wages;" to an Ohio court actually sentencing two young girls to ten years in prison for distributing pamphlets; to 137 men and women in Chicago now being tried for sedition for holding an outdoor meeting to discuss unemployment; to 900 unemployed arrested in California for being out of work; to the arrest in Milwaukee on March 6 last, of 58 men and women for making an unemployment demonstration, and in the South, workers being jailed for organizing unions.[2] And yet, the vast mass of American working men and women and the unions as well as the non-unionized white collar brigade, the jobless clerks and office help or those who tomorrow may be jobless, standing by either indifferent or fearfully or willfully silent.

But is this wise, I rise to ask, or fair—any more than is it wise or fair for the stout and entrenched corporations and individuals who have profited by the riches as well as the centuries of labor that have gone before them in this great land to cry no quarter? As I see it, the latter apparently believe that to silence, or if necessary, destroy the protester in times like these, is the way to maintain peace and prosperity, to say nothing of maintaining unmodified their personal prosperity. But is it? For certainly, the sufferers from over-production, as well as greed, are equally sure that to overcome or destroy the selfish self-centered individualist who thinks that mere money is so important to him (him and his brainless heir), is the way to economic existence for them. For certainly the guided worker along with the creative industrial and financial genius made possible the economic and socially prosperous America of today. But can the present day financial masters be made to see this? Can they be made to see that the day of financial or corporate and industrial absolutism is over? Lawyers or no lawyers, courts or no courts, police or no police, the masses today are too intelligent to long be bled for the benefit of a few. The few may not think so, but vast masses of money and huge levers of power are no longer for the unchecked use of the individual. He must and will become an agent of the many, whether he likes it or not. And the wisest and greatest among the individualists today are those who can see this clearly—not those who wish to put down and rule the many. That day is over. A new order is here, and one can see it functioning abroad. For, in Russia, we see one attempt at this solution and despite its lacks, working. And in England, where it is not—misery. But in America, no feeling as yet that a solution is necessary. Yet one is. And it must look to the reduction here and now—and that in a drastic way—of the alleged "right" of any individual, however successful or unsuccessful, to will anything in the way of property or wealth to any other who has not earned it—the abolition of an inheritance entirely. Let each beginner, after care up to the age of sixteen, earn his own way. Also, it may and probably does involve the necessity of birth control on the part of the many; also the right and the need not only to regulate corporations of all kinds and descriptions, but where advisable for the government to operate most if not all of them for the benefit of all of the people—and among some that I consider now ready to be so operated, are the railroads, the express companies (now functioning as an independent arm of government), the light and power companies, the buses and street cars, the telegraph and telephone, and unquestionably, all banks, trust and insurance companies of every description, which, as I see it, should be subsidiaries of the U.S. Treasury. After that might and should come a study of lesser manufacturing and distributing systems as have passed from regional to national stature. Also of the commandeering by the State of all men of brains and their creative energy in order that for a moderate wage, they may direct the great functions of government for the benefit of all. For unquestionably, the honor of so doing is wage sufficient. Aristotle thought so.[3] And so do I. They should, in the new economic arrangement which is to come, be used, not weakened or destroyed, as in Russia and France during the revolution. Rather they—the Rockefellers, Fords, *et. al.*, must be wakened and redirected to this greater opportunity which now confronts them—in short, and as Aristotle pointed out 2000 years ago, made to serve nations the world over—or the world itself for the honor and distinction which would and should come to them as the proper and effective servants of all. For do we not already know that it is not money, but mind, that is the really distinguishing thing in life—not possession, but brains and leadership. And cannot our economic leaders and barons be made to see that? What? Will they quarrel and wait until it is too late? I wonder! Americans are facing a world economic crisis. The hands of the clock of time point to a great change.

But meanwhile, this persecution for political and economic opinion—and this in the face of economic misery—must cease. It is not only unconstitutional here in America, but unethical and mean, and worse—idiotic! It can only inflame the masses to concerted and more than likely unwise and destructive reprisal. And who wishes that? For those who are peaceably seeking to exercise freedom of opinion, assembly and speech, whatever their views, are right. And those, who in the face of their suffering deny them these, are wrong. In sum, it is time that the world's creative economic geniuses everywhere now sit down together and take counsel in regard to the new necessities—the new order they imply—some new way of living our economic and social lives. And the men of wisdom and genius in economics, politics, direction and education, will be those who will now think what next best thing to do—however drastic the change—not to decide to fire on the ignorant, the weak, the hopeless or the defeated. Only fools and evil-doers will counsel that or stand back and announce that all is well and that there can be no change. For there can and will be change. It is here. And all courageous thinking men and women everywhere should now step forward and demand that there be thought—and after thought, action toward ushering in the new day—not merely stubborn and angry and blind use of force on both sides. The ostrich's head must come out of the sand.

Textual Note: Broadside, headed Portland, Oregon, June 10, 1930, with Dreiser's name at the foot. A manuscript draft (DPUP folder 13339) was modified slightly in revision.

1. Robert Gordon Duncan, "the Oregon Wildcat," attacked chain stores, banks, corporate businesses, and businessmen on K.V.E.P. radio, Portland. He was fined and jailed for violating the 1927 Radio Act, which prohibited "knowingly, unlawfully, willingly, and feloniously uttering obscene, indecent, and profane language by means of radio communication." The terms at issue were "damned," describing a person, and the exclamation "By God." Duncan was the first person to be convicted and to serve a federal sentence for public broadcast utterances. Dreiser returns to his case in "Mooney and America," (see 128–29).

2. Dreiser lists various protests against the distress caused by the Great Depression, many related to the "International Unemployment Day" declared by the Communist Party for 6 March 1930, and the repressive official responses. Leading Communist Party members William Z. Foster (1881–1961), Robert Minor (1884–1952), Harry Raymond, and Israel Amter (1881–1954) were arrested after police rushed a protest meeting in Union Square, New York, as protesters began to move down Broadway to City Hall. Foster, Minor, and Amter would serve six months in jail; Raymond ten. "Work or wages for the unemployed" was a Communist Party slogan of the time. Dreiser expands upon this paragraph in "Mooney and America," (see 129).

3. In his *Politics* the Greek philosopher Aristotle (384–322 BCE) argues for the importance of a small group of legislators, or political advisers, who, acting out of "virtue," help resolve the political tensions of the state. Dreiser's embrace of this idea differs substantially from Marxist thought and Communist Party policy in the 1930s, though arguably there are parallels with William Z. Foster's vision of Communist political leadership. The idea that a cadre of experts should curb the wasteful and inequitable tendencies of capitalism appears, with political overtones varying from progressivism to communism to technocracy, in Dreiser's support for figures such as Caroline Bartlett Crane in the 1900s, and later in *Tragic America*, "Challenge to the Creative Man" (1933), and "Epic Technologists Must Plan" (1936).

Mooney and America

Hesperian (San Francisco), Winter 1930.

This article was commissioned by the Scripps-Howard Newspapers as part of a campaign to free the I.W.W. activists Tom Mooney and Warren K. Billings, who had been convicted of bombing the San Francisco Preparedness Day Parade on 22 July 1916. The continued imprisonment of Mooney and Billings long after the prosecution's key witnesses had admitted perjury became a cause célèbre of American civil liberties. In "American Idealism and German Frightfulness" (see part 2), Dreiser included Mooney's name in his list of evidence disproving the existence of democracy in America. From 1929 Dreiser campaigned to secure Mooney's exoneration and release. He corresponded with Mooney and visited him in jail several times, wrote letters to successive state governors and to sympathetic celebrities such as James Cagney and Douglas Fairbanks, spoke at a "Free Tom Mooney" rally in November 1932, and contributed to two pamphlets on the case. The February 1933 American Spectator ran an article attributed to Mooney, describing his prison experiences. Mooney and Billings were finally pardoned and released in 1939, having served twenty-two years.

I am not at all interested in restating the Mooney-Billings case or why Tom Mooney should be set free. The facts have been so freely rehearsed in the past ten years at least that in one sense they constitute a chestnut. What really does interest me is the indifference—the really Imperial Roman indifference—of almost the entire body of American citizens to any and every type of ill that befalls any and every other than themselves—the voiceless indifference with which they stand by while others fail or fall so long as they themselves are comfortable or are being entertained in some ridiculous or inane way. *Vae Victis*.[1] Let the individual beware.

Is it a new trial for a pair of poverty-stricken Italians such as Sacco and Vanzetti ignorantly and blindly protesting against ills which they believe to be great? To the deuce with Sacco and Vanzetti—a pair of anarchist wops. The papers do not make the matter exactly clear. Anyhow they are Italians; they are charged with murder; and so they were hanged; very likely they are guilty; Let's go to the ball game.[2]

Is it the case, say, of Robert Gordon Duncan of Portland, Oregon, who, engaged in the business of showing up the malpractices of the chain stores of his region, was never attached for libel or false witness by the chain stores or newspapers who carried their advertising but rather "laid for" and lurked after until at last infuriated by their espionage as well as their indifference editorially, he chose to make a few insufficiently substantiated personal charges whereupon—whoop-la—out rushes the entire personnel of local editorial and legal machinery of the city and he is laid by the heels and made to pay dearly. But for what he said and offered to prove in connection with the chain stores and their methods? Don't be so dumb! Only for what he said against the individuals who were so calmly indifferent to his charges against the chain stores and their methods. That and that alone. The chain stores as well as the newspapers (who for advertising reasons could afford to blink at the evils of the chain stores) could go unwhipped of justice—

but not Mr. Duncan who could say that there was probably this and that reason for their silence. And so punishment for him—or at least arrests and trials—non-suited at last for lack of radio laws, the while the ones he denounced yelped loudest for his undoing as an unbelievable scoundrel.[3]

But do you think that this and this alone is that to which the American people is so indifferent? Consider the case of the Minnesota Gag Law—a state statute recently enacted which declares that any paper or publication which regularly publishes malicious, scandalous, and defamatory matter is a *nuisance which may be suppressed by application of the injunction process.* And already one newspaper, The *Press,* restrained from publication as a nuisance. And that restraint or suppression affirmed by the State Supreme Court from which there is no appeal save to the United States Supreme Court—yet to be heard from two years hence, say. So much for a free press.[4]

Or let us take the case of Yetta Stromberg, a former University of California student sentenced very recently to from six months to ten years in San Quentin prison for raising a red flag over a camp of workers' children in the San Bernardino Mountains last summer. And the California Supreme Court has now refused to even hear the appeal of her case![5]

Or that of William Z. Foster, Robert Minor, Harry Raymond, and Israel Amter, suffering indeterminate sentences which may run three years in New York for heading a protest march down Broadway without a permit; or that of Joseph Carr and H. M. Powers, arrested in Atlanta, Georgia, charged with "inciting to insurrection," and that carrying with it the possible penalty of death, for distributing leaflets demanding "work or wages;" or that of the Ohio court which actually sentenced two young girls to ten years in prison for distributing pamphlets; or that of the 137 men and women in Chicago recently tried for sedition for holding an outdoor meeting to discuss unemployment; or that of 900 unemployed arrested in California for being out of work; or again that of the arrest in Milwaukee on March 6 last, of 58 men and women for making an unemployment demonstration, or that of the various workers in the South and elsewhere being jailed for organizing unions.[6]

And yet as I say, the vast mass of American men and women, the unions, as well as the non-unionized white collar brigade, the jobless clerks and office help or those who tomorrow may be jobless, as well as those who have plenty but no particular bank or trust affiliations, all standing by either indifferent or fearfully or willfully silent. Not interested. Not even capable of thinking on such matters, perhaps. Yet this is a government whose welfare as well as persistence as a valuable economic and sociologic experiment demands that people do think—that they be not indifferent to the power-seeking of a selfish few; that they avoid if possible, the chains of a financial autocracy already too anxious to enslave them.

Mooney? To be sure Mooney. But he and Billings are but two other illustrations of a tragic social drift toward which almost the entire voting body of America is indifferent. Mooney. Oh yes. Yetta Stromberg. Oh yes. The Minnesota *Press*? Oh yes. The three hundred convicts burned in the Ohio State Penitentiary for the want of decent social service! Oh yes. Robert Gordon Duncan. Oh yes.

But to quote the *Philadelphia Record* which kindly sends me an editorial in which it disposes of my complaints completely, "though the trust movement began 60 years ago, the condition of the workers and the *progress of social legislation* have seen betterment." Also, "We know too, that in pooling resources, in the very building of a complex civilization we have weapons for progress in our hands." And it adds, "They promise great things."

My answer is "We have?" Also "They do?" But promise is one thing and performance is another. And may I add this: No class ever had power without abusing it.

In an earlier paragraph in the same editorial the *Record* says;

"To deny that private enterprise has been handicapped, to deny that public opinion is molded whenever possible to selfish ends by those who can profit most from the change, would be foolhardy."

Well.

Must I plead for Mooney? Let me rather plead for my entire land—a social dream that was and is now nearing its close. And for what reasons? Ignorant and selfish and brutal individualism on the part of a few. And the idle and indifferent and ignorant pleasure-seeking on the part of that vast majority that thinks that religion or life or some kind-hearted person or thing is going to do something for it.

Yes?

Well, wait and see.

Textual Note: Article commissioned by the Scripps-Howard Newspapers in June 1930; Dreiser completed it by mid-August (Harry E. Barnes to TD, 27 June 1930 and 14 August 1930, DPUP folder 5552). Published in *Hesperian* (San Francisco) 1 (Winter 1930): 2–4. DPUP folder 12213 contains a holograph manuscript (12 pages), a typescript (4 pages), and a revised typescript (4 pages). The revised typescript is used as the copy-text.

1. Latin for "woe to the vanquished."

2. Nicola Sacco (1891–1927) and Bartolomeo Vanzetti (1888–1927), Italian immigrants with strong anarchist beliefs, were convicted of the May 1920 murder of a paymaster and a guard in a robbery at a shoe factory in South Braintree, Massachusetts. For many American writers, including Upton Sinclair, Malcolm Cowley, Edna St. Vincent Millay, and Katherine Anne Porter, their case symbolized the corrosive effects of prejudice against radicals and immigrants on the judicial system. Sacco and Vanzetti were electrocuted in August 1927.

3. See "John Reed Club Answer," n1. Duncan's conviction under the obscenity terms of the Radio Act was upheld by the U.S. Appeals Court in March 1931.

4. See also "Silencing of Press by Gag Laws Flayed by Dreiser," *Progressive* (Madison, WI) 2 (23 May 1930): 1. The suppression of the Minnesota-based *Saturday Press* was finally lifted in June 1931 by a majority decision of the United States Supreme Court, as Dreiser would note in *Tragic America,* 161.

5. Yetta Stromberg (1910–?) had been convicted under a 1919 California statute banning the display of the red flag. The United States Supreme Court overturned the conviction in 1931 by a landmark decision extending the Constitutional guarantee of freedom of speech to symbolic speech.

6. See "John Reed Club Answer," n2.

On the Communists and Their Platform

October 1930.

A statement for the John Reed Club detailing Dreiser's views on the 1930 elections, which was released to the press.

I believe that the present crisis has revealed the complete inadequacy of the present major political parties. Their unwillingness to meet, or even to acknowledge, unemployment and starvation except for party and political advantage, reveals a corruption deeper than that of the widespread misuse of public funds and the graft which is apparently almost universal. This corruption strikes me as a cynical willingness to represent only the interests of the financially entrenched.

I believe, too, that the inability of Governor Roosevelt to act decisively in the present revelations of pure political corruption in New York City makes it impossible for any conscientious person to put his trust in any individual working within these parties.[1]

Unemployment appears to have been forced on the attention of the people of this state and the nation not by either of the old parties but by the activities of the Communist Party and its sympathizers. Such patchwork relief as has been offered or achieved and all wholly inadequate, appears to have followed upon the activities of the above group. More, the labor injunction which threatens the whole existence of American labor organization at this time is apparently being fought only by the Communists.[2]

For this reason, and without insisting upon my agreement with the larger aims of the Communist Party, I feel that its candidates and program represent the only current political value worth supporting.

Textual Note: Typescript (1 page), signed in typescript "Theodore Dreiser," in DPUP folder 11983. Title and date, "On the Communists & their Platform/October—1930" added in pencil in Dreiser's hand.

1. A reference to criticisms of Franklin D. Roosevelt's dependence on the corrupt Tammany Hall machine for his gubernatorial reelection campaign.

2. The Communists were campaigning against the use of court injunctions to forbid union organization and activities such as strikes, picketing, and demonstrations. The use of injunctions in this way would be outlawed by the Norris-La Guardia Act in 1932.

The American Press and American Political Prisoners

Daily Worker (New York), 9 May 1931.

Published under the editorial title "'Free the Class War Prisoners in Boss Jails' — Dreiser," this essay for the Communist Party daily newspaper articulates Dreiser's anger at the repression of labor unrest and his sense that "Communists alone" were defending ordinary Americans during the depths of the Great Depression.

What comprises the bulk of the present mass of so-called "political prisoners" in our American penitentiaries? Are they Communist labor organizers? They are! In jail? Yes! But why? If you were to trouble to look you would turn up an interesting fact, and this is that the American newspapers, mostly corporation-owned or directed, scarcely mention these cases, let alone concern themselves deeply enough to let their readers know a whit of the new greatest issue of American economic life—capitalism versus labor!

In fact, as I see it, it is the Communists, and the Communists alone, who today heed this issue solemnly enough. They and they alone, assert that economic slavery, not economic independence, has followed the growth of our enormous corporations and trusts—not the American Federation of Labor, which in my estimation, is, on the one hand, a joke, and on the other, a menace. For like all corporations, its various unions and their locals here and everywhere in America, work not for the betterment of labor in general but for the special aggrandizement of small closely-knit groups of labor grafters in particular.[1] And as for formulating and forwarding valuable economic social principles, they do not know what the words mean and do not care.

In fact, I here assert, and without fear of honest contradiction, that it is the Communists, and the Communists alone, who realize that American labor—principally non-unionized—is made the goat of corporation aspirations and the billionaires' dreams of more billions. Communist research workers—not newspaper reporters of leading or important papers, or socialists, or intellectuals, or liberals, or this or that—know, for instance, that the cotton pickers in the South receive only a dollar a day for twelve hours work, and the Jones and Laughlin Steel Corporation of Pennsylvania drives its workers twelve hours a day seven days a week at a wage of forty or fifty cents an hour. To this one group alone, such things as graft, peon-age, arrest for lack of employment when and where there are no jobs, are serious matters.

To them and to them only this constitutes capitalist anarchy. They pro-test and fight while these corporations hold their employees to low wages by selling them maybe one-half of one per cent investments in the companies that invariably take for themselves the other ninety-nine and one-half per cent and build lunatic corporation bubbles which finally end in such pan-ics as 1907 and 1929. What a dub, what a trudging numbskull must be the average worker to be so fooled and abused without riot and civil war!

Communists Alone Fight Bosses

Communists, and Communists alone these days, appear to know and pub-lish accounts of corporation power and the abuses traceable to the same. I see that by reading their papers. They see, and publish, for instance, that field workers of the southwest, their backs loaded and under heat from which many die of sunstroke, and at the same time receiving a wage of only twenty-five or thirty-five cents an hour, haven't a chance in a strike, because the Southern Pacific of that great region herds carloads of scabs into those great areas of Southern California, Arizona, New Mexico and Texas, to help break any protest they may make.

They (the Communists) have seen—and not only have seen but shown—how corporations not only try but do circumvent the proper organization of labor by encouraging total segregation of races in separate living quarters and then playing one race off against the other; as for instance, inducing the Mexicans of Imperial Valley to work in the melon fields for less money because, according to lies they spread, the Filipinos had already accepted a cut, and thereby engendering a race hatred which had no reason in fact but strengthened the position of the corporation. Here too, corporations, great landowners and hence contractors, hold back twenty-five per cent of the wages until the end of the season, and often escape with the money or give as an excuse for no pay a poor crop or drought. In this way they guar-antee the picking of the whole crop. Wouldn't it be as fair for the laborers to demand a bond or twenty-five per cent advances of their prospective pay in order to guarantee them against discharge before the crop was in? But labor, penniless and ignorant, must take what is handed it!

But if our American newspapers know these things, they prefer to ignore them and print instead inane details of fake relief for the unemployed. And yet collectively, labor is America, and without it, where would all the newspapers, corporations, bankers, financiers, and their leeches, the heirs to unearned fortune and incomes, be, I wish to ask?[2]

Yet, in the face of these known abuses, and when and where capital profits so inordinately today, when labor leaders call strikes, merely to gain a living wage, an eight hour day, and clean living conditions, they are thrown into jail, and there they stay for from three to forty-two years or from two to twenty-eight years—and there they may be kept for the entire length of the longest end. And all you have to do to bring that about is to cry Communist or Communism, and to declare that a land that was originally dedicated to liberty and equality of opportunity is being undermined. But by whom? Certainly not by the Communists, who are seeking to bring about that proper equation between strength and weakness, ignorance and wisdom, which has been the dream of philosophers, thinkers and humanitarians throughout the ages![3]

Capitalist Press Fights against Release of Class War Prisoners

And our great newspapers, like the *Los Angeles Times* (controlled by western corporations) now aim violent attacks against the release of these long term political prisoners, whose only offense is their desire to better labor conditions.[4]

In order to railroad leaders to jail in this way, though, evidence is always framed up by private detectives who spy on them, and after that, our American courts almost the land over knowingly accept such testimony. Worse, stool pigeons, such as those from the Bolling Detective Agency, who were called into this Imperial Valley case by the corporations there interested, sent the Communist labor leaders to prison.[5] Private police, hired and paid by corporations, helped to send the three Communist workers of Woodlawn, Pennsylvania, to jail. And there are innumerable additional instances. But Communists declare and justly, that this whole corporation private police and spy system should be outlawed, and what is more they are fighting to that end.

Yet in none of the hundreds of issues of the successful and widely distributed American newspapers which I have read for me, do I meet with an editorial attacking the private police system now in force, or indeed any of these shameful ills.

Rather it is always the corporations and their "rights" and plans to further debase the ordinary American clerk and laborer that are glossed over and themselves made to appear the patrons of a better life, rather than the sappers and underminers to destruction that they really are. And like the corporations, these papers and their editors and subsidizers are traitors to the original intention of this government and as such, should be tried and punished.

But to return to these Communist political prisoners. Why are they in jail? What have they done? Organized labor unions! But what of that? Is it a crime to anyone other than a grafting corporation for laborers to attempt to organize? I hold not! For that, though, men are imprisoned today in California, Pennsylvania, and elsewhere.

A Crime to Organize for Better Conditions

In the South, labor leaders are facing the electric chair for this supposed crime. Belonging to a labor union and attending its meetings is sufficient, in the Imperial Valley, according to the capitalists who rule America to warrant the arrest and brutal chaining together of 108 laborers! And in this, a country where American Federation of Labor unions and strikes are held to be in no way illegal.

But the corporations, beating up organized strikers and stopping their food supply, do not fear any laws. They are the law! And the newspapers that today know this well enough are silent. If they do anything at all, it is to soft-pedal the bitter abuses of which they know so much. And always, always they are busy publishing fictitious accounts of the plots of workers for the blowing up of plants and bridges, in order to stir up public opinion against the laborer and give the corporations excuses, in the eyes of the public, to hire more police and act more viciously.

But lastly, just how does the government decide that these labor leaders are criminal? Well, a number of the states have alien and sedition laws. But just what is "sedition"? Legally, it is incitement to discontent against the government. But mere discontent is certainly not a crime. The whole idea of democracy is supposed to be based on the right of the people to manage their government, and when their servants or officials misbehave, to protest and punish the misbehavior. But let a Communist say that today! Yet actually sedition, under its strictest definition, is no more than a commotion amounting not even to insurrection.

And what a negligible thing that should be! How really creditable and justifiable! But sedition as our corporation-controlled government sees it, does not even require an overt act. One can be arrested for nothing. Yet actually, if sedition is to be charged as a crime, it should tend to treason. But "tending" is something too vague, and is therefore not a just basis for criminal law.

Yet these criminal laws remain, constantly creating political prisoners, like Ray Peltz, sentenced in Pennsylvania for distributing pamphlets to a term of from one to twenty years imprisonment. Probably twenty years imprisonment for merely distributing pamphlets! And these sedition cases, like those of the three Communists of Woodlawn, the Supreme Court of the United States refuses even to review.[6] Yet would or do any of our great American chain newspaper corporations permit a single one of their hundreds of dailies in various cities to print a sincere attack on the basis and absolute unfairness of our sedition laws? You know not. Financially that paper would become taboo.

Criminal Syndicalist Laws an Instrument of the Bosses

As I see it, the vicious criminal syndicalism laws now in force are also as bad as those against sedition. Criminal syndicalism laws take in Communists. Why? Because these statutes apply in cases of merely advocating. No act, mind you! But advocating what? A change in governmental control through unlawful force? But what nonsense! No force that is unlawful is being used in America today. Addressing meetings, advocating a change in government or arranging such meetings, or protesting against such evils as have already undermined and subverted our government are not illegal. They are merely called so by savage, unlawful officials who take their orders from our dominant corporations. And none other.

And though Communists with labor behind them may hope to rule America, that is not, as I see it, unlawful but entirely lawful—the will (if it is the will) of those who constitute a majority. And I also believe that Communistic laws, adapted to American needs, would certainly effect the desired purpose of the Communists—a government helpful not only to farmers and to workers, but to all. And should that be looked upon as unreasonable or criminal? And should it not be arrived at peaceably? I think so.

But will this program be permitted in America? I doubt it. The corporation or capitalist everywhere today is sold to the idea that its or his reward—the reward for getting and keeping money, by whatever means or crimes—cannot be too great, whereas that of the individual without money—laborer or thinker—cannot be too little. But this is the real outrage and the great crime.

The rewards of the individual, where he is cunning and anti-social, as well as his corporation and his bank are already too great. He has come to set himself up as a ruler, not only of the lesser individual but of the government itself—the machinery and the voice of all the people—and should here and now be put in his proper place. He does not deserve to, and cannot wisely or kindly, use all of his wealth and power, and will not. And therefore it is time, since he has been endowed enough by nature with health and skill (all of which he did not and could not create) that he be compelled to share more equally the fruits of his ability with those who make the world and the condition in and by which alone he is able to function and become what he is. And if he cannot be made to see that, none-the-less—he can be forced to do that. And that is what the Communists of the world today desire, and it is exactly that that eventually they will achieve.

But suppose now, in order to be rid of this ill, the Communists do combine and by reason of superior numbers and their voting or man power decide to take over and change this government. But sure that all capitalists will call it sedition, treason, revolution, the evil and criminal overthrow of the United States. But is the United States principally composed of these laborers or of its corporations? As the capitalists see it today, the right to revolt—apparently—depends on who is doing it—not only any wrongs that may be holding or the suppression of the many in favor of the few, but rather the elevation of the few as against the misery of the many. So it comes about that it is quite all right for banks and corporations to effect a revolution in Panama, but not for the laborer and the Communist here.[7] Not on your life!

Smash the New Siberian Exile System!

Straws show how the wind blows. The *San Diego Sun* recently printed an article stating that the way to kill the Communist plague is to dynamite it out. In other words, kill those who advocate reasonable changes under that name. And corporations are violently fighting Communists and their labor leaders because they find them practical men who organize, fight and print instead of talking. Yet the scholar and theorist—still bolstered by a few safeguards—a job with some college, money, family, and the like, may talk and think, have his ideas printed in leading dailies and discussed by intellectuals. Let a Communist or ordinary laborer talk or strike or distribute a pamphlet, explaining in some rough and perhaps uncouth way identically the same political ideas or facts now distributed by many intellectuals—scholars and college professors included—and to prison he goes, and for twenty years.

But why? Because capitalism resents any thought or stirring on the part of labor; since that indicates the day is not far distant when the strong and the ambitious will have to take less—a fair reward, and the laborer will get nearer what is his due—food, clothing, fairly certain employment, a reasonable opportunity along with others to educate himself and to rest when he needs to. Is that too much? I do not see it. Yet it is from the discussion of these issues by laborers and their leaders that flow the thousands of arrests today and the scores of political prisoners. Hence our present-day American terror—our new Siberian exile system here![8]

Textual Note: Published in *Daily Worker* (New York), 9 May 1931, p. 6, under the editorial title "Free the Class War Prisoners in Boss Jails—Dreiser" and heading "The American Press and Political Prisoners." Preserved in DPUP folder 12245 are two typescript carbons titled "Our American Press and Our Political Prisoners" (each 9 pages) with revisions in Dreiser's hand, and another clean carbon copy typescript incorporating the revisions (10 pages); all are signed "Theodore Dreiser" in typescript. In addition to the added title, the text published in the *Daily Worker* includes further subheadings, corrects factual errors such as the dating of the stock market crash, standardizes Dreiser's terminology, introduces a small number of transcription errors, and makes some minor deletions. It does not incorporate the handwritten revisions on the typescripts. The historical *Daily Worker* text is selected as the copy-text, emended for transcription errors. Significant additional passages from the typescripts are given in the notes. The title "The American Press and American Political Prisoners" is supplied by Dreiser's handwritten revision to his clipping of the published version in DPUP folder 12038, and it is accepted as embodying his final intention.

1. Dreiser is probably thinking of the A.F.L.'s no-wage-cut-no-strike agreement with business leaders in November 1929, which enabled employers to cut the wages of nonunionized workers.

2. Dreiser puts this more strongly in typescript: "And yet collectively, labor *is* America, and yet without it, where would all the newspapers, corporations, bankers, financiers, and their leeches, the heirs to unearned fortunes and incomes, be? And why in hell can't they see this? I rise to ask!"

3. The following additional passage appears at this point in Dreiser's revised typescript: "Yet Americans, some of whom have been trying for years to get some of these labor leaders out of jail before the expiration of the unjust final dates of their sentences, have not as yet learned that under no circumstances should any labor or alien or sedition law have a time range of more than five years!"

4. The following additional passage appears at this point in Dreiser's revised typescript: "But our American people, and what is to be expected of them! Any economic or social understanding? To me they appear to be as dull as rabbits or moles. To me, force reigns, force and cruel, criminal and lunatic ambition which has not the least notion as to where it is going or what it really desires, though I can tell. It is going—willy-nilly—toward the general betterment of mankind and whether it likes that or not or thinks I am a fool or not."

5. Six Communist organizers among the fruit workers of Southern California had been sentenced to from 3 to 42 years in San Quentin under California's criminal syndicalism law.

6. Four Communists of Woodlawn, Pennsylvania, were convicted under the Pennsylvania Sedition Act after "seditious" literature was found in a police raid in 1926. They were sentenced to five years imprisonment.

7. Dreiser discussed the United States-backed overthrow of President Arosemena and the installation of Harmodio Arias in Panama in the article "The Right to

Revolution," (typescript, DPUP), which opens: "The right to revolution, in America as elsewhere, depends entirely on who wants the change of government. Certainly a bouffe revolution can be staged—as it just recently has been in Panama—for no other reason than that American banks and corporations were not satisfied with the existing government. Yet if Americans, slaving in mills ten and twelve hours a day, criticize the United States government because everything is so tied up that the laborer receives only a starvation wage, the criticism is 'seditious' and brings with it a prison sentence for as long as forty years."

8. Exile in the cold, northern area of Siberia was an infamous sanction of Tsarist Russia, as punishment for offenses such as theft and as a means of political or ethnic persecution. A similar practice was utilized under Stalin. The words "But why don't they arrest me?" are penciled at the end of Dreiser's second typescript.

Speech on the Scottsboro Case

June 1931.

The case of the "Scottsboro boys," nine young African Americans convicted by all-white juries and sentenced to death on weak and contradictory evidence, became one of the most notorious examples of racial injustice in the post-Reconstruction South. Haywood Patterson (1913–52), Clarence Norris (1912–89), Charles Weems (1911–?), Andy Wright (1911–?), Ossie or Ozie Powell (1916–?), Olen Montgomery (1914–?), Eugene Williams (1918–?), Willie Roberson (1915–?), and Roy Wright (1918–59), were accused of raping two white women, Victoria Price (1911–82) and Ruby Bates (1915–76) on the Southern Railroad Chattanooga-to-Memphis freight train on 25 March 1931. They were tried in April at Scottsboro, the county seat of Jackson, Alabama, in an atmosphere of extreme racial intimidation (the National Guard was called in to prevent a mob of ten thousand people from lynching the accused). Eight of the nine were sentenced to be electrocuted, and a mistrial was declared in the case of twelve-year-old Roy Wright. As the N.A.A.C.P. hesitated, the Communist Party, already involved in antilynching campaigns in the South, organized the boys' appeal and legal defense through its auxiliary, the International Labor Defense (I.L.D.). A convoluted legal process ensued, during which convictions in Alabama alternated with successful appeals to the United States Supreme Court. Eventually, after the I.L.D. had lost sole control of the defense, a controversial deal was made whereby four of the Scottsboro boys were released in 1937, but the others would remain in Alabama jails—the last, Andy Wright, until 1950.

Dreiser became involved in the Scottsboro campaign as founding chair of the I.L.D.-linked National Committee for the Defense of Political Prisoners, which viewed Scottsboro as "our immediate issue in our fight against the present epidemic of racial, industrial, and political persecutions in our country."[1] In May 1931 he authorized an open letter from the N.C.D.P.P. to Alabama Governor Meeks

Miller, describing the original verdicts as "a lynching concealed in the forms of law" and asking for a retrial. The letter was printed in the Communist monthly Labor Defender *for June 1931, opposite "Dreiser on Scottsboro," a one-page article whose theme of understanding the case by reference to the history of white racism is developed in more detail in this speech. Originally scheduled for a meeting in New York's Town Hall on 5 June 1931 (which Dreiser failed to attend), it was published in Nancy Cunard's* Negro Anthology *in 1934.*

I believe that light may come upon this Scottsboro case only by considering it from the point of view of the Negro question in the large. The Negroes, whom I do not believe to be an inferior race,[2] were viciously enslaved through outside instigation during the early days of this country. The United States as a whole, particularly the North, felt that holding and driving these humans was not in keeping with advanced standards of freedom, opportunity, and decent living. A tremendous sympathy and humanity welled up for the American Negro! Later, and as a result of the Civil War, the country tried to force this attitude upon the South. Unfortunately, attitudes not in accord with custom or mood are forced upon any people with difficulty. For that reason, the South changed little from the pre–Civil War slave standards under which they were brought up and to which they were accustomed. The drastic old slave codes of the 1830's were, after emancipation, remodeled in only a minor way. Though the Constitution gave Negroes the right to vote, this was early evaded by clauses denying this privilege to all except those whose grandfathers had voted before the Civil War. Since illiteracy has always been great, if not complete, among dominated Negroes, the voting requirement that persons must read and write has deprived hundreds of thousands. Private coercion as well put down almost every small privilege permitted at law.

These harsh statutes, and the vicious subjection of the Negro who has always been inhumanly exploited in the South, endure until this hour. And yet, I wonder if today it is not more a matter of custom rather than of real angry thought or feeling.[3] We are all so prone to continue a custom or habit long after the reason for it has been forgotten. At present, Negro tenants are held to the land by scores of brutal laws, and law enforcement tactics further forced labor and peonage.[4] Even the industrial Negro, at his first concern for his own welfare, is treated with violence. Because of its common training, the mass, united and strong, as well as the intellectuals who sit above and direct it, hold to the conviction that the Negro race is intended by Nature or God or something[5] to be an underprivileged one.

Yet these enormous class gulfs provoke a psychology terrific in its possibilities for cruelty and evil, and in its turn this becomes the very rock-bed of mob rule and mob horror. But why? Our Negro Americans did not come here. They were forced here. And since coming, have worked and worked well and peaceably. As I see them, they are the least destructive and actually the most law-abiding of all our mixed peoples.

And yet, the entire sociological background of the South today remains against them, and has a direct bearing on this Scottsboro case. The severe law, for instance, inflicting the death penalty for rape, is, in itself, a commentary on what I mean. It is so definitely aimed at the Negro male, and so very lenient to his white equivalent, who miscegenates without serious opposition.[6] But mixing the blood of a white man with that of a black woman is certainly as bad as mixing the blood of a black man with that of a white woman. The difference is that of tweedledee and tweedledum. But is the white man hanged for rape? Or do white mobs gather together to see that he is hanged? Yet this latest alleged black outrage has excited the minds of the people of the whole region adjacent to Scottsboro. The psychology of the South concerning white girls, reported alone with colored men, as they were in this case, leaves no doubt of rape to those who see the imminence of rape in the mere proximity of the two races. Black is black and white is white, and the one shall be the slave of the other. During the trials of these nine Negro boys in Scottsboro, for instance, people so fiercely believed rape had been committed, and so wanted this vicious so-called justice, founded on their prejudice, that hooting and yelling and rejoicing and applauding not only followed the verdict of death, but this outcome of one trial was being uproariously cheered while the jury for another of these boys was behind closed doors deciding as to their verdict. But is it not obvious that these 10,000 people in the yard outside the courthouse, tumultuous in their mob-unity, and with bands of music blaring forth their conception of what was fair and necessary, made the trials of the remaining Negro defendants only slightly above a lynching in the ordinary sense of the word?[7]

The entire trial, as I see it, its brevity and fierceness, showed all too plainly the underlying class viciousness of the South. I now consider that these Negro lads were convicted more on prejudice than on the evidence brought against them by the State. For one thing, a number of points were made as to who was colored and who was not.[8] The testimony which caused eight of them to receive the death sentence, was that of Ruby Bates and Victoria Price, whom they were supposed to have raped.[9] Neither of these girls made any charges until confronted by excited townspeople—and apparently forced by officials. A doctor testified that although on the day of the alleged rape at the first examination they were calm, at the second one, and by the time they had been pumped and cross-questioned insistently, they were greatly unnerved. I believe that this came from being forced to

The *Labor Defender*'s front cover gives visual form to
Dreiser's charge that the case of the Scottsboro boys
was "a lynching concealed in the forms of law."

say what was not so, or what the two girls could not agree upon. Then, too,
what little intercourse occurred, especially with Victoria Price (all somewhat
indefinite as to time), was not of such a nature as to cause either of the girls
any bodily wounds at all—only a few little bruises. Victoria Price testified
that she didn't scream, and that she delayed getting off the train until she
wanted to.[10]

Furthermore, as I learn, these two girls are reputed to be lacking in moral
discretion.[11] From reading their testimony, I know that they are ignorant,
and the older one hard-boiled and racy. The fact that these girls were in
overalls and alone on a freight train, made the very nature of their situation

provocative. Ruby Bates testified that white boys were on the train to Chattanooga the day before the alleged crime, and also when she and Victoria returned the next afternoon, white fellows hopped a car in the same city. As she said on the witness stand, Victoria Price, one of the alleged raped girls, had seen two of the Negroes previously, in her home town of Huntsville.

The only evidence of the force necessary to make intercourse actual rape, brought out by the State, was a gun or two which were in the Negro crowd,[12] but had not been fired, also one or two so-called and supposedly drawn knives, although apparently no more than jack knives. Yet Victoria was likewise carrying a knife!

With evidence so sketchy and contradictory, and with the whole case so hastily prepared and presented, and, above all, with the rule of the mob over the jury, I believe that a change of venue should now be granted; the trial moved entirely away from this frantic spirit of opposition by the people.[13]

Further, though, my interest is not only in a more sound-minded trial for these boys, but more particularly for the general broadening and humanizing of the universal treatment and condition of the Negroes, especially in the South. For up to now, this general attitude continues to practically effect an indirect form of enslavement, and because of the ruthlessness of this class difference, incites prejudice to the point where scores of cases, like this Scottsboro affair, happen, and hundreds of actual lynchings result. Yet such violent exploitation and hatred and prejudice can only provoke, not lessen, crime on both sides. Besides, by now, this Negro-lynching idea has become not only an age-old national menace, but almost an unthinking custom in the South which must be averted and cured by understanding and humaneness, not mob or judicial murder.[14]

Textual Note: Copy-text is "Speech on Scottsboro Case," unsigned revised typescript (5 pages) in DPUP folder 13342. A shorter version was published as "Humanitarianism in the Scottsboro Case," *Contempo: A Review of Ideas and Personalities* 1:6, Mid-July 1931, p. 1. A revised full text was published as "Speech on the Scottsboro Case, June 5, 1931" in Nancy Cunard, ed., *Negro Anthology* (London: The Hours Press, 1934), 271–72, using a text Cunard had been given by "the people of the *New Masses*" (Nancy Cunard to TD, 27 February 1934, DPUP). Variants are indicated in the notes.

1. TD to "Dear Friend," June 1931, DPUP.

2. Revised to "whom I believe to be a promising race with a future" in *Negro Anthology*.

3. The phrase "and that this custom is being utilized for ulterior purposes" was added in *Negro Anthology*.

4. Under the practice of peonage, laborers were kept in debt to their employers, and tenant farmers kept in debt to landowners, by the supply of basics such as clothing and agricultural supplies advanced on wages or the sale of crops. Typified by

its most prevalent form, sharecropping, this was a condition not far removed from slavery. Dreiser returned to these forms of the economic exploitation of African Americans in the South at greater length in *Tragic America*. See *Tragic America*, n. 3 (161).

5. The words "or something" cut from *Negro Anthology*.

6. Condensed to "without opposition" in *Negro Anthology*.

7. On Dreiser's own witnessing and reporting of a lynching in rural Missouri in January 1894, see part 1, "The State of the Negro," note 2. Dreiser's short story "Nigger Jeff," based on the 1894 lynching, appeals in its own way for the "understanding and humaneness" called for here.

8. "Instead of trying them as human beings, they were tried as black men." Sentence inserted at this point in *Negro Anthology*.

9. Ruby Bates and Victoria Price, poor white millworkers from Huntsville, Alabama, whose accusations led to the case. Bates would recant her testimony during the second trial of Heywood Patterson in 1933 and joined the I.L.D. campaign to free the boys, while Price maintained the truth of the charges until her death.

10. Revised in *Negro Anthology* to "The evidence of intercourse was of such nature that it could have occurred two or three days prior to the alleged crime; besides, there was almost no evidence even of this nature regarding Victoria Price, who testified that she didn't scream, and that she delayed getting off the train until she wanted to."

11. Revised in *Negro Anthology* to "Furthermore, these two girls, from affidavits gathered by the new defense, are lacking in moral discretion."

12. Revised in *Negro Anthology* to "The only evidence of the force necessary to make intercourse actual rape was that of the two girls for the State, denied by the defense for the boys, and a gun or two which were supposed to be in the Negro crowd."

13. After a successful appeal to the United States Supreme Court in 1932, Haywood Patterson and Clarence Norris were retried in nearby Decatur and reconvicted. These convictions were overturned in February 1935 by the United States Supreme Court, ruling that Alabama's practice of excluding African Americans from juries was unconstitutional. In a further round of retrials in 1936–37, the Scottsboro boys were convicted again.

14. In *Negro Anthology*: "but almost a legitimate practice in the South which must be averted and stopped. But at present, understanding and even humaneness? No, mob and judicial murder!"

Interview with Nazife Osman Pasha

November 1931.

Dreiser's response to a letter from a Turkish emigrée journalist asking questions on gender, civilization, and war. Pasha subsequently enlisted Dreiser in support of her application for asylum in the United States, but she was deported to France, from where she sent a translation of the interview published in a radical Paris newspaper.

What do I think respecting differences of the intelligence of men and women, their contributions to civilization and the possibilities of achievements in the future?

I believe there is no difference between the intelligence of men and women. To date, psychologists have offered no convincing data that women are less brilliant than men and *vice versa*. Of course, it is true that in the large, women have not accomplished as great achievements as men. However, women's part is not all on the surface. Many women of unusual mental gifts have influenced history vastly more than is realized by reading the usual summaries of it. The woman is naturally to be protected because she is the one who bears children. Her role as mother naturally puts her in the position of a comforter and aide to man rather than the one who takes the initiative or who puts the project through. This naturally brings it about that the man accomplishes the ideals and sees them through. There have, however, been notable instances of women geniuses. I cannot think of a field in which they would not accomplish as much as men. However, whether they ever will be equal with men in this sense, I question. Firstly, the ingrown prejudices of centuries would have to be overcome. Secondly, women seem happier in the subordinate role which they almost naturally pick out for themselves. I think it is perfectly true that more and more women are likely to take a hand in ruling the world. This is because silly prejudices and silly tripe are being overcome.

Do I believe that if women had ruled the world, we would have a better civilization without war and misery?

My answer is no. I consider that some of the most vicious, selfish, ruthless characters in all history have been women. I think it is these strong individualists who with their domination over the masses have caused war and misery that could be mitigated not in my opinion by the supremacy of women. Rather, I feel that both men and women in the masses of society are on the whole opposed to war from a humanitarian point of view, yet war enriches the few at the top who inspire the masses to carry it out. In carrying it out, both men and women strive with nearly equal spirit. Although men do the actual fighting, women become animated and inspired with vast organization and relief work in war.

As I view present civilization, it is on the whole unworthy of the name.

You ask if principles of civilization are based upon selfishness and hardship?

They most certainly are. The world is so organized that everywhere, except in Soviet Russia, the masses are preyed upon by the so-called constructive geniuses at the top. The rich can erect monuments, build palaces, buy yachts, *etc.*, while the masses in agony and human misery flock right around these riches and display. What is more, civilization does not seem to be working toward mitigating these outrages. On the other hand, they are even extending them not only by gaining control through industrial employment of so-called uncivilized races, but also making that control limited more and more to a few enormous trusts and cartels.

I do not consider that the World War had a noble inspiration. Rather, I look upon it as an outrageous slaughter for the enrichment of a few great corporations which supplied the vast quantities of oils, ships, uniforms, ammunition, and all sorts of equipment needed to carry it out.

Now, do I consider a civilization really complete without a universal peace?

I do not. But I do consider that a universal peace would be one of the most difficult achievements of mankind. It could never come about without equity among all men. It is difficult to conceive the high state of teaching and improvement necessary to bring this about. Without a high state of development, one race or group is bound to be oppressed and until no race is oppressed no universal peace is possible.

You ask if I consider that women's equal participation with men in handling the World's affairs may lead the world to a better humanized civilization.

I think that women should participate in world affairs as much as they want to, but I don't necessarily think that it is their participation which is going to humanize the world. Rather, I think this equity can come about only by the vigilance of the common people and the supremacy of their interests over the selfish few who control the laws.

Textual Note: Copy-text is TD to Nazife Osman Pasha, 21 November 1931, carbon copy typescript (3 pages) in DPUP folder 4762. Letter headings and address are omitted. Originally intended for publication in the Turkish daily newspaper *Aksam* (*Akcham*), and published in French as "L'éternel conflit entre l'homme et la femme (12) *Une enquête par N. Osman Pacha:* Theodore Dreiser," in *L'Intransigeant* (Paris), 30 July 1934.

From *Tragic America*

New York: Horace Liveright, December 1931.

In Tragic America's more than four hundred printed pages, Dreiser sets out his diagnosis of the ills of Depression-era America and his prescription for change. He views capitalism as a failed economic system and an unjust one, its drive to increase or maintain profits resulting in the impoverishment and distress of the majority population. Banks and industrial monopolies, whose greed was exemplified by the railroads, exercise a powerful influence not only on the government, but also on the judiciary, the police force, education, and even much of the labor movement, through company unions and the quiescent American Federation of Labor. The Constitution, like the Supreme Court, offers little protection because the framers were familiar only with the autocracy of the established church, monarchy, and aristocracy, and they could not have envisaged the autocracy of the corporation. Its guarantee of the rights of private property, once a defense against the established forms of power, Dreiser argues, now only serves to secure the interests of a corporate oligarchy (Tragic America, 154–58). Similarly, the Constitution's guarantees of states rights are used by corporations to forestall federal measures such as child labor protections. Workers are not only exploited economically, but their attempts to organize in order to resist exploitation are met with legal and often, especially in the case of Communism, violent repression. "Fundamental change" is necessary (Tragic America, 201), modeled on examples such as strong labor unions in Britain; old age pensions in Belgium; insurance for unemployment, sickness, and maternity in France; child labor protection in Germany; and education in Russia (Tragic America, 195).

Concentrating on industrial workers in early chapters, Dreiser goes on to give examples of the abuse of police powers over labor in the South as well as the North (chapters 11 and 12). In chapter 13, "The Abuse of the Individual," he makes explicit parallels: "the attitude of the Southern white to the Negro as well as that of the Southern landowner to his tenant, the 'cropper' . . . and also that of the average American corporation toward its employees, is of a similar pattern and all equally cruel and evil" (Tragic America, 229). Not only did corporations exploit labor as a class, but they also abused the individual in ways ranging from providing substandard travel accommodations in Pullman cars and motor-coaches to the continuation of the peonage system, typified by sharecropping, in the South (see 151). Chapter 21, "Is America Dominant?" goes on to assail the economic and political imperialism that extends such exploitation internationally.

Elsewhere Dreiser expands the criticisms of organized religion and charity that he had been making since the 1890s. In a lengthy chapter on "The Church and Wealth in America," he tries "to show the subtle relation of money and economic policy to religion and capital, also that capital has changed religion into a far different thing from the teachings of Jesus Christ" (Tragic America, 276). *In essence, Dreiser charges that organized religion misrecognizes social and economic problems as moral issues, consequently promoting "ignorance and submission in the working class"* (Tragic America, 247). *This moralistic dogmatism, he argues, coexists with the increasing commercialization of organized religion. On the one hand, he notes missionary activity abroad, domestic campaigns against divorce and birth control, and campaigns for a "blue Sunday" and "peace" between classes in the face of the major dislocations, repressions, and distresses of the Great Depression. On the other hand, he points to the close relationship between religion and capitalism, exemplified by the complicity of overseas missions with the opening up of access to raw materials and markets (Dreiser cites the career of John D. Rockefeller as an example of how "the oil-can followed the missionary"); he also remarks on the Churches' tax-free wealth, investment in property, use of publicity and advertising agencies, support of political campaigns and figures, and involvement in welfare provisions, such as the care of the elderly, that should properly be functions of government* (Tragic America, 257–69 and 277–96; see 154).

Chapter 19, "A Suggested Phase of Education," criticizes the individualistic and moralistic world view propagated by "religious training in the home" (Tragic America, 354) *and calls on public schools to train "children in their social relations—national and international." "Boys and girls," it continues, "should be made to see themselves as part of a great mass of people with whom they are connected and to whom they are socially, economically, and in other ways, responsible"* (Tragic America, 354–55; see revised version in "The Child and the School," 175). *Dreiser clearly had hopes that such education would bring about social change, since at one stage of composition the chapter on education was placed at the conclusion of Tragic America, where he evidently wished it to be restored in any second edition.*[1]

In the concluding chapters, Dreiser outlined a prescription for political change that was explicitly modeled on many aspects of Soviet Russia, but that differed from Communist Party policy by arguing for the common interest of working-class and middle-class Americans abused as individuals by the capitalist class, and by putting more emphasis on technocratic leadership. Dreiser reworks the Aristotelian notion of a small group of expert political and economic advisers that was suggested in "John Reed Club Answer," this time emphasizing the need to limit the material rewards enjoyed by successful capitalists and to replace them with a sense of social responsibility (see 159). Drawing on research done by party members, and clearly sympathetic to Communist analysis and aims, Tragic America stops short of endorsing Communism explicitly. In calling for fundamental economic change, the book distances itself somewhat from the total nationalization it associates with the Russian model:

[T]o relieve overproduction a really new system is needed in this country. Not Communism or Socialism, necessarily, but something similar and suited to the American temperament and certainly not with the money lords directly or indirectly reaping the profits. The present conditions are not inevitable or necessary as capitalists would have the worker believe. (Tragic America, 189)

Dreiser goes on to contest the idea that such state intervention is un-American, citing numerous examples of governments taking control over industry and utilities at local, state, and national levels (Tragic America, 329–38).

In acknowledging the national specificity of Russian Communism and trying to find ways of adapting Communist ideas for the American context, Tragic America typifies much of Dreiser's political writing in the 1930s and 1940s.

Chapter 1: The American Scene

*   *   *   *

The deep trouble with America today is that the gifted and strong individual, however self-centered and selfish and wholly unsocial, is supposed nevertheless, to remain uncurbed because he is part of a presumably wholly social state which was organized to guarantee the right of equal opportunity for all. But equal opportunity for all cannot possibly and by the very same phrase mean unlimited license for the cunning and the greedy who take advantage of that equal opportunity to establish special or, in other words, unlimited individual privileges, and the power that goes with the same, the while the remaining ninety to ninety-five per cent of the citizens of this land trudge in comparative want. And yet, that is exactly what has happened. The cunning and the strong have made great use of the land of real opportunity. They have, from the very beginning, seized upon its great perquisites as private to themselves. (I am thinking of not only millions of acres of the actual land donated to the influential, but the natural resources of the same: lumber, minerals, oils. Also of the various types of franchises, railroads, telegraph, express, lighting and the like, which have been given or stolen and now, through the wealth and power brought by the same and the private control that goes with them, have proceeded to direct the Government itself which—due to the phrase "equal opportunity for all"—has permitted them to obtain that special and private control.)

*   *   *   *

Chapter 13: The Abuse of the Individual

Corporations, the deviously won reward of skyscraper-crowned dignitaries, having catapulted their way (honestly or dishonestly) through meshes of law, public opinion, morals, theories—obviously by reason of some constructive intent on Nature's part as manifested through man—have finally reached that state of centralized power and security in America in which any attempt at opposition, correction, or even criticism, on the part of the small fry is likely to be met with drastic counter-attacks intended in quite every instance to terrify or punish and so forestall any attempt at the same thing in the future. To realize the truth of this, one need only contemplate the fierce executive, judicial, financial, as well as social, attacks on this or that opponent of the present centralization of all powers in the hands of a few. Today in America the individual is practically helpless; that is, any individual lower in rank than the top level.

* * * *

And similarly,[2] the control by corporations of prices regardless of merit or (in so far as foodstuffs are concerned) seasonal supply. In New York or Chicago or other big cities, lemons, for instance, remaining at three for ten cents, whether they be plentiful or whether the extra ones have to be allowed to rot in cars or dumped in any harbor or slough in order that this price may be maintained. And this applying to other fruits and vegetables as well. At this writing there are vast piles of farm produce rotting along the railroad tracks which stretch out into the meadows between Jersey City and Newark—carload after carload dumped because otherwise the exorbitant asking price could not be obtained from the wholesaler in New York. And this destruction of food, and in the face of millions of unemployed and thousands of bread lines, not only done openly, but widely publicized. Witness the items in all the newspapers some months ago, announcing a sham battle in California with "surplus" eggs as missiles. Thousands of crates of eggs so destroyed, and in order to keep up prices, the while children all over America were suffering from malnutrition and their parents not only unable to buy eggs for them but themselves suffering from hunger or actually dying of starvation! Is life really mad? Are all men scoundrels or fools?

It is the same with bread. Ten cents a loaf the while hundreds of millions of bushels of wheat lie stored and unsaleable! Not only that, but in the Northwest last winter, wheat used as fuel, and at the instigation of capitalists terming such measures "stabilization." Yet millions of men on the streets, with scarcely as much as ten cents wherewith to buy a loaf of bread! And though cattle-hides fall to almost nothing in price—a dead loss to the cattle-raiser, if not the packer—still, shoes remaining at from eight to fourteen dollars a pair! And let the unemployed, or he who has had his salary cut in half, do the best he can!

Worse, this destruction of necessities is not only condoned but now actually recommended and demanded by the Government itself. Have we not heard the vacuous and inane Farm Board telling the cotton-growers of the South that they must plow under one-third of their cotton crops so that the price of cotton may be increased? True, cotton has suffered great declines in price, and when it became evident that this year's crop would be large, the price collapsed below the cost of production, but should that mean the destruction of something that thousands of penniless individuals have need for? Yet as to this plowing under, the rich land-owners passing along the full burden of the decline in price to the "croppers," as demonstrated at Camp Hill, Alabama, where they cut off the food supplies of Negro "croppers" in order to force them to abandon their share of the crops before the cotton-picking season came around.[3] And later shooting them for the least offense—for stealing a loaf of bread or a purse, because otherwise—and there being now nearly one hundred thousand penniless and hungry— they might turn brave and savage and take from their grafting overlords or their alleged Government something wherewith to maintain their lives.[4] But the individual farmer, as is natural, refusing to destroy any of his own cotton, no matter how much he might approve of having the other fellow destroy his. Needless to say, and as you can see, the Farm Board's fantastic and impractical recommendation arousing only wide opposition.

But can a more insane economic system be imagined? Because there is too much food, people must starve! Because there is too much cotton, people must continue to wear rags! Or say, rather, and more truly, that because grasping corporations find themselves unable—their indecently low wage scales having practically nullified buying power as far as the mass is concerned—to command the exorbitant prices they insist on, they have nothing more to offer in the way of a solution to this economic mess than the destruction of these crops for which there is so much dire need and the starvation of those who grew them. And yet, as you can see, they have safely counted, and can continue so to do, on a fawning government to support whatever they recommend. Yet if these suggestions were not really criminal, they would appear insanely naïve.

In fact, it is true that in the United States today the capitalists having the factories and land necessary for producing them have a stranglehold on the necessities of life, for they make the price pools and agreements for keeping prices high. This enables our bankers and speculators, in order to keep up the prices of everything, to dump food on the ground to rot, to destroy crops and property in many forms, the while the jobless go hungry. Yet in the Soviet Union, where the workers collectively, through their government, are the owners (really there is no such thing as private property in Russia) every effort is made to increase production in order to improve the conditions of life for the masses. Every surplus of goods is welcomed, not as a menace to the prices of the few but as a means of further raising the standard of living of the whole population.

Not only this, but in the chapters entitled "The Position of Labor" and "The Growth of Police Power" I have cited crime after crime against the petty individual who under this great corporation-controlled government has neither voice nor recourse of any kind.[5] For, as I have just shown, not only the courts, but the police, the press, the church, the pictures and the radio, all, all have gone over to the side that has the most money and that can fight them the hardest, or, assuming them to be sufficiently subservient, do the most for them. A little brief authority, a trashy badge or uniform, or the insignia of any small office, and behold a tyrant who sees nothing but effrontery in the least desire or pleasure of any one not possessed of authority or property or power. Is it the driver of an automobile? Then it is the pleasure as well as the purpose of the largest as well as the smallest officials connected in any least way with the regulation of traffic (its assumed furtherance, not hindrance) to irritate, browbeat, delay, threaten, and all too often arrest (and for purposes of graft, fine or tax) individuals who are seeking no more than a reasonable and just use of the public roads. And since our American railroads have been seeking to drive the individual bus-owners off the roads in order to gobble up the right to operate buses for themselves, it is no uncommon occurrence to have the petty individual operator annoyed, delayed, and most inordinately fined, until at last, through downright weariness as well as robbery, he is compelled to dispose of his right and allow the corporation to function in his stead. And this by the aid of the local police, the county sheriff, the town marshal, and who not else, in quite every part of America. It is a commonplace, just as the driving out of the individual oil operator by the Standard Oil Company, or the individual coal operator by the combined mining and railway trust, was a commonplace of half a century ago.

In fact, I am now convinced that this is one country that, ever since it was conceived of as a possibility, has been steadily and deceitfully, as well as fraudulently, shunted along the path of individual and later corporate control, as opposed to its written and widely-promulgated determination to make of itself a liberal and helpful democracy in which the individual was to fare more pleasantly and comfortably than ever he had before in all the world! For here more than anywhere else in the world, I do believe,

AGAINST HUNGER—These men, women and children—miners' families—face machine guns daily on the picket line, fighting for union and wages.

The Testimony of Starvation

As Given to Theodore Dreiser by striking
miners in Pittsburgh.

*Nick Rozina, of the Kinloch mines, near
Pittsburgh, a striker, would rather take his wife
and children and starve on the streets
than return to work under the same conditions.
That is what he told Theodore Dreiser, of the
investigating committee that helped uncover
some of the horrible conditions in the coal fields
where the strike is now taking place. Dreiser is
questioning the miner — one of a score who
poured out a bitter story of starvation and conditions of peonage.*

Dreiser: How long have you been a citizen of this country?

Miner: 7 years.

Dreiser: How long a miner?

Miner: 23 years in this country.

D: Member of the U.M.W.A.?

M: From 1912 to 1927.

D: How did you like them?.

M: I didn't know any better. I thought
they was all right.

D: Did you make good money?

M: Just a living. I'm married. Four
children.

D: How long have you been in this section?

M: Since 1927. They broke the union
and cut the prices. Been living in misery
since. I got more to eat since the National Miners Union brought us out on strike
than when I was working. We organize

committees and go out and bring food
from the farmers.

D: Have they thrown you out of your
house yet?

M: Not yet.

D: Have you any money?

M: No.

D: Have you been picketing?

M: Yes, since the first of the month,
24 days.

D: Has there been any trouble since you
have been picketing?

M: Absolutely. Terrible. The deputies go out with high-powered rifles and
get strike breakers. They bring loads 3 at
a time. We call to them. "Don't go to
work, we are on strike." We dare not say
anything else. Get your head blown off.
Deputies get out of car. Point gun at one
fellow and say, "Jump in car" and take
him to jail.

D: What did you do for food up to the
time you went on strike?

M: We go every day for soup to the
Salvation Army. One and a half miles
away. Half hour to walk. The Kinloch
Mine furnishes the Salvation Army with
food. They don't give it to you now.
They want you to go to work.

D: If you went to work now, what
would you make?

M: Just same as before. Not any dif-

rent. That would be 18 cents a ton, $40
or $45 a month. If we didn't go on
strike, I would take my wife and children
and starve on the streets. I would not go
back to starve in the mines.

DEFEND THE MINERS!

*They face hunger and death every day
on the picket line. They go to jail for
bread. 600 have already been arrested.
They need relief to carry on the strike—
We must get them out of jail to carry on
the strike. The I.L.D. calls for protest
meetings against the official terror. It
also calls on all workers to raise and rush
funds to the*

MINERS' DEFENSE FUND, c-o I.L.D.
80 East 11th Street   New York City

Miners' Kids—No play. Forced to work.

151

Dreiser's visit to mining country near Pittsburgh, reported
in the *Labor Defender*, August 1931.

the petty individual has seen himself more thoroughly coerced, robbed and frustrated, and that always in favor of the cunning individual of capitalistic leanings and with a will to power.

* * * *

[*Dreiser gives examples of exploitation and forced labor, on chain gangs and under the peonage and sharecropping systems.*] But because neither the Negroes nor the poor whites dare talk much, most of these really dreadful cases never get publicity. Yet while some of the States permit men to be brought back for debt, others do prohibit planters from crossing the state lines to force men back, a fact which should be written down for their credit. On the whole, though, this Southern force and violence has its own roots, I am sure, in the pre–Civil War slavery tradition of the South; in other words, the assumed fitness of the Negro and the criminal for slavery, and for slavery only. Yet why? The Negro who works is law-abiding, and if not thrifty is at least economically independent and cheerful, a good and useful citizen. Can it be that due to his somewhat erotic nature, he is offensive to the Northern Puritan (in law, not fact), or is it merely that he is black? In part, its roots may lie in the world-old notion that freedom for the individual is something bestowed by the strong upon the weak, that might makes right, and that the strong may (not necessarily "must") direct the weak and helpless everywhere, and to the advantage of the strong. For the strong, being strong, are right, and the weak, being weak, are wrong or worthless—a doctrine to which all of the money powers of our modern world will most readily subscribe and, in reality, practice. If this and other chapters do not show this, then most certainly my statements are without meaning and of no authority.[6]

* * * *

Chapter 14: The Church and Wealth in America

* * * *

More, [*Dreiser has just been arguing that the Churches should be taxed "the same as any other self-aggrandizing corporation"*] I believe that all of the pursuits in which the Church engages in this country (except aesthetics, which they portray so meagerly, awkwardly, grossly, and unbeautifully) are actually functions of government. And if so, they should be a part of government and not of the functionings of a special and separate, if not private, group of theorists, or worse, political men of affairs seeking, via theory, and worse, revelation, to function as government. I refer to such things as hospitals, protectories, orphan asylums, schools, colleges, homes for the aged and infirm, graveyards, and industries of whatsoever nature.

* * * *

The Church itself, as much as anything, has made the spiritual life unfashionable, and hence has degraded it. Against the sole hope and inspiration of Christ, it has given way to commercial standards of corporations and just when people need a simple aesthetic and mental haven to escape from corporate speed and complexity. All in all, it has sought to become a moving factor in national life, and by so doing has defeated its purpose of spiritual nourishment. And certainly, the seeking human hearts, so lost from the Church, are something to be reckoned with. Thousands who have followed it from childhood have wakened to find it an intellectual (which includes aesthetics, of course) loss.

But let us see how the Church seeks to influence sociologically, economically and politically, and, of course, to seize power via numbers and the control of the same through faith. Orphanages, for one thing: schools, for another; Sunday schools for still another; and then hospitals, protectories, and the like. I want to speak particularly, however, of Sunday schools, schools, and homes for the aged run by churches. For first, the doctrine-flavored educational factor of the Sunday school is shockingly wide in its appeal. In 1926, 212 denominations here had 185,000 Sunday schools, with 21,000,000 pupils—only 3,700,000 less than the total enrollment of all the public schools in the United States! But what is taught in them? An aesthetic appreciation of beauty? Yes? A suggestion of the complicated nature of the organized society in which we find ourselves and the proper understanding of its functions and their value—one's benefits from as well as duties to it as one of its beneficiaries? Never! That would be putting life before death, reality above mysticism, the here and now through which we really live and suffer over and above a mythical and unsubstantiated hereafter in which we are to be rewarded for what we suffer here. Rather a deadly indifference to the correction of those same ills here and now, all reality denounced, feared, buried, the while prayer, the only thing taught in the church which might be turned to aesthetic value, is dominated by a silly, narrow code of sins, confessions and selfish yearnings or needs, pathetically doomed to unfulfillment. In short, every worthwhile phase of a proper knowledge of life evaded, the while the antithesis, dogmas relative to a mystical hierarchy which Christ never contemplated, is insisted upon. Indeed, his worded peace, order and unselfishness is almost totally ignored. Or if not, then united with dogma and rules never contemplated by him, and calculated by the Church, particularly the Catholic Church, to give it such power as to chain its adherents to slavish ignorance and obedience throughout their lives here. Yet obviously, such power cannot be for the good of the individual here on earth or his government. It is against his mind. And when that is suborned or darkened, by whatever process, what else of value can remain?

* * * *

But what are the aims and methods of procedure of these missionaries who proceed from America into China, India, Siam, and elsewhere? These are interesting, for, as you will see, they have their roots in something very peculiar here. In China, for instance, our missionaries—those of the Protestant persuasion, at least—work with the government there just as closely as do the corporations that have their origin in this land. And with the corporations there also. And are frequently as much the emissaries of American trade as of religion, and even more so. For whereas formerly the missionaries used to go to convey a spiritual message, today at least one very important phase of their purpose is to effect as well as share material or economic "blessings" for the natives, such blessings, for instance, as our very material corporations manufacture and seek to distribute as widely as possible; bathtubs, sewing machines, electric lights, and refrigerators, or in other words, anything and everything that our modern corporations make. In other words again, "Make 'em modern!" That means more business for home corporations, doesn't it? . . . And furthermore, most missionaries now believe that they should be protected with gunboats—they who supposedly represent Jesus who taught peace!

* * * *

Chapter 21: Is America Dominant?

* * * *

But now to some of the other abuses involved in this business of foreign loans.[7] Thus, for years the United States used, and is still using, her influence to keep foreign nations from making loans to Central America and the West Indies. They must deal with us or not deal at all. Nor may foreign investors trample these lands unrepelled. Concessions for their development to any but Americans are immediately vetoed. If by some ruse they are not vetoed, ultimatums stating American demands are enforced by marines, bayonets and machine guns. Thus, during July 1924, eleven Latin-American countries were officially directed in finance by Americans. Yet the misery of these foreign peoples! Their protest at our interventions! More, during recent times, the United States has, on thirty occasions, sent troops or battleships to seven sovereignties to enforce her will. And you don't call that imperialism? She has made virtual protectorates of Cuba, Panama, Haiti and Nicaragua. And look at the period of time in which the United States has maintained a government in Nicaragua although opposed by eighty per cent of its people. American marines have functioned in Nicaragua for twenty-two years. The result of this policy? The most backward of all nations there. And in Hawaii, after three thousand natives were put to death, Americans took over the customs and rewrote the Constitution. Also, when a rebellion was stirred up in Colombia some time ago, our American President took that country under our protection.[8]

To show the instability of this policy—American corporation attacks on these countries—seven of the twenty Latin-American constitutional governments were overthrown by revolution during the year ending February 1931.[9] In Argentina, Brazil and Peru no national elections have been held to obtain the will of the people of the new government and Dominican Republic elections were declared fraudulent by the courts. Now our King Hoover visits our possessions (Puerto Rico) in order to emphasize that subtle allegiance.[10] And by way of so doing, he reminds them that they are by us "endowed with liberty, freedom, self-government and individual opportunity through incorporation under the American flag." In other words, their individual opportunity to slave for an American corporation on wages too meager for a decent living! Yet the policy of Secretary of State Stimson[11] is to recognize Latin American governments whether their people approve or not. Duly elected governments there have been overthrown and the latter government recognized by the United States without people there approving said overthrown government. All the United States needs for recognition is failure of a foreign people to disapprove which means that they had no opportunity to vote and were unable to revolt. Yet recognition by this country means foreign loans to the overthrown government and hence its maintenance. Since the United States adopted this policy, there have been more revolutions than ever before in their history. So answer for yourself my question: "Is America dominant?"

* * * *

But, do we want to imitate England and Japan and the old Russia? For although England has commanded a powerful position because her financiers have "laid" for "backward" peoples, I still do not see in the British Empire any model to imitate. The idea that underlies it is passé. It will no longer work. For as we see today, the English people, millions of them, and for all their imperial sweep, take only a meager living from life while a select array of royalty and title controls and enjoys its wealth. And such royalty and title! But these so-called supermen never really care for the rank and file. They do not even understand them. It is their business, as they see it, to keep the rank and file below and themselves on top. But does it follow that the somewhat enlarged vision of the mass anywhere today is likely to accept that? I doubt it. See Spain, Cuba, Mexico, Russia. Isn't there a change at hand and for the better, not the worse? I think so.

Anyhow, I know of two things that should help break up American imperialism. The first pertains to war. Nations never fight without an issue. And always the few make the issue. As it is now, though, our American people merely follow orders, and they know it. Yet likewise they know also that this is supposed to be a free country and that men at least pretend to vote for what they want. Now declaring war is the world's greatest act of sovereignty. And whether that should be decided by the people or by "the few" (meaning the corporations who are merely after "big business") is something concerning which many otherwise not so socially well-informed are beginning to ponder. And if ever they conclude that the many, and not the few, should decide this, the dreams of the individualist will have to give way to something besides thoughts of personal profit and personal or family dominance or he will be too small for the job in hand.

And when I think of America in this connection, I wish to say: "You claim to be a democracy, yet do you realize that not one phase of your various international problems comes to a vote?" And because of this I propose an amendment to the Constitution which shall declare that war can be declared only by a vote of the people: a two-thirds majority.

In the second place, there is a way to stop not only some but all of the brutal phases of American imperialism which I have recounted in this chapter, and that is an absolute change of the economic system, so that wealth is more equitably distributed. But to achieve that, only "the many," not "the few," may declare war. After that, the many, and not the few, must proceed to enforce that equity in wealth—that is, participation in produce and such for effort expended—which is now debarred by this present control of it by the few. And when that is done, they (the many) will achieve their desire for a non-imperialistic nation and will presently present a fine native race economically fitted to pursue its personal interests and talents. And an excellent and even inspiring example that should be; something like that which the democratic-minded fathers of this country had in view when they dreamed of the thirteen colonies as a nation.

* * * *

Chapter 22: Suggestions Toward a New Statecraft

Capitalism is a failure in America today. . . . Capitalistic failure here is evidenced by the fact that no longer is economic balance maintained. I mean by that that equity of consumption does not exist here. America can produce but is unable, for want of money, to buy what it makes. In other words, the people create a wealth which in the field of consumption is denied them. On the other hand, the rich have the power to erect wastefully Empire State Buildings, Radio Cities, Chrysler Buildings, General Motors Buildings, what you will, and to build enormous mills to supply millions with food and clothing; to create automobile, radio, furniture, paint, glass, metal, lumber, coal and oil businesses sufficient for the needs of multitudes; to organize speedy transportation by steamship, airplane or railway; yet the masses are unable to obtain these commodities and facilities for their own use in any but an extraordinarily limited way.

* * * *

But what I propose is an executive power for the American working masses not unlike the Communist Central Committee in Moscow, but composed of American men and women (if there are such) who have made a thorough study of the social and economic ills that today engulf America. For you cannot escape needing brains in some form anywhere. Only instead of being in office at the instigation of monopolies, trusts and cartels, as is the case with present oligarchies, and therefore serving their personal interests only and saying to hell with the rest of humanity, the whole system must be cleansed from the very bottom, its very heart! The voice and the will of the people must again be heard if ever as yet they have been heard. All private fortunes, as in Russia, must be abolished. The idea of an unearned inheritance by any one must be ended, for it is unfair and cruel. Men must not only not hope to come by great fortunes by inheritance or chance or theft, but they must not hope to make great fortunes by what they do, since so few can do so much as to deserve a great fortune, let alone administer it wisely once they have it. Rather, let us say to them, as did Aristotle over two thousand years ago: "See, we will give you fame, the acclaim of those whom you have served and benefited!" And in addition to this honor and recognition, security and peace, but no more. For it is enough.

Yet even this proposed central authority for America must have as its sole motivation the well-being of all of the people rather than that slight aid that may slip their way after the corporation giants or lords, their wives, concubines, friends and heirs, are gorged. For how obvious it is that under private control so little is equitably distributed. Rather by favor and in willful ignorance or savage and usually erratic domination is anything done, and despite our large trusts and organizations of all kinds, unwisely, most certainly with no general view which in organized society is the very base of equity.

Yet what can alleviate this corporate grip upon America? In this book, I have shown the uselessness of reform under the present methods of production and private property. Therefore, as I see it, nothing but a fundamental change in the whole system can do it. The present foundation is crumbling; the weakness is basic—absolutely at bottom and cannot be patched up or repaired. Hence, I now ask, how is it possible to change the foundation of the American economic structure? I would answer for *the masses to build themselves new institutions*. For under our present methods the working class is being destroyed—it is dying from insufferable conditions. This class must be joined by farmers and the entire middle class whom the financial barons have bled and defrauded. The cultural influences of the middle class, with frequently slightly more leisure, must join up with the working class to whom they are far closer than they realize, and bolster it up.

For indeed, the sacredness of private property is an illusion, as shown by change and death. Hence and instead, the proposed new government must have the power to confiscate and turn into state property all of the basic industries: coal, lumber, food, steel, etc., as well as their means of transportation. Some might think that those owning stock in these corporations might be paid for their holdings, but I do not agree. In my judgment, they must take pot luck with the rest of us, fall in with the necessary changes in the spirit of our early pioneers and make a new and better scene here and now. Too long have they been the beneficiaries of inequity, and must learn, however grimly, that that is true. Let them forget the past. It has been a fine dream for the few, but an evil one for the many, and must give way. Besides, what have they to fear? The fate and the life and the living and working conditions of every other man—improved as equity would improve them. And is that so bad? Only a coward or a parasite would say so. Personally, I welcome the change.

Not only that, but this central control which now will be should have authority to confiscate such homes of the rich as well as other institutions, private, civil, religious, as might fit into any purpose of the state: educational, recreational, reformative, medical or charitable; or any other really urgent need of the new state or system. Of course, in suggesting such things, any one today is more than likely to be faced, in the capitalistic press and elsewhere, with the assurance, and without in any way consulting the masses, that the American people don't want these things! But don't they? I rather fancy myself that they do, or will!

Next, in the new constitution which I feel should supplant the old, a clause similar to that in the present Russian Soviet Constitution might, and I think would, guarantee official domination by the masses, rather than private interests, of all plans or acts. And that central authority should consistently be held to fight for the people as a whole and in a manner I shall describe.

The source of this government authority constitutes a very difficult problem, because by and large the people appear never to understand. They let whosoever will—priest, political demagogue, corporation executive, arresting and fascinating individuals out of nowhere—as in Mussolini's case—tell them anything or everything: that the country is being run for the good of the people; that this good depends on private ownership; that things are all right as they are; that a plan like this should not be developed hastily without due trial (which trial never comes about); that this plan wouldn't work, etc.—all of which is false. Yet in so far as the present situation is concerned, it would seem as though the basic facts at least must by now be seen by every one; i.e., that corporations charge prices which the public, under wages from these corporations, cannot pay; that the Government leaves the people, not the corporations, to get along as best they may; that the corporations always get value received and hence must do so for financing the activities of the two political parties which, as every one by now knows, are mere semi-annual or quadrennial circuses, intended, via red fire, oratory, scare headlines, noise and what not, to distract the attention of the marching masses from the underlying issues, which are never allowed to appear but which, none the less, have the seeming if not the real endorsement of the people. For that is the sole value of our present two-party system. And certainly, compared with that, my proposed system, working to give the utmost to every one, is infinitely better.

* * * *

Textual Note: New York: Horace Liveright, 1931. These selections are found on pages 7, 222, 224–27, 233–34, 251, 253–55, 261, 399–400, 404–6, 408–9, 412–15.

1. Note from Dreiser's secretary Evelyn Light to "HH"—probably H. H. Clauser—and unsigned telegram, DPUP.
2. The preceding complains of the high cost and poor service of railroad, street car, and bus transportation.
3. Using evidence from the pamphlet "A Statement from Governor Hugh M. Dorsey as to the Negro in Georgia" (1921), and Walter Wilson's forthcoming *Forced Labor in the United States* (1933), in this chapter Dreiser enumerates the exploitation of blacks and poor whites in the South and Southwest by the interwoven systems of chain gangs and peonage.

4. At Camp Hill, Alabama, in 1931 black sharecroppers had responded to the planters' tactics that Dreiser describes by forming the Communist-sponsored Croppers and Farm Workers Union (C.F.W.U.). The violence to which Dreiser alludes was directed toward destroying the union; a meeting in July 1931 was attacked by the local sheriff and armed white vigilantes, who killed one of its founders, Ralph Gray. Communist-organized resistance to sharecropping subsequently continued in the Share Croppers Union (S.C.U.).

5. In chapters 1 through 3 Dreiser gives examples—some from his direct observation in Harlan County, Pennsylvania, and Passaic, New Jersey, and others from his collaborator Kathryn Sayre—that are intended to show the economic exploitation of labor by American corporations and the sometimes violent repression used to maintain it. Chapter 11, "The Position of Labor," makes a case for the "disestablishment" of the American Federation of Labor on the grounds of its ineffectiveness, corrupt management, and conciliatory position with respect to the corporations, and its replacement by grassroots unions based on the workplace rather than on crafts. Chapter 12, "The Growth of the Police Power," traces the roles of state police, private detectives like the Pinkerton agency, and the deputizing and commissioning of police hired by corporations in infiltrating the labor movement, demoralizing and intimidating workers, and breaking strikes.

6. The chapter concludes by indicting corporate profiteering and price-fixing alongside the peonage and sharecropping systems as aspects of the "abuse of the individual" under capitalism.

7. Dreiser has just discussed the financial control exercised by French, British, Japanese, and American banks in China.

8. The secession of Panama from Colombia was achieved with the help of the United States in 1903.

9. There were revolutions in Argentina, Brazil, Colombia, the Dominican Republic, Honduras, and Peru in 1930, and in Chile in 1931.

10. Puerto Rico was ceded to the United States by Spain in 1898 and remains American territory.

11. Henry Lewis Stimson (1867–1950) was secretary of state in Herbert Hoover's cabinet from 1929–33.

Introduction to *Harlan Miners Speak: Report on Terrorism in the Kentucky Coal Fields*

New York: Harcourt, Brace and Company, March 1932.

In May 1931 violent conflicts erupted in Harlan County in eastern Kentucky between poverty-stricken miners and mine operators who had reduced wages and laid off large numbers of workers due to falling coal prices. In order to publicize the struggle, and to support the communist National Miners Union which was organizing in the area, the N.C.D.P.P. formed an investigative committee with Dreiser as its chair. The committee visited Harlan in November 1931 and its findings were published in book form as Harlan Miners Speak. The volume includes two hundred pages of testimony from miners, their families, a sheriff, and a prosecuting attorney, with explanatory material from other members of the committee. Among these, John Dos Passos, who did much to shape and edit the book, describes his own experiences in Harlan; Melvin P. Levy, Charles Rumford Walker, and Adelaide Walker detail the living conditions endured by the mining communities and describe how the miners were exploited and prevented from unionizing effectively; Arnold Johnson and Bruce Crawford outline how the local judiciary and press were controlled by the mine operators; and Anna Rochester provides evidence that the Harlan coal fields were dominated by "big capital" — railroad, banking, and other interests controlled by the Morgan, Insull, Mellon, Ford, and Rockefeller corporations.

Dreiser's introduction emphasizes the violent repression of the miners and their isolation, charging that not only the judiciary, the sheriff's office, and the press, but also the Red Cross, local churches, and the A.F.L. all collaborated with the coal mine operators. It concludes with a detailed critical consideration of individualism, which was emerging as a preoccupation of Dreiser's political philosophy.

In Kentucky, Dreiser and other members of the committee were indicted for "criminal syndicalism," a charge used regularly against political radicals, referring to the use or advocacy of violence as a means of bringing about economic or political change. In June 1935 a congressional investigative commission appointed by the Kentucky Governor, Ruby Laffoon, substantiated the charges against the mine operators and local judiciary made in Harlan Miners Speak, *reporting that*

> *there exists a virtual reign of terror, financed in general by a group of coal mine operators in collusion with certain public officials: the victims of this reign of terror are the coal miners and their families. . . . We found a monsterlike reign of oppression whose tentacles reached into the very foundation of the social structure and even into the Church of God. . . . It appears that the principal cause of existing conditions . . . is the desire of the mine operators to amass for themselves fortunes through the oppression of the laborers, which they do through the sheriff's office.*[1]

The reason that I personally went to the Harlan coal district in Kentucky was because from about June to November 1931, the newspapers of America carried more or less continuous reports of outrages upon the rights of not only the striking miners in that region, but apparently those of all sorts of other people inside and outside the State who sought to interfere in their behalf. I recall reading that representatives of different newspapers and press agencies, the United Press, the Federated Press, and individual newspaper men such as Bruce Crawford,[2] of Norton, Virginia, were attacked, and in Crawford's particular case, shot in the leg, the others threatened and ordered from the State, as though a portion of any State, apart from the State itself, as illustrated by this Harlan County coal district, had authority, let alone the right, to set up a military law of its own and order citizens from other States to observe it, all Constitutional guarantees to the contrary notwithstanding.

I really did not pay so much attention to this particular situation at first, because mining wars of this character in America have been a part of my entire life's experience. As a newspaper man in Chicago, St. Louis, Pittsburgh and other places, I was early drawn into this sort of thing and as early, of course, witnessed the immense injustice which property in America has not only always sought to but has succeeded in inflicting upon labor. Besides, in July of this same summer, I personally was asked by the National Miners Union to come to Pittsburgh and witness for myself the cruelties being inflicted upon the strikers of that region—Eastern Ohio, Northwest West Virginia and Pennsylvania. What I saw there of murder, starvation, extortion and the like practiced upon the coal miners by the coal operators was sufficient to cause me to openly indict the American Federation of Labor, which resulted in nothing more than a glossy and self-exculpatory denial from William Green, the present President of the A. F. of L.[3]

In late October, however, I was presented with a thirty-two page document or indictment compiled apparently by the International Labor Defense from various sources, but all relating to crimes and abuses inflicted on the striking miners in the Harlan district by, obviously, the coal operators' association of the same area. This document contained from three to five indictments to the page and covered, as usual, everything from unpunished murders (eleven all told) to the dynamiting of soup kitchens, the unwarranted search of strikers' homes, the denial of their right to join any union except the United Mine Workers of America of which they were heartily sick and to which they did not want to belong, also the denial of free speech, of the right of representatives from outside newspapers or organizations to come there and see for themselves what was going on.

Because the International Labor Defense confessed itself as in no position to evoke public interest in this wholesale brutality, it wanted to know if I, as Chairman of the National Committee for the Defense of Political Prisoners, would not organize a Committee out of the membership of the general committee of that body and proceed to Kentucky not only to question authority there as to their actions, but to see if by so doing we could not center possible attention and so modify if not dispel some of the ills being suffered by the miners there.

* * * *

[*Dreiser describes in detail how his own "counter proposal" for a widely based committee of "various representative Americans already known for their courage and their public-spirited interest in the Constitutional rights of Americans everywhere"*

*elicited just one volunteer, and how in consequence the investigative committee
drew exclusively on the membership of the N.C.D.P.P. He then describes the
committee's fact-finding visit to Bell and Harlan counties in the face of the "inimical" attitude of the local judiciary and sheriff's office, mentioning the charges
of adultery brought against Dreiser himself, and the indictment of the committee
for "criminal syndicalism."*]

My personal conclusion, after the various individuals had been examined
and the mining districts visited, was that this was a very remarkable struggle
of the American worker against the usual combination of power and wealth
in America which for so long has held him in subjection. As a matter of fact,
there I found the same line-up of petty officials and business interests on the
side of the coal operators and as against the miners, as I have discovered in
almost every other labor war or controversy that I have had the opportunity
to observe. The small town bankers, grocers, editors and lawyers, the police,
the sheriff, if not the government, were all apparently subservient to the
money and corporate masters of the area. It was their compulsion, if possibly
not always their desire, to stand well with these who had the power to cause

Dreiser during his investigation into terrorism in the coal fields,
Harlan County, Kentucky, November 1931.

them material or personal difficulties and, as against those, the underpaid and even starving workers, who could do nothing for themselves.

Possibly this practice springs from the asinine notion in America that every one has an equal opportunity to become a money master, a Morgan or a Rockefeller, although the data concerning America's economic life today show that no more than three hundred and fifty families control 95 per cent of the wealth of the country. Also, that almost every man, short of the officers and owners of our great and all-controlling corporations today, must wear the collar of one or another of these great combinations, and it is only through their favor and power that there is a chance for him or any one to improve his economic state or his social position. He must wear the collar marked with the name of his owner.

This criticism also goes for the press, the church and the public officials elected by those very people who suffer so very greatly at their hands. It is possible that here and there you may find a starving, struggling or unimportant editor who dares to exercise freedom of opinion in connection with just such things as have occurred and to this hour are still occurring in Harlan and elsewhere, but he never succeeds in prospering thereby.

In general, in so far as America is concerned, you can go into any town or city, comment vigorously on inequity in favor of the few and you will very soon find out how unprofitable that really is. Here, as elsewhere, I found, and not to my amazement any longer, the church as well as the press and public charity in all of its forms, and by that I mean the Red Cross, the Salvation Army, the Y.M.C.A. and any such related bodies as may exist, entirely on the side of the corporations as opposed to the workers.

Thus, since the corporations did not desire the miners to strike for more wages or to join a labor union which was not, as is the A. F. of L., directed by the corporations, or to read a paper such as the *Daily Worker,* which does not set forth the usual corporation blah in regard to what is necessary for the welfare of the country, these organizations, particularly where workers were on strike and in need of aid, were not willing to assist them in any way unless they were willing to bow to the demands of the corporations, i.e., in this instance, that they refuse to have anything to do with the National Miners Union, and at once ally themselves with the United Mine Workers of America, a branch of the A. F. of L.; that they cease reading the *Daily Worker* and substitute for it, let us say, the *Harlan Daily Clarion* or the *Louisville Courier Journal* and that they return to work at such wages as the A. F. of L. through its traitor union, the United Mine Workers of America, would arrange for them. Failing this, no food, no clothing, no medicine, no this, no that, for any mine worker. Rather, as I have said, jail, espionage, the blacklist, hunger, even death. In fact, this has become the accepted order in America. The corporation, organized as it is in various nation wide tie-ups, all of the industries in a given line, textile operators' association, coal operators' association, the metal manufacturers' association, and the like, seek to and do, especially for the humbler forms of labor, create a kind of slavery. The purpose of all such organizations everywhere is to prevent unionization of every kind where possible, and where this is not possible, to control such unions with a view to low, and not high, wages, with a view to company stores, even company controlled towns, and certainly company controlled notions and even religious views.

So thoroughly had all this been brought about in this particular region that the right of public meeting had certainly been denied until we arrived there. Also, the right to collect food and clothing and to distribute the same independent of the Red Cross, the Salvation Army and the Y.M.C.A. which were either indifferent to or arbitrary in their demands upon the striking miners. As a matter of fact, what followed is amply set forth in the testimony taken and the data presented in this volume by other members of the Committee.

In conclusion, however, I should like to add that what I cannot understand is why the American people which has been drilled from the beginning in the necessity and the advantage of the individual and his point of view, does not now realize how complete is the collapse of that idea as a working social formula.

For while, on the one hand, we have arrogated to each of ourselves the right to be a giant individual if we can, we have not seen how impossible it is for more than a very few, if so many, to achieve this. Also that, should it be achieved by so much as one, the rest of us would be mere robots functioning at the will and under the direction of that particular individual. It would follow then, if we had the mental strength to grasp it, that it is really not complete individualism for anybody that we need or want or can endure even, but a limited form of individualism which will guarantee to all, in so far as possible, the right, if there is such a right, to life, liberty, and the pursuit of happiness, and also an equitable share in the economic results of any such organization as the presence and harmony of numerous individuals presupposes and compels.

As it is now, we have gotten no further than the right of the most cunning and strong individuals among us to aggrandize ourselves, leaving the rest of us here in America, as elsewhere, to subsist on what is left after they are through. And if you will examine our American economic arrangement, you will find that they are not through, since by now, three hundred and fifty families control 95 per cent of the wealth of the country, and these families, their trusts and holding companies, are now not only not distributing that wealth in any equitable ratio, but even if they were so minded, they are not capable of so doing. Taken collectively, they do not constitute any central authority. And except through the functions of government which they seek to and do direct for their own private aggrandizement, they have no means, let alone any intention of so doing. More, the government, which is supposed to represent all the individualistic ambitions of all of our people, is in no position to do that. It, too, in its turn, has become one of the instruments of this central group of individuals which now directs all of its functions to its particular and very special advantage. That leaves the American citizen, one hundred and twenty-five million strong, with his faith in individualism and what it will do for him, mainly without his rent, his job, a decent suit of clothes, a pair of shoes, or food. His faith in this free-for-all individualism has now led him to the place where his fellow individualists of greater strength, cunning and greed, are in a position to say for how much, or rather, for how little, he shall work, for how long, and whether he shall be allowed to make any complaint or even seek redress in case he is unhappy or dissatisfied, ill-treated, deprived, or even actually starved. In fact, his faith in this individualism as a solvent for all his ills, has caused him to slumber, while his fellow individualists of greater greed and cunning have been seizing his wealth, his church, his press, his courts, his judges, his legislators, his police, and quite all of his originally agreed upon Constitutional privileges so that, today, he walks practically in fear of his own shadow. He cannot now any longer openly say that he is dissatisfied with his government, or that he thinks it is wrong; nor that he thinks individualism is wrong, if actually, he as yet now thinks it is wrong; nor can he any longer organize in unions which are not suborned and so controlled by the very individuals from whose economic pressure he is seeking to escape. He cannot turn to his church, because his church will not listen to his economic ills here on earth; it calls his attention to a Paradise which is to come hereafter. The present earthly Paradise, in its economic form, at least, the church blandly concedes to the very individualists of whom he now complains. Nor can he turn to his press which, by reason of economic advantages, which only those great individualists whom he has so much admired have in their keeping and can bestow, turns not to him but to these his masters. And for that reason he may not be heard. Personally, as poor as he is now, he cannot bring to the door of the press that cash return which they now demand in order to do justice to those millions whose minute and underpaid labors still constitute the source of the wealth of the treasuries which his giant overlords, once lesser individuals like himself, now control.

In sum, by his worship of his own private rights to individual advancement, as opposed to the rights and welfare of every other, he sees himself, if he is really poor and as he really is, an Ishmael in the land as well as the prosperity of the land which he creates.[4] Actually, as a worker, he is laughed at and, in times of unrest and contest, spit upon as a malcontent, a weakling, a radical, an undesirable citizen, one who has not the understanding and hence not the right to complain of the ills by which he finds himself beset. Herded, in so far as the majority of him is concerned, in work-warrens called towns, watched over as the slaves of the South were watched over in the days before the Civil War, by the spies and agents of the immense cooperative associations of wealth, in the factories and mines and mills for which he now works, warred upon by the veritable armies of mercenaries employed by these giants whom he still so much admires, in order to overawe him and subdue him; he finds himself discharged, starved, and then blacklisted and shot down when he strikes; he finds himself, as I have said before, frustrated, ignored, and denied by his church, his press, his paid officials and his supine and traitor government.

Americans today should make an intensive study of individualism as such. They will find its best exemplar in the jungle, where every individual is for itself, prowls to sustain itself, and deals death to the weakest at every turn.

The cries of the jungle today are no more and no worse than the cries of the miners in Harlan, or of the cotton mill workers of Gastonia, or the textile workers of Lawrence, or the agricultural workers of Imperial Valley, or of the masses in general.[5] They, like the zebra in the jaws of the lion, are the economic victims of these giant corporations, *still posing as individuals,* although armed to the teeth with purchased laws, hired officials, and over-awed or controlled courts. These latter are their teeth and their claws, and with these they strike, and their dead are everywhere, defeated and starved.

Again I say, Americans should mentally follow individualism to its ultimate conclusion, for society is not and cannot be a jungle. It should be and is, if it is a social organism worthy of the name, an escape from this drastic individualism which, for some, means all, and for the many, little or nothing. And consciously or unconsciously, it is by Nature and evolution intended as such, for certainly the thousands-of-years-old growth of organized society augurs desire on the part of Nature to avoid the extreme and bloody individualism of the jungle. In proof of which, I submit that organized society throughout history has indulged in more and more rules and laws, each intended to limit, yet not frustrate, the individual in his relations to his fellows.

In fact, the dream of organized society, conscious or unconscious, has been to make it not only possible but necessary for the individual to live with his fellow in reasonable equity, in order that he may enjoy equity himself.

If that is not so, why then organized society at all? If that is not so, then why the hope and the dream, in every heart, of a state in which the individual may not be too much put upon? And why in the absence of that (this desired state) *Revolution*—the final human expression of its hatred of injustice, cruelty, slavery, usury? Why our present social structure, with its courts, its legislative bodies, executives, its so-called representatives of each and every one?

If these do not indicate or spell a dream of true democracy, of helpful companionship in this all-too-disappointing struggle for existence, what does? And if that is true, then why should not this giant and rapacious individualism here in America, now operating for the whim and the comfort of a few, and the debasement and defilement of the many, be curbed or, as I would have it, set aside entirely?

New York, N. Y.
December 23, 1931

Textual Note: Introduction to *Harlan Miners Speak: Report on Terrorism in the Kentucky Coal Fields. Prepared by Members of the National Committee for the Defense of Political Prisoners.* New York: Harcourt, Brace and Company, 1932. These selections are found on pages 3–4, 10–16. The attack on individualism that forms the conclusion was first given as an address before the Group Forum, New York, on 15 December 1931, and published as "Individualism and the Jungle," *New Masses* 7 (January 1932): 1–2; and *Crawford's Weekly,* 2 January 1932, p. 6.

1. Congressional Record, 10 June 1936, quoted in John F. Day, *Bloody Ground* (Lexington: University Press of Kentucky, 1981), 303–4.
2. Crawford edited and published the radical newspaper *Crawford's Weekly* in Norton, Virginia, one of the few journals to cover events in Harlan in a manner sympathetic to the miners. Shot by a sniper while crossing a bridge in nearby Pineville in July 1931, Crawford returned to Harlan as a member of the investigative committee.
3. After visiting the mining area around Pittsburgh in June 1931, Dreiser issued a statement in which he charged that the A.F.L.-affiliated United Mine Workers of America was undemocratic and ineffective, and that it acted in collusion with the mine operators; he went on to call for the disestablishment of the A.F.L. This led to an exchange of open letters with A.F.L. President William L. Green (1873–1952), two of which are reprinted in Elias, *Letters* 2: 537–61.
4. Ishmael, Abraham's first-born son in the Hebrew Bible, is an archetype of the disinherited.
5. Strikes by low-paid workers outside of the A.F.L. unions, largely in response to employers' tightening of already harsh conditions. Cotton workers at the Loray Mill in Gaston County, North Carolina, struck in the spring of 1929; the 1929 Imperial Valley dispute is mentioned in "The American Press and American Political Prisoners." In both cases, as in Harlan, Communist-organized unions became involved. The most famous "cry" from Lawrence, Massachusetts, was the 1912 strike led by the I.W.W.

America

After 18 June 1932.

This previously unpublished short essay brings together many strands of Dreiser's political thinking in the 1930s—that capitalism was inefficient and gave rise to antisocial, individualistic values, and that a new form of social organization was needed to promote humanistic values. Here that mode of organization is conceived of as "socialization" on principles of "social equity," as advocated by Communism.

The present crisis of the world, and specifically that of the United States, is something more than a mere crisis of politics and economics, and it will not pass with this depression. The reason it will not pass is because the depression is a mere symptom of ills which do not spring from the absence of fat profits and prosperity for a few against the leanness if not actual want of the many, but from the fact that we have come to the place where fat profits and mere money lordship for a few, and enforced financial mediocrity for the many do not make room for the new ideas and opportunities of the many as against the ignorant, wooden-headed and ridiculously vain and pretentious and entirely dull tyranny of those who have the cunning and brass to make and keep money. They lack the brains wherewith to grasp its social significance. In short, we are faced today by the need of new social forms, new mental directions and interests, and, in consequence, a new social code.

But how to get these in America? For here today, as quite everywhere else in the world, outside of Russia, our present economic system is based on the exploitation of the many for the profit of the few.

Worse, there is no social interest, and hence no social planning toward which national as well as private social success and profit should be directed. And there are so many basic social needs as well as necessary changes to effect them, waiting. Among them may be cited:

1. Socialization of medicine, dentistry, etc.
2. Socialization of transportation.
3. Socialization of communications.
4. Socialization of mines.
5. Socialization of farming.
6. Socialization of all other industry.
7. Socialization of industrial and educational science.
8. Socialization of education.
9. Socialization of the arts.

10. Socialization of eleemosynary activities in connection with
unemployment, illness, insurance, mental and physical defectives,
all of which are supposed to be covered by hospitals, sanatoria,
resorts, pensions, furloughs, and treatments of various kinds.

But as to these, *in regard to them*, what are our overlords of the profit-
motive thinking, let alone doing? Or their dumb followers, the intellectuals,
professors, editors, writers, journalists, scientists, religionists, etc.? Instead
of grasping their importance, and frowning on or, better, vigorously opposing the overlords in their dull and brutal program, they ape and follow
them, and will continue unless deflected and prevented from so doing by
the masses below, from whom they humbly take their money, position and
rating in the world. And so we see inequity, dishonesty, cunning, cruelty
and hateful and shameful indifference and self-indulgence, flowering into
bank accounts, and clothes and houses and lands and servants and ballyhoo
as to proper social engagements and connections—the right golf club or
tennis court, the right resort, the right club, the right college, marriage,
secret order, the right church, and what not, and so bringing on the ever-
broadening curses of slums, sectarianism, mental and social abuses, ending
finally in the untouchables of crime and beggary.

In truth, our intellectuals or thinkers, so-called, of any standing with
the press, churches, universities, etc. encourage, and really *only* encourage,
the leadership of the cunning and the greedy, whose responsibility ends
with getting and keeping—not at all with thinking intensively of what a
world or a race that can accumulate wealth apart from eating, drinking and
pleasuring itself, can do with it.

In short, the present economic system is based on this subordination
of human and, by the same token, its mentally creative values, to those
of anarchic self-assertion. Get and keep. Do not encourage or multiply or
fructify the forces of the mind. Forget that human, and by human I mean
mental, growth is first, and that mere physical or social comfort is last—in
fact, that human growth, the encouragement and so multiplication of the
higher powers of man is the main business of living. It is for that reason at
this time that the true lover of humanity and the up-building of mind should
announce himself as an advocate of the program and policies of the Communists, wherever and should oppose all other programs—particularly here
in America, where they parade under the names Democratic, Republican,
Socialist, and seek, solely and with not the least inkling of the mental as
well as economic changes afoot in the world, to retain control and power.
They should oppose the profit motive to the death, set aside inheritance
as robbery which it is, and insist that every man make a life for himself but

no other, that if a man and a woman bear children, they urge and compel them to start with all other children of the nation at scratch, and make lives and characters for themselves as did their parents or, at least, primary ancestors before them.

Mr. Gene Tunney, the retired world's heavyweight prize-fighting champion, once said, I believe, that he could go into a haberdashery, whip the salesman, and walk off with a dozen shirts, but that he would be arrested at the door, and punished, as he should be. "But," he added, "men steal things through the use of brute brains and get away with it. What is worse, they are held in high respect."[1] And that is true, or the recent congressional investigations of the banking business and the stock market are without significance, their sworn testimony registered without truth or meaning.

And hence it is that although you now see being partially enforced a five-day week and a six-hour day, and a minimum wage of 40 cents an hour, you hear nothing of any national efforts toward the socializations previously listed. Nor any word yet of the government itself taking over the railroads, the telephones, the telegraph, the radio corporations, the power trust, the gas trust, the national bus lines and airways, and operating them equitably and generously for all. For that would immediately dispose of that immense and brutal system of special interests, private ownership and private inheritance and privilege, never worked for or earned.

In short, the plain, old, material and greedy profit system for the few which now holds in thrall the cunning and the cruel (never the wise or artistic or humanitarian) and which seeks by mere money and show and the name of it to have its victors recognized as giants, mental and social, whereas, at bottom, they are mere economic factotums, who once and for all should be placed in their equitable state in this world, and nowhere else, should be dispensed with. It does not and cannot, by anything its cunning and dishonest exemplars do or seek to do, honestly come by or use even a fraction of the immense sums which, by way of interest or plain old usury or, in other words, legalized thievery, which now, by political and financial control of all the machinery of politics and law, it is able to collect and control.

Treason! Anarchy! The subversion of all law and order and equity, do I hear someone say? Certainly treason and anarchy, but only to one idea—the profit-grabbing one. No other. And that not on the part of those who denounce these social grafters and their ways, but on the part of the robbers and grafters at the top who denounce those who would end their inequitable rule.

As things stand today in America, our parties and their conventions represent only political organizations for practical, political, and economic aid to our special American financiers and money-trust masters, their corporations, courts, judges, police and subservient unions in every walk of life, but never to the people at large. Our parties and their followers and promoters represent today only spineless and characterless newspapers; a money directed and debauched educational system; churches that promote a heaven anywhere but on earth, the one place where, if anywhere, it honestly belongs; a government by and for corporations, their principal bond and share-holders, who cruelly and brutally take money and work from the many in order to socially deify and make fools and snobs of the children, and the grandchildren of those who thus primarily steal, rob and even murder. It is our financial history. And our *financial history* is *our history*.

Rampant greed and hypocrisy in high places; unfairness to the working classes, constant exploitation of all classes below the millionaire level, the worship of false ideals and utterly vapid values.

The Big Bruisers of Business.

It is my doctrine as well as those of others that today the acquisitive or profit instinct ought to be policed just as muscular strength or brute strength generally in some walks of life, at least, has been policed. The big bruisers of business and money should be taken to the public's police station. Greed and cunning should be shackled—and heavily.

The marvel to me is that every thinking individual, from the topmost levels of the rich to the poorest of the poor, cannot see the wisdom and equity of social equity which would arrange all this,[2] that it can only make, on the one hand, for the destruction of idle, cruel and wasteful sybaritism of the profit-motivated few and, on the other hand, for the development of those natural and valuable powers of man which will result in an equitable and respectable state and its mental progress.

Textual Note: Undated essay, completed after 18 June 1932 from internal evidence. Copy-text is the 7-page typescript in DPUP folder 11909 headed "America" in Dreiser's hand, selectively emended by reference to the untitled mixed holograph and typescript (15 pages, DPUP folder 11908).

1. Quoted from Edward Angly, "What's the Matter with the United States? Gene Tunney Finds Rampant Greed and Hypocrisy among Reasons Nation Is Taking Count," *Herald Tribune*, 18 June 1932 (clipping in DPUP). Gene (born James Joseph) Tunney (1887–1978), who had been heavyweight boxing champion from 1926 to 1928, explicitly distances himself from state socialism but is quoted as advocating "state control of the acquisitive instinct" and unemployment insurance, and flaying "poisonous parasites" of the stock exchange, hypocrisy in American society, and prohibition.

2. This rather awkward phrasing replaces Dreiser's earlier formulation "cannot see the wisdom and the justice of Communism."

The Child and the School

American Spectator, April 1933.

As a member of the American Spectator's *editorial board from November 1932 to February 1934, Dreiser tried to push its address to a cosmopolitan intellectual readership toward the left. Here he adapts material from* Tragic America.

As I see it, the training of children in their social relations—national and international—should be the main function of our public schools. Boys and girls should be made to see themselves as part of a great mass of people with whom they are connected and to whom they are socially, economically and in other ways responsible as co-sharers in all the benefits of that immense mass co-ordination known as organized society. Early and clearly, it seems to me, they should be apprised of its immense ramifications and duties, of which they must be a part, however humble, connected with it all by the fact that they live in a house built for them by others, ride in automobiles manufactured for them by men like their fathers, eat food grown by farmers, shipped by railroad clerks, cooked by their mothers—and in return for all this, that it is their duty as well as their father's to help to build houses for others, build roads, do *something*. In sum, children must be made to see that they are only a few members of a wide race with other little boys and girls all over the world. They must be taught that neither the necessities nor the more interesting and pleasurable phases of their lives can be had without the contributions of all of the individuals of the world working to supply them.[1]

Instead of being taught submission and weak servitude to God, as a philosophy of life, children should be taught their rights. One would think, in going through school, that the individual American citizen had no rights. No mention is ever made of them. I would, at the outset, instruct pupils concerning their property rights. They should know certain things, as, for example, that notice should be given before eviction; that when a place is rented by the week, there must be a week's notice to leave before anyone can be put out, or with a rental by the month, a month's notice. This would save a lot of corporate abuse to the worker and his family.

More, children today should be filled with knowledge of that which is the most important of all: the real basis of organized society. A man is supposed to receive from society in return for his work the necessities and comforts of society as provided by other members of the community. If the people but understood this and were alive, the poor and the middle classes would not be so submissive to their oppression by our present-day corporations—or their predecessors, the divine-right masters of the past. Yet although the

Church has long made oppression of the poor a sin, it has done nothing, so far as I can see, to lessen it.

Textual Note: American Spectator 1:6 (April 1933): 2. Revised and condensed version of material from *Tragic America*, chapter 19: "A Suggested Phase of Education," 354–55; 363–64; 364–65.

1. Drawing on his visit to a Russian school in 1927, in *Tragic America* Dreiser had expanded this thought as follows: "In fact, everything that comes up in the classroom or in connection with education in general, should be explained to the children in its relation to this social organization of which they are a part. Should a little boy or girl bring the teacher flowers, it should be asked: 'Do people like flowers; why do people like flowers?' etc. Thus should the school training concerning society replace the old, meaningless, because unthoughtful, religious training of the home" (*Tragic America*, 355).

Editorial Note on the New Deal and Soviet Policy

American Spectator, August 1933.

This unsigned editorial typifies the American Spectator's *habitual tone of "clever" irony, into which Dreiser tried to inject a leftwing political perspective.*

The Editors patriotically note that, whereas President Roosevelt's proposals in regard to the national control of railroads, banks, industry, farming, shipping, the unification of operations in the purchase of all raw materials, their manufacture and sale, stabilization of prices, uniform accounting, the thirty-hour week or five-hour day, etc., constitute economic and social statesmanship of the first American order, the same proposals and their practical enforcement in Russia constitute the Red Menace and, if advocated here by Communists, involve arrest, imprisonment, fines, expatriation, and deportation.

Textual Note: American Spectator 1:10 (August 1933): 1.
    Title supplied by the present editors. Attributed on the basis of the editorial policy of the *American Spectator,* which required agreement of each of the editors for publication, and of Dreiser's interest in the relation of the New Deal and Soviet policy.

The "Is Dreiser Anti-Semitic?" Correspondence

September–December 1933.

The front page of the September 1933 American Spectator *featured an "Editorial Conference (With Wine)," in which the five editors discussed the "Jewish question" with a mixture of flippancy and seriousness. Dreiser expressed admiration for Jewish literature and culture, achievements all the more remarkable given the* long-standing repression of Jews, and speculated on possible solutions to what he called the "anomalous" position of Jews dispersed across different nations. These possible solutions include the introduction of "handicaps" to curb Jewish shrewdness and intellectual ability, referring to the ethnic quotas proposed by the Pennsylvania Bar Association; the assimilation of Jews into mainstream America; or Jewish nationalism. Dreiser is quoted as articulating a position close to the early American Zionism of his friend Ludwig Lewisohn (1882–1955), who is mentioned in the "Symposium":

> I would ask the Jew with all his ability and his wealth and admiration of power, with all the genius he shows when he enters an alien land and becomes a powerful factor in its welfare, or its domination, I would ask him, I say, personally to consider whether in just plain fairness to nations that want to be themselves, that don't care to be dominated by a church or race or theory of life, and are not, in short, as clever as he is, why he shouldn't step up before the peoples of the world and ask for just such a territory in which to develop a nation of his own and with which he could deal on the basis of his own genius in all lines. With the Jews nationally so placed, we could deal [with them], just as they could deal with every other nation in the world. And by degrees all should benefit from their very great ability to organize and construct. What I cannot understand is their present objection to doing so. But this may be the result of their scattering in historic times, and it may, for all we know, be presently overcome by the Jew himself.[1]

Resisting the trivializing comments of his fellow editors, Dreiser insists upon the prestige of Jewish cultural achievement and attempts to initiate a serious discussion of the tensions caused by ethnic solidarity. James Branch Cabell concludes the discussion by satirically suggesting that "America present the American Jews with the State of Kansas. Thereby, in the first place, we might rid ourselves of Kansas; in the second place, of the Jews; and in the third place, we might happily establish in the heart of America a source not only of aesthetic development but of financial support."

The Symposium drew a concerned response from Hutchins Hapgood (1869–1944), author of The Spirit of the Ghetto (1902), one of the first authentic studies of American immigrant life by a nonimmigrant. Harvard-educated and descended from New England Brahmin stock, Hapgood affiliated himself with the non-Communist liberal left. He wrote to the American Spectator editors appealing to them as fellow liberals and warning of the danger of seeming to indulge nativist prejudices. His letter was passed on to Dreiser, and a heated exchange ensued, the bulk of which Hapgood eventually published in The Nation for 7 April 1935, under the title "Is Dreiser Anti-Semitic?" The pertinent correspondence is printed in full below.

Dreiser vehemently denied that his opposition to Hapgood's "liberalism" could be equated with anti-Semitism, and went on to clarify and modify his position in a statement to the New Masses *(see 199–200) and in a June 1936 letter to* The Nation, *published as "Mea Culpa!" (see 204–8).*

Hutchins Hapgood to the Editors of the
American Spectator, 4 October 1933

Editors of the American Spectator
Gentlemen:
When I read the Jewish symposium, in the *American Spectator,* I had a feeling that it was to be regretted. But at first I passed it by with the idea that it was only a sort of editorial amusement—the way editors get together over a cocktail and a little half-serious talk.

But when I talked to a Jewish friend of mine, a painter, who had never been troubled by the Jewish question, and who had led the life of an artist, who had no felt nationality; and when I saw that he had suddenly and violently discovered that he belonged to the Jewish race, partly because of the Hitler epidemic and partly because of the article in the *American Spectator,* that article seemed not as innocent in its results as I had hoped.

The editors of the *Spectator* are no longer young, and no doubt are a part of the liberal past. Their values are the values of our traditional culture. It is difficult to think that these values are dispersed, almost overnight, by the shock of the recent nationalism that has overtaken the world.[2] It is to be hoped that the Symposium is but a temporary and rather thoughtless gesture; for at a time when the peace and sanity of the world is troubled and threatened, we need all the convinced liberals we can muster. True liberals are not reactionary to any forward movement. Norman Thomas for example although a Socialist, is also a liberal.[3] It is probable that by this time some of the Russian Communists are liberals, without ceasing to be Communists. But a liberal, if he remains a true liberal, can never act against the fundamental morality of a slowly worked out emancipation of the individual from racial, nationalistic and religious prejudices.

The legitimate struggle today is between groups divided on economic policy and interests. Other points of struggle—national, racial and religious—are throwbacks and barbaric remnants, and so obscuring and harmful.

At a time like this, we liberals cannot afford to approach the immediate passions of the time in any spirit that is not serious. We should consider that it would take very little added emphasis on the side of national and race feeling as a basis for special privilege on a large scale, to plunge the world into a more destructive war and depression than that from which we are struggling to recover.

If we remain true to our liberal faith, we shall, I am convinced, and at no distant day, have cause to congratulate ourselves that we did not yield to a moment of nationalistic madness. Not to yield thus tests not only our liberalism, but also the independence of our individual judgment, as opposed to majority pressure.

Hutchins Hapgood

Theodore Dreiser to Hutchins Hapgood,
10 October 1933

Dear Hapgood:

Your letter to The Editors of The American Spectator, although answered by Boyd,[4] has been turned over to me.

Liberality has always had a dubious standing in my mental court. It is so easy to be liberal, when there is nothing to be illiberal about, but, on the other hand, it is so easy to pose a few problems to the liberal which will cause him no end of trouble.

Let us say that it is necessary to sustain a liberal attitude toward sectarianism. Well, a mild form of religious sectarianism would not work much harm, and might be liberally treated. Supposing your liberalism were faced by a rising tide of Mohammedism in the United States, as it is actually faced by a rising tide of Catholicism, and before it all, not only a little, of what you deemed true liberalism would be certain to go down. What about liberalism in that instance?

Or, let us take, for instance, the rising tide of color. I like the Negro as much as anyone in the world. I believe he is honest, I think he is industrious and I think he has gifts which, particularly in the matters of vitality, humor, if not romance, the white race lacks. It is entirely possible that a blend is not only possible but desirable and even unescapable. But if the people of England—I am not speaking of South Africa, which does not concern me very much, or Australia, or any of her outlying provinces—but if the people of England, I say, were faced by a rising tide of color, how do you suppose the English liberal would feel about it, and, if he opposed it, would there be any justification for it? It would be interesting to know. His temperament and the institutions which are the result of it reflect one very interesting state of historic life. The occupation of England by Negroes would certainly result in an entirely different state of affairs. Should the one, without argument, and for the sake of liberality, be abandoned for the other? It makes an interesting problem.

Let us take the divine right of kings, and its final smash. According to your theory of liberalism, the divine right of kings should never have been disturbed and, by the same token, should be flourishing in whatever philosophic or tyrannical form it might have assumed, until this hour. It was really overthrown by illiberalism, as the divine right individualist saw it. It would be interesting to know what liberalism would say to that.

In the same line, you can take the Jewish question. Liberalism, in the case of the Jew, means internationalism. He is to wander where he pleases, and retain, as he does, his religion and race-characteristics without change. In America, Jewish temples are multiplying about as rapidly as Catholic churches and, thank God, they are a little more artistic. The Jews, despite all argument to the contrary, are multiplying in number. It is admitted now that there are at least 2,400,000 in New York City. In other cities, they bear the same ratio to the population. They do not, in spite of all discussion of the matter, enter upon farming; they are rarely mechanics; they are not the day laborer of the world—pick and shovel—they are, by preference, lawyers, bankers, merchants, money lenders and brokers and middlemen. If you listen to Jews discuss Jews, you will find that they are money-minded, very pagan, very sharp in practice and, usually, in so far as the rest is concerned, they have the single objective of plenty of money out of which they build a fairly material surrounding.

The profession of the law is today seriously considering, in such states as Pennsylvania, New Jersey, Oregon, limiting the number of Jewish lawyers and, as they see it, for a very definite reason. The Jews lack, if I read the Pennsylvania Bar Association correctly, the fine integrity which at least is endorsed and, to a degree, followed by the lawyers of other nationalities. At least, that is the charge. Left to sheer liberalism, as you interpret it, they could possess America by sheer numbers, their cohesion, their race tastes and, as in the case of the Negro in South Africa, really overrun the land.

Well, if liberalism means that you are to accept that change without thought, without opposition, bow to whatever is coming without trying to stay it or keep what you have, well and good. There is no reason for anybody saying anything. But if that is not to be done, then some consideration by at least someone must be given to what befalls a given state, and also whether anything can be done to maintain one type of civilization, or life, or racial life, as against another type of civilization or racial life. If the liberal says that is *not* the thing to do, there are many who would still consider themselves fairly liberal who say that it would have been better to preserve Greece against the Romans or barbarians than to stand by and see it overrun by Rome and, actually, even later by barbarians. If these are fair examples of true liberalism, I decline to endorse it, and I think it is a fair criticism, because I believe that ideals are not garden weeds. They do not just take care of themselves; they are inspirational and have to be maintained by enthusiasm and by sacrifice. It is the same way with social organization; it has to be maintained against these invasions, or there will be no organization. If the liberals say not to bother, but to let this other organization come in if it would, well and good, only that does not seem to be reasonable, and certainly it is not admirable nor desirable.

In this particular symposium, I did not say anything which should cause an intelligent Jew to quarrel with my position. I simply said that I saw no reason why a race as gifted, as definite, as religious in its predilections should not be willing to occupy a country of its own, and what is wrong with that argument, I still fail to see.[5] The Jew insists that when he invades Italy or France or America or what you will, he becomes a native of that country—a full blooded native of that country. You know yourself, if you know anything, that that is not true. He has been in Germany now for all of a thousand years, if not longer, and he is still a Jew. He has been in America all of two hundred years, and he has not faded into a pure American by any means, and he will not. As I said before, he maintains his religious dogmas, and his racial sympathies, race characteristics and race cohesion as against all types or nationalities surrounding him wheresoever.

For that reason, I maintain that it is the hour in which *laissez-faire* liberalism might be willing to step aside at least to the extent of suggesting or even advising the Jew to undertake a land of his own. I say this because I am for nationalism as opposed to internationalism. I think that differences in nations in the world will always exist, and that it is interesting and better that there should be differences, if for no more than the matter of entertainment and of developing new characteristics through the various mediums which differences invariably give rise to.

So what?
Theodore Dreiser

P.S. It just occurs to me that the Jewish artist who was made so conscious of his Judaism is very likely the same artist who expressed the opinions which I quoted. I am not sure, but I think so. If it is so, it is very interesting.

Hutchins Hapgood to Theodore Dreiser,
18 October 1933

Dear Dreiser:

I have your letter of October 10th; and to say that I am surprised and disappointed is to put it mildly. I thought, as you know, that the original symposium about the Jews, in the *American Spectator,* was unfortunate in its probable results. But I did not think that what you wrote there amounted to definite anti-Semitism.

This letter of yours, however, is a clear expression not only of anti-Semitism but of intense nationalism in general. If you hadn't signed the letter I might have thought that it was written by a member of the Ku Klux Klan or a representative of Hitler.

It makes no difference whether you attach value to the Jews or not, and you evidently do attach value to them. It makes no difference whether you like the negroes or not, and you apparently do like them. It makes no difference whether you like the Catholics or not. It makes no difference whether you like the Mohammedans or not.

But it does make a difference, as an indication of your state of mind, what you want to have done about these nations, races and sects. I will not discuss the Mohammedans or the negroes; they seem to me at present too remote for any useful discussion. And for the sake of simplicity, I will leave out the Catholics, for the time; although I think it is safe to say that the differences of religious opinion can be handled only by thought and cultural experience.

The Jews are the subject of our discussion. Your statements about the Jews are far from being true. If your statements about the Jewish population in the United States were true, there would be more Jews in the United States than there are in the whole world, including the United States.

You say that the Jews "do not represent the day-laborers of the world, but are by preference lawyers, bankers, brokers, merchants, money-lenders and middlemen."

But as a matter of fact the very great majority of Jews in the United States are laborers. They constitute a very large majority of the needle-workers and the sweat-shop workers here. The poor Jews in New York throw into complete shadow the wealthy Jews, so far as numbers are concerned. It is equally true also that the non-Jews are, "by preference lawyers, bankers, merchants, money-lenders, brokers and middlemen."

The non-Jews are not by preference day-laborers, needle-workers, nor sweat-shop workers.

Again you say, "If you listen to Jews discuss Jews, you will find that they are money-minded, very pagan, very sharp in practice . . . and usually have a single objective, of plenty of money."

Of how many non-Jews, I will ask, are these things also true? Meanness, stupidity and sharp practice, are as universal as the more sympathetic qualities, and equally distributed among the nations and races. These things are individual characteristics, not national or racial.

You also state that the Jews keep their religion and racial characteristics. On the contrary, one of the most marked things about the Jews is that they drop their religion in the second generation after reaching America, and that they would be more than willing to drop their race, if the non-Jews allowed them to do so. The "race," whatever that may be, has been kept alive by the unfriendly attentions of the non-Jews. Certainly the Jews would have been much more nearly assimilated, were it not for the fact that for a great many years they were penned up together in ghettos, and were the object of fanatical outrages, which of course helped still more to keep them together.

Now by the attitude that you express in your letter, which is a frank statement that you would like if possible to have the Jews removed from America, you do something which would strengthen their racial and national consciousness.

However, if all you say in your letter were true—which is far from being the case—your attitude is, in the real sense of the word, barbarous. You go back on our cherished civilization, on what has been painfully attained during hundreds of years. A part of our culture is the recognition of the evil of religious and racial intolerance and persecution, and no man who is a part of our civilization can safely ignore it otherwise he is either ignorant or an agent provocateur, and therefore a danger to the peace of the community, for, in a time like this it is easy to stir up trouble. And for you, who ought to be a leader in our civilization, to take this barbarous attitude, is to me inexplicable on any decent ground. Ignorance, as I have said, is the only tolerable excuse, and even that is hardly tolerable.

It is true that barbarism lies only a little way beneath the surface of civilization. As Freud said in a little book which I think he called *War and Death*,[6] man in his barbaric condition hates everything not himself and wants to kill it. No matter how civilized he becomes, the instinct to kill the stranger, the foreigner, the Jew and so forth, persists, and when civilized restraints are removed, bursts out again with terrible violence.

What nobler faith can civilized man cherish, than that which opposes this destructive instinct? What better colors can they follow?

Dreiser, go back to your novels; cease to occupy yourself with "labor" or with any other broadly social activities; for neither by education nor by character are you qualified, and can therefore do only harm.

Hutchins Hapgood

Theodore Dreiser to Hutchins Hapgood,
28 December 1933

Dear Hapgood:

Two months ago, I had your reply to my letter, and would have answered it except for pressure of other matters which, in my case, is great. I hasten to do so now not because, as you seem to indicate in your latest, that I fear publicity for my letter.[7] After all these years, I feel you do not know me. I underwrite all of my opinions as well as convictions, and now stand by what I wrote as written. The single purpose of this letter is to take up some of your counter-charges and arguments, and see what they amount to.

One of them is that I exaggerate the number of Jews in the United States. I do not think so. It is true that the census for 1927 shows the total Jewish population in the United States as 4,288,000 as against a total population of 118,000,000, but the accuracy of this can certainly be questioned, particularly in the face of the fact that so many Jews deliberately pass as Americans, using American names and, to a degree, this would be further qualified because of the number of half-Jews and quarter-Jews who, none the less, because of their Jewish blood, adhere racially and religiously with Jewry. I notice that the World Almanac gives the Jewish population of New York City in 1927 as 1,765,000 and that of Chicago as 325,000. Anyone who has observed New York, Chicago, Cleveland or Los Angeles on a Jewish holiday or, more particularly, on their religious fast and feast days, would know that these figures are ridiculous. New York is practically deserted. You would think that all but one third of the people had retired to their homes and, in Chicago, the impression is that at least one third of the life, if not more, had departed from the city, which would certainly bring the Jewish population there to over a million. Besides, these figures are 1927 as against 1934.

Another of your deductions from my letter is that I would like to have the Jews removed from America. I said nothing about removing them, and I actually think that Germany, in assaulting, torturing and robbing them, and driving them forth without means or a land of their own to go to, acted not only without social justice, but without wisdom. A decent way, if they felt that they could not live with them, would have been to negotiate with them, and the powers of the world for land and social opportunities of an equal character elsewhere. In fact, a great opportunity for statesmanlike posing of a difficult national as well as international problem, if it was one, was lost by not entering into negotiations with the German Jews as a people, and then and there posing the problems seemingly so irritating to the German people. What with the wisdom and genius of the Jews on the one hand, and German as well as the associated statesmanship of the other nations on the other—for foreign aid could and should have been secured—a peaceful and, what is more, very likely an illuminating and generally beneficial solution of the difficulties might have been reached. As it is, Germany now stands indicted of barbarism, and that indictment will not be easily set aside. Certainly it could have done no harm to publicly and internationally thrash out this age-old quarrel between the Jews and the people with whom they have found themselves associated. For I hold that either they are to be accepted and joined up peacefully and fraternally with all nations everywhere, or they are not. And if not, then most certainly they should have been provided not only with an important and suitable territory of their own in which to display their social genius, but also with the means to transfer themselves. Otherwise no decency. And if that is related to "removing" them in the sense that you use the word in connection with my letter, then you are welcome to that use of it—but none other.

What really should be done, if the various nations now quarreling with the Jew and his internationalism wish to be fair, is for them to call an international conference with all Jewry and therein thrash out all the problems now seemingly worrying so many of them as well as the Jews and by wise counsel on the part of all reach as acceptable a program as possible. I see no other honest or fair way to deal with the Jews. And they, scattered and quarreled with in so many places and nations, should be the first to welcome it.

As for dismissing the problem of the Negro and the Mohammedans as too remote for any useful discussion—you may recall that we unjustly enslaved the Negro after bringing him here, and then fought a war to free him and, to this hour, have not truly freed him. And yet with some thirteen million of him under a general social ban, you call that remote. It seems to me very immediate, and one of the things that some day or other will have to be faced by a white world—whether by intermarriage or repatriation or, as you vaguely put it, "by thought and cultural experience" (a phrase, by the way, which means absolutely nothing to me, since it may mean anywhere from a day to a billion years of time and thought and cultural experience) I cannot say.

As for Catholicism (not "the Catholics" as you incorrectly put it) it represents a problem in mental liberation and at this hour is up and straining for solution in Spain, Mexico—indeed in every country where there is thought as to the wisdom of opposing disestablished dogma with ascertained knowledge. Yet you say of that, "It can only be handled by thought and cultural experience." Well, maybe, but over how many millions of years? The Russians, in so far as the eastern equivalent of Catholicism is concerned, swept it away, and rightly, as I see it, and in favor of ascertained knowledge as against "revealed truth." In Germany, there is a compromise in favor of keeping the masses ignorant. Here, we dawdle, as we dawdle with all problems until angered by delay or chains or legal fictions which we cannot peacefully dispel, we resort to the arbitrament of arms. It is the fool's way. Better an open and free discussion—a public and free re-examination of the intentions as well as the intellectual proclivities and tendencies of this nation as it now is rather than a piddling and dawdling reference of it to future thought and cultural experience. We are fairly at the crossroads now. And now is the time for us to choose our mental direction. As I see it, disestablished dogma should bow before ascertained knowledge. And only ascertained knowledge should be taught the child by the state. If Catholicism disagrees with that, its schools should be closed and its children educated by the state.

In connection with this, and my discussion of the Jews, you assert that "the most marked thing about the Jews is that they drop their religion in the second generation after reaching America, and that they would be willing to drop their race if the non-Jews allow them to do so." Primarily, I would like to have the opinions of ten different Jews in various walks of life, religious, legal, commercial, artistic, labor, and the like, and see how heartily, if at all, they would agree with you. I have noted the growth of architecturally aesthetic Jewish Synagogues, America over. I note the current call for the re-establishment of the Saturday Jewish Sabbath. I note the appearance of New York and Chicago at such times as the Jews enter upon their religious observances of the Passover and related race and religious days, and I am not ready to believe what you say. I think you are blinking realities because you greatly admire and strongly sympathize with a brilliant and gifted people. My own observation as to the Jew's tendencies in this respect is different. More, I greatly respect their race and religious solidarity even though you personally proceed to dismiss the Jewish race as a myth. I quote you: "the 'race,' whatever that may be." Imagine! Then there are no Semites and hence no anti-Semites. Be reasonable. In the next sentence, you say, "certainly the Jews would have been much more nearly assimilated were it not for the fact that for a great many years they were penned up together in Ghettoes and were the object of fanatical outrages which, of course, helped still more to keep them together." Perfectly true. But if there are no Jews—if "the 'race,' whatever that might mean" does not exist, as your line seems to indicate, then against what nation or race, if any, were the outrages committed?

You call me barbarous and anti-Semitic—even "Jew-hating and Jew-baiting." As you please, but I am supposedly barbarous and anti-Semitic because in the face of all the attacks upon the Jews, their crucifixion in Germany and elsewhere, I rise to assert that these very gifted and highly integrated and self-protective people are, whatever their distinguished equipment, mistaken in attempting to establish themselves as Jews, with their religion, race characteristics, race solidarity and all, in the bosom, not of any one country or people, but rather in the lands and nations of almost every country the world over, the while they assert that they are not Jews but Germans, Frenchmen, Englishmen, Americans, Russians, Poles, Hollanders, Italians, Hungarians, Turks, Romanians, what you will. It is not reasonable. It is not the way—especially since, being as gifted as they are, they so rapidly rise to power and affluence wherever they go. To say the least, it is provocative of comment and in all too many cases of jealousy, the jealousy of the not-so-clever and gifted of those who are so much more clever and truly gifted in so many ways. And, though I be counted barbarous and anti-Semitic and what you will, I now rise to assert that, having grown in wealth and numbers and ability and distinction the world over, it is time for them, as well as wisdom, to realize that they are, after all, a dispersed and, in many ways, annoyed race or put upon nation, and that, as such—and anti-Semitism being what it is today, culture and liberality to the contrary notwithstanding—they should now take steps to assemble and consider their state and their future. There are lands as well as nations—international statesmanship being what it is at this hour—which should be willing and able to furnish them forth not only with an entirely adequate country, but with the loans and equipment necessary to start them upon an independent and, as I see it, certain-to-be successful and even glorious career as a nation. And to that I should think—the Zionist movement being what it is—they should be willing and even anxious to subscribe.

But, not wanting that, some anti-nationalistic, if not anti-social feeling or mood animating them, why not a program of race or nation blending here in America—the type or kind of race or nation blending that has been in progress here since America was founded, and between the English, French, Germans, Italians, Poles, Hungarians, Russians, Swedes, Chinese and others. They have all come as members of separate races and nations, yet slowly and surely they have been absorbed in that strange and perhaps worthless people, the dub American. As Shaw urged only recently—why not every Jewish male forced to marry a Gentile female, and every Jewish female a Gentile male?[8] Would not that solve this very vexing question of how the Jew is to be disposed of among the various races and nations of the world?

But if not that, then perhaps the Jews will rise and say what they think should be done to allay this very obvious international bitterness. And I, for one, should like to know what their answer would be.

Theodore Dreiser

Textual Note: The correspondence is in DPUP folder 2507. Copy-texts of Hutchins Hapgood to the Editors of the *American Spectator*, 4 October 1933, and Hutchins Hapgood to TD, 18 October 1933, are taken from the original typescripts. Copy-texts of TD to Hutchins Hapgood, 10 October 1933, and TD to Hutchins Hapgood, 28 December 1933, are taken from carbons of fair copies produced in response to Hapgood's proposal to publish them, emended for sense and transcription errors by reference to carbons of the originals. The texts have been standardized. Clean texts are presented, spellings corrected, and addresses have been silently removed.

1. "Editorial Conference (With Wine)," *American Spectator* 1:11 (September 1933): 1.

2. A reference to the *American Spectator* editors' generational interpretation of rising political extremism in Europe: "All over Europe at this moment [young men] are rushing about in black, brown, green or red shirts, raising their arms in Roman salutation and obeying, as usual, the behests of a spellbinder who can stir up those mob emotions which are apparently their only substitute for thought." Editorial, *American Spectator* 1:7 (May 1933): 1.

3. Norman Thomas (1884–1968) was the leader of the Socialist Party from 1926–48. His thought mixed the Christian Social Gospel, anarchism, and Marxism.

4. Ernest Boyd (1887–1946), one of the five originating editors of the *American Spectator*.

5. Dreiser's adoption of this Zionist position in the *American Spectator* editorial conference is quoted in the headnote to this selection.

6. Sigmund Freud, *Thoughts for the Times on War and Death,* trans. A. A. Brill and Alfred B. Kuttner (New York: Moffat, Yard and Co., 1918).

7. Hapgood had written to Dreiser on 15 December 1933 proposing the publication of their first exchange of letters. He closed, "If I do not hear from you giving me your consent to publish your letter to me, I shall publish my letter to you in any case. If you write, I'll include your reply in the publication." Hutchins Hapgood to TD, 15 December 1933, DPUP.

8. The precise source of this comment has not been found. George Bernard Shaw's "Preface on Bosses" to his 1936 play *The Millionairess* ironizes Hitler's anti-Semitism as follows: "All Germans are not Mozarts, nor even Mendelssohns and Meyerbeers, both of whom, by the way, though exceptionally desirable Germans, were Jews. Surely the average German can be improved. I am told that children bred from Irish colleens and Chinese laundrymen are far superior to inbred Irish or Chinese. . . . Only the stupidest or craziest ultra-Nationalists believe that people corralled within the same political frontier are all exactly alike, and that they improve by in-breeding."

Flies and Locusts

Common Sense, December 1933.

Common Sense *was a political monthly started by Alfred M. Bingham (1905–98) and Selden Rodman (1909–2002) in December 1932 with the aim of promoting a "definite and practical program which is at once thoroughgoing in its objectives and American in its appeal."*[1] *Attracted by their attempt to forge an anti-capitalist alternative to the New Deal out of the technocracy and farmer-labor movements, Dreiser contributed four essays to the magazine in 1933–39. "Flies and Locusts" was subsequently included in the* Common Sense *anthology* Challenge to the New Deal *(1934), alongside contributions from technocrats and "third party" exponents like John Dewey, Lewis Mumford (1895–1990), and Upton Sinclair (1878–1968), the labor activists and educationalists A. J. Muste (1885–1967) and J. B. S. Hardman (1882–1968), and Max Eastman*

(1883–1969), *who had been a political ally of Dreiser's during World War I, and was now a supporter of the exiled Leon Trotsky (1879–1940). In his introduction to the volume, Dewey characterized Bingham and Rodman as believing that "there is something like a second American Revolution looming ahead. And while it may not be 'the Revolution' to the disciples of Marx, it should none the less allow no truckling to capitalism."[2] In his contributions to* Common Sense, *Dreiser argues that the competitive aspects of capitalism, and the American ideology of individualism, stifle human creativity, progress, and produce massive inequality. Echoing the ideas of Thorstein Veblen (1857–1929) concerning the "instinct of workmanship," Dreiser emphasizes the transformative potential of creativity and invention, and the wastefulness and inequality of capitalism, in ways that were consonant with Bingham and Rodman's intended address to industrial workers, farmers, and middle-class technocrats, as well as scientists, inventors, and cultural producers.*

Here in the West, as well as in other parts of the world, we still cling to the theory that only by promising the individual unrestricted wealth and privilege against poverty, frustration, and defeat of the many, can we further the development of society. And governmentally we actually proceed to define what type of individual this is to be: the industrialist, the banker, the stockholder, and the investor. Without these, society will fail!

But throughout history the world has owed its progress more to the impulse to look upon profit as something apart from gold. The satisfaction of inherent humanitarian impulses looking toward the happiness or improvement of others has been another type of profit. One of the greatest impulses to create springs from curiosity, the mental necessity to discover or to solve this amazing riddle of our existence. Another is the very humane one of attempting to solve or eradicate not only our own personal ills, but those of others. Consider Christ, St. Francis, Pasteur.[3] In the main, the achievements springing from these impulses or desires have not received gold for a reward, very often not even applause or notice, and yet such men have rendered services so enormously superior to the third and fourth-rate mentalities that have stepped forward via the industrial system that there is no comparison.

And yet, what do we actually see? The present cry of the self-centered individualist whether of the industrial, banking, or merely hoarding class, is that if the profit system in its wildest form is not retained, the incentive to creative action will be destroyed. Mr. Hoover, throughout the desperate years of '30, '31, '32, was satisfied that only by placing more and more resources in the hands of the bankers and the masters of wealth generally was mass prosperity to be revived. These, regardless of their lunatic theories, greed, waste, and dishonesty, were to be refortified against the results and losses which they had brought upon themselves and others. They were to be saved and retained, though the millions of people betrayed by them starved or died.

And to a modified extent, that theory is being pursued by the Roosevelt administration. Our great industrial leaders agreeing to this modified version are to be heartened by the certainty of profit for themselves and their investors, to continue the creative activities of which, for some mysterious reason, they are assumed to be the substance, not the mere expression. But the creative impulse in every field existed long before the present high-powered capitalistic era had appeared, and not always for profit.

For instance, against the discoverer of the lever, about which Archimedes wrote, put Mr. Henry Ford's development of the cheap automobile. The inventor of the lever, whoever he was, probably sought to solve the problem of the lever as much for the satisfaction of exercising his mind as a thinking machine, as for the honor of being known as a great inventor. Perhaps also he desired to advance life, and so help his fellowmen. Who knows? Mr. Ford thought of his cheap car for reasons of personal profit. If one can accept historical records, the reward of the inventor of the lever was little more than the distinction of having achieved his purpose. Mr. Ford's is what we see.

If one is to return to the early world for other illustrations, one would have to ask after the intellect that achieved the wheel, and what was its possible reward; or the arch and keystone, the water wheel, the plow, the arrow, the sail, the windmill, compass, pulley, ladder. We do not know, of course, but to this hour the Morgans and Rockefellers take their share of profit from these things.

Taking the modern world as we know it, we find it a product of the brains and labors of the underpaid and, frequently, from a material point of view, unseeking geniuses. Howe, who invented the sewing machine; Watt, the inventor of the steam engine; Fulton, who invented the steamboat; Edison, who invented the incandescent bulb, the phonograph, the moving picture; Madame Curie, who discovered radium; the Wright brothers, who gave the world the airplane. In fact, we know that Leibnitz, the great mathematician, took no patent for his differential calculus, to which all modern science and invention is indebted, nor yet Sir Isaac Newton for his theory of gravitation. And the great John Tyndall, leading English experimental physicist of his day, once exclaimed, on hearing of a new theory that pleased him, "Thank God, it will not produce any material results. No one will ever be able to take out a patent and make money on it." He loathed the mind that worked solely for money.[4]

Leaving the world of inventions, one can pass directly and with stag-gering force to the world of science in general, the distinguished creative thinkers and discoverers in all mental realms. But where in these realms, and to which we actually owe the whole vigorous modern scene, is the plutocrat, the coupon-clipper, the individual who, unless he is sure of a thousand percent profit, will stop his great labor, and let the world die?

Actually, one must descend from the Himalayan mental and character heights occupied by such minds as Newton, Faraday, Helmholtz, Darwin, Pasteur, Beethoven, Loeb, Einstein, not to the valleys of ordinary human achievements occupied by the professional and educational classes, but infinitely lower, before one comes to the growling, thieving, contesting and even murderous depths occupied by the profit seeker.[5] And how do you find him? As the one who is first compelled to lay aside every dignity and principle motivating these others before he can possibly achieve the profits which he claims for himself. Certainly. And by what right? Invariably, by the "right" of trading upon the ignorance, innocence, liberality, fear or necessity of others who are, in the main, glad to give the world that which the profit seeker immediately proceeds to capitalize as his own. Otherwise, how would one explain the enormous divergences in the fates of the discoverers of the automobile, the telephone, the telegraph, the radio, and the money success of such companies as General Motors, General Electric, the Standard Oil, the Bell Telephone Company, Western Union, the Radio Corporation of America, their overlords, stockholders, and principal investors?

And yet in the face of this unshakable and beautiful truth that genius in the main creates, discovers, and presents almost charitably to the world what it has to give, you have here and now our present world of brokers and middlemen of the thinnest stripe intellectually and morally, our bankers, speculators, politician-promoters and industrialists generally, their stock-holders, lawyers, judges, executives. And all proclaiming the doctrine that they must be permitted to gather where they have not labored, and reap where they have not sown, or civilization will surely fail.

Flies. Locusts. The function of thought, discovery, and invention is to strengthen and advance the mental and physical and social position and welfare of man. The function of industry is to apply the thoughts, discover-ies, inventions and industry of man to the natural resources of life and to convert these into forms suitable for the use of man, to feed, clothe, and entertain him on his march. But in these modern days, this simple and quite secondary process has become a huge network of middleman activity, of conversion, involving as it does the lives and comforts of almost two bil-lion people. And because of the huge network of equipment and activity involved, as well as by reason of the exorbitant profit motive which has been permitted to creep into every stage and phase, there has been brought about not the apotheosis of the thinker, the inventor and discoverer, but these larvae and locusts, these moneybags and their bankers, politicians, office-holders, judges and lawyers. And so we have the spectacle of the few mentally and socially incompetent, but, nevertheless, wealthy and comfortable, set against the millions of unemployed, untrained, unused and often hungry. And this when the very function of conversion should be the one to bring about their employment, education, social and mental happiness. Yet as the manufacturing or converting interests have grown from local to national and from national to international proportions, the problem of unemployment and crime has grown until now we see it in almost full flower, with war, penitentiaries, asylums as its major accompaniments. And so we have the millionaire (instead of the thinker, the scientist and the inventor) held as first among men, entitled to all the sycophancy and fawning slavery of government and office to his every wish and even to the applause and awe of the cheated and disfranchised whose bread he eats and the fruits of whose labors he hoards as gold.

Not the worker but himself is to have the whole advantage of invention and improving thought in every form. He and not the worker or the worker's government will patent the machine, the process, the new and improved way for multiplying labor, and then use that very government of the millions, its police, army, navy, legislature, executive and legal processes to enforce his claim to the same, and to all the profits of the same. And this is called individualism, instead of graftism or locustism, and the millions or masses of all nations are ordered to fight and die for its preservation, to march under its flag and sing songs to its glory and honor.

The spectacle is fantastic, the argument that of a trickster and a thief. It is to set aside as nothing, or worse, a crime to be opposed with war and destruction, that great, sound and by now successful experiment, the Soviet Union, with all that it has achieved in merging into one colossal entity the intellect and the naturally creative impulses and inventive vigor of all of its immense population, and the using of those for the development as well as the permanent comfort of that population. It is to write down as a crime that the men who work with their hands or minds should ask for an eight-hour day, a five-day week, or a minimum wage. It is to be written down that a pension for the aged, free care for the sick and the injured in the great labor of making life possible for the millions, free education and training of children, the pensioning of soldiers after war, the improving and sanitation of the homes and cities of the people, and the guaranteeing to all of periods of rest and pleasure, are burdens which may not be paid for out of the adequate labor of all, but must in order to make more good for the few in control, be left undone, or, at best, half-done, the while these flies and locusts in the guise of bankers, industrialists and the leisured and titled classes take their fill of what these guarantees would have cost—they and their heirs and assigns, forever. Flies and locusts. Thieves and robbers these, who, strong, yet sly and dishonest and cruel, seize upon the age-old machinery of life and exact interest or profit for their own and not life's use.

Yet if the world were going to fail, as the individualist now claims it will without his greed and heartless interference and direction, it would have so failed long before these hoarders or Midases appeared on the scene. For it has never been pushed forward by the lone profit motive as such, the mere right to eat, drink and walk in material splendor before others, but by the mental enthusiasms and curiosities and wonders of these better and so much more generous minds which have led them—our Aristotles, Galileos, Leonardos and Faradays—to study and results for the sake of those studies and results. To argue otherwise is to ignore the whole evidence as well as the true course of history. It is also to argue against the whole and almost timeless struggle of man toward the organized society of today of which he is the beneficiary; a society which should offer to every man a decent chance to work and live.

Textual Note: A shorter version was published in *Daily Mirror* (New York), 1 August 1933, pp. 19, 31. This version first appeared as "The Profit-Makers are Thieves" in *Common Sense*, December 1933, pp. 20–22, with editorial introduction and subheadings. A corrected text, with editorial introduction and subheadings removed, was printed as "Flies and Locusts" in Alfred M. Bingham and Selden Rodman, eds., *Challenge to the New Deal* (New York: Falcon Press, 1934), 53–58, and this is used as the copy-text.

1. Unsigned (Alfred M. Bingham and Selden Rodman), "*Common Sense:* Prospectus of a New Magazine," DPUP.

2. John Dewey, "Introduction," in Bingham and Rodman, eds., *Challenge to the New Deal*, vii.

3. Louis Pasteur (1822–95), French chemist and bacteriologist who proved the germ theory of disease and invented the process of Pasteurization.

4. Inventor Elias Howe (1819–67) contributed much of his income from his sewing machine patent to the Union army during the Civil War. Also Scottish engineer James Watt (1736–1819); Robert Fulton (1765–1815); Thomas Alva Edison (1847–1931); discoverer of radium Marie Curie (Maria Sklodowska) (1867–1934); flight pioneers Wilbur Wright (1867–1912) and Orville Wright (1871–1948); German rationalist philosopher and mathematician Baron Gottfried Wilhelm von Leibnitz (or Leibniz) (1646–1716); British scientist Sir Isaac Newton (1642–1727); and Irish physicist John Tyndall (1820–93).

5. Michael Faraday (1791–1867), English physicist and inventor; Baron Hermann Ludwig Ferdinand von Helmholtz (1821–94), German physiologist, physicist, and mathematician; and Jacques Loeb (1859–1924), the physiologist whose physio-chemical explanations of human conduct heavily influenced Dreiser in the 1920s.

"They Shall Not Die" Indicts North
as Well as the South

New York Evening Post, 24 March 1934.

In December 1933, a third trial in Alabama reconvicted the Scottsboro boys. Dreiser supported a further appeal to the Supreme Court, donating a manuscript to raise funds and reviewing They Shall Not Die, *a play on the Scottsboro case by John Wexley (1907–85), which opened at the Royale Theater on Broadway on 21 February 1934.*

If the South Exploits the Negro, the North
Does the Same to Its Workers in Factory and Mine

Criticism of so dramatic and moving a presentation as "They Shall Not Die" must necessarily limit itself to a question of fact: is it a truthful representation or not? In regard to this, there is not only the court record of the trial, voluminous newspaper reports, but better still, the first decision of the United States Supreme Court, which set aside the verdict of the lower court on the ground that a fair trial had not been provided.[1] With this established, there can only remain the matter of bringing this powerful dramatization of this ghastly travesty on justice to the attention of the largest number of people. Personally, I am convinced that if seen by enough people, their natural resentment toward the coarse and inhuman race prejudice, which has brought about this travesty, will tend to frighten, if not actually shock the sensibilities of the perpetrators into something resembling at least outward fairness. For I, personally, have no hope that any present appeal to Southerners as a whole, to relax their fierce antipathy toward the Negro as an equal before the law, if not an equal in social or economic import, will have any weight whatsoever.

They, our American Southern white citizens, do not appear willing at any time to consider the vast injustice done the Negro by the South in the first instance. They do not seem to be willing to recall that in the first place he did not come here of his own accord but was seized and dragged here in chains. Next, once here, he was most brutally enslaved by a race that intended nothing but evil in regard to him. He was sold as animals are sold, and whipped as animals are whipped, in order to labor as animals labor, with no other real reward than enough food and shelter to keep him useful. That injustice, that horror, endured for 150 years, until a nation far beyond the confines of the old South decided that under liberty as an emblem, and an ideal, it could not endure. Two million men fought to establish that, and the nation bled until it was sick.

And yet, since then, and despite that staggering arbitrament, slavery, not only in the form of labor, but of race. The South, even though it will now consider the Negro a man, instead of an animal, will not consider him a fellow citizen before the law, much less an equal. Yet to insure justice or equity in life, it is not necessary to consider every man your equal. Few do that in any walk whatsoever even when looking upon their superiors. What is necessary, whether considered as an equal or not, is that a certain minimum of privileges must be allotted to every one in any form of organized, democratic society, if that society is to endure. And once that minimum is fixed as it has been fixed intentionally at least, by the American Constitution, it should be respected. One thing I charge, that has caused this minimum to fail of respect, not only in the South, but in the North, is the American-old doctrine of stalwart individualism, the right of every one, to all the privileges and power which he can possibly, and by whatsoever process, acquire, and that, regardless of the rights and privileges of any other individual. And that is not democracy. It is junglism.

In fact, despite the Constitution, which really speaks of liberty, equality, and fraternity, giants have grown, and have been encouraged to grow, while the single individual with but his two hands to depend on, has been encouraged to believe that not only is he equal to them mentally in cunning and brutality, but that he is an equal before the law, which they control, and more, co-sharer in all the wealth and prosperity of America. In short, slyly and dishonestly, he has been confronted by the more cunning and the totally ruthless, who have either by force, as in the South, or by the intricacies and dishonesties of the law in the North, lifted themselves into absolutely impregnable positions of power and wealth. So much so, that even to this hour, and with Mr. Roosevelt in the chair, they say, "Go," and men go, or "Come," and men come. And they order by exemptions how men shall work, and where, and under such and such conditions, and for such and such wages, while they, organized as companies, trusts, holding companies, and even the Government itself, manipulate all national privileges for their personal benefit. So it has been, and to this hour, so it still is, N.R.A. or no N.R.A. They pile up staggering fortunes, build Rockefeller cities, leave billions to incompetent and worthless heirs, and are worshipped in America as the leisure class, and then say, that unless this order is accepted permanently, imprisonment, torture, and even death shall be the portion of those who deny them.

I, as well as every other living American has seen all this with his own eyes, if he has had eyes to see. In consequence, I say that, this play, "They Shall Not Die," at this time, is of the utmost importance, not only to the South, but to the North, and not only to the East, but to the West, and it should be shown as here presented, in every city, town, and village in America. If sectional opposition should seek to interfere with its presentation, that opposition should be officially counteracted. For when we come to the bottom of it, it is really no greater indictment of the South, than it is of the North. If the South exploits and tortures the Negro, the North does the same to its workers in the coal mines, steel mills, and basic industries. And so long as this national belief in free and unlimited individualism and sectionalism endures, there can be no equity for the worker. There can be only class power, class privileges, for the few, and class suffering, class hatred on the part of the many, for those who by ruthless cunning and jungle power afflict him.

It is for that reason that I urge all Americans to see this play, call for it to be done in the movies, and then see to it that it is shown in the form in which it has been presented here in New York. And once so shown and seen, may the social significance and wisdom of it move all in this nation to appropriate action.

Textual Note: New York Evening Post, 24 March 1934, p. 8. Selectively emended by reference to Dreiser's revised typescript, "They Shall Not Die" carbon copy typescript, DPUP folder 12332. The title and subheading are editorial from the *Evening Post*.

1. *Powell et al. v. State of Alabama*, 287 US 45 (1932). The Supreme Court ruled that the Scottsboro defendants' rights to competent legal counsel under the Fourteenth Amendment had been denied by the State of Alabama, and it sent the cases back for retrial.

Contribution to "Where We Stand"

International Literature, July 1934.

Dreiser's contribution to a symposium organized by International Literature, *the Moscow-based organ of the International Union of Revolutionary Writers, on the occasion of the Soviet Writers Congress.*

1. What has the existence and achievements of the Soviet Union meant to you? (What changes were made in your way of thinking and in the character of your creative work by the October Revolution and Soviet construction?)

I have watched, with the profoundest interest, the inception and growth of the U.S.S.R. To do this, and remain in thought uncolored and in work uninspired by its tremendous and humane concepts and their gradual achievement would, I think, be impossible. I have not, since my first analytical understanding of its processes and results, been anything but despairing of the miserable and degrading inequity fostered by the capitalist system, but while this condition was plainly and at once evident to any honest inquirer, to combat it he had only the phantom and so often derided weapon, theory.

With the advent of the U.S.S.R., and even throughout the struggle of its early years, there was provided that most instructive and unanswerable reference, an example, and now a successful one. Here, for all the world to see, was a nation which said, in effect: By our system, the producer, not the provider of capital, shall benefit, and benefit by every equitable and comfortable condition of life which the genius, the art, the sciences, the general humanitarian forces of the human mind can conceive and practice. And, inevitably, this enlightenment became not only a beacon for Russia alone, but, as well, a keen searchlight, mercilessly investigating and exposing the tricks, the vanities, the greed-created conflicts, the dreary prejudices, and the wastes and frustrations of the profit system. And to this precept and this exposing beam, I have looked and found support and encouragement in creative work.[1]

2. What is your opinion of Soviet literature?

Because translations are not readily available, I am not as familiar with all phases of Soviet literature as I could wish to be. But I am aware of the most representative work, and, lately, have been particularly interested by *International Literature*. I find, for one thing, satisfaction in the present trend toward a literature which is not wholly and solely propagandist, or, better, which does not concern itself entirely with the minutiae of doctrine. I do not at all question the extreme necessity for this insistence on Soviet principles and technique while there was still need of utilizing every field to demonstrate and educate and to triumph over the ancient prejudices and inertias which held captive so great a part of your nation. But now, when so much of this work has been accomplished, and particularly since the years have given you a new generation whole-heartedly bent on the preservation of its incalculable advantages over the rest of the world, it is refreshing and vitalizing to find that your writers can and do turn to an easier and less limited expression, and to the task of giving the world a more generously rounded picture of your life—and to which it can look only with envy.

There are superb and uplifting connotations to the vast, humanitarian projects you have initiated. And they are so plainly antipathetic to any economic background other than the one you provide that, conceivably, their presentation to the world can safely be made without undue emphasis as to their origin, leaving the easy discovery of that to the onlooker.

One phase of your literature which has recently engaged me is the work of your humorous writers; a wider appreciation of those sportive and ludicrous elements which, to the Slav, constitute humor, suggests a not inconsiderable field for a more flexible attitude toward other phases of your life.

3. What events and cultural processes in capitalist countries are especially attracting your attention?

Those events and processes which seemingly mirror some phase or other of the larger economic outlook of the Soviet system. But in this connection, my attention has paused in every case not so much before the event itself as before the mental processes which saw fit to introduce it. I refer, for one thing, to the vast governmental projects in the United States which at present represent the source of so much pother in the press as to a new deal. When, even to the capitalist class itself, it became to some extent obvious that the continuance of its huge return was dependent upon something other than the mere urgent motive of its own greed, they bestirred themselves to provide the appearance of concession to the mass—to seek the charm which, hung about their necks, was to ward off further evil. We have had, as a result, their *public* acceptance of the N.R.A., not in itself a wholly invaluable plan, since it copies your minimum wage and maximum labor time, but without any of the other advantages which your workers enjoy. Its chief purpose is to provide work for more workers, but not at wages that spell a decent living or provide means for using the shorter hours. Yet patriotic banners were hung; a huge parade in New York City indulged in. But labor is still underpaid and the profiteers are still in the saddle. And they are still comfortably waiting for the return of the good old thousand percent profit days. The one thing that really astonishes me is the naïve expectation, on the part of the masses, of real benefits to come. But from where I fail to see, unless capitalism can be swept away.

To illustrate what I mean, there was recently printed here a report by Joseph Eastman, Railroad Coordinator,[2] and blazoned by headlines in the papers purporting to announce that he favored governmental ownership of the railroads—one of the most flagrantly money-hungry of industries. But a reading of the report itself, compounded of the most guarded and sterile phrases, makes it plain that Mr. Eastman recommends nothing of the sort; that in fact he advises only the most tender and expensive attentions to the railroads to insure the continuance and extension of their gigantic grafts and greeds.

Yet, not only here in the United States, but almost universally is the shadow substituted for the substance. Outside of Russia, there is no true fulfillment anywhere for the masses. Italy, France, Germany, England, here, it is the same. In the United States there have been active protests in certain farming sections against shamefully inadequate return; also the dissenting voices of some student bodies to a program which graduates them for no more noble purpose than to starve on a park bench; but that is all. The people have not suffered enough, or they lack leaders. In short, the vast need of the mass to free itself of wolfish greeds and the chimeras of religion remains unanswered.

As to your postscript requesting mention of stories characterizing relations among intellectuals, there are no such stories here—and damned few intellectuals.

Textual Note: Copy-text from "Replies by Theodore Dreiser to Queries of *International Literature* for Special Number: All Russian Conference of Soviet Writers," DPUP folder 1532. Published as "A Symposium: Where We Stand: Theodore Dreiser," *International Literature* 3 (July 1934), 80–82. The *International Literature* symposium was introduced by an editorial note summarizing the three questions in slightly different terms, as follows:

On the occasion of the Soviet Writers Congress the secretariat of the I[international] U[nion of] R[evolutionary] W[riters] addressed three questions to prominent writers in a number of countries. The questions were:

  1. What influence has the October revolution had upon your work?
  2. What do you think of Soviet literature?
  3. What problems interest you most at this time?

Below we present the answers of a number of American and English writers.
In the next issue we will print the answers of writers from France and Denmark, to be followed by letters from other countries.

Dreiser's response was followed by those of Malcolm Cowley, Louis Adamic, Granville Hicks, Corliss Lamont, Joseph Kalar, John Strachey, A. P. Roley, and Naomi Mitchison.

  1. The closing two sentences of this paragraph, present in Dreiser's carbon copy typescript, are cut from the published *International Literature* text.
  2. Joseph B. Eastman (1882–1944) had been charged by President Roosevelt with modernizing the railroads under the terms of the Emergency Railroad Transportation Act passed in June 1933.

Dreiser Denies He Is Anti-Semitic

New Masses, 30 April 1935.

Hutchins Hapgood's accusations of Dreiser's anti-Semitism in The Nation *(see "The 'Is Dreiser Anti-Semitic' Correspondence," 176–88) caused consternation on the Marxist left. The* New Masses *sent a delegation to discuss the matter with Dreiser on two occasions and printed the results in the 30 April 1935 issue. Dreiser's statement is boxed and separated from a longer, anonymous article, which recounts heated conversations between Dreiser and the* New Masses *representatives, who included Michael Gold, whose friendship with Dreiser was ended by the incident, and the prominent African American Communist and vice-presidential nominee, James W. Ford (1893–1957).*

Dreiser's Statement

New York, April 1935

Of course I make a distinction between the classes. I draw a distinction between the Jewish worker and the Jewish exploiter. Everybody knows that I am an anti-capitalist. I identify the interests of the Jewish worker with the interests of all the other workers. What you have just read by Lenin on the Jewish question[1] meets with my full approval. And if my letters are used by the Nazis as propaganda, I repudiate such use. I have no hatred for the Jew and nothing to do with Hitler or fascism.

My interest in Communism is that it will equitably solve the relations of man, and I emphatically repudiate any inference in my writing that will be interpreted as counter to this.

DREISER

Textual Note: Copy-text from *New Masses*, 30 April 1935, pp. 10–11.

1. The introductory article quoted from Lenin's 1919 speech "On the Jewish Question" as follows:

> It is not the Jews who are the enemies of the toiler. The enemies of the work- ers are the capitalists of all lands. Among the Jews there are workers, toilers; they are in the majority. They are our brothers, comrades in the struggle for Socialism because they are oppressed by capitalism. Among the Jews there are kulaks, exploiters, capitalists, just as there are among the Russians and every other nation.
>
> The capitalists are tireless in their endeavours to stir up enmity between the workers of different faiths, different nations and different races. The rich Jews, just like the rich Russians and the rich of all countries, are united in trampling upon, oppressing and dividing the workers.

Contribution to "What Is Americanism? A Symposium on Marxism and the American Tradition"

Partisan Review & Anvil, April 1936.

The central question posed in this Partisan Review *symposium was whether the "native" American revolutionary and radical traditions personified by Tom Paine, Eugene Debs, and Bill Haywood were too individualistic to be compatible with Marxism and Russian Communism. This was a vital debate one year into the Comintern's Popular Front policy, which the* Partisan Review *fully supported at this point, and one which resonated strongly with Dreiser's reflections on the campaigns of the 1930s. His response gives short shrift to the notion of revolution-*

ary literature that the Partisan Review *editors had also wanted to put into play, suggesting a firm break between political and literary activity.*

Americanism, as I see it, is an illusion of national individuality, held by the great mass of our people in more or less emotional form, through which ideas of reform, of government, of social systems, of art, etc., can be focused; essentially, it is the emotional, intangible, and often unconscious frame of reference with which most Americans compare whatever ideas they have or come into contact with. Americanism involves the associated illusions of such words as: individualism, the land of the free and the home of the brave, liberty, self-made man, pioneers, this is the best country in the world and you ought to be proud you were born here, the stars and stripes, etc. As I think of it, it is these deeply rooted, powerful associations, close to the very essence of feeling, and as such a positive force. It grew out of the cultural conditions of Western Europe, and is opposed to it in the same way that an acorn is opposed to an oak.

Because I think of it this way, I am inclined to believe that in questions and problems of bringing about a social revolution, the most practical thing is to enlist this feeling, if possible, in the cause of reform and revolution. As I see it, the reforms and revolutions, the changes from capitalism to socialism and communism, are inevitable and inherent in the very nature of things; and if identifying these changes with this powerful emotional force of Americanism will make these changes and processes of adjustment easier for the great mass of people, and correspondingly easier to bring about, then surely the American radical movement should make itself as far as possible free of European associations, and as American as possible in terminology, leadership, and general form. If this American tradition is said to be only a symbolization of the brutal struggle to obtain individual riches—what then? Communism itself is best defended on the very same grounds. Individual riches are nothing but a relative illusion.

Although it is certainly clear that American cultural traditions have very obvious Western European roots, and that there has never been any change of importance here in America that was not preceded by a change of the same kind in Europe, it is a part of Americanism to resent any present influence and connection with Europe. And it is for just this reason that Marxian ideology would do well to fit itself to such an adaptable form—our revolutionary tradition—even if it has to lose its own identity.

As for revolutionary literature in this country, I think it is sadly lacking in anything comprehensive enough to suggest the combination of a present-day social revolution with a large and broad view of Americanism in art forms, which would have the widest effect and most powerful appeal. I object to the absolutist reform type in writers, as this characteristic is limiting to the artist and antagonizing to the reader. Revolutionary writing certainly might well include a favorable view of, and in fact a synthesis with, Americanism.

Textual Note: Partisan Review and Anvil 3 (April 1936): 3–4. The published version accurately reproduces Dreiser's revised typescript in DPUP folder 12453.

Epic Technologists Must Plan

National E.P.I.C. Magazine, June 1936.

E.P.I.C., the End Poverty in California movement founded by Upton Sinclair, was in 1936 attempting to widen its influence across the nation. The more middle-class technocracy movement, which had come to national prominence in 1932–33, took up some ideas of Thorstein Veblen to advocate that business should be taken over and run by engineers. In this article Dreiser seeks to bring them together, with the hope of spurring the advocates of technocracy into political action. Dreiser had several personal contacts with Sinclair and the technocrat leader Howard Scott (1890–1970) in 1935–36.

Technocracy and its leaders seem to prefer the position, mysterious and intangible as it now is, of not aligning themselves with any party with political aims.[1] When some one has waved the magic wand and changed the balance of power in the material situation of the country they will step in and run things.

However unfortunate their attitude, the facts remain that they have an idea, which is so universally applicable and in many ways so unoriginal, that any plan for social reform, although including the political aspect which Technocracy rejects, is at liberty to incorporate it. And what is even more important, no plan for social reform will be able to succeed without it in-corporating this idea in some form, so that if the idea is not included under the name Technocracy, it must be included under another name. I have only to say that I think the attitude of Technocracy is unfortunate not only because they have already worked out their idea and so well, but because the idea has certain associations in connection with the name Technocracy which make it unnecessary to go into long explanations concerning it, as will be necessary in building up the idea under another name.

It would be well, in my opinion, for E.P.I.C. to hasten to appoint some committee of its own, including scientists, engineers, and practical men from every field of production of raw materials, manufacturing, distribution, etc., and to have them work out a real plan of operation which would be based on the present available men, factories, stores, laboratories, mines, mills, etc., and present needs. This plan should be one that is constantly being refreshed and altered and perfected and studied, so that it could be put into effect immediately, as soon as the political side of the E.P.I.C. program has succeeded

I am aware that E.P.I.C. has, of course, approached its ideas with the socialization of industry, etc., as its goal. But I do think that its most practical and available plans have been and are much more aimed towards means to this goal rather than to the end. And I do feel that no amount of idealism, good-will, and fine but hazy generalizations will take the place of a definite, practical plan, which deals with the situation as you will find it, with the problems as you will have to meet them, with the personalities and customs and habits of wanting and buying and selling as they are. What, for example, supposing E.P.I.C. won a state-wide election, and had a whole state to ad-minister, would it do? Is there any plan, inclusive and coherent and definite for such a situation? There certainly should be one. For the administration of the business and industry of a large group, spread over a wide geographical area is not one of those bridges that are best crossed without forethought. This type of administration needs careful planning, a group of experienced leaders who expect and are trained to work in harmony.

In order for E.P.I.C. to be more than a social reformer's dream, in order for it to be a practical success, in my opinion it must adopt the methods of technology, and plan accordingly. As the Technocrats point out their plan is the fundamental aim of socialistic reform groups. But as they have failed to point out, their aim cannot be achieved except through some social reform group, and in my opinion, one like E.P.I.C. which uses political methods. So that if E.P.I.C. would incorporate a very definite program including by name, what and where and when they would do, into its political program, it would assure itself of success in the second step of its plans. This second step which is nothing less than the end in view, must be definite and practical and applicable, or else all the present efforts will become useless and empty.

Textual Note: National E.P.I.C. Magazine, June 1936, p. 12.

1. Upton Sinclair initiated the E.P.I.C. movement in 1933, having previously stood for office as a radical Socialist. Its program centered on bringing land, industrial production, and money under the control of state-appointed experts. Dreiser had supported Sinclair's bid for election as governor of California on a shared E.P.I.C./ Democratic Party platform in "The Epic Sinclair" (see Further Reading).

Mea Culpa!

The Nation, 17 June 1936.

Dreiser wrote this letter to The Nation *in response to Benjamin Stolberg's article "The Jew and the World," (*The Nation, *17 June 1936, pp. 766–70), a Marxist and psychoanalytical exploration of anti-Semitism and Jewish identity. Stolberg explains anti-Semitism psychologically as "an expression of social guilt" that enables non-Jews to rationalize the economic exploitation of Jews. Ironically, while any significant Jewish identity has been diffused by the diaspora, Stolberg argues, the dominant American culture clings to the "myth" of Jewish racial purity. Hence Jews are presented with the "fantastic [i.e. imaginary] alternative of 'segregation' or 'assimilation,'" that is, either "professionalizing" their Jewishness, or "passing" according to the dictates of "bourgeois prejudice." Stolberg therefore concludes that the problem of anti-Semitism will only be resolved when class society is replaced by social democracy.*

Dreiser's letter appeared alongside responses from Archibald MacLeish, Franz Boas, Clifton Fadiman, H. G. Perelmuter, and others. As in the Hapgood correspondence, Dreiser initially defines "the Jewish question" as an issue of religious and ethnic particularism, to which assimilation and self-determination present imperfect answers. Then in a shift of perspective, he describes anti-Semitism not as the product of tensions between a host culture and a transplanted ethnic group, but as a victimizing psychology within the host culture. Dreiser acknowledges his own complicity with this endemic prejudice and asks forgiveness. Reiterating his respect for Jewish culture, Dreiser finds his earlier hopes for the creation of a Zionist homeland all but crushed by the ethnic, military, and political tensions emerging in the mid-1930s.

Dear Sirs:

Thank you for sending the advance copy of the Stolberg article. I think I have seldom seen such an astute and penetrating discussion of this question. And, what is more, it leaves the commentator little or nothing to say but yes or no. My answer is mostly yes, with a little change in the emphasis of his argument.

Many people forget that under the heat and storm, the fighting and stress and argument which go with the Jewish question in our present day, there are biological and physiological factors and trends at work which have a far larger if unconscious weight in settling the matter. These basic activities underlie and finally determine race questions; the Jewish question in the last analysis is a biologic question. And what we know of the history of races taken over the period of historical time points to the fact that races intermarry, lose their identity, are merged or submerged in the welter of the peoples with whom they come in contact. Of course, none of this mingling goes on, or ever went on, without a great deal of mental and physical torture, persecution, warfare, governmental restriction, social ostracism, and all the cruelties which our consciousness can invent to waggle futilely in the face of a natural fact. Probably there is no individual alive on the earth today in the dim, forgotten shadows of whose ancestry there are not many individual experiences of just such a type as would occur today in a marriage between a Jew and a Christian. And so, if we wanted to, or could, wait a thousand years or so, we might see the last of this so very troublesome problem. The Jews, who because of the accident of their peculiar history have kept their identity as a race in the minds of many, would be no more; perhaps one might say then, that "my great-grandfather twice removed was a Jew," as one says today, "One of my ancestors came over with William the Conqueror," and with just about as much truth.[1]

However, the Jewish problem is today a great problem, and one which brings no one any great pleasure. It would be an intellectual and emotional triumph to have a "fair" attitude. I can hardly believe that any discussion of it does any good, including this. The only profit in taking an attitude is a social one, like liking birds' nest soup in China. Nearly everyone, nevertheless, has an attitude on the Jews. And nearly all these attitudes are emotional, and many deeply so, and are much more difficult to change than an ordinary appetite, but are as inevitably acquired. As for me, I have mine, an attitude[2] which leads me to suggest certain things with regard to the solution of the Jewish problem, and probably these are as futile suggestions as any.

It is well known that I have said that I regard the Jews not as Americans, or Germans, or French—but as Jewish Americans, Jewish Germans, Jewish Frenchmen, and, as a consequence, as thinking and acting not entirely as Americans or French or Germans, but as Jewish Americans, etc. I never said that as a race (in its entirety) I wholly disliked and distrusted them. I have paid my compliments to very, very many and still do, Stolberg among them. I would be wholly ungrateful and unreliable if I said differently. Like the bourgeois in Stolberg's article, I have many Jewish friends.[3] Nonetheless, even among these I have heard some damn portions of the race as this or that, in other words, affirm a number of my charges. And Stolberg points out this sort of action as a characteristic of the problem as a whole.[4] And yet, although their words on occasion have proved emotional fuel to feed my possibly unreasoned attitude, I doubt if they have any more right to say what they do than I. Their opinions are like those of a self-diagnosed patient. Also, when they disagree with me, hold out for the immensely superior social and intellectual qualities of their race, and deny the validity of certain experiences which I have had, well, I don't change then, but only hold on to my attitude with increasing force.

I admit that my attitude is in part emotional. I have said I have had a certain kind of typical experience with Jews, especially in practical matters, and of unvarying consistency. In consequence, I admit that I am likely to believe unquestioningly instances of the same kind when I hear them from others. Probably I am likely to add to this certain things relating to the way some of them live, parts of their culture, etc., which displease me and evoke in me sometimes a half-conscious emotional mass, which I feel as disagreement, rage, and so on. No doubt today I look for what I dislike in Jews, and dislike what I would normally pass over in another. *Mea culpa!*[5]

At a time like this, when social unrest, nationalism, jingoism, etc. are so rampant, an attitude like mine might in some group, somewhere, lead to a pogrom, to social persecution of the very cruelest and bitterest nature. Yet this is decidedly what I do not want. Rather I have been always seeking some solution. For in the day of violence the obvious causes would not be the real ones. We in America might have as false justifications as there have been in Germany. We would have, of course, economic jealousy as a base. But still, there is always the much more powerful factor of the intangible fanaticism against the scapegoat through which we must always rationalize our unfulfilled desires and our disappointments. *Mea culpa!*

Unlike Stolberg,[6] I myself do not think that Communism will do away with the Jewish question. Unless it can take away whatever economic necessity there is for jealousy, and for finding scapegoats, and make marriage between Jews and others unstigmatized by either side, it will do no better than Capitalism. I do not believe that Communism will help the Jewish question by encouraging Jewish nationalism and separatism.[7] Racial, cultural, and religious separatism will lead to just as much division of opinion as there is today.

I can well sympathize with the despairing confusion of the Jew who is at once proud and humiliated. His culture is as good and perhaps better than any. But from his side he will be humiliated as long as he is proud. And from the other he must, for his own sake, be proud as long as he is humiliated.

I once thought that if all the Jews could move into a large country of their own, and build up for themselves a national and cultural unity of which they could be proud and which all the world would respect, that would be a solution. But of course, that idea is impractical in the extreme.[8] I really think today that the sufferings and persecution which this question entails are inevitable; that it is a kind of war, perhaps, which increases in fury until some final solution—perhaps only after years of heartrending, bitter, stupid, even insane cruelty, which I personally would hate to see, have come and gone. Oi! Oi![9]

There is nothing anyone can do. Social life, economic life, for all of us, whether in connection with the Jews or any other group, runs a bitter, unsettled course. This may sound like defeatism for certain liberal groups. Still their liberality is just as much a part of the constant conflict as is my opposite conviction. "Pardon is the word for all."[10]

THEODORE DREISER
Mount Kisco, N.Y., June 17.

Textual Note: The Nation 143 (4 July 1936): 25–26. A final draft of Dreiser's letter to *The Nation*, presumed dated 17 June 1936, is not among his papers at UP. A draft headed "15 June 1936/Mount Kisco, New York" (3-page typescript, with numerous pencil revisions in Dreiser's hand), is preserved in DPUP folder 4363. As best representing Dreiser's final intentions, the *Nation* text has been used as the copy-text, selectively emended for punctuation and sense by reference to the draft letter dated 15 June. Dreiser's capitalization has been silently restored.

1. Stolberg had argued (p. 776) that "those quarrelsome Siamese twins, Jewish separatism and anti-Semitism, have succeeded in keeping alive an illusion of Jewish endogamy and racial purity. But no matter how carefully we may weight Jewish vital statistics by all sorts of sociological factors, it still remains true that every Jew living has had an incalculable number of millions of ancestors since the last Fall of Jerusalem. Only historically sidetracked peoples such as Icelanders or African pigmies have remained hermetically sealed by their environment; and even there the seal no doubt has been broken many a time. But the racial purity of the Jews, the most diffused of all groups, is obviously only a myth."

2. In draft Dreiser had added at this point, in handwriting which becomes difficult to decipher, "based on many personal experiences and not a little [word unclear: love(?)]." TD to *The Nation*, 15 June 1936, DPUP.

3. "The average American agrees with the cracked notion of the professional Jew that the Jews as a whole are a lot brighter, abler, shrewder, and altogether superior fellows. Then he agrees with the equally cracked notion of the Jew-baiter that they are invariably greedier, greasier, louder, and more crooked than their fellow-citizens, and of course a much poorer fire risk. And just to show that he accepts both fantasies quite impartially, he smugly remarks that some of his best friends are Jews" (Stolberg, 768).

4. "Even though thousands of Jews may 'pass,' the Jewish problem remains. For bourgeois 'assimilation' is not assimilation to social democracy but to bourgeois prejudice. The Jew who becomes assimilated to bourgeois society, thereby becomes assimilated to bourgeois anti-Semitism. . . . Denial is not cure. To be Jewish is not a secret vice but a social absurdity" (Stolberg, 769–70).

5. This Latin phrase meaning literally "through my own fault" was popularized in Western society through the "Confiteor" or confession of sins at Roman Catholic Mass. The phrase was added to this and the succeeding paragraph comparatively late in the composition of the letter, after the 15 June draft.

6. Stolberg's article (p. 770) concludes as follows:

The only way to solve the Jewish problem is to solve the great problem of social and industrial democracy.

That is why I have found, to my amazement, that the little Jewish tailor who shouts in Yiddish in his Socialist or union local is far less race-conscious than the big German-Jewish banker whose family has been here for a century. Unlike the banker, he does not want to join a club to snub others. He wants a society which everyone can join in security and justice. He may not get such a society for a long time to come. And when he gets it, it will no doubt have its terrible faults. But at least he is on the way. You've guessed it: The answer is Marxism!

7. From 1934, the Birobidzhan region, situated in the far south east of the Soviet Union, was designated as the "Jewish Autonomous Oblast," the national homeland of Soviet Jewry, with Yiddish as its official language.

8. In April 1936, riots had erupted in Jaffa, starting a violent three-year period known as the Arab Revolt. Dreiser had been grappling with the Palestinian dimension of the Zionist question since 1930, when the Jewish Telegraphic Agency asked him to comment on the British policy restricting Jewish land ownership in Palestine. Dreiser asked for more information, and eventually responded as follows:

> "Thanks for giving me the opportunity of reading the various articles in the Jewish Daily Bulletin.
>
> My final conclusion is that the pros and cons of the situation—where they do not cancel each other—show reasonable claims on both sides. The chief problem involved appears to be one of sincerity, and from the data before me I am not able to decide as to this. In consequence, I can only say that I hope for a satisfactory outcome for the Jewish people, since that seems to promise beneficial results to the Arabs also."

TD to Jacob Landay, 15 November 1930, DPUP.

9. The phrase "have come and gone. Oi! Oi!" was added after the draft dated 15 June.

10. Dreiser cites Voltaire's definition of tolerance in his *Philosophical Dictionary:* "What is tolerance? It is the consequence of humanity. We are all formed of frailty and error; let us pardon reciprocally each other's folly—that is the first law of nature." Voltaire goes on to argue that "if it were permitted to reason consistently in religious matters, it is clear that we all ought to become Jews, because Jesus Christ our Saviour was born a Jew, lived a Jew, died a Jew, and he said expressly that he was accomplishing, that he was fulfilling the Jewish religion. But it is clearer still that we ought to be tolerant of one another, because we are all weak, inconsistent, liable to fickleness and error."

Statement on Russia and the Struggle against Fascism in Spain

September 1936.

Dreiser urges the Soviet Union to come to the aid of the elected leftwing government of Spain, under military attack from General Franco's fascists. In August 1936 he had written a short statement intended for the New Masses, *in which he "congratulate[d] the people of Russia, France and other countries who have given aid, both in money, men, materials and encouragement to the Spanish people in their fight to save themselves."*[1] *By September, British and French governments were campaigning for "non-intervention" in Spain, a strategy Dreiser calls upon Stalin to reject.*

At this time, when fascism is dragging its net of terror and oppression across the face of Europe, I look to Russia as the savior of justice and equity in the world, and I will greet that day with joy when Russia at last sides openly, and with the force of arms, if need be, with the rights and needs of the workers of Europe. As it stands now, their only refuge and hope of salvation lies in Russian strength, potential and actual, moral and physical. From this side of the world and from what I know of the situation, that day must come soon, or the cause of equity in Europe may well be lost. I, therefore, urge the Russian people and the Russian leaders to lose no time in taking this step. The success of their own inevitable battle may depend on their taking part and at once in this present one in Spain.

Textual Note: Untitled typescript, (1 page) headed "Sent to Walt Carmon—for Russian newspapers. September 19, 1936," in DPUP folder 4464. Title supplied by the editors.

   1. Theodore Dreiser, "Statement on Spain for the *New Masses*, August 1936," typescript, DPUP.

Contribution to Symposium, "Is Leon Trotsky Guilty?"

Modern Monthly, March 1937.

V. F. Calverton's Modern Quarterly, and its successor Modern Monthly, were significant radical journals in the late 1920s and 1930s. Like Bingham and Rodman in Common Sense, Calverton's emphasis on "Americanizing" communism helped pioneer Popular Front ideas in advance of their adoption by the Comintern, as well as promoting discussion among nonaligned communists and radicals. Simply by participating in the journal's symposium on Trotsky, Dreiser distanced himself from Moscow and the Communist Party. The symposium raised three of the most controversial topics for the contemporary left: respectively, the significance of Stalin's purges and show trials within the Soviet Union; Trotsky himself; and the impact of Stalin's repression on the Soviet Union's international position and reputation.

   1. To me, they are very confusing. But somehow they seem characteristic of what might be called the Russian temperament. If it is true that all these confessions were made without undue pressure, and in the spirit of a "confession" then I think that the trials represent a real triumph of the spirit of self-abnegation, of the realization on the part of the confessed conspirators

of the enormity of the anti-social activities they had been contemplating and of their own, individual inability to justify themselves and their plans. On the other hand, there are so many strange and curious factors, and so much more factual explanation that needs to be made before I can really believe this myself, that I do not know what to say. It is hard to believe that in this day of unbelief any man would willingly and knowingly sacrifice his life, which is, as he now realizes, the only thing which he is likely to have, for the sake of an idea or scheme, of which he is the self-acknowledged enemy. And still, I believe that it is possible for the innate inconsistencies of thought and desire to be so developed that their very existence becomes perilous to the individual's sanity and ordinary instincts. Under the pressure of a denouement, and of the imagined or real pressure of mass feeling, public disgrace, and personal moral confusion, a man is likely to defy all ordinary rules of psychology, and elevate himself to a martyr's place.

2. As for Trotsky,[1] I believe that he is probably guilty of all the charges made against him. On the basis of his past history, I believe that he is capable of planning the very vastest schemes for social organization and personal aggrandizement. Do not forget that Trotsky is a man of extraordinary ability, and that he has probably suffered greatly from the humiliation of not being in a position to use it. He wanted to run Russia and he probably hates Stalin and wants to ruin him for standing in his way. However, I do believe that there is a possible explanation of his activities which, in a way, justifies them from the Communist point of view, if not from Stalin's. This is merely hypothetical, of course. I think that Trotsky counted on an inevitable war, and that he surmised (and rightly) that Russia, Japan and Germany would be an unbeatable combination. He was going to win over Germany and Japan by concessions of Russian territory and privileges, and was going to discredit and disorganize the present regime in Russia by means of sabotage and terrorism. And after managing to get into power in Russia and with the coming of the war, the confusion of ideas and conditions which he may have counted on as following it, he may have planned to turn all three countries to Communism, with himself at the head. Remember that it was over the question of world revolution and foreign policy that Trotsky and Stalin disagreed in the first place, and it was through the failure of the Chinese Revolution in 1928 that Trotsky was forced at last to get out of the Russian regime. If he could have succeeded with his plans, he would have realized his two dreams—a world well on the way to a Communist organization, and himself as the leader. Let me emphasize here that I have no basis for such a hypothesis as this except my idea of what Trotsky is like as a person and his past record.

3. I think the Moscow trials have more or less confused the definitely favorable attitude toward Russia that was growing in this country. On the one hand, it has marked the Russians as more capable than any other nationality of proceeding by devious, subtle, fanatical methods, incomprehensible and unjustified to the western mind. On the other hand, it has put the present Russian regime in the position of an established government defending itself from the attacks of a revolutionary minority; this in a way puts this regime, for once in its life, in the position of fellow-feeling with other conservative but threatened governments. I think though, that it is likely that the long-run result of this trial and the disclosures made in connection with it, will not interfere with the old trend.

Textual Note: Published in *Modern Monthly* 10 (March 1937): 5. Copy-text from untitled typescript signed Theodore Dreiser (2 pages).

  1. One of the most important leaders of the 1917 Russian Revolution, Leon Trotsky later clashed with Stalin both personally and over political strategy, advocating "permanent revolution" against the latter's "socialism in one country." After his enforced exile from the Soviet Union in 1929, Trotsky became a focus for many communists alienated by Stalin's authoritarianism, opportunism, and Russian-centered perspective.

From "A Conversation:
Theodore Dreiser and John Dos Passos"

Direction 1 (January 1938).

Dreiser and Dos Passos discussed the American political scene on 17 December 1937, under the shadow of disillusionment with the Soviet Union due to Stalin's repressions. They speculate upon putative leaders of the emergent American Labor Party, such as Fiorello LaGuardia (1882–1947), miners' union boss John L. Lewis, and Roosevelt's secretary of agriculture Henry A. Wallace (1888–1965), and they discuss the growth of the far right. Dreiser praises Upton Sinclair and the E.P.I.C. movement, which he describes as a secular development of the American tradition of utopian communities such as Brook Farm, Oneida, and Harmony. This leads into a discussion of the means by which progressive social change may be brought about, focusing on education, fundamental economic change, authoritarianism, freedom of the press, and religious belief such as Quakerism.

* * * *

Dos Passos: Five years ago, a great many Americans pretended to be very hopeful about what happened in Russia. I think now because of this terrific terror, because of the fact that the terror has to keep on, and keeps going on, people feel that something is not working there.

Dreiser: Well, I was strong for Russia and for Stalin and the whole program, but in the last year, I have begun to think that maybe it won't be any better than anything else.

Dos Passos: Well, though, look at the achievements of the French Revolution, a great many survived through the period following Napoleon. I think a great many of its achievements are still going on.

Dreiser: Yes, and a great many achievements of the Russian Revolution are right here with us. We're indebted to them for a lot of things—40 hour week, W.P.A.—I mean for public works—the dole, because they had the dole over there from the first. Wages and laws, control of farming. This bill that's up now. That would never have come in this country except for Russia and 1917, at least not in our day.[1]

Dos Passos: No, I think all the achievements of the Russian Revolution have been made, and have been absorbed into history. And I still don't understand what's happening there . . . .

Dreiser: And damned if I do. They claim that they give the Russians a liberal education, you know, a technical education from farming and dairying up. They also give them training in the arts, the natural approach to the arts, pertaining to the theater, the libraries, and gymnastics, health, diet—all of that is supposed to go with being a Russian. But what seems to be lacking is the question of ideology, of what they are to think. And they *are* to think that any other form of government is insane and that everybody outside of Russia is worse off than they are, that they are less miserable than anybody else. I know that to be a fact. Still, that may be only a temporary condition, an attempt to achieve cohesion and unity. It has been how many years now? Twenty years, and they have done that much, but it's just a question in my mind whether they'll do more, or whether Russia will be liberalized. Maybe they do want to have a little religion, or greater class differences, or a little more money—less standardization in life, you know.

Dos Passos: Yes.

Dreiser: I don't really think that that question can be settled for another five years, or ten.

* * * *

Textual Note: Copy-text from *Direction* 1 (January 1938): 2–3, 28. This excerpt is found on page 3.

1. Dreiser lists New Deal measures such as the flagship Works Progress Administration (1935) and what would become the Agricultural Adjustment Act of 1938, which institutionalized farm income support. His argument that the Russian Revolution by its example had promoted "equity" and democratic values throughout the world is rehearsed in more detail in "I am Grateful to Soviet Russia" (see Further Reading).

PART FOUR

1938–1945

Historical Commentary

The main focus of Dreiser's political writing after 1938 was dictated by the international tensions that culminated in World War II. He campaigned against 1930s militarism and on behalf of victims of new military technologies, such as the civilians bombed in Spain and China. Dreiser maintained his support for the foreign policy of the U.S.S.R., frequently defending Russia as the world's best hope of an egalitarian society. Alongside these issues and campaigns, Dreiser's political philosophy evolved into its more explicit and multifaceted form, ranging values of "equity," "humanity," "mental creativity," and respect for other cultures against capitalism, material acquisitiveness, imperialism, and militarism.

Until Pearl Harbor, Dreiser viewed it as being of prime importance for the United States to keep out of what he saw as the imperial rivalries between Britain, France, Germany, and Japan. In 1940 and early 1941 he campaigned intensively, speaking at antiwar rallies, making a radio address to the American Peace Mobilization in November 1940 (see "'U.S. Must Not Be Bled for Imperial Britain'—Dreiser" in Further Reading) and publishing a succession of antiwar articles, many of which he had printed and distributed as broadsides: "The Soviet-Finnish Treaty and World Peace," the most succinct statement of his analysis up to April 1940; "Theodore Dreiser Condemns War"; and "This is Churchill's 'Democracy'" (see Further Reading). This effort culminated in January 1941 with his second full-length political book, *America Is Worth Saving*. When its antiwar message was overtaken by Germany's invasion of Russia, Dreiser effectively suppressed his own book and called for aid to the Soviet Union and the opening of a second front against the Axis powers.[1] After Pearl Harbor, Dreiser supported the war effort ("Writers Declare: 'We Have a War to Win!'") and in 1944 recorded two speeches on behalf of the United States government that were broadcast to the peoples of Europe after D-Day (see 279–86). In his last year, Dreiser formally applied for membership in the Communist Party just as it was reconstituting itself after Earl Browder's collaborative "Teheran policy"; and in the shadow of the atomic bombs dropped on Hiroshima and Nagasaki, he looked to international education and cooperation to help secure world peace.

This output combines an evolving understanding of international relations as they shifted, sometimes at a rapid pace, with a fairly stable political philosophy. Much of Dreiser's political output until May 1942 is dominated by the urgency of resisting the United States's going to war. At the same time, essays such as "War Is a Racket" and "Equity between Nations" concretize and add detail to his 1930s preoccupations with the pursuit of equity and opposition to individualist ideologies, extending them from national to international relations—"fair play will not come between nations, until fair play between capital and labor in the various nationalities has been established." To these larger themes Dreiser now added a kind of cultural relativism that combined suspicion of self-serving claims for Western "civilization" with a respect for non-Western cultures, bolstering all of them with the idea that improved technical knowledge brought about the possibility of abolishing scarcity. During the Great Depression—in *Tragic America* and pieces such as "Will Fascism Come to America?"—Dreiser had indicted capitalism for its deliberate destruction of commodities, especially foodstuffs, in order to guarantee or maintain profits. Early in the war, he was suspicious that Roosevelt had connived at keeping American workers in conditions of scarcity in order to shore up the finances of the British Empire.[2] In the 1940s, culminating in the late article "Interdependence," Dreiser recast his criticism of capitalist wastefulness according to a more hopeful belief in a potential economy of abundance.

America Is Worth Saving, Dreiser's most substantial political work of this period, was hastily written, and its pacifist message became obsolete within months, yet the overall focus of the book reflects many themes found in his novels and other writings. In a central chapter titled "What is Democracy?" Dreiser returns to questions of competition and social progress that informed his magazine work in the 1890s and 1900s, and the novels *Sister Carrie*, *The Financier*, *The Titan*, and *The Stoic*. Acknowledging that social progress has depended on a "cruel" and "brutal" mechanism of competition, Dreiser denies that this legitimates social Darwinism, the notion of society as a site of struggle between individuals, which is adopted by Frank Cowperwood, protagonist of *The Financier* and *The Titan*. "What was efficient for nature's purposes when we swung from bough to bough by our tails," Dreiser suggests, "is no longer efficient when all of life, because of our acquired store of knowledge, is organized socially." Whereas in the Cowperwood novels he explored how selfish individuals might yet be responsible for major productive and creative contributions to society, "What is Democracy?" takes a more holistic perspective that he would strive to articulate in the late novels *The Bulwark* and *The Stoic*. Conceptually, it is as if the mysticism that had run alongside the naturalist novelist's sense of determinism is now seen as shaping determinist mechanisms so that they ultimately work for social progress. Still, in his political writing at least, Dreiser is more concerned with the utility of ideas than with grand philosophical frameworks. In an era where productive capacities have the potential to eliminate scarcity, he argues, capitalism, social Darwinism, and the "theory of rugged individualism" are outdated ideas promulgated by vested corporate interests in order to resist change, "very handy to those who sought moral justification for sitting on the kettle of progress."

Similarly, Dreiser's opposition to 1930s militarism was orientated in support of the Soviet Union's foreign policy, but it drew directly from existing strands in his political philosophy. Here too, the sense of powerful, indifferent forces determining human activity associated with Dreiser as a novelist, and articulated in the *Ev'ry Month* editorials in the 1890s (but questioned as early as 1904's "The Cradle of Tears"), gives way to a moral critique of social Darwinist apologetics. In the previously unpublished "War Is a Racket," Dreiser explicitly denies that the cliché of the struggle for existence "red in beak and claw" is an accurate model of animal life, still less of human society and international politics. Wars are not caused by conflicts over resources, he argues, but by efforts to exert dominance. He questions the high reputation accorded to Alexander the Great and other military leaders of antiquity, and he calls for nationalistic and militaristic values to be replaced by "equity."

Dreiser's pacifism was also rooted in his hostility toward Western imperialism; this was manifested during World War II in his resistance to the propagandistic deployment of notions of "civilization" and, linked with this, in a respect for non-European cultures. These are the central themes of two essays completed shortly after the outbreak of war in September 1939, "The Dawn Is in the East" (see 253–57) and "Civilization: Where? What?" (see 257–58).

In 1939–40, Dreiser's opposition to United States involvement in the war tearing Europe apart was shared by many Americans. However his antipathy toward Britain and continued support for Russia even after its August 1939 non-aggression pact with Germany became known, were unusual even on the left, as was the cultural relativism that gave them philosophical underpinning. In rejecting the self-serving discourse of "civilization" deployed on behalf of the Allies, he resisted acknowledging a qualitative distinction between the British Empire and Nazi Germany—"Hitlerdum and Hitlerdee" as he put it out of frustration at what he perceived as Allied hypocrisy in a 1941 interview.[3] Dreiser regarded the aristocracy and financiers of the British Empire as posing the most powerful threat to democracy until Hitler's Germany invaded Russia in June 1941. Nevertheless, he was a frequent critic of Nazi authoritarianism and anti-Semitism from 1933 (see the *Historical Commentary* to part 3 and "Statement on Anti-Semitism," 250–52).

The importance of the Spanish Civil War (1936–39) in shaping Dreiser's pacifist stance in 1940–41 should not be underestimated. In a speech before an international audience of diplomats and ministers at the 1938 Anti-Bombardment Conference in Paris, later published as "Equity between Nations" (see 229–34), Dreiser made one of many impassioned appeals for aid to Chinese and Spanish Loyalist civilians, victims of new war technologies that enabled the large-scale bombing of cities. Like many on the American and European left, Dreiser regarded the great powers' refusal to help the elected Spanish government defend itself against fascist aggression as a betrayal of democratic principles. Afterwards he reflected:

> When I first arrived in Paris to attend the conference called by Bonnet of France and Lord Cecil of England, against the bombing of open cities, I was greatly surprised to find that the conference was a sort of diplomatic maneuver to reconcile other nations to England's attitude of Hands-off— the making of humanitarian phrases without humanitarian aims. In some measure, this prepared me for the attitude of Chamberlain and Daladier in the Czechoslovakian crisis. This indifference of certain powerful individuals representing England and France, to the fate of the Spanish government. A protest against Hitler's treatment of Catholics, but no protest against Franco or Mussolini's bombing of the open cities was allowed.[4]

From Paris Dreiser traveled to Spain to see for himself the effects of bombing carried out by nationalist forces and their fascist allies, later reporting on his experiences in a series of newspaper dispatches and speeches (see "Loyalist Spain—July 1938," 239–50). Such experiences cemented his view that as capitalist empires, Britain and France were afraid of Russia both as a national rival and as an example of the social relations precluded by capitalism. That democratic Spain had been abandoned was a signal that British and French governments preferred to let fascism triumph rather than make common cause with the Spanish left and Russia, a sign even that they regarded the fascist dictatorships of Hitler, Mussolini, and Franco as useful defenses against the spread of communism, as British commentators quoted in *America Is Worth Saving* had said. Their appeasement of fascism and isolation of Russia were thus responsible for Stalin's entering into the non-aggression pact with Hitler, details of which emerged in the early days of the war.

Throughout this period Dreiser's support for Russia was constant but critical, as it had been since 1931. He drafted or allowed to be published under his name various short, topical pieces supporting aspects of its foreign policy or commemorating Soviet anniversaries.[5] On several occasions he rejects Communist aims and strategy. A July 1942 telegram urging the opening of a second front with Germany in order to relieve pressure on Russia claims that "the whole world wants a second European land front except Hitler and the ruling class of England," whereas Comintern policy presented aid to the Soviet Union as indivisible from aid to Britain.[6] The statement went unprinted in the *New Masses,* which had requested it. In May 1945 Dreiser telegrammed Josef Stalin directly, asking for urgent "clarification" of Soviet policy in regard to the reconstitution of the Polish government and expressing the wish that "our two great nations should grow in friendship."[7]

Dreiser's attitude toward the Communist Party of America likewise continued to be one of critical support. In the 1940 presidential election campaign he spoke and broadcast in favor of the party's candidate, Earl Browder. When Browder and his running mate James W. Ford were excluded from the ballot in many states, Dreiser protested breaches of civil and voting rights, pointing out the irony of suppressing minority parties at home while opposing fascist dictatorships abroad.[8] "I'm not a Communist," he declared, introducing Browder on the radio,

> and I don't agree with the entire program of the Communist Party. But I can read; and I know that here in America the Communist Party has come out against the war-mongering and war hysteria of the Roosevelt-Willkie platforms. Also I know that the Communists in their platform have a program for keeping this country out of war—that they attempt to face the problems of our own people, the problems of how to put our people back to work, of how to wipe out the shame of hunger amid plenty, of how to spread some of the vast wealth of the nation to the people who produce it. As a result, the Communist Party is being gagged; and the people in 24 states, including the State of New York, are being denied the right to vote the Communist ticket if they so desire.[9]

While at times he did accept the label "communist," Dreiser always rejected the application of the Russian model of communism to America, asserting the need to allow national differences to shape the means of achieving "equity." His 1940 broadside defending Russian foreign policy, "Concerning Dives and Lazarus," prominently quotes William Jennings Bryan's famous speech to the 1896 Democratic Convention: "You shall not press down upon the brow of labor this crown of thorns: You shall not crucify mankind upon a cross of gold." In a long interview with Harry Bridges, undertaken to publicize the veteran longshoreman organizer's fight against deportation, Dreiser cites approvingly Bridges's comment that "when you are anti-labor, you are anti-American."[10] *America Is Worth Saving,* as its title suggests, is concerned primarily with the welfare of the United States, and it appeals explicitly to values embedded in the Constitution and the

Declaration of Independence, not Marxism-Leninism. In a July 1940 letter to his agent William C. Lengel, Dreiser states explicitly that he "had no . . . intention" to "make a Pro-Communistic appeal out of the book." Rather, he argued, returning to a long-standing preoccupation with the mass versus the individual, governmental intervention was necessary to curb excessive corporate power and genuinely enable individualism: "what we need is greater opportunity for individual enterprise—and if we don't get that we're going to have a nation of money controlled and directed robots. . . . Perhaps some new and more democratic form of government will have to be worked out—a government composed of four or five new but popularly authorized branches or divisions governing or having charge of such things as [science, production, distribution, education, the arts, public welfare, and defense, which] might swing the mind of the nation back to individual initiative, individual competition for place in the national service, and individual pride and satisfaction in a fair and humane degree of individual achievement of money, fame, honor, and social comfort."[11]

The principle of adjusting class analysis according to national differences became Communist Party policy with Earl Browder's short-lived Teheran doctrine of 1944–45. The party dissolved and re-formed as the Communist Political Association, aiming to work within the Democratic Party in anticipation of postwar coexistence between capitalist and communist nations. Initially Dreiser welcomed this major shift in orientation, but when Browder's strategy was successfully challenged by William Z. Foster, he sided with the latter. It was Foster's reconstituted Communist Party that Dreiser would eventually join in the summer of 1945 (see "Theodore Dreiser Joins Communist Party," 287–91).

Alongside his very public engagement with international relations, and after his peace campaigning wound down in December 1941, Dreiser espoused numerous campaigns on matters of political policy and individual welfare. He pamphleteered on issues such as the political affiliation of the Writers' League of America, the existence of a free press in America, and, reiterating concerns that went back to the *Delineator* days if not to the 1890s, on the need to fund provision for child welfare out of national taxation, not charity.[12] While he passionately opposed what he considered to be Franklin Roosevelt's war-mongering and Anglophilia, Dreiser praised many New Deal policies and engaged positively and directly with the administration. He called for the creation of a secretary for the arts in the presidential cabinet, and he corresponded with the White House about ideas for a National Transportation Department and on Spanish war relief (on which topic he met with the president); he also demanded a detailed national program for children, the "seed corn" of America's future.[13] In addition, Dreiser wrote to officials on behalf of prisoners threatened with extradition or convicted of homosexual offenses; challenged Governor Schricker of Indiana to stop the persecution of C.I.O. workers by Indiana State troops and hired vigilantes; sent a message of support to striking dock workers; and met and corresponded with Mme. Chiang Kai-shek, wife and English translator of the Chinese premier.[14]

This combination of activities reflected a fundamental attitude to political organization evinced in the late poem "What To Do" (see 286), where Dreiser contrasts individual activism, imagined as quietly heroic, with abstracted "groups," "committees," and "government." In a companion piece titled "Interdependence" (see 291–93), written shortly before his death, Dreiser develops his sense of cultural relativism into a commitment to international diversity. There he places his hopes for future peace in personal engagements with the individuality of others across the globe, under the economic conditions of abundance newly made possible by technological advances. Echoing the widespread but short-lived optimistic internationalism of the immediate postwar moment, "Interdependence," like "What To Do," recalls Dreiser's 1896 definition of genuine charity as existing only "in the heart, the eye and the hand of one toward the suffering and woe of a visible *other*."[15]

Notes

1. Theodore Dreiser, "'Nothing So Important to American People now as Aiding U.S.S.R.'—Dreiser," *People's World* (San Francisco), 2 July 1941, p. 1; "Come All Ye who are Weary and Heavy Laden," typescript, DPUP; Telegram to *New Masses*, 24 July 1942, DPUP.

2. Theodore Dreiser, "Interview with Harry Bridges," typescript, 48–49, DPUP.

3. "Radio Interview with Theodore Dreiser," Interviewer: Edward Robbin; KMTR Hollywood, 1 February 1941; printed version, p. 4, DPUP.

4. Theodore Dreiser, "Barcelona in August," *Direction* 1 (November-December 1938): 5.

5. For example, Theodore Dreiser, "Lenin," *International Literature* 4–5 (April-May 1940): 82; "The Meaning of the U.S.S.R. in the World Today," *Soviet Russia Today* 9 (November 1940), 23, 47; and "Armenia Today," typescript, DPUP.

6. TD telegram to *New Masses*, 24 July 1942, DPUP.

7. TD to Josef Stalin, 16 May 1945, DPUP.

8. Theodore Dreiser, Statement to National Committee on Election Rights, 9 October 1940, DPUP.

9. Theodore Dreiser, Radio broadcast on KHJ Los Angeles, 29 October 1940, carbon copy typescript, p. 2, DPUP.

10. "The Story of Harry Bridges," *Friday* 1 (4 October 1940): 2.

11. TD to William C. Lengel, 17 July 1940, pp. 1, 2, DPUP.

12. See Further Reading and "Theodore Dreiser and the Free Press" (259–63).

13. TD to Adelaide Bean, 22 January 1940; TD to Franklin D. Roosevelt, 23 August 1938, 1 September 1938, 19 September 1938, and 2 January 1939; TD to Eleanor Roosevelt, 19 March 1942. All in DPUP.

14. TD to Culbert L. Olson, 14 March 1940; TD to John G. Clark, State of California Board of Prison Terms and Paroles, 27 April 1940; TD to Governor F. Schricker, 4 April 1941; TD to National Maritime Union at San Pedro, 1 December 1945; TD to Mme. Chiang Kai-shek, 3 July 1944. All in DPUP.

15. Theodore Dreiser, "Reflections," *Ev'ry Month*, November 1896, p. 6.

Further Reading

"The Soviet-Finnish Treaty and World Peace." *Soviet Russia Today* 8 (April 1940): 8–9; also printed as a broadside, "Concerning Dives and Lazarus," March 1940.
"Theodore Dreiser Condemns War." *People's World* (San Francisco), 6 April 1940, p. 7; also printed as a broadside, "War," April 1940.
"Letter to S. Bayard Colgate of the Boys Brotherhood Republic, 16 July 1940"; published as a broadside, "A Request and an Answer," July 1940.
"The Story of Harry Bridges." *Friday* 1 (4 October 1940): 1–8, 28, and *Friday* 1 (11 October 1940): 14–17.
"'U.S. Must Not Be Bled for Imperial Britain'—Dreiser." *People's World* (San Francisco), 12 November 1940, p. 6; also printed as a leaflet, November 1940.
"This is Churchill's 'Democracy.'" *New Masses* 38 (18 February 1941): 35–36; also printed as a leaflet, "Concerning Our Helping England Again," February 1941.
"To The Writers' League of America." Leaflet, May 1941.

War Is a Racket

1937–39

The title of this unpublished essay echoes Major General Smedley D. Butler's anti-corporate, anti-imperialist speech and 1935 book, War Is a Racket. *Butler had warned against 1930s militarism on the basis of the corporate profit and human loss of World War I. Taking up these themes, Dreiser adopts a more philosophical approach and a longer historical perspective, citing a range of historical figures to personify negative, militaristic, and imperialistic tendencies on the one hand, and creative, cooperative values on the other. Contrary to Darwinistic notions of struggle, Dreiser argues, it is only such peaceful values that bring about evolutionary progress. This struggle over values takes on urgency in the midst of the international tensions that would lead to the outbreak of war, at a time when the League of Nations's policy of "collective security" was put into crisis by technological developments such as aerial and submarine warfare.*

Apart from a really worthy cause that the world in its days of peace would substantiate, war is a racket. With very few exceptions, all wars throughout historic times have been rackets. That is, they have been erratic, selfish plunder plans on the part of individuals or nations, and in both cases, underlying the mood of the nation or the individual making such plans, have been greed and vanity—vanity that only greed, and a determination to brutally frustrate, dominate or destroy one another, that is, either nations or individuals, could explain. You need only to read the story of historic wars, from that of the Trojan War down, to know that.

We read of great wars and great generals, but until our Civil War, fought to free the American Negro slaves, and some earlier and purely defensive wars, I doubt if there has been an honorable war—let alone one great, in a moral sense. Of course you read of the rise of Assyria and Persia and Greece and Rome and Spain and England and France and Germany and Russia, and more recently Japan. But on what terms? For hope of what great result? Justified by what? Success? Development? Advancement for the masses of mankind? Never. Then for whom? The masses of the victorious nation— or their leaders? Which? Well, read the history of all wars and learn that almost without exception what you read of is the vanities and the greeds of nations and individuals who have wished and determined, by any processes whatsoever to outstrip their neighbors or even their distant and unfamiliar contemporaries. But to what private end? To improve themselves mentally or others? You know that is not so. All that the Assyrians, the Persians, the Egyptians, the Greeks, the Romans and so forth, could write on their monuments after their wars and victories, was that they had come, murdered, destroyed or subjugated, and then left.

In our schools the children still read of Alexander the Great, but my question is "GREAT" for what? For starting out at the age of twenty or twenty some odd years to conquer the known world of his day—the Asiatic world to the east of him? And impelled by what? The desire to improve the East? Or, to say and prove that he had conquered, that is, that he had subdued the known world? That and nothing else. But to what end? To carry Greek enlightenment over the world that he conquered? If you think so, read the history. Already his father, Philip of Macedon had subjugated and really destroyed the old and really distinguished Greek world. Besides that, Alexander carried nothing of import into Asia. Nothing. There is no evidence to show that anything that was in Asia Minor, or India, or Persia, on his arrival there, was beneficially altered by him. And there *is* evidence, plenty of it, to show that what was there was injured by his coming. But this was equally true of other conquerors before his time—Darius and Xerxes,[1] who sought to conquer Greece. Ashurbanipal,[2] who appears to have wiped out a great nation—the Hittites—but to what profit? None that anyone can see.

But after these and Alexander, consider only the long line of Roman Generals, Republican and Imperial, who made Rome Great. Did they not make war in order to tax and enslave other tribes and nations—the Greeks, Egyptians, Germans, and Britons? And who not else? But to what end? Well I will tell you. To allow Rome to live on slaves and robbery. But once she was finished (destroyed by her own luxury and excesses—not the luxury of her masses, but her classes) came other peoples or nations and their so-called leaders, the Goths, the Huns, the Germans, the Spaniards. And all doing what? Well, just what Rome did, only not as forcefully or terribly. But apart from that, exactly what civilization had Rome to offer her victims? Or her imitators who came after her? Culture? She knew nothing of it—at best what she borrowed from Greece. What she had to offer by way of ex-ample was trade and show, and that based on plunder and slavery, whereas Greece, left to itself, could as easily, and better, have established culture without war and plunder. Greed and vanity gave Rome a dominance, which, instead of enduring, to the welfare of the world after Rome's fall, perished with it. Actually all that Rome did was to awaken the envy, the hatred, and a desire for revenge and plunder on the part of all the peoples that it conquered, or who remembered it. And yet it is supposed to have spread enlightenment!

Really, the only enlightenment worthy of the name, in the ancient as well as the modern sense, came not from its captains and kings who were seeking their own fame and pleasure, but from the lesser individuals of all ancient nations, who, tortured by the iniquities and the inequities that they saw about them, set about seeking equity.

Indeed, before Rome, during its life and afterwards, only such individuals as Anaxagoras, Plato, Aristotle, Christ, Marcus Aurelius, Buddha, Lao-tzu,[3] and others who were not interested in wars but peace and the development of the human mind, brought anything of value into the world. These indi-viduals, one and all, felt life to be best furthered and advantaged, not by war and plunder and death, but by cooperation and construction on the part of minute individuals, who, hidden away from so-called great affairs, lived to think and study out the welfare of man, and to act and write as they lived. As a matter of fact, if you will read the lives of the really great men of the world, its thinkers, inventors, artists, travelers, educators, explorers, men of medicine, law, the arts, governments, and so forth, you will see for yourself that it is they and they only who have done the really valuable things for the world. That is, invented and planned for the betterment and the wel-fare of man, not these others. And they were not warriors or conquerors or members of the leisure or the ruling classes. And they did not seek fame or applause, but only the happiness of culture and social improvement. I defy you to produce evidence to the contrary.

Not only that, but it is these people—not the fighting and ruling classes—who from the beginning and by their studies of life and its history, our early and late great naturalists, scientists, inventors and investigators of every kind, who have helped man move upward. And by their work and the progress that they, and not these others, have made possible, has man climbed to where he is. They, as opposed to these others, have proved that life is not necessarily red in beak and claw and must live by murder and death, but rather that there has been operating throughout all time, an adaptive as well as creative process which is by no means wholly individualistic and selfish and brutal and cruel, but on the contrary, cooperative and social. And more, that it is by this process as much, if not more than the other, that not only animals but vegetables, flowers, birds, trees, insects, slowly, and by some inner impulse than outward force or cruelty, have tended to build and fit themselves most graciously and even peacefully into their surroundings.

True enough, there has been a struggle for subsistence quite everywhere, and not a little death. But that struggle has not by any means related itself exclusively, or even evenly, to contests with individuals as intelligent and formidable as themselves. In most cases, it has consisted of more lively and intelligent and alert forms living not on their equals—that is, individuals like themselves and capable of suffering as much as themselves or more, but rather on very minute, and insofar as sensory capacities are concerned, relatively insensitive growths—vegetable and animal—the capacity of which to suffer was and remains so very much less that their destruction or use for food cannot be looked upon as war or murder. Far from it. Is it murder to cut grass, or to grow corn or potatoes or wheat grains and eat them? Well, man has mostly survived and developed on these things—not the flesh of animals, let alone the blood of his fellow men. The last appears to be needed only for the purpose of making Alexanders, Hannibals, Attilas, Genghis Khans, Napoleons, vainglorious brutes and murderers all.

Furthermore, the power of these lesser creatures I have just spoken of, except as food to aid in the matter of constructing any such thing as civilization, was, if at all, almost infinitesimally small. They were not, insofar as we can see, tending toward any such social, or human life as we know. More than that, if you look at all the animals truly useful to man in his upward climb, you will note that they have not been slayers like tigers and wolves, but helpers in the best sense of the word—killing nothing of importance to sustain themselves, and yet at the same time aiding man, not so much as food but as servants in his struggle to sustain and enlighten himself. I refer to the elephant, the horse, the cow, the sheep, the zebra, and some others. As for the beauty of life, which helps man to live, that has been much contributed to by birds, flowers of great beauty, trees, and some insects that have helped protect the fruit tree and bush. To be sure, the really ferocious and destructive flesh-eating animals are the most formidable, but by no means have they ever been so numerous, and have usually been matched and destroyed by others of their own kind. And not only that, but as to their utility, it would appear from the way society has dispensed with them that they are not necessary to the beauty or the happiness of the world. As a matter of fact, except for the business of sustaining and entertaining themselves, they seem to have generated only fear and terror and misery to types that sought to progress by more peaceful means. The creatures or creations that tended to make life really possible and worthwhile have been trees, flowers, grass-eating animals, birds, fish, and races of men who have struggled with the soil and advanced by the arts of peace—not war. If you will read Darwin, Huxley, Humboldt, Haeckel and others,[4] you can judge for yourself whether the slaughter and war programs of the world's individualists have ever as yet helped make the world what it is today. Never. And they will not keep intact what life has achieved so far. Never.

Yet curiously enough, only man, the vain, selfish, egoist, and no other, has, as he has progressed in so-called wisdom (really not in understanding of what may contribute to his mental but rather his material satisfaction and lusts and greeds) developed those phases of greed and cruelty and murder which have made life the hell that it is. Like wolves and tigers and lions, these have preyed and tended to prey on their fellow men within and without their native lands and so to bring on the enormous struggles and slaughters that have tortured and betrayed the world. And not for sustenance either, mind you, but for the glory and the vanity of war and slaughter or conquest—and little else. And more, their plotted slaughters have rarely, if ever, been based on the fact that their means of subsistence were fading or passing, but rather that those means were increasing, and that by reason of the energy and patience and strength of the masses under them—so much so that once these means were plentiful enough, these braggarts and wasters at the top could then afford to use the surpluses created for them to strike down, not only the masses beneath them, but their neighboring rivals, and for the sole purpose of more power. To be able to say, "I am the Lord of all I survey. Besides me who is there to lift his head?" Yes, by that process, in our modern as well as in the ancient state, have the people been enslaved, tortured and bled. Only today, in place of Kings, Queens, Emperors, and Tsars—the old world General or savage conqueror like Attila or Genghis Khan—we have the modern industrialist and his subject state—that is, our capitalists, their bankers, paid agents, lawyers, courts, judges, police, armies, navies, and what not—who now have so-called elected Presidents or Dictators to do their bidding, and who not only enslave and rob the people as before, but indulge in all the old-time rivalries for plunder which bring about such wars as the last great one—or the one that NOW threatens the world in Europe and Asia.

But for what? The development and uplift or at least welfare of man as against wild nature? Never believe it. Now, as throughout recorded history, your individualist—whether capitalist or Dictator, here or abroad, is plotting and fighting not for sustenance or to preserve his country or his people or their welfare, but singly and solely to increase his authority and his vanity over all the life about him. That and nothing less and nothing more. If you doubt it, for God's sake read history, American as well as European. As I said before, the lone exception was our great Civil War in which the Americans of the North fought the Americans of the South to prevent them from enslaving more and more Negroes. As terrible as that was, it remains the only respectable war known to men.

But now I maintain that we have reached the place where we do not need either these egotists, their vanities, or their wars to further either the honor or dignity or the success of man, In fact, as I said before, the real improvements in connection with the knowledge, the comfort, the happiness and the ideals of man, have come, not from these tigers and wolves, but from individuals who have neither desired nor promoted war—men and women who have been interested in, have even been entertained and charmed, by the opportunity for laboring and developing and perfecting the equipment of man for a happier, more colorful, more beautiful and peaceful life than has ever yet existed in the world before. And it is time that the world understood this and that these people are allowed to show what they can do. They have been and remain, not only tillers of the soil, builders of homes, artificers of all kinds of useful and necessary things, but also our explorers, educators, scientists, physicians, architects, poets, philosophers, naturalists, geologists, chemists, physicists, inventors, traders, writers, and equitable and order-seeking officials, if not their rulers, everywhere. And they have worked diligently and sacrificially in all the fields and all the times of life. It is these—not the Alexanders, the Caesars, the Xerxeses, the Attilas, the Napoleons, and so forth—who have really built the world that we know. And it is time that we turned to them and away from these others who have only disturbed and delayed life in its onward march. Indeed, our last and greatest war that was fought between 1914 and 1918 was nothing more than the outgrowth and the outcome of all the lunatic and baseless and petty vanities and jealousies and vainglories that have bestridden and tortured the world since history began. And more, it proved, and how clearly, how futile has been all the time and energy and invention and enthusiasm devoted to this wasteful and murderous pursuit of power and acclaim. For now, and at long last, as you can read in any daily paper, our leading war powers—Japan, England, France, Italy, and even America, startled by the steady and terrific progress of their own machinery for fighting and what

228 • *Theodore Dreiser*

it means to them, as well as their enemies in their chase after power and dominance, are at last seeing and admitting that by their own plans and schemes to destroy each other, they have come to the place where they are as likely to destroy themselves as their enemies. Indeed, the last war proved that well enough—only, suffering from the old war germ, they have gone on putting their faith in airplanes and submarines and the death ray and the gas bomb, only to find that now, with the airplane and the submarine to convey all of these things at three hundred miles an hour, they cannot really protect themselves, particularly while they are so busy seeking to destroy their enemies. They cannot protect their cities or their people. France cannot protect Paris or Lyon. England cannot protect London or Liverpool. The United States knows that New York, Chicago, San Francisco, indeed any city you choose to name, cannot protect itself against the airplane, and that in hours, not days, these will be in ashes. Japan will lose its Kyoto, its Nagasaki; Russia its Moscow and Leningrad. Italy its Rome, Milan, Naples, Florence. And so at last, because of their crazy dreaming of and planning for conquest, they have come to the place where they are beginning to be afraid, and are now thinking of some method by which their tricky, and as yet biased, League of Nations may rule out of war the airplane and the submarine! Imagine!

Yet that fact alone should establish my contention that war, predatory war as such, created and backed as it is by our present day insane and brutal rivalry for individual wealth and power, has run its course and that if the world is to be saved, progress preserved, and man permitted to straighten out his life and make it something less than the hell it now is, war will have to be eliminated and the business of progress turned over to the people—the temperaments that have always done the most for it. And unless that is done, and quickly, there will come a long long period in which man will strive, and perhaps in vain, for the joys and the comforts of a social order that at one time—this hour in which we are living no less—was measurably within his reach.

Textual Note: Undated typescript (14 pages) signed Theodore Dreiser in typescript, with title "War Is a Racket" in Dreiser's hand, in DPUP folder 12477.

1. Darius I (548–486 BCE), king of Persia, whose expedition against Athens was defeated at Marathon in 490 BCE; and his son, Xerxes I (519–465 BCE), who ordered the destruction of Athens in 480 BCE but ultimately failed to conquer Greece.

2. Ashurbanipal (or Assurbanipal), better known by the Greek form of Sardanapalus (669–640 BCE), belonged to a dynasty that consolidated the Assyrian empire, involving, in part, the defeat and dispersal of the Hittite empire, which had occupied much of modern-day Turkey and northern Syria.

3. Greek philosophers Anaxagoras (c. 500–428 BCE), Plato (427–347 BCE), and

Aristotle (384–322 BCE); Roman emperor and philosopher Marcus Aurelius Antoninus (121–80 BCE); and Lao-tzu, also called Lao-Tse or Lao Zi (c. 604–531 BCE), Chinese philosopher and founder of Taoism. The significance of these figures for Dreiser lies in his view of them as pursuing "the development of the human mind" untrammeled either by the pursuit of military glory and power or by what he saw as the mystifying moral codes associated with organized Christianity.

4. Charles Darwin (1809–82), Thomas Henry Huxley (1825–95), Alexander von Humboldt (1769–1859), and Ernst Haeckel (1834–1919) were prominent figures of evolutionary theory and social Darwinism, who had strongly influenced Dreiser in the 1890s. The argument for the importance of peaceful cooperation for evolutionary "progress" is primarily associated with the Russian anarchist scientist Peter Kropotkin (1842–1921), especially his *Mutual Aid: A Factor of Evolution* (1902).

Equity between Nations

Address before the World Conference for Action on the Bombardment of Open Towns and the Restoration of Peace, Paris, 23 July 1938.

The Rassemblement Universel Pour La Paix was founded in September 1935 by British and French politicians in response to fascist Italy's invasion of Abyssinia (Ethiopia). Its stated objective was to rally support for the peacekeeping activities of the League of Nations, and it appealed across the political spectrum from communists to British conservatives. The R.U.P. called the 1938 Paris conference to protest the bombing of civilian populations in the Spanish Civil War and by Japanese forces in China. In his speech, Dreiser encourages diplomatic efforts aimed at restoring peace, while insisting that deeper changes in individual attitudes toward wealth, "class hatreds," and "cut throat individualism" are necessary to tackle the causes of nationalistic domination and war. The speech was subsequently published in the progressive literary and political magazine Direction *under the title "Equity between Nations."*

The work of the two American Committees that asked me to come here as one of their representatives is really aimed to abolish war and establish democracy.[1] The phrases "peace and democracy" and "war against war and fascism" actually include the hope of stopping the bombardment of innocent civilians, whether they be women and children or unarmed workers or merchants or professionals in what ever fields they may be. At bottom the campaign is for fair play or legal conduct between antagonists, however just or unjust their antagonisms may be. To this end the Committees I represent seek to arouse favorable public sentiment the world over. More, they ask for money, not only for the injured and the homeless, but for men and women workers, to take this money and aid to them, wherever they are, in Spain or in China.

Dreiser addresses the World Conference for Action on the Bombardment
of Open Towns and the Restoration of Peace, Paris, 23 July 1938.

This particular conference, as I understand it, has been called to devise
ways and means of doing all of these things. Some people, like Mr. Blum[2]
in France and Lord Halifax[3] in England and our own Secretary of State, Mr.
Hull,[4] are wondering, how for instance, Italy and Germany and Spain, the
Loyalists and the Rebels, the Chinese and the Japanese can be harmonized.
How to initiate mediation between them, to get them not to do the things
they are doing.

Only the other day, when the King[5] was here, your premier, Mr. Daladier,[6]
your ex-premier Mr. Blum, Mr. Herriot,[7] your president of the chamber, and
Lord Halifax agreed sadly, that mediation could be undertaken only by the
five Great Powers. By them, I assume, they mean: Germany, Italy, France,
England, and Russia (if they are willing to concede that Russia is a Great
Power), or possibly, as someone said, by England single-handed. I don't
suppose, in view of the present attitude of the United States, that they feel
that they can interest it.

However, I can tell you, a real majority of the American people would
like to see their government do something about all this. And it is actually
the work of the League of American Writers and the American League
against War and Fascism, to persuade the people of America to compel
their government to do this. And they are certainly making progress. Public

sentiment against dishonest and unjustified war and oppression is very strong in America. It is not as strong as it was in the days of slavery or when Royal Spain was oppressing Cuba, but it can well become so.[8]

In England, if I read the events in that country correctly, there is now developing among the English masses an opinion which may, and I hope will, force the responsible executives of that government to be less soft spoken about the horrors, which they see and about which they have done little or nothing. That I am right as to this, seems to me to be confirmed by that meeting here in Paris that I was just talking about. Because there Lord Halifax told his French questioners, that the bombardment of open towns in Spain and China had deeply moved public opinion in England. But he also said, that it was no easy matter to reform.

It will never be an easy matter. And fair play will not come between nations, until fair play between capital and labor in the various nationalities has been established. Nor will it come, until the majority of individuals of all lands and nationalities stop pinning their faith to wealth, and by that I mean individual wealth as against national wealth, as the only way to secure for them, individually, comfort and safety. For individual wealth leads to the grouping or union of the possessors of such wealth as against those who have not so much, in order that they may retain it, regardless of all others. And this leads directly to those class hatreds that divide and weaken nations internally and—externally—to cause them to war on other nations which have more than they have or which seek or seem to seek (as they think) to prevent them from obtaining what they desire. In other words, as nations, it leads to internal and external quarrelling, injustice and inhuman wars such as we see today.

But when any one says that, the individual replies: "Well, that is all right. But if I don't take care of myself, no one else will." And until men of good will and good sense the world over sit down together and think out ways and means of making their governments deal fairly between the strong and the weak, the intelligent and the unintelligent, the cunning and the innocent, he will certainly struggle to take care of himself in any way that he can, honestly or dishonestly. The masses, and by that I mean all the individuals of the masses, must learn that they can only expect a fair reward for what they do *if they insist and see to it, that every other individual receives a fair reward for what he does.*

In America we say: "fifty-fifty" and the masses really want our representatives and our executives to see that this "fifty-fifty" is secured to all. Our Constitution calls for it and our present president, Mr. Roosevelt, is quite cautiously trying to bring it about by democratic means. However, there as everywhere else in the world, he has the strong and the greedy and the lazy and the vain, who happen to have the majority of the wealth of the country, or would like to have it, to deal with.

These do not want fair play as between them and the man who has little or nothing. They insist on trying to be giants in a world that consists only of little men, for certainly we are all of us little men, and we have not yet solved exactly how to establish equity. But when we begin trying, you will not have England seizing India, Italy Abyssinia, Japan, China, the United States the Panama Canal, as they did at first, but you will have an effort to bring the means of subsistence and the opportunity of self-development to every individual the world over. And when you have that, you will not have a world in which men are almost compelled to seize each other by the throat in order to live. But my feeling at this time is that, if a Great World War can be avoided, it is entirely possible that some world conference, such as this one would like to be, will bring about a plan, that may help all nations to avoid this old cut throat individualism. And for this reason this particular world conference—because of the thought and the feeling for men of all nations that prompts it—has enormous significance for me.

This hall is small, the number of people here is not many, but the word that could go out from here, might be so wise, so valuable, that it would move millions of people. For what I read and hear in many places today leads me to believe that many many people are weary, and more than that, disgusted with this silly struggle for enormous individual wealth and enormous individual power. For, as you can see for yourself, these things can no longer mean really anything in a world, where millions realize, that no one man anywhere is so very different from any other and where they are beginning to see, that to do the really great things in life, the good things, the helpful things, the beautiful things, the individual does not need great wealth or great power. He only needs to represent the wealth, the power, the intelligence, and the needs of all of the people. And what is more, considering all of the people that have to be dealt with today, neither great wealth, nor great power can rest in the hands of any single individual. Because no individual can possibly wisely handle all of the things which great wealth and great power demand of him. He must have help. He must have the information, which has never yet resided in any one individual and never will.

Wisdom and knowledge exist only in the minds of all of the people— not in those of just a few. You may know medicine, I don't. And millions of other people don't either. You may know engineering, or law, or surgery, or chemistry, or how to make tools, or how to build a house, or even how to lay a water pipe in the street. I don't. And probably not a man or a woman in this room knows much more than a little of any of these things. But in all of the minds of all of the people of the world today, including as these do, all of the knowledge that has been gathered by their ancestors and worked out in the form of habits, customs, implements, materials, machines, architecture, art and the books that describe these things, are to be found the knowledge and the wisdom by which we live or seek to. So that no one man anywhere nor any single nation anywhere can claim to know all this, or how to arrange life for everybody, everywhere. Besides there is so much to be known, that no one, no individual, nor any single nation anywhere, knows or can know all that is to be known.[9] We have yet to learn and we must be humble and cooperative in the search.

And for that reason individual vanity and individual greed leading as these often do (through the vainglorious and the greedy groups they invoke), to national vanities and national greeds must be curbed. For these provoke international hatred and wars and so injure man as a whole—stop his progress—wipe out his achievements as they frequently have and may still do.

So let me repeat, that since most of the knowledge of today is not in any individual nor any group of individuals but is rather in books written by dead men, piled up in libraries or laboratories and willed by them to us without charge, it is neither wise nor fair of any of us to be so vain, greedy, self-seeking, or intolerant as some are. This building, this city, all of the processes by which we live, by which this nation and every other nation lives, was willed by other generations to this generation. You did not pay for this street outside any more than you paid for this hall or the Atlantic Ocean. You found it here. It was given to you. And no one should be charged too much for what was already here, when he came. That is why I feel that more fair play must come into life. We are—all of us—co-heirs of all that is. We should find ways and means of sharing peacefully what has been given us by nature and other men, without fighting, without bombing cities, without murdering women and children and people, who do not want unjustly to take anything from anyone.

I hope that this World Conference will be able to make a few suggestions which may appeal to the individuals of all nations, and more, move them to endeavor to work this out. I hope it will make France and England and the United States and all other countries get busy and make their religions, Catholic, Protestant, or whatsoever—their Red Crosses, Salvation Armies, and other charitable organizations or groups begin earnestly to aid the Loyalists, the Chinese, and those despised and afflicted everywhere. I thank you.[10]

Textual Note: Address before the World Conference for Action on the Bombardment of Open Towns and the Restoration of Peace, Paris, 23 July 1938. Copy-text is the signed typescript (7 pages) with revisions in Dreiser's hand in DPUP folder 13378, selectively emended by reference to one mixed holograph and typescript (DPUP folder 13377) and three further typescripts and carbon copies in DPUP folder 13378. Published, without the two closing sentences, and with minor editorial revisions, as "Equity between Nations," *Direction* 1 (September–October 1938): 5–6, 11.

1. Dreiser's travel expenses were paid by the League of American Writers and the American League for Peace and Democracy, formerly known as the American League against War and Fascism, liberal organizations led by a minority communist membership.

2. Léon Blum (1872–1950), socialist prime minister of France in May–June 1936 and March–April 1938.

3. Lord Halifax (1881–1959), British foreign secretary from 1938 to 1940.

4. Cordell Hull (1871–1955), secretary of state under Roosevelt from 1933 until 1944.

5. Alfonso XIII (1886–1941), deposed from the Spanish throne in 1931 and exiled in France.

6. Édouard Daladier (1884–1970), socialist prime minister of France from April 1938 until 1940.

7. Édouard Herriot (1872–1957) remained president of the Chamber of Deputies until the Nazi occupation in 1942.

8. Dreiser refers to popular support for military action during the American Civil War (1861–65) and in support of Cuba during its war of independence against Spain in 1895–98.

9. This sentence is condensed in *Direction* to "Besides, there is too much to be known."

10. The closing lines, from "or whatsoever" to the end, are handwritten additions to the typescript.

American Democracy against Fascism

Speech to the Conference of the International Association of Writers for the Defense of Culture, Paris, France, 26 July 1938.

Dreiser addressed this gathering of leftist writers' associations immediately after the anti-bombardment conference.

What is the attitude of the United States toward Fascism?

I must say first that America is still far from being a democracy. Before President Roosevelt's election it was wholly dominated by a powerful if not numerous group of financiers that desired, and still does, to rule it fascistically—for itself, its "sixty families"[1] and not for the people. But to disguise its purpose, it speaks of America as a *Democracy*. And what is slyer, *in all of the legal proceedings* of each and every one of its corporations and banks it speaks of each one of them as an *individual* (!) not as a *corporation*. Our Supreme Court was induced to rule that all our corporations are individuals, like you and me.[2] Thus our Railroads, Express Companies, Power & Light Companies, General Motors, General Electric, the Duponts, the Standard Oil and Insurance and Mortgage Companies are each and every one of them *individuals*, with all the rights of an individual plus those of a corporation, and you can only sue them as individuals—not as giant corporations.

And so as individuals—not corporations—they between 1928 and 1931 sought to take control of America. In these years Mr. J. P. Morgan organized his *America Incorporated* and divided the shares of that *Company* (this one not an individual but the United States itself) between sixty or seventy of our leading corporations. They in their turn as shareholders or directors were to "appoint" a secretary, who in his turn was to be elected President of the United States.[3] We were still to have our Senate, our House of Representatives and our Supreme Court—"the one place on 'God's Foot Stool'" (meaning the Earth) where (as Ex-President and Ex-Chief-Justice Taft[4] once boasted) "adequate" and exact justice could be secured by all. *But their tool, Mr. Hoover, was not reelected.* His rival, Mr. Roosevelt, won. And he has proceeded to "save" our democracy such as it is (and it is better today than it was) first by exposing the above plan and next by surrounding himself by that much scoffed at *"Brain Trust"*—economists, sociologists, agronomists, engineers, labor and financial experts, etc.—who at once sought honestly to save the country from ruin.

From Russia, principally, they proceeded to borrow the five-year plan, the six or seven hour day for labor, a national housing plan, but not the nationalization of railroads, express companies, telephone and telegraph and power and light companies. However they did begin building national automobile roads, to inaugurate national water and forest preserve projects and to restore our outworn soils. And with these in full view in Russia, Roosevelt began at once to try to re-employ the twenty million men and women in America who were by then out of work. Also to save for the small depositors, where he could, some of the money they had deposited in our many *looted* and closed banks.

To be sure he did not dare inaugurate the communistic state, that is, a full imitation of what had been done in Russia. He did not believe for the moment that the American people, however wretched they were, would follow him that far. As a matter of fact, since 1917 so great had been the capitalists' uproar against communism and the "Reds" that they had succeeded, through their newspapers, churches, politicians, radio and moving picture mouthpieces, in making a majority of our American farmers and laborers, our clerks and "white collar" men half, (not wholly) believe that all communists were criminals—and that they only lived to rob, burn, murder, and steal what others, not they, had created; and once having done that, to turn them into voiceless frightened slaves, working day and night for a Communist Central Committee and its bureaucrats, who were paid to rule them. Every rumor or fact in connection with a shortage of any kind in Russia was exaggerated into the total absence of almost everything relating to an endurable life.

But Roosevelt, in announcing that he intended to *make* work for some 20,000,000 unemployed and all but starving Americans, had to go slow. For the cry was at once raised that he was a "Red"—that he proposed to communize the United States, to do away with *"individual initiative"* and worse *"individuality."* The *Constitution* was to be flouted! The creative "genius" of the country was to be smothered. Americans, little and big, were to be made serfs. He—Roosevelt—became a little frightened and moved cautiously— much too much so, since he had both houses of Congress behind him. So much so, that by going slow, he permitted these capitalist snakes, their lawyers, judges, courts, purchased state legislatures, newspapers, moving picture producers and radio and what not, to crawl out of their holes, warm up, and as in the fable of the peasant and the frozen snake,[5] to attempt to strike the friend who had warmed them.

But, by degrees, Roosevelt had learned where his friends were and where enemies. And by continuing to employ the unemployed on national projects he finally restored a degree of prosperity. That is, by February 1937 living conditions in America were becoming once more moderately endurable if not good. Then suddenly and by pre-arrangement—as all of our workers and clerks now believe—the large corporations and their banks and holding companies decided to end this progress by shutting down mills, reducing wages, and throwing out laborers. In Wall Street, their so much admired barometer of all success, they began to sell their own America Incorporated shares "short"—to cry down their own properties, to—where possible—move their mills out of the country. But it did not work. Finding himself and his followers *"sold out"* in this way and unemployment increasing, Roosevelt now decided to cease attempting to placate the corporations and proceeded, with the consent of Congress, to set aside four billion dollars more—$4,000,000,0000 of the nation's future taxes—in order to re-employ the now once more unemployed. With this money he proposed, with the consent of Congress, of course, to continue the various water, power, land, and reforestation projects, but, in addition—and which is really more important—to undertake a national re-housing or slum clearance work—very much needed in America—and better yet, to stop paying a weekly dole to the men and women whom the corporations would not employ, and so keep them idle. Instead he determined to find employment for them in some form so that they would not lose their skill and their spirit *as* laborers.

To this end he secured the passage of the Wages and Hours Bill[6] which, as they say in America, "put a floor under wages and a ceiling over hours" so that no one—child or man—can now be paid less than 25 cents an hour, nor be made to work more than eight hours a day.

But this is exactly what our American corporations do not want. They want, truly, to introduce as much labor saving machinery as possible in order to cut down labor costs, while, at the same time, having the government not put these men to work in any competitive industries, but instead having it pay them a very small dole—too small to live on—and so let them sicken and die or loaf like convicts do in prison—in other words prevent them from interfering with business. That is what they call prosperity *for them*.

However, all these things done or not done do not by any means make a democracy. Ninety-five per cent of the wealth of America still belongs to five per cent of our Americans. The others have little or nothing—get 25 cents to $2.00 a day—if so much. Yet in spite of all this Mr. Roosevelt or his party (the Democratic Party) will not take the railroads and run them, nor the telephone or telegraph companies, nor Standard Oil, nor any of the big corporations. That would be un-American, unconstitutional—Red. Instead, these and the banks, the real money yielding organizations of the country have to be left in private hands so that *"individual initiative"* shall not be destroyed—that *"individual initiative"* that, today, can only "result" in our masses working for the corporations—the "Sixty Families"—instead of the government. They do not want the government to build good houses for the working men, at the government's expense. That would increase their taxes, take away their right to charge high rents. Nor do they want any more money spent on water power or electricity producing dams. That reduces the profits of the Electric Companies. Or to help the farmers to improve their land or to fix prices below which their products—wheat, corn, cattle—may be sold—because these things injure the Packing Business. They are still, all of them, strong not so much for the old jungle game, where the stronger wins against the next strongest, but for the absence of any competition of any kind, in other words slavery. They would like slavery again in America—white slavery. And if they can get it they will.

So we have not so much a Democracy in America as a *war* for one. And while it is not an open war with guns and gas, as in Spain and China, it is a semi-private one—with guns and gas around the various factory towns. All our corporations are strong for a big army and navy to be used of course *at home* or abroad while the average American is not. Our multi-millionaires control at least 70 per cent of our newspapers, the radio, moving pictures and, of course, most of our judges, lawyers, police, and all of the hundred or two hundred thousand "socialites" (our leisure or royal class) which desires workers to serve them and keep them comfortable. And they use, and are using still, all of these agencies and forces to subvert the masses. Only labor, under such a man as John Lewis,[7] or the "Reds," or agitators, such as the communists, socialists, etc. fight for democracy in America today. They want a fair deal for labor and are determined to get it. But they have little money, few publications—and free speech or free distribution of pamphlets or hand-bills on the streets, or in halls, as well as uncensored publication of "radical" ideas in newspapers and magazines or over the radio or through our moving pictures is becoming more and more difficult. We have our Hitlers and Mussolinis, little ones, on every hand. For a price they are ready to serve the money crowd in any way that they can. And they are so doing.

What the outcome of all this will be I can't truly say—no one can. But I firmly believe that in spite of the money trust, the steel trust, the telephone trust, the railroads etc., the rank and file of America will yet make their government represent them. At least, as yet we have no Hitler and no Mussolini, and we do not want one. Nor any British aristocracy either. We want all Americans living in good houses, wearing good clothes, eating good food and reading fair minded and intelligent magazines and newspapers and books. We want a free stage, free movies, a free radio, free music and if we continue to feel as we do now—a majority of us all—we will get them. Also our Negroes, our Jews, our Italians, Germans, Japanese, Chinese, Malays, and all others will also be free as long as they love true freedom not for themselves alone but for everybody.[8]

Textual Note: Speech to the Conference of the International Association of Writers for the Defense of Culture, Paris, France, 26 July 1938. Copy-text is the latest of three carbon copy typescripts (7 pages), with revisions in Dreiser's hand, in DPUP folder 11913. Signed in typescript "Theodore Dreiser" with "House Mt. Kisco, N.Y. Paris. France. July 26 1938" appended in Dreiser's hand.

1. Dreiser refers to Ferdinand Lundberg's exposé of super-rich dynasties using tax records, *America's 60 Families* (New York: Vanguard Press, 1937).

2. The legal precedent of regarding corporations as persons, based on the Fourteenth Amendment to the Constitution, was set by the U.S. Supreme Court's 1886 decision in the case of *Santa Clara County v. the Southern Pacific Railroad*. The legal recognition of corporate personhood has subsequently been qualified but remains controversial.

3. The leftwing conspiracy theory outlined in this paragraph is unsubstantiated. Allegations of a "business plot" to remove Roosevelt by military force were examined by the McCormack-Dickstein Congressional Committee in 1934.

4. William Howard Taft (1857–1930), president from 1909 to 1913 and chief justice between 1921 and 1930.

5. In the fable, attributed to Aesop, a peasant or farmer is bitten fatally by a half-frozen snake he has picked up and warmed in his bosom.

6. The Fair Labor Standards Act, signed into law by Roosevelt in June 1937.

7. John L. Lewis (1880–1969), miners' union leader and cofounder in 1935 of the militant C.I.O., reconstituted by 1938 as an explicit rival to the A.F.L.

8. An instructive formulation of Dreiser's sense of an inclusive America and the basis on which he predicated that inclusiveness.

Loyalist Spain—July 1938

Address at a Benefit Dinner for American Relief for Spain, organized by the League of American Writers, Hotel St. Moritz, New York, 15 September 1938.

Immediately after the Paris conferences, Dreiser briefly visited war-torn Spain at the invitation of its Republican government, where he observed the damage inflicted by Nationalist, Italian, and German bombers, and met with Republican political leaders. Back home, he campaigned on behalf of aid for Spanish civilians, making speeches and publishing three syndicated articles. He also wrote directly to President Roosevelt asking him to authorize relief, to be split equally between areas controlled by Republicans and Nationalists. This speech, Dreiser's most detailed and polished account of his visit to Spain, was the centerpiece of a fundraising dinner organized by the League of American Writers. Too late to affect the outcome of the war, Roosevelt did authorize shipments of flour to Spain in December 1938.

In Spain, for me at least, everything was remarkably interesting—down to the last details of living. I suppose this is partly true because we are all interested in how war affects people. But war makes its own atmosphere—a sort of feeling in the air, which arrives almost instantly after you cross the border from France to Spain. In the car with me were a photographer, entering to make pictures of the fighting, a government chauffeur, my guide, and others. All we strangers confessed to experiencing this feeling at once. It was a sense of impending danger—some dreadful thing that might, yet might not, occur.

Spain is beautiful. In the north as one leaves France it is mountainous and pastoral, with small farms, herds, and shepherds, little towns, donkey carts, and the eternal peasantry. Everyone there seemed to be going about his business as usual. But, in Spain, I was deeply impressed with the danger of air-raids, and the infectious sense of fear which follows such a probability.

In France, for instance, the flight of birds of any kind conveyed no suggestion of anything save poetry—birds flying over a river, or singing, or making a picture in the sky. But here in Spain, once you were in it, even the sight of a blackbird or a crow flying over a field, suggested—what? Did you not know? All soon mentioned this—that that was the way the war planes might come into view from anywhere at any moment—flying, like birds.

Entering Spain we drove through town after town—hamlets and villages with plenty of evidence of what already had been in this line—the broken and shell-spattered walls of houses, the heaps of ruins here and there, the closed shops and stores. We drove through one little town where one end of the street seemed to me to have been crushed to nothing. But, it was another place, quite a large town called Gerona,[1] that interested me most. Here there was a very large central square surrounded by the shops and restaurants of the town. I suppose, in ordinary times, the Spaniards sit out in this square, afternoon and evening, for there are many benches and chairs and trees. But, at the time we entered, a large trench had been dug down the middle. A bomb shelter was in the process of making, to which the people could hurry once a warning siren sounded. These sirens sound about five minutes before the bombers actually arrive. Warning of the coming of war planes is phoned into towns and cities by the farmer and outlying residents over whose regions they pass. The raids are sometimes short, sometimes long, depending on the objectives. One raid or a series of raids on Barcelona continued for three days, the war planes leaving and returning almost hourly.[2] During that time nearly 1500 people were killed, and many, many buildings in different parts of the city were destroyed. The week before I arrived thirty people were killed.

These bombings frighten some people, make others resigned, and still others defiant and hateful—and of course, there are many dead and wounded after each raid, many houses, shops, factories and so on blown up—much fruitless and profitless damage done. The hotel in which I stayed had its kitchen partially wrecked before I arrived.

But, of course, it is not only in bombings that the effect of the war is seen. There is by now the terror of starvation, homelessness, of being cold in winter, of being helpless to maintain life in almost any way, for this prolonged conflict has exhausted many of their original resources. At the time I was there people did not have much to eat, mostly vegetables, for all I could see. No meat, no sugar, no butter, no milk. For most, no good clothing.

As for Barcelona, I was amazed by the really great beauty of that city. It was built principally since 1900, and it is or was, despite its relatively small size—900,000—one of the fine cities of the world. Most of the buildings are new. There are offices and apartment houses most originally and pleasingly designed. There are many very beautiful old houses. Some old palaces. A very beautiful city hall. And all arranged in such a mixture, and with such distinction, that I wish some of the people responsible for the messes we call our cities, could see. Although we boast of our towers and plumbing and our facilities and conveniences, I have never seen a better combination of art and convenience than Barcelona presents. It has charm and the added grace of being beside the sea. And before this present war it had a number of great docks which permitted the entry and departure of many large vessels, and for it to hold the very important commercial position it did hold. So you can imagine how doubly destructive it was to have this city bombed.

A great power plant which supplied the people with light and power and transportation was wrecked. That means no light, no trolley cars, no elevators. Also, in places, the streets have been torn up, buildings shattered, windows broken, and so on. In addition, in order to provide some protection to the masses, there have been dug under the streets some five miles of serpentine subways. This compulsory physical defacing of something so rare and lovely as that city is really enraging.

But, relatively speaking, the wreck of the city is nothing compared to what has happened to the life of the inhabitants all over Loyalist Spain. Their railways and highways bombed, their ports blockaded, and their trade and food ships sunk, their businesses, of course, have been ruined. Therefore, by now, the people are mostly too poor to buy. They cannot even buy the things they have to sell.[3] There are few shops. Most factories are closed. There are few if any new clothes, no automobiles beyond those needed by the officials of the army, government, doctors, hospitals, police, and so on; no supplies, none of the things which seem essential here. You simply cannot get anything. In the early morning, and again early in the afternoon, you can see the poor people, the women and children, old men, and very young boys, going out, solemn, distrait and yet dignified, to the country. They carry bags and baskets. Their purpose is to buy directly from the farmers or peasants what they cannot buy in the city—food or a little wood with which to build a fire. And, in the evening, about five o'clock, you will see them coming back with perhaps a head of cabbage or two heads of lettuce; perhaps a few sticks of wood, for there is little fuel now, no coal, or gas. And then, later in the evening, in the poorer quarters, you will see them cooking their things over little fires built in the old style charcoal burners, but now resting on their balconies or in the doorways. Some of these people, particularly the older ones, looked so forlorn and downcast, especially where a part of their old homes had been blown to pieces and they were living, cooking, sleeping in what was left.

As for the one-time better-to-do people, the former middle class, (the truly rich having long since fled), they did not seem to me to be so much better off. To be sure, their cooking was done inside—they did not sit ruefully in the ruined doorways; but wherever you saw them you saw people looking as though they were straining to make ends meet. I saw individuals who reminded me of one-time clerks, storekeepers, minor officials, teachers, professors, and so on—their wives and children. Their clothes looked to me as though they had endured all they could in the way of face-saving wear. Such thin coats or trousers, such old hats, in so many instances! Mostly, none! And such worn shoes! But bustling about as though things were not quite as bad as they obviously were. And on foot, almost always, since of course taxis and streetcars or buses have long since gone the way of war.

I had been put up at one of the two principal hotels, the Ritz, and even there, as I can testify, was nothing except the outer details of a once prosperous life. That is, there was still the original furniture, hangings, some towels—but no good sheets. All cotton cloth has been commandeered for the hospitals and the army. The one-time very pretentious dining room was still serviced by waiters in long black coat-tails and white shirts—but there was no soap, none in all Loyalist Spain, so I heard, other than in the hospitals or at the front, or the institutions that cared for the wounded and children. Already an epidemic of skin diseases was feared. I myself caught the itch while I was there. But don't worry I have since recovered.

By the way, everything about the Ritz was a contradiction in terms. For instance, the marvelous silver tray on which one miserable bun and a cup of black juice called coffee was served! And the beautiful elevators which did not run! And the palatial lobbies, designed for gaiety and show but now filled with the hustle and bustle of newspapermen and the superficial buzz of worried officials and foreign observers! These last, together with writers, playwrights, artists and what not from different countries, plus officers and some aviators on leave for a day or two, seemed to me, to contribute the only feeling of ease, if not security, to be found in the whole city. For they could truly come and go as they chose—bombing permitting—but not the others. But, just the same, the natives, real, suffering citizens, contributed the real color, of course. Incidentally, I want to say I had no trouble, in their hotels, in picking up news—all I really wanted, from both sides of the fighting lines—both as to Franco's[4] world and that of the Loyalists. And I did.

But here in Barcelona, as I noticed, almost no one, outside of those in hospitals, the army and so on, has any meat. All the meat goes to the soldiers. Instead of meat, the Spaniards use a kind of gourd which tastes like meat fat. They broil this as we do meat, and then cover it with seasonings and vegetables and so make a tasty dish. However, the bread is very obscure as to origin. One does not ask what it is made of. And as for butter, pastry, wine, beer or even sparkling water? No. Supplies of these had run out as I entered. Nor are there any cigarettes. They are luxuries. In short, it is a long story of scarcity, of deprivation, of helplessness. And for an appalling number, of starvation, and the prospect of disease and death.

For in all Loyalist Spain there are now about twelve million people. In Franco's realm another twelve million. Of these, in the Loyalist realm, three and one half million are refugees, people without anything at all. And among these, there are about half a million children. Because of this number and with most of the physically able men in the army, and the number of those who cannot support themselves constantly increasing, only much suffering can result. And these people cannot improve their conditions, for nearly all the materials to work with—cotton, iron, coal, wood, chemicals, and so on, are now lacking.

The need for aid from without, immediate aid, if a great disaster is not to befall Loyalist as well as Rebel Spain is necessary. For although you may not know it, neither Mr. Hitler nor Mr. Mussolini appears to have agreed to finance fully a real rebellion in Spain. What appears to have happened is that one or both of the gentlemen said to Franco some two years ago— "See here. We're willing to finance you to a good start in Spain. That is, we'll get you in there with an army and supplies for say five or six months at the most. After that, if what you say is true, that you can conquer Spain in seven or eight months at the least, you ought to be able to live on the country, make your conquered citizens do the rest." And so he has been trying to do. But, as everyone knows by now, things haven't worked out quite right. There have been setbacks and defeats.[5]

While I was in Barcelona, I went to the principal war hospital. This was one of the most beautifully designed and built hospitals that I have ever seen. It has plenty of light and air, and is so pleasing to look at that if getting well were merely a matter of charm, no one would be sick there for very long. In fact, in the hospitals, if nowhere else, one more nearly approaches the ordinary standards of life, because all Loyalist Spain makes sacrifices for the sick and the armies. I talked with one of the surgeons and he told me how the hospital was run, how the soldiers were brought here from the front line hospitals, if they had a chance for life; how taken care of.

Afterward, in this hospital, as I could see, the soldiers and sick prisoners—for there were many of them—did have fairly adequate supplies. But so difficult to get! And running out so fast! For ordinary people there is almost no medicine. All the ordinary metals and chemicals are used for the army and the very sick people in the hospitals. The same with bandages, and medical supplies in general. It was emphasized to me over and over by the people in charge that compared with the need, their supplies were insignificant.

In the face of all this deprivation and suffering, and the array of threats and fears for the present and the future, the fear, for instance, of bombing, of starving, of having nothing in the future, of losing one's family, of not being able to provide for one's children—all fears which harass and threaten these people constantly—their attitude is one of the most heartening and cheering facts with regard to people anywhere, under any conditions, that I have ever seen. This suffering, instead of developing a defeated mood, appears to me to have brought out something strong, something not to be beaten down. The whole time I was in Barcelona, although the condition of the people was as I have said, and worse, not one single person approached me to beg! Consider that and the almost whimpering throngs which we have in our large cities. In spite of the long record of cruelties alleged to have been inflicted by Spaniards on others, I cannot but respect the way in which they stand up under cruelties inflicted on them. The Spaniard, to me at least, now seems to have a kind of proud dignity and reserve, something which humiliation and poverty cannot erase. It is handsome. It is respectable. In their rags they are proud and maybe cold. And they fight. And they do not quit. Why do I admire that? Why do you? If you do? As for myself, I don't know why, but I do like to see men stand up under injustice and defy the world. To die defying, if need be. To me it is swell!

The third day I was in Barcelona I got an invitation from the Loyalist chiefs to come and dine with them. You must know that, practically, there are two Loyalist governments in Spain, since it has been cut in two by the Rebel army.[6] But in Barcelona are Azaña, the president, del Vayo, the minister of state, and Negrin, prime minister and minister of war, in short, most, if not all, of the original democratic government which functioned prior to the war.[7] In the late afternoon I went to del Vayo's office and we sat and talked about various affairs. He is a stocky, elderly man, earnest and I am sure, sincere. The office is in a new and well-equipped building, quite handsome. And all about were posted plenty of soldiers, going here and there, standing on guard, and so on. Mr. del Vayo is a civilian. Later we went to Mr. Negrin's house for dinner and had a long talk.

Both del Vayo and Negrin told me a great deal about conditions before the war and what they were trying to do for Spain now. Del Vayo said that the main objective of his government, before the war, was to modernize Spain, to bring it the latest inventions, good roads, machinery, to introduce education and so on. As everyone knows, the government which existed before that was, if not opposed to innovations of any sort, at least too torpid and corrupt to try to help Spain. Azaña and del Vayo and Negrin are not politicians such as one finds in most places. They are much more the type of professional man, or professor. Negrin was and still is, I suppose, a doctor. Now, although they are quite polished and diplomatic, you can sense very easily the sincere and disinterested attitude which intellectual people often have toward politics. They told me that, so deeply was the cause of the war embedded in the hearts of the Spaniards that, if they, the heads of the State, should now decide to surrender and give up the fight, the people, they thought, would object and choose new leaders. More, that people of so much courage deserved to win—to have the kind of government they liked. And to illustrate this, they told the story of how, in planning the recent push across the Ebro toward Valencia, they were both so discouraged to think that they would have to enter on another battle or campaign, really, without the necessary equipment which such heroic fighters deserved. They knew positively at the time they planned the offensive, they said, that Franco had 521 planes. And in the same sector, they had only three. However, they figured, that with as many as 25 or 30 planes they could at least make a showing that would give the impression, to their own troops, that they were not without planes. And so they did their best to try to persuade several foreign powers to supply them with sufficient equipment to enter on this contest. But they could get no help. And so, Mr. del Vayo decided, the only thing to do was to tell his soldiers what the situation was. At that time the soldiers were already deployed along the north bank of the Ebro and their natural assumption was that, as in all previous battles, they would be reinforced by planes. Del Vayo told me that he spent several sleepless nights considering this problem. Should the men be deceived—left uninformed as to the truth of their predicament? He decided no—and finally, in the afternoon preceding the attack, he went to the front and collected the officers and men and told them exactly what the situation was—that they would not be supported by planes. And he left it to them, as to whether or not they could or would fight in such circumstances. "Their response," he said, "amazed me. To a man they agreed that they should fight anyhow. They would fight the airplanes with rifles and machine guns. It is a brave and wonderful people we have behind us," he said to me.[8]

Negrin and del Vayo are emotionally deeply concerned over the prospect of increased suffering. They said that since they cannot and will not give up, that the war will not be ended before another year or year and a half, whatever the outcome.[9] Accordingly, they have this terrible problem of feeding and clothing people who cannot help themselves.

One thing that impressed me tremendously about del Vayo and Negrin was the faith they have in the Loyalist Spaniards. Negrin, who is quite a good writer, has written many of the addresses and appeals which are not only printed and distributed but quoted in posters plastered on the walls and fences of Loyalist Spain. Here is one:

> Spaniards! We are fighting with full regard to the will of the nation. We are fighting to insure the independence of Spain. Be of good heart. The right of our magnificent Spanish heritage has come down to us from men who have sought the good and the freedom of our people. Fight on! Sacrifice! We are not failing. We will win and Spain will be one great free people!

In the face of their many difficulties and lacks, this kind of thing seems to me—well—beautiful.

However, both del Vayo and Negrin went on to tell me more about the ideals of their Loyalist government. One thing which struck me was the fact that they are not against Catholics or religious freedom. But they do want the right to establish a school system which is free of all denominational bias. Nor do they want a government run by any religious group. They would like to have something like what we have over here, where no religious group is supposed to have control. I think there is a lot of difference and propaganda aroused on this ground, and that people who are religious criticize the Loyalists falsely when they say they are anti-religious.[10] One interesting thing, to me at least, is to compare the Loyalist point of view toward religion with the Rebel. Franco, I learned, for instance, is planning to have a completely Catholic school system and ideology. God, as interpreted by the Catholic Church, is to rule Spain. But, in addition and more than that a complete Catholic direction of affairs. He says he does not want Fascism, Hitler Fascism, that is. But from that, I gather, that the Catholics are thinking of what Hitler did and is doing to the Catholics in Germany. So the whole thing is still curious, if not plain. For, in Paris at the International Peace Conference which I attended in July, and which was called to oppose fascism, there were a great number of priests come from France, Rebel Spain, Belgium, and so on, to protest against Hitler. But, when some other delegates wanted to protest against Mussolini and Franco, they threatened to leave the meeting. To off-set this, the anti-Francoites had got a Spanish peasant woman, know as La Pasionaria,[11] who has been very important in arousing the peasants of Loyalist Spain to that cause, to attend the meeting. But the chief sponsors of this international peace meeting, Messr. Paul-Boncour and Lord Cecil,[12] together with various attending pro-Franco delegates, would not have her. They denied her admission to the platform. But I can tell you, it all but broke up the meeting! And not only that, but although she was barred there, she did speak later at a meeting over which I presided, of the International Association of Writers for the Defense of Culture.[13]

Again, in Barcelona, there are three thousand priests and five thousand nuns, so I was told, being supported by the Loyalists, living on and eating of what they had. Because of that, I asked del Vayo and Negrin why they didn't send these priests and nuns to the other side, and ask Franco to support them; but they said that that would be looked on as a black outrage against religion! It would do the Loyalists great harm. Yet, as I pointed out, to imprison and starve Loyalists on the Rebel side was looked upon as quite all right.

Quite right, they said, but still it would do more harm than good, although both most strongly feel, as they said, that denominational religions ought to stay out of the government. And I myself cannot see what the Catholics have to lose under the Loyalists except their real-estate and their wish to rule. Besides, after all, as a religious organization, are they supposed to be so very much interested in real-estate? I hope not! I pray not![14]

Del Vayo and Negrin both told me that they had had some aid from Russia and from other governments in a less overt way, but not enough to make any decisive difference. In fact, that they had been terribly disappointed by the shift in attitude exhibited by England and France since the beginning of the war. France has had 50 million pesetas in gold, sent there for safekeeping, by the Loyalist Government. But do you think the Loyalists can get it? It seems that recently the Loyalists wanted to use some of the money they thought they had in France for the purchase of supplies. But when Franco heard about it, he threatened to hold the French government responsible for the money, in case he won. All the same, the money does belong to the de facto government which is Loyalist. The French told the Loyalists to sue in the French courts for the money and such a suit was begun. But of course, their case will never be decided until after the war is over and then it will go to the de facto government, which may be Franco's.[15]

But long ago both Negrin and del Vayo were forced as they said, not only to convince themselves that no help was coming from anybody, but to tell their people so, and thereafter to rely on themselves for food, for arms and for money. This meant rationing in the strictest sense, because otherwise they could not have endured. But it has also brought about the social picture I have described. Loyalist Spain, for all of its courage and fighting ability, is on the edge of famine—famine this winter. Get that! And it must have help! But from where? Who is to provide it? It is true that already there are various agencies at work. But not enough. England has given ten thousand pounds to one agency. The labor unions in England are being asked to raise one million pounds—five million dollars. But will they? Both del Vayo and Negrin told me that if real help—that is large scale help could be secured from anywhere they would be willing to see it impartially distributed by some non-Spanish committee, not only fifty-fifty between Loyalist and Rebel Spain, but fifty-fifty between Catholic and non-Catholic on both sides. In other words, they were willing and anxious to feed all starving Spaniards in all Spain which I think is fair enough. But how? By whom? Has this group here any suggestion to make? Can the American people—Catholic, Protestant, Jew, Gentile, White, Black, be interested? I wonder.

There is one final point I wish to make in connection with this Spanish situation and with ourselves here tonight, and here it is. It used to be that people laughed at the Methodist Wednesday Culture and Missionary Society as it gathered to pack barrels of food or tracts for the poor heathen in darkest

Africa, or India, or China. Some of our writers used to poke fun at what they described as the American heathen trying to uplift the foreign heathen, the point being that we Americans were not "spiritually" justified in these goings on. And it is true that these American societies, as we all know, flourished in the midst of poverty, oppression, corruption, cruelty and so on, amidst conditions which might have been selected by those very societies, had they had mentality enough, for their religious and moral attention. But instead, and stupidly enough, as I see it they insisted on looking outward instead of inward, across the seas, because looking across the seas was easier and more glamorous, the while they remained blind to conditions at home.

But are not we today, just as apt, for one reason and another to neglect to look at the beams in our own eyes here, while we concentrate on the motes in Europe? Which is not to say that the Spaniards are not to have help. They must have help and if we, or people like us, don't give it to them, no one will, and they will starve or perish in some frightful way.

But, when we give it to them, don't let it be with any of that smug glow that suggests that such conditions can never come here, or are not made here. This country is, to wars and international affairs, something like the arctic is to weather conditions. It is a world weather-maker and is becoming increasingly so. Over here is concentrated power, money, and ability. And we cannot say to ourselves any longer that we are not responsible for what happens as a result of our policies, no matter how innocuous and righteous they may look.

Mussolini said the other day that the United States handed out sermons with one hand and arms with the other. And I think that is true. As long as we continue to have trade and banking and financial relations which, whatever our justification, whatever ancient right we appeal to, have the effect of continuing in power governments and policies which we whole-heartedly disapprove of, and which openly threaten to bring about the war we so much dread, we cannot take the position of innocent and harmless people. I refer to the idea of shipping arms to Germany, or Italy. Or war materials. Or chemicals of any kind, anywhere. We may say, what is wrong with trading with a country at peace? It is perfectly legal, is it not? But— what do you suppose anyone buys guns, or chemicals or war materials for? The implication is so clear. Of course, it is about forty years too late to say this. But still here it is. And what about it?[16]

Textual Note: Address at a Benefit Dinner for American Relief for Spain, organized by the League of American Writers, Hotel St. Moritz, New York, 15 September 1938. DPUP folder 13383 contains two typescripts, here designated TsA and TsB. TsA (14 pages) is headed in pen "Loyalist Spain—July 1938." It is mostly double-spaced, with revisions in Dreiser's hand in pencil and in pen, and it is signed and dated in ink at the bottom, 15 September 1938. TsB (9 pages), with typed heading "Spain—July 1938," is mostly single-spaced, and it is almost a clean copy, which has been marked up in the left margin for delivery as a speech. It is signed in typescript at the bottom of the final page. TsB incorporates almost all of the pencil revisions made on TsA, but none of the revisions made in pen. We conclude therefore that TsA was the first to be typed, and was used, as revised by Dreiser in pencil, as the basis for TsB. TsB may then have served as the text for the speech itself. Subsequent to the production of TsB, Dreiser seems to have returned to TsA and revised it in pen. The revised TsA has therefore been selected as our copy-text. Revisions are numerous but rarely substantial.

1. Gerona (Girona, in Spanish), situated in the Catalūnya region of northeast Spain.

2. Barcelona, at the time the capital of Republican Spain, had been subjected to bombing raids by Nationalist, Italian, and German planes since December 1937.

3. Dreiser seems to be referring to the inability of traders and retailers to obtain goods to replenish their inventories.

4. General Francisco Franco (1892–1975) was the leader of the Nationalist forces, and after victory in 1939 he became dictator of Spain.

5. At this point the following passage is marked for cutting: "Hence the problem—which is almost as much Rebel as Loyalist—certainly nearly so. So that if one or both are to be aided, it must be speedily from somewhere. No single ship is going to do it. I can tell you that. The problem is much larger."

6. Nationalist forces had fought their way south and east to the coast in May 1938, cutting off Catalūnya in the northeast from the areas of central and southern Spain controlled by the Republicans.

7. Manuel Azaña (1880–1940) had become president in May 1936, following the left coalition's victory in elections held in February. Alvarez del Vayo (1891–1974), was minister of state between 1936–37 and 1938–39, and Juan Negrin (1889–1956) had been prime minister since 17 May 1937.

8. The Battle of the Ebro, a counter-offensive undertaken between July and November 1938, proved to be a military disaster for the Republicans, largely because of their lack of air support.

9. In fact Barcelona fell to Franco in January 1939, followed by Madrid in March; the Republicans surrendered in April 1939.

10. Although the Republican government was generally anticlerical, on 1 May 1938 Negrin had published a conciliatory "thirteen point" program which promised full civil and political rights, and freedom of religion.

11. Dolores Ibárurri (1895–1989), known as La Pasionaria ("the passionflower"), was a Communist Party deputy in the 1936 Spanish government and became famous for her speeches rallying resistance to the Nationalists during the Civil War.

12. Joseph Paul-Boncour (1873–1972), socialist politician and delegate to the League of Nations, who had been the French secretary of state until April 1938. Lord Robert Cecil (1864–1958), English Conservative Party statesman who was president of the League of Nations Union from 1923 to 1945 and a cofounder of the R.U.P.

13. Dreiser had described the furor over La Pasionaria less circumspectly in his address to the National Council of the League of American Writers on 24 August:

"There was turmoil and uproar over the fact that the committee in charge of the International Peace Conference did not think that her presence was needed and that she ought not speak because, the argument was, that she did not have any intelligent comment to make on this thing, no data on fascism or liberalism, and that all she could do was to tell about the difficulties in Spain, and they did not think that was important so she didn't get on the program, but because of all the commotion she caused the result was even better: they were ready to blow up the place and it really almost wrecked the evening meeting." ("Address by Theodore Dreiser to the National Council of the League of American Writers," 24 August 1938, pp. 2–3, DPUP.) La Pasionaria subsequently addressed the 25 July meeting of the International Association of Writers for the Defence of Culture, chaired by Dreiser.

14. The following text is marked for cutting at this point: "I would like to add here that both Negrin and del Vayo feel that conditions among the people in Rebel Spain are just as bad as they are among the people of Loyalist Spain, the population of both regions being the same. But all this brings up the problem of foreign aid."

15. The bulk of the Spanish government's gold reserves had been sent abroad, to France and Russia, in order to buy armaments and supplies. When the pacifist Daladier succeeded Blum as French premier in April 1938, the money there was effectively frozen. On 6 July the French Court of Appeal rejected a claim from the Spanish government for the return of gold valued at around $37 million. It was eventually claimed by Franco's Spain in the 1950s.

16. The closing direct question was a late addition. In draft the speech ends as follows: "Of course it is about forty years too late to discuss this. But still there it is."

Statement on Anti-Semitism

From *"We hold these Truths . . ." Statements on anti-Semitism by 54 leading American writers, statesmen, educators, clergymen, and trade-unionists*, March 1939.

This small book was made up of responses to a circular issued on behalf of the League of American Writers that asked two direct questions: "What do you know about anti-Semitism in this country?" and "What would you do to stop it if you were chosen to lay down a program?" Most contributors, like Dreiser, viewed anti-Semitism in the context of ethnic prejudice and persecution more generally. Langston Hughes, for example, argued that even New Deal policies were infected by racism and cautioned that "it seems that those of us who seriously wish to keep Nazism out of America have to start not by keeping it out at all, but by putting out a lot of it that's already here—and has been here a mighty long time. Is still another monster coming? Damn! A dragon has long been present."

Dreiser's comments demonstrate some continuities with his earlier discussions of anti-Semitism but suggest a new and urgent understanding of its roots and how to oppose it. The appeal to "equitable legal procedure" to arbitrate tensions between different ethnic, religious, or national groups echoes his criticism of German barbarism in the 28 December 1933 letter to Hutchins Hapgood (see "The

'Is Dreiser anti-Semitic?' Correspondence," 184–85). Here, though, Dreiser dispenses completely with the idea that the "race solidarity" of Jews is a cause of anti-Semitism. Instead, building on the self-reflexive understanding of prejudice in "Mea Culpa" (see 204–8), Dreiser argues that the roots of persecution lie in the resentment felt by individuals at perceived injustices that in reality arise from nothing more than ethnic and cultural difference. Having despaired in "Mea Culpa" of his previously preferred Zionist solution, Dreiser expresses qualified hope in the "collective mass results of . . . respective individual energies" in order to extirpate anti-Semitism and other forms of persecution.

Today, world society, because of the illuminating data furnished by thousands of years of social experience, as well as the more integrated and clarifying knowledge of life and how to live it gathered by science, should at least have arrived at, one would hope, the place where it could function without barbarism—these constant resorts to persecution, individual and social murders, or war—and the endless forms of physical and mental cruelty that come from religious or racial prejudices. Personally I do not believe in social torture of any group, or race, or sect for reasons of difference in appearance or creed or custom. Where these latter involve what other sects or creeds look upon as inequities of social procedure, these same should be dealt with civilly via equitable legal procedure.

But how to overcome or dissipate these extensions of ancient ignorance, delusions, illusions, prejudices and what not that protrude from ancient days into our bright new realm of knowledge? Cannot the sects or races be cured of their sometimes aggravating, sometimes savage determinations to preserve or extend themselves by war or boycott or persecution or robbery? It is quite plain, of course, that no social or religious or racial problems can either humanely or equitably be solved that way. It is not a question of an eye for an eye or a tooth for a tooth—but an eye for no eye, a tooth for no tooth. Mostly the alleged crimes relate to passing differences in language, dress, information, beliefs, customs. You do not eat as I do; pronounce my native tongue as I do; dress, walk, talk, or respond as fast or in the same way to this or that, as I do. Hence you are accursed. You should not live in the same world—at least the same land or city with me. Out! I cannot endure you and I cannot wait for you to change. Is not that the mood of many races, tribes, groups, creeds, sects, nationalities at this hour—or at least of their leaders?

Yet the social, religious, national or racial problems are never really solved in, by, or through such a mood. Instead, wars, persecutions, cherished hatreds, and social and legal inequities of all descriptions follow. Consider the warring sects in India at this hour.[1] The social and religious hatreds in

Europe, America and Asia. And all of this in the face of modern science—the verified realities of political, social, economic law!

Just now it is the Jews in Germany, the Negroes in America, the democratic-minded Loyalists in Spain, the backward in China, the swart Fellaheen in Egypt, the Moors in Africa, the Czechs in Czechoslovakia,[2] who are being seized upon and exploited, restrained, oppressed or murdered—each according to some theory as to their unfitness on the part of some other nation or group, as often as not, really more often than not, for economic purposes; the desire and hope of profit on the part of the exploiters.

But how to overcome all this? By urging the victims to fight back and helping them so to do. Of course. By advertising said inequities and iniquities to the entire world, and propagandizing against them and their perpetrators. Of course. That more equitable governments or nations and races should be asked not only to protest but to bring such pressure as they can—making war even on the authors of inequity or iniquity is also right.

But—at this point—the equitable individual continuing to do his best to bring all equitable peoples and governments into active opposition against the inequities and iniquities, can he do more? No—nothing. Improvement from there on depends on the collective mass results of his respective individual energies. But so far these have not been sufficient to stop these several outrages. They are still with us. I am, of course, for the general abolishment of these outrages, wherever. And I so urge and have urged. If all will do as much there is at least the hope that these various ills will be ended. A majority must combine to bring it about. And I am strong for such a combination in all of these cases. The record of my personal appeals over many years proves this. What more would you have me say or do?

Textual Note: Copy-text from *"We hold these Truths . . ." Statements on anti-Semitism by 54 leading American writers, statesmen, educators, clergymen, and trade-unionists.* New York: The League of American Writers, March 1939, pp. 45–47.

1. The tensions between Hindus and Muslims in British-controlled India would lead to its partition into India and Pakistan at independence in 1947.

2. In addition to Nazi persecution of Jews, Dreiser cites racism in America, the Nationalists' suppression of the Spanish Republic in the Spanish Civil War, the 1937 invasion of mostly peasant China by industrialized Japan, the continuing military and political domination of Egypt by Britain, ongoing French and Spanish colonialism in Morocco, and the 1938 partition of Czechoslovakia by Hitler's Germany, which was followed by full-scale annexation in March 1939.

The Dawn Is in the East

Broadside, November 1939.

Written for a symposium in the radical magazine Common Sense, *and submitted on 15 September 1939, twelve days after Germany's invasion of Poland had precipitated World War II. Dreiser's response to panic about the future of civilization is to criticize Christian and Western European notions of such fears for being at best narrow, and at worst self-serving and propagandistic. After invoking Einsteinian theories of relativity to challenge Western orthodoxy, Dreiser looks to the East for alternative forms of civilization, citing the historical achievements of Chinese, Japanese, Indian, and Egyptian cultures and the ostensibly more equitable industrial development of Russia. This underwrites a view of the war as a struggle for power between rival nations, negating British and French claims on democracy, recognizing German aspirations to some extent, and suggesting the paramount importance of Russian security. Dreiser also looks to Eastern philosophy and religions for ideas about selfhood that dispense with the self-serving moralizing he associates with Western culture, expressing an interest in Buddhist and Hindu traditions that also informs* The Stoic (1947).

Dear Mr. Dreiser:

The Editors of *Common Sense* would like from you your opinion as to whether the present war in Europe is likely to end civilization as we know it at this time in America, Europe, and elsewhere.

Very truly,
COMMON SENSE
315 Fourth Ave., N.Y.C.

No, I do not believe that because of the present storm in Europe (if it is still storming when this arrives) "civilization" is going to wind up on this earth. I should like to say here that that word also has a dubious ring to me—somewhat like that of a counterfeit fifty-cent piece. It is so freely used by so many people of such varying degrees of mentality, experience, environment, and what not. The mildest religionist, asserting the most fantastic dogmas as to our origins, government, and hereafter, will threateningly insist that his assertions represent true civilization. At the same time the profoundest students of chemistry and physics will announce that the universe is running down—i.e., that its future is in danger, when none thus far has ever been able to guess its past. Oh, yes, someone (I won't swear it was either Jeans or Eddington[1]) guessed that it might have been a giant star or whole thing that blew up and its fragments are now speeding pell-mell into space—chaos, some unworthy end of some kind I suppose. But I can't help thinking that we are a part of that sad finish and have been (man, anyhow), say for two or three hundred thousand years. And the funny part of it is that during all that time we are supposed to have been evolving and improving—building this thing called *civilization*. And before that arrived, as I read, there was the origin and evolution of species—certainly a seemingly mental and technically progressive sort of process leading up to (they say—not *me* but *they*) us. Well, anyhow, here we are and now we're going to decay—or pass.

Of course, personally, I doubt that. I know there were the dark ages running from the fifth to the thirteenth centuries, but only in Western Europe. Don't forget that. For in China during all that time as the records show there was a quite satisfactory and as many seem to think, a beautiful *civilization* (Confucius, Lao-tzu, The Golden Rule) which endured until only yesterday with (to my way of thinking) the loveliest art and architecture and costumes and social and philosophic arrangements and acceptances which hold me in respectful and more, loving awe to this day.

And before China and Japan (the latter a derivative of China) was India with the loveliest of all speculations and conclusions as to the origins of life here on this earth—Brahma, Buddha—speculations so profound and humane as to have powerfully influenced all modern European philosophy—Kant, Hegel, Schopenhauer, Goethe, Nietzsche and our own Emerson ("If the Red Slayer Think He Slays")—and now promises to reconcile itself or be reconciled, with all modern chemistry and physics, and so bring us to know that intuition and research are, after all, not so remote from each other in their sources as the earlier chemists and physicists of our time would have had us imagine.[2]

But either before or parallel with India was Egypt with Amun Ra and Isis and Osiris and its movingly soothing and kind Book of the Dead, seeking to console man for this "Strange Interlude" here.[3] And after Egypt, Greece. And after Greece, Rome. And only then the dark ages. (Dogmatic, not true, Christianity—remember.) But immediately thereafter the renaissance in Italy. New life in England, France, Germany, the Netherlands, and then America; the arrival of the machine or the scientific age, and with it, modern Europe, the French Revolution, the American Revolution, our own Civil War to free the slaves, and more recently, the great Russian Revolution, which in my judgment may yet repay the world for all the horrors it endured between 1914–1918.

Wild?

A radical?

A Red?

As you please.

Just now, however, our Western world seems inclined, as in the dark ages, to live only on propaganda. No one reads the Russian papers. It is a crime. No American paper will publish a truthful line concerning the enormous work being done there—the new world being made; the work and modern living conditions and palatial working conditions being provided there for all. Nothing as to the universal schooling from Bering Strait to China, from Archangel to Persia (Iran) and Afghanistan.[4] No mention of the railroads, bus lines, airplane routes, telegraph, telephone, radio—the new and completely modernized agricultural system, the dozens of universities, research laboratories, giant manufactories, industrial cities and towns that have sprung up over Russia. Only now—and *only* now—you hear *at last*, and grudgingly—but even from Mr. Winston Churchill, first Lord of the English Navy, that Russia is today the first military power in the world. Only no one tells you *how come* . . . If all was chaos and brutality and fear, up to yesterday, how—from where—the means to feed, clothe, equip, drill twelve million men—and with a few of them fighting battles from which the today so much respected Japanese withdraw in disorder and seek peace?

Why?

Because long haired Bolshevik savages or lunatics are in charge?

If so, why are England and France sending delegations to Moscow to seek aid? Because they are brainless incompetents?

It was Winston Churchill, who in 1928, told me when I came out of Russia that the idea was all wrong—that it would not work and that *seven* years would see the end of it.[5] Well, it is eleven years and now, *to Mr. Churchill himself*, it is the first military power in the world. Why? Is Mr. Stalin doing it single handed? Or has he? Or, is it possible that there are rejuvenated and encouraged and maybe even inspired Russian masses—175,000,000 strong— who believe that the horrors of social inequity such as I saw in England last summer (August) and before that in 1926, and before that in 1912 (labor getting as little as 12, 15, 18 shillings a week) (a cocktail costs 2 shillings in London) to say nothing of what I saw last summer in France (labor getting as little as 60 cents a day) and before that right here in America, in St. Louis, Kansas City, the deep South, in West Virginia, Pittsburgh, Chicago, Paterson, Fall River, the mining towns of Utah and where not else—labor getting as little as fifteen dollars a week and less—should end. (If you will go back to the start of the sentence you will find that this *should end* refers to what the Russian millions may be thinking. It got lost on the way.)

Anyway, when you ask me whether I think this thing called civilization is about to collapse, I want to know what you mean by civilization. The economic and social brutalities I have been seeing all my life in Europe and America, to say nothing of Egypt, Africa, India, China, the South seas, South America, Mexico, and where not else? Or the so-called brutal barbarism now extant in Russia? If the former, my answer is that most likely it will—this so-called civilization in Western Europe plus the greedy capitalistic system in the United States which works so closely with capitalism the world over.

As for Germany and Herr Hitler, I am convinced that once she is satisfied as to her particular position in the sun—neither entirely dominant nor yet second to any, she will think of a more humane and creative program in regard to the Jews. For we cannot always have Herr Hitler with us. He, too, must die. And there can be no question that, since the sinking of the Spanish Armada, England has been determined not only to rule the seas but to see to it that no power capable of rivaling her should endure on the European continent. Hence the wars and rumors of wars—the Napoleonic, the Austro-German, French-German,[6] and finally the great world war from which England did not emerge as the lone victor although she wished to think so. And there is plenty to the German contention that she was entitled to a place in the sun. Also that after Versailles[7] she could get no justice from the League of Nations because of British-French domination. And certain it is that a nation that could in the face of England and America, build up the pre-war Germany of 1914 and since 1918 the present post-war Germany is not one of dunces or lunatics. It is seeking a place in the sun—its intellectual place, only like England, it has felt that it must fight for it.

Well, all wars come to an end. The old world that England and America knew before 1914 has gone. Submarines and airplanes make battleships expensive targets. No one country is likely to be able to rule the seas or the world for some time. Such being the case, an agreement should be reached and will be—a friendly agreement to exchange products and ideas—without harm—one to the other, that or an armed neutrality—each one ready, gun in hand.

Ordinarily it is the former that comes about. People get tired of war. But also, apparently, after a time they get tired of peace, because peace after a time seems to breed stagnation, or silly vanities and notions such as only war can blow away. At present the British-French position is that a world in which Germany seeks an equal place in the sun with Britain and France is intolerable because the Germans (and Russians) are not fit for it. The German and Russian positions are that they are and will.

A shift from either or both the assumed intellectual and financial aristocracies and so superiorities of some of our western powers—England, France, Germany,[8] America, even, will do everybody good. Hence, as I see it, the dawn is in the east. Civilization will not pass. It will proceed in a new form.

Textual Note: Copy-text from broadside "The Dawn Is in the East," 1939, based on *Common Sense* 8 (December 1939): 6–7. Submitted by Dreiser to *Common Sense* on 15 September 1939 (TD to Alfred M. Bingham, 15 September 1939). A slightly different version containing several transcription errors appeared in *International Literature* 11 (November 1939): 109–11. Typescripts and carbon copies are in DPUP folders 1194 and 11999.

1. English physicists and astronomers James Hopwood Jeans (1877–1946) and Arthur Stanley Eddington (1882–1944) did much to establish and popularize Albert Einstein's theories, notably in Eddington's *Mathematical Theory of Relativity* (1923).

2. The "red slayer" is ultimately a reference to Siva, God-as-Destroyer, one of the personifications of God in Hinduism. Dreiser cites the opening line of Ralph Waldo Emerson's poem "Brahma" (1857). In a 1940 letter, in which he quotes further from the poem, Dreiser suggests that Eastern philosophies and religions give a sense of a "universal soul" containing all wisdom and creative power that was compatible with modern science. This Dreiser finds a source of inspiration, in contrast to what he sees as the preoccupation with moral judgments about good and evil individuals found in most Western and Christian ideas. (TD to Dorothy Payne Davis, 18 July 1940, DPUP.)

3. Amun Ra, Isis, and Osiris are deities from ancient Egyptian mythology. Osiris is especially connected to legends of death and rebirth and is hymned in the final part of the ancient Egyptian funerary text *The Book of the Dead*, more properly called *The Book of Coming Forth By Day*. "Strange Interlude" refers to the span of human life on earth, and makes a sidelong reference to Eugene O'Neill's play of that title, first produced in 1928.

4. That is, from the westernmost to the easternmost borders, and from the northern to the southern extent of the territory of the Soviet Union.

5. Dreiser interviewed Winston Churchill (1874–1965; later British prime minister and celebrated war leader) in London on his way back from Russia in January 1928. See "Dreiser Back from Russia; Praises Soviet," *New York Herald Tribune*, 22 February 1928; repr. in Rusch and Pizer, *Interviews*, 165–67.

6. Wars between European states: the Napoleonic Wars from approximately 1803 to 1815, the 1866 Austro-German war, and the Franco-Prussian War of 1870–71.

7. The 1919 Treaty of Versailles, which officially ended World War I, and whose punitive treatment of Germany contributed to the instability of the 1930s.

8. Germany was added to this list subsequent to the preparation of the surviving typescripts and is absent from the version published in *International Literature*.

From "Civilization: Where? What?"

Late 1939 or early 1940.

As in "The Dawn Is in the East," Dreiser's concern with civilization in this unpublished essay is occasioned by contemporary appeals to defend the Allies in World War II, appeals that Dreiser regards as mere camouflage for the self-interest of established imperial powers France and Britain. In the passage excerpted here, he develops the strand of cultural relativism expressed in the earlier essay, questioning Western notions of civilization and arguing for the validity and sophistication of different cultures. After this passage, Dreiser returns to the immediate politi-cal theme, arguing that the Allied powers' failure to intervene to defend Spain and Czechoslovakia against fascism in 1936–39 nullifies their claim to be more "civilized" than Germany.

* * * *

But really this matter of being civilized or uncivilized on this minute star, the earth, is a most puzzling matter. Bad feeling and war and propaganda aside, there appear to be—in time of peace—a number of quite acceptable "civilizations"—Hindu, Chinese, British, American, Japanese, German—if not Russian, for none of the Western powers (civilizations, I mean—excuse me) appear to be willing to accept sovietized Russia as civilized. It is too kind to the workers—the hand laborer as well as all others—who work or think or invent or lead.

But apart from these, to me at least, there appear to be a number of oth-ers, not one of which to our Western "civilized" powers would be accepted as "civilized" in their sense of the meaning of the word. For instance, in Australia, where there are many tribes that represent the "civilizations" of the Stone Age still living, each Stone Age hunter must have an enormous amount of land to support him and his family. Game is scarce—so is water. Besides, these fine brown fellows with their spears must know in infinite detail the habits, varying with the seasons, of animal life. This takes great intelligence and knowledge which anyone of appreciation, intelligence and knowledge must respect. It is not savagery any more than knowing how to farm or install plumbing or electric fixtures is savagery—in fact it is more difficult and requires more so-called mental ability than, maybe, the aver-age plumber or electrician dreams of. He goes by a method and practice book or has someone to teach him. So has the Stone Age man. An older man or woman. And put down in Australia, or some parts of Africa, the average American or European, with his own, but not this Stone Age man's knowledge, would not last a week.

Yet, we of Western Europe and America, as you know, talk loftily of our organized society; its civilization, science, morality, charity—this and that. But the Australian Stone Age man meets his problems as thoughtfully and considerately as any American or European anywhere.

* * * *

Textual Note: Undated essay, presumed late 1939 or early 1940. Copy-text is the 14-page typescript in DPUP folder 11974 headed "Civilization: Where? What?" bearing Dreiser's signature in pen. This excerpt comes from pages 4–6.

Theodore Dreiser and the Free Press

Broadside, September 1940.

This essay is Dreiser's withering response to an invitation from the trade publication Editor and Publisher *to submit an article "emphasizing America's fortunate position, with respect to a free press in a world of tyranny and censorship." It contains brief lists of those Dreiser considered heroic, villainous, or "mental and social peanuts" at the time.*

Hollywood, California, Sept. 18, 1940

EDITOR & PUBLISHER
1700 Times Building, Times Square,
New York City.
WALTER E. SCHNEIDER,
Associate Editor:

Your letter of September 9, 1940, outlining the plan of "the newspapers of the nation" to "bring home to America the blessings of her free press" by the "observance of a National Newspaper Week, October 1 to October 7" and selecting me among others for the honorable task of preparing "a brief expression of appreciation of one of the most vital bulwarks of American freedom, an uncensored press" is before me. What between sheer awe of the corporation gall which unquestionably prompts and no doubt finances this industrious labor of yours, and wonder as to how, at this late date, I still come to be on your National Corporation sucker list I am fairly flattered— not flattered.

For as you know, or should, I was in the service of various American newspapers as a reporter and traveling correspondent for five years of my life; also editor in chief of four advertising kept magazines for five years more[1]—so I ought to know something about the blessings of a free press. And again, before I was ever a newspaper man even, I was a citizen of Chicago when Mr. Cleveland sent 3,000 Federal troops into the city to protect the robbing and thieving railways of that day from their underpaid and ill used workers, and I noted then with interest and some rage the editorial and news barrage laid down by the leading papers of Chicago and elsewhere in behalf of the suffering railways and against the workers.[2] And ever since, wherever labor has been employed and has struck for decent treatment, I have noted and frequently written about the zest with which our liberty loving press invariably sprung to action in behalf of capital and violently against labor. Also in favor of every criminal monopoly program of our corporations since.

I assume, of course, that you never heard of a book of mine called *Newspaper Days*—nor another called *Tragic America,* promptly suppressed after one month of circulation and a sale of 5,000 copies.[3] But I wrote them, you should come to know, to expose the very lack of this liberty loving press in our national life and at the same time the criminal doings of our national monopolies which today—at this late hour—having grown finally ponderous with stolen money and so supremely authoritative in our American affairs of government and liberty, prompt, if they do not directly finance, such a brassy burst of propaganda as your letter outlines. Really if it weren't because of awe inspired by this latest corporation gall stone cast at a long suffering public, I would shout with laughter at your stupidity. For as you know—and so you mean—that the corporations of America which control our newspapers and radio as well as our politicians, a large majority of our judges, our state legislators, congressmen, governors, mayors, police, chambers of commerce, banks, ministers and small loan controlled merchants everywhere, are now planning to stage this fake demonstration of ours with the hope of either frightening or fooling the genuinely liberty-less masses into imagining that there may be somewhere in America at least a percentage of the people who can say what they think and read what they would like to read without job or financial loss in some quick and drastic form. In fact the gradual suppression of free speech, free assembly, free publication of anything not agreeable to corporations, their banks and their 60 would-be royal—or better—Tsaristic families—is so plain to the really thinking people in America—as well as those who are so directly deprived of the speaking, reading and public assembly rights as to be moved to protest, that veritable corporation press and radio blitzkriegs have to be indulged in, in order to frighten them into silence. Consider the corporation work of a political stooge like Dies.[4] Or the labors of such geniuses of liberty as Mayor Hague of Jersey City,[5] Father Coughlin of the Catholic Church,[6] Lieutenant Hynes of the Los Angeles Police and Chamber of Commerce hook-up on our West Coast,[7] to say nothing of endless others. Who or what was it that cut Anita Whitney[8] off the National Don Lee network here in Los Angeles on Friday, September 14th last, or denied the C.I.O. radio time in San Diego on the same date? And why didn't our National Free Press carry these facts as news?

Try, if you choose, to get some favorable mention or any mention of any innocent labor objective in the *New York Times* or *Tribune,* any Philadelphia paper, any Pittsburgh or Chicago or Kansas City or Los Angeles or San Francisco or Portland or Seattle paper. I have tried. These corporation lice are of one mind and one pocketbook, and liberty of the press to them means liberty to praise the works and schemes of our American and International corporations and the schemes of their families and their children and their children's children and no others.

If Americans knew how far we have already gone toward abolishing our democracy they would rise in anger now in defense of their most precious possession. But millions don't know, because the only sources of information they have deliberately keep them from knowing. The National Federation for Constitutional Liberties[9] has issued a statement listing the grossest recent newspaper suppressions showing that:

"Only one large newspaper in the country printed anything about the petition to discontinue the Dies Committee which was signed by 100 outstanding Americans including six college presidents;"

"Only two or three papers printed the 'Defense of the Bill of Rights' issued by 62 prominent Americans;"

"Scores of protests against the Dies Committee and against conscription by C.I.O. and A.F.L. unions were unmentioned in the press;"

"About 2% of the press mentioned the State and City conferences against anti-alien bills, in which delegates representing millions of Americans participated;"

"Most papers suppressed altogether the American Bar Association Bill of Rights Committee's warning to the nation against certain Congressional actions;"

"More than 300 leading American writers issued a declaration against American entry into the war—it was ignored."

And to that let me add that when some six thousand delegates from 40 states, representing many millions of Americans, made the trek to Chicago in September for an American Peace Mobilization[10]—probably the most remarkable spontaneous demonstration of its kind in our history—hardly any newspaper mentioned it, and those that did dismissed it in a few lines as "Communist," merely because some of those taking part had been given a Red label by the preposterous Dies.

Actually if this were a really liberty protected country—one not ruled and stifled by a heartless and greedy band of profiteers, you and your paper might well be charged with fraud in this instance, and, if you ventured to take a court oath in behalf of your innocence, convicted of perjury.

Very truly,
THEODORE DREISER

P. S. How would it do if instead of your Free Press Week you were to celebrate a Controlled Press, Radio, and Public Speech Week? Think of how in some such corporation owned or politically controlled centers as Rockefeller City or Jersey City or Pittsburgh the assembled beneficiaries of the same could sit and listen to readings of congratulatory messages concerning the success of British or Corporation propaganda throughout the nation the past twenty years or longer. Special phases of these would certainly deal with the recent brilliant Polish, Finnish, Norwegian, Belgian and French "victories" that filled our American papers, news reels and radio preceding their collapse. Also the huge corporation success in excluding from or smearing in all American papers any and all advocates of democratic liberty and prosperity for the masses such as the late Senator Borah,[11] the former Senator La Follette,[12] the former Governor of Michigan but now present Supreme Court justice, Frank Murphy,[13] the brilliant advocate of technocracy, Howard Scott, the brilliant and honest labor leader, Harry Bridges,[14] the hero of the first transatlantic airplane flight, Lindbergh,[15] etc., etc., etc. These coupled with the brilliant ballooning of such mental and social peanuts as Warren Harding, Calvin Coolidge, Alf Landon,[16] Martin Dies, Wendell Willkie,[17] and endless other corporation or Wall Street stooges, ought to make such a week worth remembering. The idea is hereby presented—not charged for—which fact should endow it with some value to our greed stricken financial wreckers with the compliments of, yours truly.

Textual Note: Untitled broadside, 18 September 1940; repr. as "Theodore Dreiser And the Free Press," *People's World* (San Francisco), 2 October 1940, p. 5. Original correspondence in DPUP folder 1726. The original letter from *Editor and Publisher* reproduced on the broadside is omitted.

    1. Dreiser worked as a junior reporter on newspapers in Chicago, St. Louis, Toledo, Pittsburgh, and New York between June 1892 and the winter of 1894–95, and edited the magazines *Ev'ry Month* (1895–97), *Smith's* (1905–6), *Broadway* (1906–7), *The Delineator,* as editor-in-chief of the Butterick company's "trio" of mass-circulation fashion magazines (1907–10), and *The Bohemian* (1909).

    2. In July 1894 President Grover Cleveland sent federal troops numbering between one or two thousand and twenty thousand (the figure remains debated) to Chicago to suppress the strike initiated by workers at the Pullman railroad car factory outside the city. At the time, Dreiser was working as a newspaperman in Pittsburgh, where, according to his autobiography *Newspaper Days* (New York: Liveright, 1922), he was struck by the dejected atmosphere two years after the violent suppression of the strike at nearby Homestead.

    3. In *Newspaper Days* Dreiser abhors the "moralistic mush" favored by newspaper editors and makes specific criticisms of newspapers' poor coverage of labor issues. There is no evidence that *Tragic America* was officially suppressed. According to Dreiser's files it sold 4,371 copies in 1932, and a further 236 by March 1934 (DPUP).

    4. Martin Dies Jr. (1901–72), Democratic congressman, anticommunist campaigner, and, from 1938 to 1945, the first chair of the Special Committee Investigating Un-American Activities (later the House Un-American Activities Committee).

5. Frank Hague (1876–1956), mayor of Jersey City, N. J., from 1917 to 1947, epitomized the corrupt municipal politics known as "bossism." Hague actively suppressed labor organization in the 1930s.

6. Father Charles E. Coughlin (1891–1979), Roman Catholic priest and radio broadcaster. Anticommunist and anticapitalist, Coughlin embraced fascism and anti-Semitism from 1936.

7. William F. Hynes (1896–1952) was the leader of the "Red Squad" of the Los Angeles Police, founded in the 1920s in order to disrupt leftwing labor meetings and demonstrations at the behest of the corporate-funded Better America Federation.

8. Charlotte Anita Whitney (1867–1955), suffragist, political radical, and Communist Party supporter.

9. Dreiser's statement to the 9 October 1940 meeting of this organization amplifies several of the points made here.

10. The American Peace Mobilization was formed in 1940 to continue the antiwar campaigning of the American League for Peace and Democracy. Dreiser's November 1940 radio speech on its behalf was published as "'U.S. Must Not Be Bled for Imperial Britain'—Dreiser." See Further Reading.

11. William E. Borah (1865–1940). A progressive Republican; as chair of the Senate Foreign Affairs Committee from 1925 to 1933, Borah had favored diplomatic recognition of the U.S.S.R.

12. Robert M. La Follette Jr (1895–1953), progressive Republican senator and defender of organized labor.

13. Frank Murphy (1890–1949) championed civil rights on the Supreme Court, warning in 1944 that by sanctioning the forced relocation of Japanese-Americans, the court was falling "into the ugly abyss of racism."

14. Harry Bridges (1901–90), founder of the International Longshoremen's and Warehousemen's Union and by this time a C.I.O. activist, was interviewed at length by Dreiser in August 1940 (see Further Reading) and is quoted in America Is Worth Saving, 266–67.

15. The aviator Colonel Charles A. Lindbergh (1902–74) was a prominent member of the noninterventionist America First Committee. In America Is Worth Saving (202), Dreiser would excoriate Lindbergh, along with industrialists Henry Ford and James D. Mooney, for allegedly accepting Nazi honors.

16. Alf Landon (1887–1987), unsuccessful Republican presidential nominee in 1936.

17. Wendell L. Willkie (1892–1944), a long-time Democrat who left the party out of opposition to the New Deal and ran unsuccessfully as the Republican presidential nominee in 1940.

From *America Is Worth Saving*

New York: Modern Age Books, January 1941.

Written between June and September 1940, Dreiser's second full-length political book, America Is Worth Saving, *is primarily aimed at persuading Americans to remain neutral in the face of the war in Europe, which had begun in September 1939. Dreiser views the conflict as a trade war between imperial and would-be imperial nations, promulgated by international capitalists, arms manufacturers, and industrialists. In chapter 14, "Have English and American Finance Cooperated with Hitler to Destroy Democracy?" he blames British foreign policy for the rise of fascism, quoting the views of English newspaper proprietor Lord Rothermere that the Nazis were "Europe's guardians against the communist danger."*[1] *By deliberately keeping Russia isolated and weak and refusing to defend democratic governments in Spain and Czechoslovakia, Dreiser argues, Britain and France have forfeited any claim to international aid. Against the forces of international capitalism and of British imperialism, Dreiser argues passionately for American democracy to be reinvigorated, conceiving of this as an alternative to entering into another bloody war.*

The political significance of the antiwar message changed dramatically when Hitler's Germany invaded Russia in June 1941. Dreiser subsequently refused permission for his attacks on England in America Is Worth Saving *to be reprinted by the isolationist America First organization, and he completely disowned the book's pacifist conclusions when Japan attacked Pearl Harbor in December 1941. Despite these shifting historical circumstances, and the possibly substantial but unquantifiable contribution of Dreiser's assistant Cedric Belfrage (1904–90) to the finished book, the affiliations and hopes expressed in* America Is Worth Saving *contribute to an identifiably Dreiserian political trajectory. Grappling with the immediate challenge of mobilizing a prolabor, antiwar movement, Dreiser updates the critique of American exceptionalism made à propos of Woodrow Wilson in 1917's "American Idealism and German Frightfulness," vociferously opposes imperialist and capitalist exploitation, and argues that labor agitation should be recognized as being firmly at the center of the best traditions of American politics. The book reiterates the arguments Dreiser had been making since 1929 about the inefficiency of capitalism and the manipulation of ideas about democracy to serve the interests of big corporations and finance. Critical as it is of corporate-dominated America, the book nevertheless orients itself by reference to the democratic values that make America "worth saving." In key chapters such as "Has America a 'Save-the-World' Complex," Dreiser filters elements of exceptionalist ideology through his anticlericalism and commitment to creativity and social utility, to make some of his most penetrating analysis of the contradictions and potential of American democracy.*

In a central chapter of political philosophy titled "What is Democracy?" Dreiser argues that the ruthless competitive struggle for existence beloved of social Darwinists is obsolete. His emphasis on social solidarity and the possibilities offered by a post-scarcity economy picks up on his 1938 appeals on behalf of bombed civilians, and these ideas would form the foundation of his hopes for the future of mankind during the darkest hours of World War II.

Chapter 4: Has America a "Save-the-World" Complex?

* * * *

We are a peculiar and perverse-seeming people. Balzac said that the death by famine or plague of millions of Chinese was as nothing for the average Western citizen compared with the headache of someone in his own household. That has been more or less true everywhere except in the United States of America, where the exact opposite is the case. Our hearts bleed for the Chinese. We have enjoyed this sensation so much that we long supplied Japan with the iron to torture the Chinese a little more, and the oil to take Japanese planes to the altitudes from which it can most effectively be hurled.[2] This makes our hearts bleed more gushingly than ever. We reach down into our patched jeans and are overcome with the sense of our benevolence.

It is for beautiful abstract words that we prefer to perform our national Salvation Act—words like Democracy and Christianity. The thought of all the heathens in benighted tropical lands gives us insomnia, and the forcing of our beliefs upon them we regard as nothing less than our duty. Few things have shocked America more than the return from the Marquesas Islands of Herman Melville, the great American novelist of a hundred years ago, shamelessly proclaiming that he had not only done nothing to save the Marquesans but actually admired their way of life.[3] Had Melville set to work to raise a fund for a Salvation expeditionary force he would have been a hero, and his fellow-citizens would have denied themselves to contribute. But we did not want an author, we wanted a missionary; and we killed Melville as a writer by treating him as a social leper.

Last year alone we spent over $20,000,000 on missions to make the poor savages Christian. It was reported at the Missions Conference of North America in June that thirteen million Christians had been baptized, in China and elsewhere. Upon this remarkable achievement as it concerns China, Pearl S. Buck has commented:

> Christ has not become a part of the Chinese life . . . We can have no assurance that if we withdrew from China today there would be any more permanent record left of our religious presence these 150 years than is left there of the old Nestorian church—a wind-blown, obliterated tablet upon desert land.[4]

That was highly un-American of Mrs. Buck. It is not our national custom to probe deeply into the errors and miseries that arouse our pity—to attack the causes at the roots with a view to permanent improvement. We rush in precipitately with money and with our sons and daughters, and draw up the balance sheet much later, if at all, to find that we have bought nothing except salve for our conscience.

We were the only people in the world willing to go to war to end slavery. Hundreds of thousands of our men died for that noble cause—and today we examine the "freed" South and see the Negroes slightly less illiterate, but in basic needs as badly off as they were before the Civil War: without clothing and food, without a vote, without civil liberties, living in pigsties. No matter: "theoretically," slavery has been abolished.

For more than a century we have crusaded against the Demon Rum—with money, with "Face on the Barroom Floor" propaganda, with axes, with the lifetime devotion of well-meaning men and women, and finally with laws. We are proud to have "abolished the corner saloon." In its place we, still the thirstiest people on earth, have three chromium-plated "cocktail bars" in every block.

Our best people have "saved" art. In 1866 it was reported in *The New York Times* that three thousand "artists" in Belgium alone were living on wealthy American patrons, who purchased caricatures of celebrated paintings sold as originals. If we ever had a good artist here he had to go to Europe to be "discovered" by Americans.

Our Billy Sundays and Moodys and Sankeys "saved" millions of American sinners for the Lord, and their successors, the Aimee McPhersons, are still at it.[5] Nevertheless America still holds the unchallenged laurels as the world's leading criminal nation.

We whimpered with horror at the tales of Turkish atrocities in Armenia, and especially at the goings-on in Turkish harems, and sent emissaries to save Turkey's womenfolk from worse than death.[6] At the very same period the vast red light districts in our own country were passing almost unnoticed. St. Louis, when I was in the newspaper business there, had four lines of houses a mile and a quarter long which were all brothels. In Pittsburgh, where churches were particularly numerous, and where just then the miserably underpaid miners striking for a living wage were being shot down in cold blood, it was the same. Idealistic Americans of those cities gave their all for the unfortunate females of Turkey.

Smart people soon began to get wise to the potentialities of the American Salvation Racket. The English caught on to it long ago and exploited it for all they were worth. If people were starving in a British colony, and there were rumblings of revolt, England didn't have to do anything about it. It was easier and cheaper to get America's Salvationeers on the job. In China the English fostered the opium trade for their own profit, manufacturing addicts by the million, while at the same time piously welcoming American missionaries sent to save the addicts from themselves.

In America thousands of leeches burrowed their heads into the racket, promoting themselves excellent incomes as collectors of Salvation money. The shrewd editor of a religious paper lifts that publication from nothing to several hundred thousand circulation by exploiting Salvationeers. All he has to do when the growth begins to lag is to find a new famine or massacre or epidemic—not in America, of course—or send a reporter to describe the distressing conditions of the savages in Africa. A week after the crusade is launched, a mountain of letters containing cash and checks is piled on the long editorial tables—and wholesalers are doubling their orders for his paper.

There was just one thing Americans were not ready to save—the financially oppressed of our own people in America. Only in the last few years has sympathy for our own oppressed and starving begun to dawn. That is not because we are hard-hearted. We are a genuinely charitable people.

It is a simple matter of geography. Geography made England the cradle of the industrial age and of the revolt against feudalism. Geography gave Americans our pathological concern about Christianity in China, Democracy in Cuba, Democracy in Europe—great abstract causes for which we will give and fight without pausing to think who is really profiting by it, or that these things cannot be imposed from without. Geography gave us our blind spot concerning the wrongs and miseries of our own people.

How? Because the America of our fathers and grandfathers was a promised land, an undeveloped land containing riches for everyone, to which they had escaped from the wars and tyrannies of their homelands. It was so far from Europe, as distances went then, that it seemed in another world. It was so big and so new that up until quite recently, when I myself was at school, possibilities of overnight wealth for the humblest citizen still existed. There was still some undeveloped land to be had in the West. Excitement as to what fortune might easily bring to the enterprising was still in the air. No matter how badly things went, no matter what sufferings the millions in Eastern cities were already then enduring, no matter how little physical abundance the millions enjoyed, there was a strong hangover of mental abundance. Heaven was just about eight hundred miles west.

And the people who felt this mental abundance were mostly sober religious folk who had taken the Sermon on the Mount to heart. In America they had not yet known want in the European sense—poverty and degradation made almost unbearable by the sense of hopelessness. Hope there still was. But they remembered what it had been like in the old countries, or what their parents had told them it was like; and when they heard of the

Press advertisement for *America Is Worth Saving*.

terrible sufferings abroad they were moved not only to pity but to a desire to give something as a thank offering for their escape to the land of hope. If they had been hard-pressed themselves—or if, though hard-pressed, they had been without hope—they would not have cared. In the republics of Central and South America, with their peon traditions, nobody cared.

What we did not then realize—what we have only begun to understand in the last decade—is that the American Cinderella saga was not a story to be indefinitely continued. So far as the vast majority were concerned, it ended inevitably with the end of free land in the West, when the land was all gobbled up by banks and corporations and was only available to the poor man on a basis of more or less serfdom. There were no longer opportunities after that for the ordinary man and woman in the realm of producing society's basic needs. Such opportunities as there were existed now in the realm of luxuries and of distribution and finance. The time had come, as it had come in every European country, when the creative man who produced things was firmly relegated to the bottom of the social heap, while the uncreative man who sold things was laden with rich rewards.

Chapter 10: Has England Done More for
Its People Than Fascism or Socialism?

* * * *

The new "American" code earmarks Nazism and Communism together as "alien isms," even to discuss which with attempted detachment is more heinous than for a nineteenth-century schoolgirl to discuss sex. But imperialism, the system in implacable opposition to which our forefathers placed our Constitution, is apparently *not* an "alien ism." We are asked to be hotly in favor of it, because our Wall Street gangs are jealous of the swag England has got out of it and would like us to shed our blood to get them a slice.

However, I intend to exercise my constitutional privilege, while I still have it, of discussing this question. We need not jump into the morass of theoretical argumentation about Fascism and Communism. But if we are to get our ideas straight we must consider the results of those systems and scale "free" England down to its correct proportions in comparison. For we are told that one is white and the other is black, and therefore we must all root for the white like good little children of Mr. Roosevelt. As far as I am concerned—and I believe this goes for most Americans, despite all the earnest efforts to stifle free thought—that kind of totemic mystification simply will not do.

* * * *

The point is that a government which Americans should support (but which our present rulers can be relied on to betray, as in Spain and China) is one that *raises* the masses' share in the rising national income, *reduces* their working hours in line with the advance of technology, steadily *increases* their effective democratic rights. Those are things that England cannot claim to have been doing in the past twenty years. Nor have we Americans any right to look superior about it when we contemplate the present trend in our own land. But in the most typically American (in my sense of the word, not Mr. Dies'[7]) period of our history we did come nearer to doing those things than any European nation; and that is still the ideal firmly planted in our Constitution. It has always been and still is the only ideal worth fighting for.

But now we have to move on once again to the British Empire. It is an unreal approach to our comparison to confine it to England, which contains less than 10 per cent of the people under English rule. To fight for England is inevitably to fight for the Empire as it exists now—at least until England's rulers take the opportunity India has offered them to show a change of heart. And when we look at the Empire, what edge can we now give England over Nazi Germany?

We find anti-Semitism rampant in Palestine, anti-Hinduism rampant in India. No, of course the English are not officially anti-Semitic or anti-Hindu—it's the Arab and Moslem minorities. But try as they will, the English cannot find evidence of such rioting in Palestine before the British Mandate, or in India before the East India Company.[8] We find standards of living which would have been unimaginable to men in the barbarian state of development.

* * * *

What people as a whole want, so far as my observation goes, is more food and more houses and more clothes and more leisure and more opportunities to use that leisure pleasantly and advantageously. The facts show that the Russians, having abolished the dividend system, are now getting these things at a faster rate of progress than has ever been recorded in history. But perhaps that doesn't prove anything, or does it? And, of course, there may well be things in Russia that are bad and to be avoided, such as whatever it was that caused the famous purges and the attack on Finland.[9] Granted: but are we so feeble-minded, is England so feeble-minded, as to be unable to choose between good and bad? Does the whole experiment have to be labeled "poison" and avoided like cyanide, because there are chunks of grit in the mixture?

* * * *

Chapter 11: What is Democracy?[10]

* * * *

Philosophers' dreams of "freedom" are necessarily limited by the contemporary limitations of man's power to produce abundance. So in Plato's *Republic* everything is held in common—by a select group of loftier souls, who spend their time in thought while the slaves toil to feed them.

* * * *

With the Industrial Revolution in England, the Aristotelian imperialist-"democracy," the dream became clearer and bigger in the minds of William Morris, George Bernard Shaw, and H. G. Wells.[11] It was caught up by poets and thinkers in the new rich land of America, by Whitman, Henry George, Edward Bellamy.[12] All these believed with Rousseau and Kant that the law of man's nature is social and that the Good is social good—that which serves the common interest.[13] But others, the servants and beneficiaries of things-as-they-are, stood ready to distort the new and dangerous theories. Had not Darwin shown that man had evolved from the monkey through natural selection and survival of the fittest? Very well then: since it was desirable for the fittest to survive, the precept most useful to society was every man for himself and the devil take the hindmost.

The theory of rugged individualism going onward and upward forever—retained to this day by privileged persons in all lands and particularly in America—was very handy to those who sought moral justification for sitting on the kettle of progress. But it ignored, as one critic puts it, the consideration of "what happens if everybody bolts for the exits in a theater fire." It ignored the implacable and basic law of social existence. What was efficient for nature's purposes when we swung from bough to bough by our tails is no longer efficient when all of life, because of our acquired store of knowledge, is organized socially.

* * * *

So in the civilized world moving toward more democracy and more freedom—or rather, more sense of freedom, since we can never be free of nature's laws—the tendency of nature has been to let the homunculus run a long struggle and see what he can get. His pleasures or his troubles arise from the fact that he always ends by wanting more than he is entitled to, which in a scarcity economy means that others must do with less than they are entitled to in order that he may have more. But from nature's point of view up to now that has been good, for by that struggle between individuals and groups the living world has developed: its pleasures, pains, surpluses, and seeming but not real deficiencies—for in nature is everything ready to be discovered. As science today knows, we need only to search and find out—enjoying life as best we can as we go.

Cruel, yes. The creative force is quite brutal in its methods. It gives Edison the power to create something new almost every day while to a man born next door it barely gives the ability to sweep a floor. It gives one woman an ugly face and body, and her cousin such beauty that men lay everything at her feet and she need not stir. It is a cruel dictatorship and at the same time a recklessly bountiful genius. It gives the opossum a score of young and the ability to feed but twelve, so that the weakest must fall from the pouch and perish. It produces as many as 500 million mackerel eggs during a spawning time on a square mile of ocean surface, and condemns 999,996 in each million to die before they live. But also it decrees that from the putrescence of death shall always come new and yet more abundant life.

The point is that out of this struggle the onward-and-upward movement has come. Hence it is absurd to say that "capitalism," the system of competitive struggle for the available turkey and gravy, is absolutely "bad" and "undemocratic." It is equally absurd to say that it is absolutely "good." It was the system best adapted to nature's unfolding purpose, and gave us as much democracy as the traffic would bear, at a certain stage of our development—just as primitive tribalism was best adapted to that purpose in ancient Polynesia before the missionaries came, in India before the English came, and among the American Indians before we barged in. Such systems could and did persist until the people knew about other systems geared to the demands of progress—and then they were doomed.

Our present competitive system based on scarcity was as inevitable as sunrise. The champions of it are entirely right in pointing out that it has made us what we are today. But the question now is: What are we today? Does it function efficiently any longer? Do we like the reflection of ourselves in the mirror?

The question is, whether this system's displacement by something else has not, with scarcity at long last potentially ended, become as inevitable as sunset.

The best of all definitions of democracy is that it is the knowledge of necessity. Knowledge is death to the old, and new life springs from the putrescence. The advance of democracy is no more than the advance of knowledge.

In order, then, that there shall not be plenty for all in our era, there must be ignorance on the part of most.

In order to continue suffering for the want of things that can now be produced in endless quantities, the mass of the people must remain ignorant of their existence; or at least ignorant of how to extract them from nature and, once extracted, how to distribute them so that a few cannot, for reasons of selfish display and vanity, prevent the many from sharing what is enough for all.

The extent therefore of our national ignorance of these things is the extent of our lack of democracy.

Chapter 13: What are the Objectives of American Finance?

* * * *

What developed finally with this, [the internationalization of capitalism by the first decade of the twentieth century] of course, was understandings and conferences between American, British, French, German, and other groups or phases of finance in the important countries of the world. With this went the problem of their protection, by either their native land or the land which each or both had invaded. And for that, of course, in case of international financial quarrels, both armies and navies were necessary. Hence armies and navies to threaten Mexico, China, England, Japan, Germany, anybody and everybody who chose to interfere with any English or American corporation. So, even before the first great World War, you had the picture of American and British and German and other agencies of finance invading various alien countries with the money of their native lands; and once there, employing the cheapest labor, charging the highest prices, competing sometimes even with their own native land by underselling themselves in their native lands.

Yet, at the same time, in case of any quarrel concerning or danger to their property anywhere, expecting and calling upon their native country to help them. English warships arriving in Venezuela in 1895 to demand payment of loans that were made to Venezuela in order to secure an interest in the asphalt lakes.[14] The Guggenheims exacting international intervention on the part of America in connection with the passing determination of Chile to seize their copper mines or make them pay better wages.[15] The Standard Oil Company calling upon the United States to protect its interests in Manchuria at the time that Japan seized that country, in Mexico, in Central America, etc.[16]

The only eventual object—if one looks acquisitive international finance squarely in the eye—being the eventual domination of the world by some one international financial group, with so-called nations as mere local forms or puppets, under their control, but with the avowed purpose to do what?

Pay better wages to all the laborers in the world wherever? Advance the education or technical training of the millions here in America or England or elsewhere? Build them better houses? Provide state medicine for the millions of the underpaid and sick? State hospitalization? Assured labor for those able to work? Old-age pensions for those who have worked and are no longer able to do so? Food, clothing, shelter, education for the children of widows or the orphans of the dead? Establish peace and plenty for all? What do you think?

Do you truly think their hearts or minds are touched or appealed to by any such objectives? If so, study the newspapers and radio speakers of our day. Or are they blazing with that same old individualistic vanity which causes them to look on private and personal possessions and supreme power as the be-all and end-all of human existence? Imagine!

If you look at the first great World War in which 40,000,000 people died from starvation or other causes, and after which America as well as Europe sank into twenty years of poverty and fear—and realize that it was nothing more than a quarrel between the financial leaders of England, Germany, and such other powers as England could influence, as to which was to have the financial domination of Europe and Africa and Asia, and nothing more and nothing less—you can judge for yourself. There was no Jewish question in 1914 and there is none now in so far as these warriors are concerned. Neither is democracy, human liberty, nor any other truly and socially respectable thing being fought for. Power, wealth, dominance for one or the other is all that is sought. And England cares no more for America than she does for Germany or India. She is out for herself and so are our American financiers. But not the American people.

This latest war that is raging in Europe is about just that: the determination of Germany, after twenty years of sufferings due to its defeat in the first war, to recapture at least some of the power that it once dreamed of obtaining. The determination of England, which has one quarter of the world—and when I say England, of course I mean its financiers, not its undernourished masses—to see that not one acre of its quarter of the world is yielded or lost to its rival financial mechanism that will control Germany if Germany wins. And although, as you know, it prates of saving civilization and democracy, it has no such purpose in mind, for it is a financial oligarchy of the worst type and, as I have shown in another chapter of this book,[17] it has never been anything but that. Victorious, it does not intend to free the 380,000,000 Hindus whom it causes to live on a cent or two a day; nor does it intend to do anything for the blacks of its various colonies in Africa and elsewhere, who at this time slave for a mere pittance to grow its sheep and wool, its tobacco, its coffee, its cattle and rubber, any more than it intends to improve the condition of the working man in Canada or Australia or British South Africa, or British Guiana or England, or Honduras, or anywhere in its quarter of the world.

It has not done so and it will not do so because, as I have shown, the British Empire is built on the theory of the dominant 3 per cent whose obligation is to no one but themselves. And as for our American financiers, if you can judge by what they do and not what they say, you can see that their objective is precisely the same.

* * * *

Chapter 15: Can the British Empire Endure?

If I have been at pains to point out how wretched England makes the existence of hundreds of millions of its subjects—if I have challenged anyone to explain just how those subject peoples could be any worse off under, say, the Nazis—it has not been done to satisfy any personal animosity against the English, nor to demonstrate that the individual Englishman is "evil" by comparison with individuals of other races. If America had an empire like the British Empire, you can depend upon it that the inhabitants would be in precisely the same condition. Indeed, you have but to look at Puerto Rico— where the people are starving and without democracy and where only the other day (according to the Associated Press) two native political leaders were arrested and charged with the crime of "making speeches and publishing letters"—to see that in such colonies as we now possess we do exactly what England does in India, Africa, and the West Indies. We do it on a smaller scale of course, because our possessions (you will, by the way, find nothing in our Constitution about our ever having any possessions) are few. But the net results of imperialism by whomsoever practiced are and must be the same, without the slightest relation to the benevolence that may or may not glow in the hearts of the rulers. The imperialist economy makes it necessary for the subject peoples to be held back from normal industrialization—and at that point man clashes with nature, and we know who is bound to win in the end. You cannot get the peoples of colonial Britain—nine-tenths of all the people ruled from London—excited about the "threat of falling under the Nazi heel." They have nowhere to fall, since they are under a heel now, and no matter who owns the heel it feels just as uncomfortable under there.

Chapter 16: Will American Democracy Endure?

* * * *

The greatest democratic tradition of America is the tradition of Labor. Our people are given to "spontaneous mass movements and sudden manifestations of tremendous violence, especially when peaceful or lawful channels seem blocked." They do not resort to such violence until they are convinced that it is the only alternative to far greater and more ruthless violence by the enemies of labor. The tradition comes down through John Brown, through the Know-Nothings of the '50s, the Anti-Renters and Barn-Burners, the Molly Maguires, the Green Corn Rebellion, through "Coxey's Army" of '94 and the Bonus Army of more recent years.[18] The flame has only been fed by the savage anti-labor violence of the Haymarket Affair, of Ludlow, Wheatland, Gastonia, Centralia, Harlan County, Homestead, Lawrence, Everett, and the Memorial Day massacre of Chicago in 1936. The cry back of all these movements has been: "We'll make democracy work!" And if it were not for the American spirit in the common man through all these events, then indeed there would be no hope for America.

* * * *

Chapter 19: What Should Be the Objectives of the American People?

* * * *

This is not to say that the poor in America, as elsewhere, do not spend the great majority of their time thinking about money. For how can they forget it—how can money stop haunting them through every waking moment—as long as they suffer from lack of the basic needs while those same are being destroyed or the people who could produce them are forcibly denied the right to possess them? Actually money is not the love of the poor man's life but the curse of his life. Extreme need distorts all his other values and exaggerates the value of the wealth possessed by others. Poverty is like the 2,000 diameter power of a microscope. When your pocket is empty the sight of a man going into an automat for a two-bit dinner makes you wildly envious. I know too well from my own experiences how belittled and humiliated the poor man feels. To subject any willing citizen to such hunger and want is social dynamite, not only when the man is poor, but later when and if he begins to get money by some means or other. For when he has a little wealth in his hands and sees what he can do with it—when he sees the almost lunatic gratitude with which his handouts are received by the less fortunate—it gives him a wholly unnatural and unsocial and so undemocratic sense of grandeur and power, in fact turns him into a ten-cent lord, a ward-heeler, an aristocrat of the alley, a Mayor Hague. And then let those who have not fared so well in the jungle we call civilization watch out!

* * * *

Wherever we look, we come back to the Declaration of Independence and the Constitution as the anchors of our democracy and welfare. We do not want an empire, we want democracy. The ideal of democracy is the highest humanity ever developed. It will withstand any propaganda from within or without if the people can only be satisfied that the ideal of the benefit of ALL, including the under-privileged, is fixed on the horizon. To speak of democracy flourishing and being saved or advanced in war is like speaking of a fish flourishing out of water. The only air in which democracy can breathe is peace, and it must be free air and abundant air, in which all ideas regardless of labels and origin can be expressed. Fighting "isms" is merely fighting symptoms, not the cause. Give the "isms" rein and they will stand or fall by what common sense there may be in them for America.

The Constitution is not concerned with "isms" but with the right for every man to speak his mind together with his neighbor's right to disprove his contentions if he can.

We must get a little sense in our heads at this late date and use our perfectly specific Constitution and Declaration of Independence as the only acid test of a man's loyalty to democracy, instead of persecuting, as we are now doing, the very people who stand up for those national charters.

We must make an end, however ruthless the means that have to be employed, to the possibility of individuals and small groups accumulating and inheriting huge sums of money, which they inevitably use to suborn the government and to get us into foreign wars by the eternal search for more profit.

We must make this the criterion regarding what should and should not be done in the exploitation of our own land: Does it or doesn't it add to the general wealth of the whole community? We must stop courting scarcity as if it were the most desirable of bedfellows.

We must make the Constitution work—all of the Constitution—or we will never have democracy. We must do it in a fully conscious and methodical and speedy way because if we don't it will come to fighting in our streets between brother and brother.

For as Tom Paine pointed out, what an old sage, Archimedes, said in the dawn of civilization about the mechanical powers may be applied to reason and liberty: "Had we a place to stand upon, we might raise the world."[19] America plus our Constitution is certainly a place to stand on to raise democracy into being. Let us save America and democracy by not joining in this foreign bloodbath, but rather by showing the world in our own example how democracy can work.

Only the mass can get America out of the mess. Not a small group of a few thousand crusaders. America will be on the road forward, solidly and unmovably on the road, when a great throng of people comes out on the streets of our cities with the Constitution and Declaration of Independence as their banners and the un-American monopolists will see them and will say: "That's America."

Textual Note: New York: Modern Age Books, 1941. These selections are taken from pages 36–40, 125, 130, 139, 148, 149–50, 152–53, 180–82, 213–14, 238–39, 279–80, 291–92.

1. Lord Rothermere in the *Daily Mail* (London), 28 November 1933, quoted in *America Is Worth Saving*, 195. The *Daily Mail*, a mainstream newspaper owned by Rothermere, explicitly supported fascism in Germany and in England in the early 1930s.

2. Dreiser refers to the supply by American companies of raw materials that enabled Japanese military aggression toward China in the 1930s.

3. Herman Melville (1819–91), author of the fictionalized travel narrative *Typee: A Peep at Polynesian Life* (1846).

4. The writer, activist, and humanitarian Pearl Sydenstricker Buck (1892–1973) frequently reminded Americans of the cultural specificity of China, where she spent much of her life until the early 1930s. She refers to the Assyrian Monument discovered in Xi'an province, an eighth-century relic of the (Assyrian) Church of the East, popularly known as the Nestorian Church.

5. William Ashley "Billy" Sunday (1862–1935) and Dwight Lyman Moody (1837–99) were successful evangelists; Ira David Sankey (1840–1908) was a gospel singer and composer who toured with Moody; and Aimée Semple McPherson (1890–1944) was a Pentecostal evangelist of a later generation.

6. Dreiser refers to the violent abuse and forced expulsion of Armenians carried out in Turkey during World War I, during which an estimated one to one and a half million Armenians died.

7. A reference to Martin Dies's chairmanship of the Special Committee to Investigate Un-American Activities. In February 1941, Dreiser told an interviewer that "Americanism, as I understand it, with apologies to Mr. Dies, means precisely giving equal chances to *all*, and nothing else." Rusch and Pizer, *Interviews*, 306.

8. In a preceding chapter Dreiser accuses Britain of deliberately fomenting religious tensions in India and elsewhere in order to maintain its imperial control (103–4). Conversely, due to the recognition of such differences in the Soviet Union's federal system, he claims that the "racial minority problem" and the "Jewish problem" have "gone with the wind" (143).

9. Stalin's purges of rivals within the Soviet Communist Party culminated in three major show trials in 1936–38. Russia invaded Finland on 30 November 1939, initiating what would become known as the Winter War, or Russo-Finnish War. Following its conclusion in March 1940, Dreiser defended the right of the U.S.S.R. to take such steps to defend itself against the hostile intents of capitalist nations. See "Concerning Dives and Lazarus," in Further Reading.

10. A condensation of this chapter first appeared as "What Is Democracy?" *Clipper* 1 (December 1940): 3–7.

11. Dreiser refers to the more expansive notions of democracy made possible for socialists such as William Morris (1834–96), George Bernard Shaw (1856–1950), and H. G. Wells (1866–1946) by the exponentially increased productive capacity of industrialised Britain, as compared with the "imperialist-democracy" of slave-holding classical Athens.

12. Dreiser emphasizes the importance of the abundant resources of America to inspire poets and thinkers Walt Whitman (1819–91), Henry George (an early influence cited in "The Day of Special Privileges," see 36), and Edward Bellamy (1850–98).

13. Jean-Jacques Rousseau (1712–78) argued in *The Social Contract* (1762) for the surrendering of individual rights to the collective "general will," which by definition represents the common good. In the *Groundwork to a Metaphysic of Morals* (1785), Immanuel Kant (1724–1804) framed the "Categorical Imperative"—"Act only on that maxim which you can at the same time will to become a universal law."

14. This incident was part of a long-running dispute between Britain and Venezuela, principally over territory and mineral resources claimed by Britain in what is now Guyana.

15. The Guggenheim Brothers had taken control of the Chuquicamata copper mine in Chile in 1912. The Chilean copper industry remained in the hands of United States-based multinational corporations until it was nationalized in the 1970s by the government of Salvador Allende (1908–73). Allende was subsequently removed and killed in the C.I.A.-sponsored coup that brought Augusto Pinochet (1915–2006) to power.

16. After Standard Oil interests in Manchuria were threatened by Japanese invasion, Secretary of State Stimson sent an official note of protest to Japan in January 1932. The Mexican oil industry was nationalized in 1938.

17. Chapter 7: How Democratic Is England? and Chapter 8: Has England Democratized the Peoples of Its Empire?

18. After the abolitionist leader John Brown (1800–1859), Dreiser lists, respectively, a nativist political movement of the 1850s, leaseholding farmers who successfully protested the manorial system in upper New York State from 1839–46, a group of radical Democrats active in New York State from the 1830s to the 1850s, a secret organization of Irish miners in the Pennsylvania coalfields who came to prominence in a series of controversial trials in 1876–78, a 1917 rebellion against conscription by poor Oklahoma farmers in association with the Socialist Party, a protest march on Washington led by populist Jacob Coxey (1854–1951) in 1894, and another march on Washington by between 11,000 and 31,000 World War I veterans and their families in 1932.

19. The introduction to the second part of Thomas Paine's *Rights of Man* (1792) opens as follows: "What Archimedes said of the mechanical powers, may be applied to Reason and Liberty. 'Had we,' said he, 'a place to stand upon, we might raise the world.'"

From "Writers Declare: 'We Have a War to Win!'"

Sunday Worker (New York), 21 December 1941.

In the aftermath of the Japanese attack on Pearl Harbor and the United States's declaration of war on Japan, the Sunday Worker *printed several "expression[s] of opinion on what American writers can do to help win the war against the Axis." After Dreiser came messages from Upton Sinclair and Millen Brand (1906–80).*

The Japanese invasion of the United States of America at dawn on Sunday, December 7, 1941, speaks for itself. I think that President Roosevelt was absolutely correct when he said that they had adopted the thug tactic—of sneaking up with a lead pipe instead of honestly stating their claims and intentions—and that this principle must be knocked out of them, at whatever cost to our nation. You cannot let thugs run loose in ordinary society.

I think that there is something mentally wrong with any group in any nation that seeks to perform an unsocial act. After all, the tradition of chivalry is worth something. Many people have standards that they will not tarnish; there are certain things that they will not do because these things would be inequitable. When the principle of raw force is introduced, the standards of a decent world have gone to hell—if they are allowed to get away with it.

I believe that all Americans ought to be willing, not only to cooperate with, but to serve the officials of this government to produce a united front, and to make effective any orders or plans for the safety of the public, and the confusion and destruction of the enemy. It is very obvious that the Japanese are willing to cooperate with and even die for their government. And I believe we ought to be in exactly the same spirit, for we have a country that is democratic in spirit, and once its dream of real democracy is made effective, it can actually democratize the whole world. It has constructive and creative skill, and everybody that is here now ought to have that in mind—NOT JUST TO WIN THIS WAR BUT TO MAKE A BETTER WORLD FOR THE INDIVIDUAL IN EVERY WALK OF LIFE.

And by the same token, I am opposed to powerful countries, when they are in power, refusing the benefits of progress and civilization to any group. And whether or not we do it, or Hitler does it, or England does it, or the Mikado does it—it makes no difference. It ought to be stopped. Grant the same measure of equity to everybody. Enforce the Golden Rule. Implement it.

The American writers in this crisis should certainly realize their serious responsibilities and show by example and not by talk, that this is what America stands for—with the hope of influencing people in other walks of life to exactly the same attitude. The light and casual mood that has pervaded the minds of the people of this country for some years past must come to an end. The play mood, based on wealth, however accumulated,[1] has even invaded our training camps. And the sooner our boys in the army and navy get down to brass tacks and pay less attention as to who is the queen of the May, the stronger our national defense will be. Even the Student Union at the University of California at Los Angeles commented upon this fact.

We have a war to win. We have principles of justice and freedom that we must defend. We have a dream of democracy that must endure. It is time for all Americans to get to work—to make, if possible, an equitable world for the generations that are yet to come.

More than that they cannot do. Less than that they should not do.

Textual Note: Sunday Worker (New York), 21 December 1941, section 2, p. 6.

Dreiser's message, dated 12 December 1941, was in response to a telegram request from the *Daily Worker*, dated 9 December: "Would like statement by air mail maximum five hundred words on Japanese attack on United States and what American writers can do in this crisis" (DPUP). Copy-text is Dreiser's carbon copy typescript (3 pages) in DPUP folder 1390, which carries several minor revisions in pencil.

1. The opening part of this sentence is a pencil revision to the typescript, replacing the single word "Glamor" in the *Sunday Worker* text.

Broadcast to the People of Europe

Recorded May 1944.

In anticipation of D-Day (6 June 1944), the allied landings in Nazi-occupied France that started the counteroffensive against Hitler, Dreiser recorded two broadcasts for the Office of War Information. This, the first, was specifically aimed to counter Nazi propaganda claims that doubtful public opinion and low morale in the United States were holding up the invasion. It was subsequently printed in Direction, *which reported that Dreiser's voice was "heard many times throughout Europe, translated into many languages the week before D-Day."*

I have just come across the country[1] . . . this great America of ours . . . and I wish you could have been with me. You would have seen, as I did, in railway stations, on trains, in hotels, on the streets . . . an amazing display of youthful vigor, enthusiasm, youthful, yet manly love of country. . . . In sum, millions of the finest type of fighting men, who seek nothing so much as the day and hour when they can try their young strength, their American vitality and brains, their American alertness and inventiveness, against the Nazi brutes, whom they do not fear but whom they abhor, as do all Americans. For what we now know of Nazi principles and practices has inflamed us with the desire to eradicate those principles as well as the criminals who practice them.

If you could cross America with me you would see scores upon scores of training fields. Endless divisions that are fair-sized armies . . . marching and drilling in the immense camps in every state of the union. The great wagon-trains with their military equipment. The enormous factories and yards in which everything from ships to airplanes, submarines to tanks, rifles to long-range, heavy artillery are made. Indeed, enormous factories which are minor cities in themselves, from which are pouring out not only ammunition and bombs, but clothing, preserved foods, surgical and medical supplies . . . tents, jeeps, field hospitals and so forth. In fact, I have seen a long, almost endless train go by, stop, and begin to unload cars, trucks, equipment of all kinds . . . until, in a few hours . . . a whole tent city spread out as far as I could see. Presently, men were being called to a meal, over loud-speakers installed throughout the camp. This tent city, I thought as I saw it, is a demonstration of what our men will soon be setting up in Europe.

There is another side of America's war spirit that I should show you in connection with every military center I have visited. You would see new and great armies of women soldiers and nurses, mentally and physically equipped to follow their fighting men not only through the jungles, but, if necessary, to the graves which they may be destined to occupy.

Last but not least, you would and should see the armies of civilians, in every occupation, in every walk of life, who have geared themselves to war . . . and now to invasion . . . who are working for it, hoping for it, ready for it. Retired businessmen, housewives who have given up their comforts to work in factories. Young girls who work in hospitals to relieve nurses for war duty. Boys who work after school hours, in shops and on farms, to release men for the service.

In millions of little homes across America, as I am talking to you now, are farmers coming in from their fields. War workers coming home from factories. Almost the first thing they do is to turn on their radios and listen, as you are listening. They are waiting for news of the invasion, as you are. They are thinking of their boys . . . of the jobs they have to do . . . the fighting, the dying, the killing of the Nazi hordes, as they land and advance into your countries, one by one. They know the price that they, these American fathers and mothers, will have to pay, in lost sons and husbands, in hours of harder work and sacrifices at home.

I personally have been a witness to particular scenes of farewell and departure that have touched me as though the parents and their boys were of my own flesh and blood. A mother, for instance, who, at the moment of parting, turned and ran back . . . only to turn again . . . her eyes wet, and saying . . . "but I mustn't cry, darling, and I won't any more, but I'll be loving you all the time. My heart is going with you." And again, a crippled father, watching the family car moving away from the door—his son and his bags, and a sister within—hobbling down to the gate, and from there to the nearest corner in the hope of obtaining one last glimpse of his sturdy son and heir. This boy is overseas now, awaiting the hour of invasion. His family is one of the millions that have but one desire . . . and that is . . . NOW to get the job done . . . by any and every means in their power. To fight at home, to speed invasion, and to crush the Nazi horror forever.

For America glows with the force and enthusiasm of a great and war-ready people, who are determined that Hitler and his criminals shall unconditionally sue for peace. . . . Americans are a great people, a gay people, a fearless people. Cracking jokes, and at the same time making sure that, to the last millionth of an inch, the equipment they prepare is true and fateful, spelling death to our enemies. America is the one country that can say . . . WAIT AND SEE.

Textual Note: Copy-text is the typescript "Special Events Recording," "Title: Theodore Dreiser Re- American Morale" (3 pages), in DPUP folder 13411. Published as "Broadcast by Theodore Dreiser to the People of Europe," *Direction* 7:3 (July 1944): 4.

1. That is, from Dreiser's home in Hollywood, California, to New York.

Broadcast to the People of Germany

Recorded week of 29 May–3 June 1944.

This is a second speech Dreiser prepared for the Office of War Information, intended for broadcast once Allied forces had reached Germany's borders.

As an American of part-German descent, I feel strongly about the situation confronting the German people after this war.

Before the last war, Germans were looked upon as producing some of our best types of citizens. German-Americans are, for the most part, industrious, orderly, socially responsible, recognizing their obligations and taking a constructive part in community life.

My own father came to this country as an immigrant from the little town of Mayen on the Moselle river in Germany. He and another German, Carl Fischer (who later became head of a music house[1]), walked their way westward, peddling small articles as they went. My father gradually worked his way up in the woolen business and founded two woolen mills, one in Fort Wayne and one in Sullivan, Indiana. He came to be considered a wool expert, and his advice was sought even after he had retired and was over eighty years old.

My father and Carl Fischer left Germany because they did not want to be conscripted into the armies being formed in those days by Bismarck, who dreamt of conquering Europe as Napoleon had done.

I do not think that desire for conquest and cruelty are inherent in the German nation as a whole, any more than they are in any nation of people continuously trained for war. It was Napoleon who first stirred up German and possibly Prussian ambition when he demonstrated that it was possible to conquer Europe through military force. England was rapidly expanding at that time, having taken unto herself almost one-fifth of the globe, and it is perfectly true that Germany did not have a place in world affairs appropriate to her abilities and equally rapid industrial expansion. Germany's desire for a place in the sun, or *lebensraum*,[2] drove her to try military conquest—in sum you have Bismarck and the young Kaiser Wilhelm[3] copying Napoleon, and Hitler copying Kaiser Wilhelm, as well as Napoleon.

It is not the fact that Germany has been a warring nation, even since the days of the Romans, that causes the peoples of the world to think of not forgiving her. It is the horror of the Nazi rule and of the Nazi principles—the cruel, unbelievable bestiality practiced by the Nazi leaders, and the new type of warfare they have developed, directed not only against the soldiers of their opponents, but against old people, women and children. The systematic torture and starvation of millions of human beings, including even many of their own people—the mass murderings of hostages chosen at random, of whole village populations, of thousands upon thousands of helpless and often heroic Jews, of children shot down or bled to death—

It is these things that civilization will never forget—

These things make me shudder and grieve to think that I am a part-German—

It is these things that the Germans of the future must take into their intellectual considerations and stamp out of the German mind and soul. For the Nazi poison has sunk deep and spread far and wide over the world. But it is still the German people of the future that can best exterminate it at its source. As terrible as the record is, I still believe that they can do this. Also, I believe that the world will give them a chance to do this if, at once, NOW, they repudiate their Nazi leaders and the Nazi-minded citizens among them; if they abandon and turn them over without reservation to justice and punishment for their crime against humanity. Then I feel they will be forgiven. For should the German people as a whole be made to suffer for the Nazi crimes—the agony inflicted by Nazi-German armies over the face of Europe and beyond? No. I think not. For masses are always seized and dominated by the few, just as the poor are. At the same time I feel that the German people should pay in part, in fact suffer a great deal so that they will never again follow a Hitler into world carnage and disaster . . . but they *have* suffered already—they are suffering now and yet are only beginning to suffer what is still to be their share before the invasion is over and the Nazi war machine is smashed . . . .

However, suffering alone is sterile, unless it inspires action of some constructive sort. . . . And because of that I feel that for the next twenty years at least, German scientists and technicians and efficiency experts and their thinkers in general, should devote their time to showing the world what Germans can do to contribute to a just peace. Let German doctors and artists and writers and statesmen show what they can do to put Germany back in her place among civilized nations. Let German democrats see what they can contribute to help solve the problems that will confront all of humanity together—

For there are German democrats! I have seen them, here, amongst our own German-American citizens—and amongst the thousands of exiles from Nazi-dom who have enriched our country in the past years—men like Einstein, Thomas Mann, Heinrich Mann, and countless others. . . . [4]

And don't let us forget that there is a German underground, too, fighting as it has fought, for twelve years against Hitler. Many of its best fighters have been tortured to death or starved in concentration camps. But many live on—some even in the German army. Tales trickle to us continually of their efforts—they have helped organize bands of saboteurs among the foreign labor battalions in Germany—and by many other means, sought to throw sand in the Nazi war machine. They have been too weak to break it down from within without more pressure from outside, but underground resistance in Germany has never ceased to function, run its own presses, radio stations, etc. and cooperate with the underground in other occupied countries. For many German inhabitants have considered that Germany itself has been an "occupied" country since Hitler took his stranglehold on German democracy in 1933.

Personally, I believe that Germany can produce democratic statesmen and citizens who will willingly work with the United Nations, to stamp out Nazism and fascism in Germany and elsewhere. . . . In sum, I believe that Germany can again prosper and take her place as one of the great, constructive nations of the world, if once and for all, she abandons her dreams of domination of others—and the last vestiges of the Nazi LIE.

But it is not only a question of what the German people can do—

The world, as a whole, must figure out some new scheme by which all industrious and constructive peoples can develop themselves, without having to drive others out—without having to fight over a piece of land.

If equitable trade agreements are worked out—and a fair distribution of the world's goods, and the money benefits therefrom, is arranged—in sum, if economic justice is established, then Germany should have her place in the world scheme, the same as any other nation or conglomeration of peoples. . . .

Just as a try-out, let's have a few hundred years of the Brotherhood of Man!

Textual Note: Copy-text is the typescript "OWI BROADCAST, recorded week of May 29–June 3, 1944," (2 pages), in DPUP folder 13412. Noted as being from F. O. Matthiessen. Title supplied by the editors

1. Founded in New York in 1872, Carl Fischer Music remains a music publishing house of the first rank.
2. Literally "living-space," the desire for which was used in Nazi rhetoric to legitimate Germany's territorial expansion.

3. Kaiser Wilhelm II (1849–1941), King of Prussia, and Emperor of Germany from 1888 to 1918.

4. Thomas Mann (1875–1955) and Heinrich Mann (1871–1950), celebrated novelists of the decline of European high culture, who left Germany on Hitler's accession to power in 1933 and eventually settled in the United States.

What to Do

Free World, March 1945.

With Apologies to Lyov Tolstoy[1]

>Storm
>Storm
>Storm
>War
>Want
>Misery.
>
>And each asking of the other what to do
>And so
>Groups
>Committees
>Government.[2]
>In the meantime one
>A small-town editor writes the truth about profit and starvation.[3]
>And one knocks at a broken door and when it opens hands in a loaf of bread.
>And one, step by step, all day long, walks to this laborer and that saying united we stand, divided we fall.
>And one, the workers' friend, says Vote, Speak, for you are the Government, By you your leaders rise or fall.
>And one, the educator, says to the child, A.B.C. and to the adult, Learn! Know that the world grows smaller!
>And one, the minister, says to all, Love thy neighbor as thyself.
>And one, the lover of his fellow man says Take, from each according to his ability; Give, to each according to his need.
>And so from the heart comes the answer
>Of him who does and serves
>That by degrees,
>A new and better world
>May be made.[4]

Textual Note: Copy-text from *Free World* 9 (March 1945): 10. A typescript carbon copy draft is in DPUP folder 13041.

1. In his 1886 book *What To Do?* or *What Then Must We Do?* Leo Tolstoy (1828–1910) criticized organized religion and the Tzarist Russian authorities. Tolstoy's ideas on the need for one to perform some of the labor necessary for one's existence, and on nonintervention in evil, or nonviolent resistance, were widely influential on activists whom Dreiser admired, from Jane Addams to Ghandi.

2. "Governments" in draft.

3. Possibly a reference to Dreiser's friend Bruce Crawford, editor of *Crawford's Weekly,* who had joined the Harlan County investigative committee in 1931.

4. In draft, Dreiser had the following: "The answer must come from the heart/ Of him who does and serves/So by degrees/Making the new and better world."

Theodore Dreiser Joins Communist Party

Daily Worker, 30 July 1945.

Having worked closely with Communist Party members and linked organizations for much of the period since 1930, Dreiser's decision formally to join the party was less a commitment to follow its discipline than a gesture of support at a time of uncertainty both nationally and internationally. Party Secretary Earl Browder had interpreted the 1943 Teheran agreement between Roosevelt, Stalin, and Churchill as guaranteeing the "co-existence" of capitalism and communism. In May 1944, under what became known as the "Teheran Doctrine," the C.P.U.S.A. was dissolved and reconstituted as the Communist Political Association, which helped campaign for Roosevelt's reelection. Dreiser initially welcomed Browder's vision, lauding his book Teheran and America *as "such a clear illumination of our path in war and peace," the "sanest and most honest and helpful that I have ever read."[1] Developments such as the increase in labor unrest in early 1945 and the succession to the presidency of Harry Truman, who proved less sympathetic than Roosevelt to leftwing organized labor, along with a more nationalistic stance in Moscow, undermined Browder's position. In July 1945 the Communist Party reconstituted itself with William Z. Foster as its leader, at a meeting that also accepted Dreiser's application for membership. Dreiser subsequently wrote Foster, praising his "demolition of Browder's compromises."[2] This formal letter of application reflects Communist propaganda priorities in style, tone, and much of its content, and it may have been ghostwritten in part or whole, possibly by John Howard Lawson (1894–1977), who had helped persuade Dreiser to join the party. Nevertheless the themes of anti-imperialism and criticism of red-baiting are common in Dreiser's output after 1930, and the tone and many turns of phrase echo his other attempts to envision a peaceful and equitable postwar world in 1944–45.*

Hollywood, California
July 20, 1945
William Z. Foster,
New York, N. Y.

Dear Mr. Foster:

I am writing this letter to tell you of my desire to become a member of the American Communist organization.[3]

This request is rooted in convictions that I have long held and that have been strengthened and deepened by the years. I have believed intensely that the common people, and first of all the workers,—of the United States and of the world—are the guardians of their own destiny and the creators of their own future. I have endeavored to live by this faith, to clothe it in words and symbols, to explore its full meaning in the lives of men and women.

It seems to me that faith in the people is the simple and profound reality that has been tested and proved in the present world crisis. Fascism derided that faith, proclaiming the end of human rights and human dignity, seeking to rob the people of faith in themselves, so that they could be used for their own enslavement and degradation.

But the democratic peoples of the world demonstrated the power that lay in their unity, and a tremendous role was played in this victory by the country that through its attainment of socialism has given the greatest example in history of the heights of achievement that can be reached by a free people with faith in itself and in all the progressive forces of humanity—the Soviet Union. The unity of our country with the great Soviet Union is one of the most valuable fruits of our united struggle, and dare not be weakened without grave danger to America itself.

Communists all over the world have played a vital part in welding the unity of the peoples that insures the defeat of fascism. Theirs were the first and clearest voices raised against the march of aggression in China, Ethiopia, and Spain.

Dr. Norman Bethune, the great pioneer in saving war wounded through the use of the blood bank, died in China helping the free peoples of that country withstand the Japanese hordes years before the democratic countries came to their aid.[4] His dying request was that it be made known that since many years he had been a Communist.

Out of the underground movements of tortured Europe, Communists have risen to give leadership in the face of terror and all-pervading military suppression. Tito of Yugoslavia won the admiration of the world for his leadership of his people to victory.[5] The name of Stalin is one beloved by the free peoples of the earth. Mao Tse-tung and Chou En-lai have kept the spirit of democracy and unity alive in China throughout the years that divisive forces have split that country asunder.[6]

In the United States, I feel that the Communists have helped to deepen our understanding of the heritage of American freedom as a guide to action in the present. During the years when fascism was preparing for its projected conquest of the world, American Communists fought to rally the American people against fascism. They saw the danger and proposed the remedy. Marxist theory enabled them to cast a steady light on the true economic and social origins of fascism; Marxism gave them also a scientific understanding of the power of the working people as a force in history which could mobilize the necessary intelligence, strength, and heroism to destroy fascism, save humanity, and carry on the fight for further progress.

More than 11,000 Communists are taking part in that struggle as members of the armed forces of our country. That they have served with honor and patriotism is attested to even by the highest authorities of the Army itself.

More and more it is becoming recognized in our country that the Communists are a vital and constructive part of our nation, and that a nation's unity and a nation's democracy is dangerously weakened if it excludes the Communists. Symbolic of this recognition was the action of the War Department in renouncing discrimination against Communists in granting commissions. A statement signed by a number of distinguished Americans points out that "the Army has apparently taken its position as a result of the excellent record of Communists and so-called Communists, including a number who have been cited for gallantry and a number who have died in action."

It seems to me that this ought to discredit completely one of the ideological weapons from the arsenal of fascism that disorients the country's political life and disgraces its intellectual life—red-baiting. Irrational prejudice against anything that is truly or falsely labeled "Communism" is absurd and dangerous in politics. Concessions to red-baiting are even more demoralizing in the field of science, art and culture. If our thinkers and creators are to fulfill their responsibilities to a democratic culture, they must free themselves from the petty fears and illusions that prevent the open discussion of ideas on an adult level. The necessities of our time demand that we explore and use the whole realm of human knowledge.

I therefore greet with particular satisfaction the information that such leading scientists as the French physicist, Joliot-Curie, and the French mathematician, Langevin, have found in the Communist movement, as did the British scientist, Haldane, some years ago, not only the unselfishness and devotion characteristic of the pursuit of science, but also the integration

of the scientific approach to their own field of work with the scientific approach to the problems of society.[7]

I am also deeply stirred to hear that such artists and writers, devoted
to the cause of the people, as Pablo Picasso of Spain and Louis Aragon of
France, have joined the Communist movement, which also counts among
its leading cultural figures the great Danish novelist, Martin Andersen Nexö,
and the Irish playwright Sean O'Casey.[8]

These historic years have deepened my conviction that widespread membership in the Communist movement will greatly strengthen the American
people, together with the anti-fascist forces throughout the world, in completely stamping out fascism and achieving new heights of world democracy,
economic progress and free culture. Belief in the greatness and dignity of
Man has been the guiding principle of my life and work. The logic of my
life and work leads me therefore to apply for membership in the Communist
Party.

Sincerely,
THEODORE DREISER

Textual Note: Copy-text from "Theodore Dreiser Joins Communist Party," *Daily
Worker,* 30 July 1945, p. 5, selectively emended by reference to TD letter to William
Z. Foster dated 20 July 1945, (3 pages), DPUP folder 1199. Apparently this letter
was typed on Dreiser's letterhead at the Los Angeles office of the Communist Party
in June and early July 1945 (see Elizabeth Glenn to TD, 10 July 1945, DPUP folder
1199). Revisions were made to the first and final paragraphs in the *Daily Worker*
text, which reflect the organization's reconstitution as the Communist Party from
the Teheran-period Communist Political Association. "Fascism" is capitalized in-
consistently within prepublication and published texts and has been standardized
according to the lower-case usage of the first page of the typescript letter.

1. TD to Earl Browder, 28 September 1944, DPUP.
2. TD to William Z. Foster, 16 August 1945, DPUP.
3. In prepublication form the letter is addressed to, and applies for membership
in, the Communist Political Association, the name adopted during the period of
the Teheran Doctrine.
4. Canadian-born Norman Bethune (1899–1939) worked as a surgeon in the
Spanish Civil War in 1936–37 and with the army in China in 1938–39, where he
died of septicaemia contracted while operating on a wounded Chinese soldier.
5. General Tito (born Josip Broz; 1892–1980) led the most effective partisan resistance to Axis occupation of what became in November 1945 the Yugoslav Federal
Republic. A Communist who had participated in the 1917 Russian Revolution,
Tito would as leader of Yugoslavia break with Stalinist policy in 1948, founding
the "nonaligned" movement.
6. Mao Tse-tung (or Mao Zedong, 1893–1976) and Chou En-lai (or Zhou Enlai,
1898–1976) were at this time communist leaders of the successful resistance to
the Japanese invasion of China. They became, respectively, chairman and prime

minister of the People's Republic of China after ousting the Nationalist government of Chiang Kai-shek in 1949.

7. Prominent scientists Jean Frédéric Joliot-Curie (1900–1958), who joined the Communist Party during his time in the French Resistance; Paul Langevin (1872–1946), who had been a prominent antifascist since 1934; and John Burdon Sanderson Haldane (1892–1964), chair of the editorial board of the London *Daily Worker*.

8. Pablo Picasso (1881–1973) had joined the communists after the liberation of Paris in 1944; Louis Aragon (1897–1983), the surrealist poet and novelist, adopted communism in 1930; Martin Andersen Nexö (1869–1954) is best known for *Pelle the Conqueror* (1906), which describes working-class life and the labor movement; Sean O'Casey (1884–1964) is known for plays such as *Juno and the Paycock* (1924) and *The Plough and the Stars* (1926).

Interdependence

Free World, September 1945.

In the last work to be published during his lifetime, and under the shadow of the atomic bombs dropped on Hiroshima and Nagasaki, Dreiser places his hopes for the future of humanity in three postwar possibilities: "abundance"—equitable economic development taking full advantage of technology and international trade, and free from the artificial manipulation of markets to ensure profits; "international education" and contact between individuals, whereby the recognition of individual and cultural differences is the crucial step in forging a common humanity; and political internationalism, culminating in a "Federation of Countries." The expansiveness of this approach is signaled by Dreiser's choice of examples from sources of which he had previously been critical: Wendell Willkie, whose own internationalist perspective had been strengthened by wartime experience; and the British agents of Dreiser's detested British Empire, at least by reference to the account of Jawaharlal Nehru, hero of the struggle for Indian independence.

While a great deal has been said on the subject of scarcity and plenty, abundance, as a basis for national life, has never been tried. Russia has come nearer the actual goal than any other country in the world. But even in Russia, due to enormous natural obstacles, the ideal of abundance for all is still in the evolutionary stage.

Everything we have today is built on scarcity and the incentive of actual physical need. But this age of scarcity has failed dismally. And, as Willkie pointed out in his worthy book *One World* we need expansion of trade to provide a new basis for our whole social structure.[1] And the structure must be based on abundance instead of scarcity.

However, only the mass can get the world out of its present mess. People. Interdependence. A new understanding between peoples all over the world is what is needed. And how are we to get that? First, the need is so great and the danger of the destruction of civilization so apparent and so close at hand, that men everywhere have begun to think of ways and means of surviving through contact and understanding each the other. As someone said, if we get scared enough we will move. And it looks as though that time were at hand.

But when I speak of the mass I speak of the individuals of which the mass is made up. We must understand the necessities of many individuals. For, as Jawaharlal Nehru said in his book *Toward Freedom*,[2] where he points out that after all he had received better treatment as a prisoner from the British than did many other Indians, because the English knew him as an individual who had attended their schools in England and so had studied the various subjects they had studied, and was looked upon as different; whereas to an individual of another nationality—Chinese, Burmese, Scotch, or whatsoever—having been seized upon by the English and trained as an official or a soldier of Great Britain, or a unit of one of its armies sent to govern or control him or the people to whom he belonged, he was little more than nothing, someone to obey whatever he was told to obey or, refusing, to be shot down, or thrown into solitary confinement, as he was.

In sum, the important point that Nehru stresses in regard to all this is that, without some degree of understanding by all everywhere, your fellow man everywhere, although a social unit, not so vastly different to yourself, is not acceptable to you or the other nationalities of the world. For the want of a little international education! Or for want of training not exactly like that which you have received he becomes an outcast, an individual subject to suspicion. Someone of whom it is assumed, however ignorantly, that he may injure you; not, for instance, that you injure him.

Thus the soldier, stiffening to attention, drops his humanity, and, acting as an automaton, shoots and kills inoffensive and harmless persons who have done him no ill, for he cannot, or will not, think of himself as an individual *then*, nor will he consider as individuals those crowds whom he beats down or shoots. In other words, as soon as one begins to think of the other side as a mass or a crowd, the human link seems to go. We forget that crowds consist of individuals, of men and women and children, who love and hate and suffer. And we must develop our intellects so as to think of this when we speak of the mass of this or that far off country. We must begin to think of "people" and persons, their ways, customs, shortcomings and difficulties, their differences and talents,—not as inexplicable automatons. For only in this way will we ever come to understand that we are brothers under one sun.

As in the beginning of this country when we were fighting, one colony against another, until a Federation of States was formed to stop, by force if necessary, the constant warring on each other, we must form and develop a Federation of Countries which are not imposed one upon another, but interwoven. People must move into other countries. They must study strange and unfamiliar ways and customs and try to learn from them. They must learn to understand, and wish to, their fellow men on this globe. For in this way, and this way alone, can just laws be adopted and enforced to keep the peace in the interest of each individual in each country. For to know and to understand is to love, not to hate.

Textual Note: Published in *Free World* 10 (September 1945): 69–70. Copy-text is the carbon copy typescript (3 pages) in DPUP folder 12125.

1. Wendell L. Willkie's bestselling *One World* (New York: Simon & Schuster, 1943) promulgated a democratic internationalism in which the United States would work alongside other nations, including the Soviet Union, with the aim of "the creation of a world in which there shall be an equality of opportunity for every race and every nation" (84). Dreiser had written to Willkie praising the book, but urging that he challenge economic inequality with more urgency (TD to Wendell Willkie, 28 June 1944, DPUP).

2. *Toward Freedom* (New York: John Day Co., 1941) is the autobiography of Jawaharlal Nehru (1889–1964), leader of the Indian National Congress Party and prominent in the movement for independence from the British Empire. Nehru was the principal architect of India's secular constitution and became independent India's first prime minister, from 1947 to 1964.

INDEX

abundance: and democracy, 278n11; and freedom, 270–71; hopes for future, 216, 217, 221, 264, 291–92; and war, 226; and westward expansion, 267

Abyssinia. *See* Ethiopia/Abyssinia

Act for the Suppression of Trade in, and Circulation of, Obscene Literature and Articles for Immoral Use (1873), 89

Addams, Jane, xviii, 9, 43–44, 287n1

Africa: British imperialism, 58, 72, 274; indigenous knowledge, 258; missionary activity, 247–48; press attention, 267. *See also* Egypt; Ethiopia/Abyssinia; South Africa

African Americans, continuing marginalization of, 32–34, 87n1, 185; civil liberties, 266; compared with corporate oppression of workers, 147; economic exploitation, xxi, 143n4, 151, 154; as evidence of American democratic myth, 83; exclusion from juries, 144n13; opportunities, 34n1; and prejudice, 111, 143, 154, 252; in South, 140–41, 147, 154, 194–95; white fear, 32–33. *See also* lynching; peonage; racism/racial oppression; Scottsboro boys; sharecropping

African Americans, cultural richness, 33–34, 34n4

agency, sociopolitical, xxiii, 6

Agricultural Adjustment Act (1938), 212n1

Ainslee's (magazine), 6

Aksam (Turkish daily), 146

Alabama. *See* Scottsboro boys

Alaska, 64, 80n22, 80n24

Alexander III of Macedon (Alexander the Great), 66, 81n27, 217, 223

Alfonso XIII (Spain), 39, 40n2, 230, 234n5

alienation, 8, 19–20, 21, 23–24

Allende, Salvador, 279n15

Alsace, 62

Álvarez del Vayo, Julio, 244–47, 249n7

"America" (Dreiser, 1932), 171–74

"America, Europe, and Cuba" (Dreiser, 1895), 13–14

America First Committee, 263n15, 264

America Is Worth Saving (Dreiser, 1941), xii, xxvii, 45, 263–77; advertisement for, 268; American values invoked, 219–20; British appeasement of fascism, 218; "Can the British Empire Endure?" 274–75; Dreiser's suppression of, 215; "Has America a 'Save-the-World' Complex," 264, 265–68; "Has England Done More for Its People Than Fascism or Socialism?" 269–70; "Have English and American Finance Cooperated with Hitler to Destroy Democracy?" 264; summary, 216–17, 263–64; "What are the Objectives of American Finance?" 272–74; "What Is Democracy?" 264, 270–72; "What Should Be the Objectives of the American People?" 276–77; "Will American Democracy Endure?" 275

American Art Galleries, 35n4

American Bar Association Bill of Rights Committee, 261

American Birth Control League, 89

American Civil War. *See* Civil War (U.S.)

American democracy: effect of moralism on, 67; and individualism, 270–71; and labor movement, 237–38, 264, 275; as myth, 67, 68–69, 77, 83–86, 128, 152–54, 234–35, 261; and New Deal, 235–37; potential of, 264, 269, 276–77, 280; powerlessness of, 46; and socialization, 85; vs. true democracy, 59; and war, 158; and wealth inequality, 57. *See also* American exceptionalism; democracy

"American Democracy against Fascism" (Dreiser speech, 1938), 234–38

American exceptionalism, xii–xiii; and America's global role, xix, 265–68; vs.

278n8, 293n2; and civilization, 253; independence struggle, 291, 293n2; missionary activity in, 156; partition with Pakistan, 252n1; population, 93; religious tensions, 251–52, 252n1, 278n8; spiritual tradition, 254
Indianapolis, Indiana, 27
Indian National Congress Party, 293n2
Indians/Native Americans, 14, 50, 51, 83
individualism, xvii; in activism, 200, 221; and American democracy, 270–71; and American exceptionalism, 201; and capitalism, xix, xx, 111, 112, 171, 189; *vs.* collective wisdom, 232–33; *vs.* communism, xix, 46, 96, 111, 200; and corporate power, 112, 124, 192–93, 220; as dynamic force, 109; efficiency of, 86; *vs.* equal opportunity, 149; *vs.* equity, 109, 196, 216; and materialism, 125, 273; as myth, xii, xx; and New Deal, 236, 237; as outdated idea, 217; and race, 195; and selfishness, 158, 189–90, 227; and social Darwinism, 271; and social injustice, xxi, 111–12, 130, 163, 167–69; and war, 145, 226, 229; and wealth inequality, 166. *See also* big man, the
"Individualism and the Jungle" (Dreiser, 1932), 170
Industrial Revolution, 270
Industrial Workers of the World (IWW), 50n1, 69, 82n35, 170n5. *See also* Mooney, Tom
Ingersoll, Robert, 94
inheritances, 124, 125–26, 159, 172–73, 195, 277
insurance, 59, 79n9; in France, 147; socialization of, 126, 172; for unemployment, 110, 113, 147, 174n1
intellectuals, xviii–xix, 172, 224–25
Interborough Transit Commission (New York City), 87n2
"Interdependence" (Dreiser, 1945), xxv, 216, 221, 291–93
International Association of Writers for the Defense of Culture, 246, 250n13
internationalism, xviii, 221, 291, 293n1; and Judaism, 185; *vs.* nationalism, 181. *See also* cultural relativism
International Labor Defense, 110, 115, 139, 144n9, 164

International Literature (magazine), 116, 119, 196, 197, 199
International Longshoremen's and Warehousemen's Union, 263n14
international relations, 64, 116, 215–16, 220, 229–33. *See also* cultural relativism
International Unemployment Day (1930), 127n2
International Union of Revolutionary Writers, 196, 199
"Interview with Nazife Osman Pasha" (Dreiser, 1931), 144–46
inventors/inventions. *See* art; creativity; science
Iron and Fuel Company, 82n34
"Is Dreiser Anti-Semitic?" (*Nation*, 1935), 118, 176–87, 199
Islam. *See* Mohammedism, Muslims
"Is Leon Trotsky Guilty?" (Dreiser, 1937), 119, 209–11
Italy: arms supplied to, 248; as Great Power, 230; imitation of German autocracy, 75; imperialism, 72; invasion of Abyssinia (Ethiopia), 35n4, 229, 232; and military technology, 227–28; renaissance, 254; and Spanish Civil War, 243; WWI, 56, 62, 65
"It Pays to Treat Workers Generously" (Dreiser, 1899), 6

Jackson, Andrew, 76
Jaffa, 208n8
James, William, 13
Jamestown, Virginia settlement, 51, 55n1
Japan: autocracy, 59, 68; bombardment of China, 215, 218, 229, 231, 265, 269; and civilization, 253, 254; invasion of China, 229, 232, 252, 252n2, 265, 277n2, 290n6; invasion of Manchuria, 273, 279n16; and military technology, 227–28; naval heroism, 81n29; and "open door" policy, 65, 81n25; as potential hostile nation, 56–57; and Soviet Union, 255; and WWI, 61, 67–68, 74–75. *See also* Pearl Harbor attack
Japanese Americans, relocation of, 263n13
Japanese imperialism: American complicity, 45; in China, 62, 65, 74, 77–78, 232; U.S. arms sales, 116; and WWI, 62, 65, 72, 74–75; and WWII, 215

Jeans, James Hopwood, 253, 257n1
Jefferson, Thomas, 50, 64, 76, 80n23
Jennie Gerhardt (Dreiser, 1911), xxiii, 89, 293
Jersey City, New Jersey, 263n5
Jesus Christ, 224
"Jew and the World, The" (Stolberg), 204–6, 207n1, 207nn3–4, 207–8n6
"Jewish question," 118, 176–77, 178, 180, 181, 200, 200n1, 204. *See also* anti-Semitism; Jews/Judaism; Zionism
Jewish Telegraphic Agency, 208n8
Jews/Judaism: and assimilation, 207n4; in Germany, 181, 184, 186, 188n8, 252, 256, 284; as laborers, 182, 200, 200n1, 208n6; myth of racial purity, 182–83, 186, 204–5, 207n1; populations, 180, 184, 186; and religion, 186; separatism, 207n1, 208n7; tolerance, 208n10. *See also* anti-Semitism; "Jewish question"; Zionism
"John Reed Club Answer" (Dreiser, 1930), 110, 123–27, 148
John Reed Clubs, 113, 123, 131
Johnson, Arnold, 163
Joliot-Curie, Jean Frédéric, 289–90, 291n7
Jones, John Paul, 68, 81n32
Jones and Laughlin Steel Corporation, 132
judiciary: and labor repression, 110, 134–35; powerlessness of, 46; prejudice in, 130n2; reform of, 117. *See also* corporate power; Supreme Court (U.S.)
Juno and the Paycock (O'Casey), 291n8

Kalinin, Mikhail Ivanovich, 103, 105n7
Kansas City Star (newspaper), 81n33
Kant, Immanuel, 254, 270, 278n13
Karsner, Rose, 115, 119
Kennell, Ruth, 96
kings, divine right of, 179–80
Know-Nothings, 275, 279n18
Kraft, Hy, 120n22
Krog, Fritz, 11, 34
Kropotkin, Peter, 229n4
Ku Klux Klan, 45, 181–82

Labor Defender (monthly), xxi, 110, 111, 116, 140, 142, 153
labor disputes: corporate circumvention, 133; dramatization of, 43, 48–50;

Dreiser's support, 4, 221; Gaston County, North Carolina strike (1929), 169, 170n5, 275; and Great Depression, xx, 110; Imperial Valley farmworker dispute (1929), 133, 134, 135, 169, 170n5; increase in, 287; *vs.* individualism, 111–12; Lawrence textile workers strike (1912), 50n1, 82n34, 82n36, 170n5, 275; New York garment workers strike (1896), 5; Pittsburgh miners' strike, 266; and press, 259; tobacco worker rebellion (1907), 117. *See also* corporate power; Harlan, Kentucky coal region
labor organizing, 109; and anticommunism, 116; as best American tradition, 237–38, 264, 275; and Communist Party, 131, 132, 132n2, 170n5; *vs.* corporate power, 137; and Jews, 208n6; and New Deal, 115; powerlessness of, 23–24, 46; and press, 133–34, 259, 260–61, 262n3; and race hatred, 133; as right, xix, 113. *See also* farmer-labor movement
labor organizing, repression of, xxi; corporate influence on unions, 167, 168–69; and individualism, 192–93; in legal system, 110, 124–25, 129, 132, 134–38, 147, 275; lynching, 69, 82n35; municipal repression of, 263n5; police/militia role, 45, 81n34, 110, 134–35, 147, 153, 162n4, 162n5, 221, 259, 262n2, 263n7; and press, 110, 134–35, 135–36; violence, 110, 113, 162n4, 162n5, 164, 237–38, 259, 262n2, 266, 275; and WWI, 43–44, 69. *See also* Harlan, Kentucky coal region
Labor Research Association, 112, 117
labor: Dreiser's experience with, 17; exploitation of, 20, 147, 154, 162n5; invisibility of, 8; in Soviet Union, 96–97; Tolstoy's ideas, 287n1. *See also* "The Toil of the Laborer" (Dreiser, 1913); wages; workday length restriction; working class
Laffoon, Ruby, 163
La Follette, Robert M., 262, 263n12
LaGuardia, Fiorello, 211
Landon, Alf, 262, 263n16
Lane, Franklin, 44, 62, 66, 77, 80n14, 83n45
Langevin, Paul, 289–90, 291n7
Lansing, Robert, 77, 83n45

Progress Administration, 212, 212n1.
See also Great Depression
Newlands, Francis Griffith, 75, 82n41
Newlin, Keith, xxviii
New Masses (magazine): 1928 elections,
46–47; Dreiser's statement on anti-Sem-
itism, 118, 178, 199–200; individualism,
111–12; and second front in WWII, 219;
Spanish Civil War, 208–9
New Republic (magazine), 46, 116, 121
Newspaper Days (Dreiser, 1922), 260,
262n2, 262n3
Newton, Isaac, 190, 193n4
New York Call (newspaper), 8, 17, 25
New York Central railroad, 17
New York City: Jewish population, 180,
184, 186; and New Deal, 198; protests
in, 127n2; racial injustice, 34n3; and
Schools for Mothers, 29; Tammany Hall
machine, 11, 46–47, 84, 87n2, 131,
132n1
New York Evening Post (newspaper), 194
New York Foundling Hospital, xxiii, 7–8
New York Society for the Prevention of
Vice, 44
New York state, 32n3, 63–64, 219
New York Street Car Monopoly, 84, 87n2
New York Telegram (newspaper), 121
New York Times (newspaper), 116–17, 260,
266
New York Tribune (newspaper), 260
New York World (newspaper), 94
Nexö, Martin Andersen, 290, 291n8
Nicaragua, American imperialism, 157
Nicholas II (Russia), 80n15
Nietzsche, Friedrich, 254
"Nigger Jeff" (Dreiser, 1901), xxiii–xxiv,
32, 34n2, 144n7
nonaggression pact (Soviet/German), xxii–
xxiii, 217, 218
nonviolent resistance, 287n1
Norris, Clarence, 139, 144n13
Norris–La Guardia Act (1932), 132n2
Northcliff, Lord (Alfred Harmsworth), 77,
82n44
Norway, 62, 65
nostalgia, xii

obscenity. *See* censorship; moralism
O'Casey, Sean, 290, 291n8

Office of War Information, 281, 283
oil, 74, 265, 279n16
old-age homes, 155
Oneida community, 211
O'Neill, Eugene, xviii, 117, 257n3
"One Woman's Civic Service" (Daggett),
27n2
One World (Willkie), 291, 293n1
"One Worldism," xxv
"On the Communists and Their Platform"
(Dreiser, 1930), 131
"On the Jewish Question" (Lenin), 200n1
"open door" policy, 65, 81n25
opium trade, 266–67
orphan asylums, 10, 154–55
"Our Government and Our Food" (Dreiser,
1899), 6
over-production, 123, 149
Ovington, Mary White, 34n3

pacifism, 215–17, 228; and Communist
Party, 219; and cultural relativism, 217,
292–93; *vs.* individualism, 232; and
Pearl Harbor attacks, 264; sharing of
resources, 233; and Spanish Civil War,
218; WWI, 72–73. *See also* peace
pagan, as political outlook, 59–60, 74,
79n10, 180
Page, Walter Hines, 77, 83n45
Paine, Thomas, xiii, 50, 200, 277, 279n19
Pakistan, 252n1
Palestine, 208n8, 270
Palisades Interstate Park, 32n3
Panama, 116, 138n7, 157, 162n8
Panama Canal Zone, xxviii, 57, 63, 79n1,
80n18, 162n8, 232
Paris, Treaty of (1763), 80n20
Paris, Treaty of (1783), 80n21
Partisan Review & Anvil (monthly), xxii,
200–202
Pasha, Nazife Osman, 144–46
Pasionaria, La, 246, 249n11, 249n13
Pass, Joseph, 116
Passaic, New Jersey, 162n5
Pasteur, Louis, 189, 191, 193n3
Paterson, New Jersey, 50n1, 69, 81n34
patriotism, 3, 5
Patterson, Haywood, 139, 144n9, 144n13
Paul-Boncour, Joseph, 246, 249n12
peace, 112; and abundance, 221; after

76; reform of, 5; and social change, 148, 175–76, 211; in Soviet Union, 105n2; and women, 16. *See also* education/educators

public transportation/transportation industry, 88, 126, 152, 160, 161n2, 171. *See also* railroads

Puerto Rico, American imperialism, 157, 162n10, 275

Pulitzer newspapers, 13, 94

Pullman railroad car factory (Chicago), 262n2

purchasing power, 123, 151

puritanism. *See* moralism

Quakerism, 211

racism/racial oppression, xviii, 32–34, 109, 252; compared with corporate power, 147, 195–96; as danger to community, 183; and exploitation of African Americans, 140, 154; and Great Depression, xx, 110; and labor movement, 133; and liberalism, 178, 179; and myth of Jewish race, 182–83, 186, 204–5, 207n1; and New Deal, 250; "race suicide," 10, 11, 93, 94n1; and relocation of Japanese Americans, 263n13; and Scottsboro boys, 111, 139–43, 194–96. *See also* African Americans, continuing marginalization of; lynching; peonage; sharecropping

Radek, Karl, 99–100, 105nn4–5

radio: corporate control, 124, 235, 237–38, 260; Radio Act (1927), 127n1, 129, 131n3

Radio Corporation of America, 191

"Railroad and the People, The" (Dreiser, 1900), 6

railroads, 117; Dreiser's employment with, 21–25, 25n2; German nationalization of during WWI, 75; and Harlan coal region, 163; Harriman's control, 32n3; high fares, 88, 161n2; labor disputes, 259; and New Deal, 237; poor accommodations, 147; corporate control, 124, 149; *vs.* small transportation operators, 152; socialization, 75, 113, 126, 176, 198, 199n2; treatment of poor workers, 6; trusts, 152

Rakovsky, Christian, 99–100, 105n4

"Random Reflections on Russia" (*Dreiser Looks at Russia*), 103–4

rape, 141

Rassemblement Universel Pour La Paix, 229, 249n12

Raymond, Harry, 124, 127n2, 129

"Realization of an Ideal, The" (Dreiser 1923), 25n1

Reconstruction Finance Corporation, 110

Reconstruction (magazine), 25, 83

red-baiting, 287, 289

Red Cross, 116, 163, 166, 167

Red Menace, 176

"Red Scare," 43–44

Reed, John, xviii

"Reformer, The" (Dreiser, 1920), 46

religion, xvii, 9, 287n1; and birth control, 90–91, 93; commercialization of, 147–48, 152, 235; and hypocrisy, 51–52; and immigrants, 182–83; and legislation, 88–89, 89n2; and liberalism, 179; missionary activity, 148, 156, 247–48, 265–67, 278n4; and orphanages, 10; and poverty, 175–76; and press, 68–69; religious education, 38, 40, 154–55, 175, 186; repression by, 163, 166; *vs.* science, 185–86; as self-deception, 89, 94, 130, 168, 174, 199; and social change, 211; in Soviet Union, 185, 208nn7–8. *See also* Catholic Church/Catholicism; Christianity; eastern philosophies; Jews/Judaism; moralism

religious intolerance, 179, 251–52, 252n1, 270, 278n8

Republican Party, 4; 1916 elections, 79n8; 1928 elections, 46–47; 1932 elections, 122n1; 1936 elections, 263n16; 1940 elections, 263n17; money influence, 172, 173–74

Republicans (Spanish). *See* Spanish Civil War

Revolutionary War (U.S.), 80n18, 80n21, 81n32, 254

Richelieu, Cardinal, 76, 82n42

"Rights of a Columnist: A Symposium on the Case of Heywood Broun *versus* the New York *World*" (*Nation*, 1928), 94–95

Rights of Man (Paine), 279n19

"Right to Kill, The" (Dreiser, 1918), 89

JUDE DAVIES is Professor of American Literature and Culture
at the University of Winchester. He is the coauthor of *Gender,
Ethnicity, and Sexuality in Contemporary American Film* and author
of numerous articles on Theodore Dreiser and literary naturalism.

The University of Illinois Press
is a founding member of the
Association of American University Presses.

Composed in 10.5/13 Goudy Old Style
by Jim Proefrock
at the University of Illinois Press
Manufactured by Thomson-Shore, Inc.

University of Illinois Press
1325 South Oak Street
Champaign, IL 61820-6903
www.press.uillinois.edu